US INTERVENTION POLICY AND ARMY INNOVATION

This book examines how the US Army rebuilt itself after the Vietnam War and how this has affected US intervention policy, from the victory of the Gulf War to the failure of Somalia, the Bosnian and Kosovo interventions and the use of force post 9/11.

This volume sets out to analyse the changes in US military intervention strategy by examining two separate issues: the nature of the US Army as it rebuilt itself after the Vietnam War, and the attempts by the US to establish criteria for future military interventions. Richard Lock-Pullan first argues that US strategy traditionally relied upon national mobilisation to co-ordinate political aims and military means; he subsequently analyses how this changed to a formula of establishing militarily achievable political objectives prior to the use of force. Drawing on a vast body of material and on strategic culture and military innovation literature, the author demonstrates that the strategic lessons were a product of the rebuilding of the Army's identity as it became a professional all-volunteer force and that the Army's new doctrine developed a new 'way of war' for the nation, embodied in the AirLand Battle doctrine, which changed the approach to strategy.

The book finally gives a practical analysis of how the interventions in Panama and the Gulf War vindicated this approach and brought a revived confidence in the use of force while more recent campaigns in Somalia, Kosovo and Bosnia exposed its weaknesses and the limiting nature of the Army's thinking. The legacy of the Army's innovation is examined in the new strategic environment post 9/11 with the operations in Afghanistan and Iraq.

This book will be of interest to students of strategic studies, international relations and American politics as well as to military professionals.

Richard Lock-Pullan is a Roberts Research Fellow in the Department of Political Science and International Studies and the Centre for Studies in Security and Diplomacy at the University of Birmingham. He was formerly a Senior Lecturer in the Defence Studies Department at King's College, London at the UK's Defence Academy. He has published extensively on US security policy, strategy, innovation and security studies.

CASS SERIES: STRATEGY AND HISTORY
Series Editors: Colin Gray and Williamson Murray

This new series will focus on the theory and practice of strategy. Following Clausewitz, strategy has been understood to mean the use made of force, and the threat of the use of force, for the ends of policy. This series is as interested in ideas as in historical cases of grand strategy and military strategy in action. All historical periods, near and past, and even future, are of interest. In addition to original monographs, the series will from time to time publish edited reprints of neglected classics as well as collections of essays.

Military logistics and strategic performance
Thomas M. Kane

Strategy for chaos
Revolutions in military affairs and the evidence of history
Colin Gray

The myth of inevitable US defeat in Vietnam
C. Dale Walton

Astropolitik
Classical geopolitics in the space age
Everett C. Dolman

Anglo-American strategic relations and the Far East, 1933–1939
Imperial crossroads
Greg Kennedy

Pure strategy
Power and principle in the space and information age
Everett C. Dolman

The Red Army, 1918–1941
From vanguard of world revolution to US ally
Earl F. Ziemke

Britain and ballistic missile defence, 1942–2002
Jeremy Stocker

The nature of war in the information age
Clausewitzian future
David J. Lonsdale

Strategy as social science
Thomas Schelling and the nuclear age
Robert Ayson

Warfighting and disruptive technologies
Disguising innovation
Terry Pierce

The fog of peace and war planning
Military and strategic planning under uncertainty
Edited by Talbot C. Imlay and Monica Duffy Toft

US intervention policy and army innovation
From Vietnam to Iraq
Richard Lock-Pullan

US INTERVENTION POLICY AND ARMY INNOVATION

From Vietnam to Iraq

Richard Lock-Pullan

Routledge
Taylor & Francis Group
LONDON AND NEW YORK

First published 2006
by Routledge, an imprint of Taylor & Francis
2 Park Square, Milton Park, Abingdon, Oxon OX14 4RN

Simultaneously published in the USA and Canada
by Routledge
270 Madison Ave, New York, NY 10016

Routledge is an imprint of the Taylor & Francis Group

Transferred to Digital Printing 2006

Typeset in Times
by Keystroke. Jacaranda Lodge, Wolverhampton

British Library Cataloguing in Publication Data
A catalogue record for this book is available from the British Library

Library of Congress Cataloging in Publication Data
A catalog record for this book has been requested

ISBN10: 0–7146–5719–0 (hbk)
ISBN10: 0–415–40787–7 (pbk)

ISBN13: 978–0–7146–5719–6 (hbk)
ISBN13: 978–0–415–40787–8 (pbk)

TO PENNY,
WITH ALL MY LOVE
AND
IN MEMORY OF
PETER ERIC PULLAN, AFC
1924–1992

'Nature herself was proud of his designs
And joyed to wear the dressing of his lines.'

CONTENTS

PREFACE

This study examines how and why US military intervention strategy changed after the Vietnam War. It argues that US strategy traditionally relied upon national mobilisation to co-ordinate political aims and military means, and changed to a formula of establishing militarily achievable political objectives prior to the use of force. Employing strategic culture and military innovation literature, it argues that the strategic lessons were a product of the rebuilding of the Army's identity and perception of its role and utility as it became a professional all-volunteer force after the Vietnam War. The Army's new doctrine developed a new 'way of war' for the nation, embodied in the AirLand Battle doctrine. The Weinberger doctrine was the formal acceptance by the executive of the Army's formula. The Panama intervention and the first Gulf War vindicated the lessons the Army drew from the Vietnam War, and brought a revived confidence in the use of force. The failure in Somalia exposed the weaknesses and particular nature of the lessons drawn from the war, and derailed the Clinton administration's intervention agenda. The revival of the Weinberger doctrine under Clinton showed that the Army's understanding of its professional identity and operational doctrine was fundamental to the US's military intervention strategy, and provided its norms and constraints in the new strategic environment. The US's response to the events of 11 September 2001 showed the strengths and limitations of the Army's approach with its trends of a technological approach to war and an avoidance of 'nation building'. It significantly shaped the nature of US policy.

ACKNOWLEDGEMENTS

Like many first books, this has had a long gestation and has required much good fortune over the seven years of writing. My luck in working for King's College London at the Joint Services Command and Staff College (JSCSC) and in being a postgraduate at the University of Birmingham is a considerable intellectual debt. In particular, the advice, support, enthusiasm and interest provided by my PhD supervisor Dr David H. Dunn was considerable, greatly appreciated, and well beyond his formal responsibilities. He and Dr Terry Terriff opened, and continue to open, many vistas for me with a generosity that is extraordinary. Professor Erik Goldstein, in both his Birmingham and Boston incarnations, was a wonderful mentor and host. The School of Social Science at Birmingham, and the ESRC (R00429824537) kindly supported the research financially, whilst the Defence Studies Department at JSCSC provided study leave. Rich amounts of material were provided by the US Embassy, the libraries at JSCSC Watchfield and Bracknell. the Royal Military College of Science (RMCS) Shrivenham and the universities of Birmingham, Keele, Boston and Johns Hopkins. I am grateful to the helpful staff at each establishment.

This research would not have been possible without the very generous co-operation of all the people who allowed me to interview them, many giving large amounts of time and material. My genuine thanks to them. I would like to mention in particular the patience shown in the face of my simple questions by Generals Starry and Richardson. I would like to pay tribute to my former colleagues Drs Robert Foley, Greg Kennedy, Nial Barr, Tim Bird, Rod Thornton and Jon Robb-Webb, for all their advice and comments. I would like to thank Air Vice-Marshal Professor Tony Mason, Dr John Bourne, Colonel Richard Iron, and many students and colleagues, especially serving US Army officers, for their time, ideas and advice. Having Nick Lock to chat to was a great boon. Dr Rehan ul-Haq, Professor Forest Hansen and Reverend Mark Woods proved themselves true Knechtians. Without John Conway and Nigel Philips, I and this book would be very different. Of course, the responsibility for what is written remains mine alone.

Some earlier versions of this study first appeared, wholly or in part, in article form. I would like to thank the editors for their help and permission to reproduce the material here: 'Civilian Ideas and Military Innovation: Manoeuvre Warfare and

Organisational Change in the US Army'. *War and Society* (Vol. 20, No. 1 2002) pp. 125–47; '"An Inward Looking Time": The US Army 1973–76'. *Journal of Military History* (Vol. 67, No. 2 2003) pp. 483–511; and 'Learning the Limits of Virtue: Clinton, the Army and the Criteria for the Use of Military Force'. *Contemporary Security Policy* (Vol. 24, No. 2 2003) pp. 133–56.

A family which has two children during the period of writing a PhD, and the subsequent book, requires a prodigious amount of sustained support from family and friends. We were very lucky in receiving enormous amounts of help from Meg and Andrew and from my mother and Peter – without whom this book would have been inconceivable. They all know how grateful I am. In the future I hope that Hannah and Freya will understand why I wrote it. I wish to thank Hannah publically for suggesting the book's title. My greatest thanks are to Penny, whose generosity of spirit made my return to academia possible, and it involved her becoming virtually a single parent. My debt is beyond accounting. This book is dedicated to her and to the memory of my father, who began my interest in military and political issues by showing me just how important they were.

ABBREVIATIONS

AAR	After Action Reports
ACE	Allied Command Europe
ALB	AirLand Battle doctrine
ARTEP	Army Training and Evaluation Program
ARVN	Army of the Republic of Vietnam
AVF	All-Volunteer Force
C^4I	Command, Control, Communications, Computers and Intelligence
CALL	Center for Army Lessons Learned
CAP	Combined Action Platoon
CAS	Combined Arms and Service School
CIA	Central Intelligence Agency
CJSC	Chairman, Joint Chiefs of Staff
CINC	Commander in Chief
CINCPAC	Commander in Chief, Pacific Comand
CMTC	Combat Maneuver Training Center
COIN	Counter-Insurgency
COMUSMACV	Commander, USMACV
CONARC	Continental Army Command
CONUS	Continental United States
CORDS	Civil Operations and Rural Development Program
DCSOPS	Deputy Chief of Staff for Operations
DIA	Defense Intelligence Agency
DOD	Department of Defense
FEBA	Forward Edge of the Battle Area
FOFA	Follow-On Forces Attack
FLOT	Forward Line of Troops
FM	Field Manual
FRUS	*Foreign Relations of the United States*
FY	Fiscal Year
IDAD	Internal Defense and Development
IED	Improvised Explosive Device
JCS	Joint Chiefs of Staff
JRTC	Joint Readiness Training Center
JSTARS	Joint Surveillance Target Attack Radar System
JV2010	Joint Vision 2010
LIC	Low-Intensity Conflict
MAAGV	Military Assistance and Advisory Group, Vietnam
MACV	Military Assistance Command, Vietnam

MNF	Multi-National Forces
MOOTW	Military Operations Other Than War
NATO	North Atlantic Treaty Organisation
NGO	Non-Governmental Organisation
NMS	National Military Strategy
NSA	National Security Agency
NSC	National Security Council
NTC	National Training Center
NVA	Army of North Vietnam
OCS	Officer Candidate School
OER	Officer Efficiency Report
OMG	Operational Maneuver Group
OODA	Observation–Orientation–Decision–Action
OOTW	Operations Other Than War
OPFOR	Opposing Force
OPMS	Officer Personnel Management System
PAVN	People's Army of Vietnam
PDD	Presidential Decision Directive
PDF	Panamanian Defense Force
PGM	Precision Guided Munitions
QDR	Quadrennial Defense Review
QRF	Quick Reaction Force
RDF	Rapid Deployment Force
REDCOM	Readiness Command
RMA	Revolution in Military Affairs
ROE	Rules of Engagement
SAC	Strategic Air Command
SACEUR	Supreme Allied Commander Europe
SIOP	Single Integrated Operational Plan for Nuclear War
SOCOM	Special Operations Command
SOF	Special Operations Forces
SOLIC	Special Operations, Low-Intensity Conflict
SOUTHCOM	Southern Command
TAC	Tactical Air Command
TAF	Tactical Air Force
TRADOC	Training and Doctrine Command
UMT	Universal Military Training
UN	United Nations
UNITAF	Unified Task Force
UNOSOM	United Nations Operations in Somalia
UNPROFOR	United Nations Protection Force
USACGSC	US Army Command and General Staff College
USARV	United States Army, Vietnam
USMACV	United States Military Assistance Command, Vietnam
USMC	United States Marine Corps
USSOCOM	United States Special Operations Command
VC	Viet Cong
VOLAR	Volunteer Army
WMD	Weapons of Mass Destruction

INTRODUCTION

The use of military force is a key feature of international politics, particularly in the early twenty-first century. Nations use the powerful tool of military forces to be their 'fists of statecraft', enabling them to intimidate and dominate the decisions of other people and states.[1] But it is a complex problem and strategy is the study of the practice of 'the art of distributing and applying military means to fulfil the ends of policy'.[2] A mechanistic formula of setting political ends and using military means to achieve them is insufficient to make strategy, as the presence of an enemy who reacts means that war is more than mere administration.[3] In fact 'the entire realm of strategy is pervaded by a paradoxical logic of its own'.[4]

An over-reliance on either the political aims or the military means can destabilise a strategy and ultimately be fatal for a state. In the early nineteenth century, little regard was paid to military advice and the task of the military was to win wars after they had been declared, leaving strategy dominated by politics.[5] However, the growing intricacies of European warfare meant that the political–military relationship became more involved.[6] For example, Barbara Tuchman famously argued that the First World War was triggered by the German military machine's failure to adapt to the changing needs of the Kaiser once it had been mobilised.[7] In this case, the military means defined the political ends with catastrophic results for the Kaiser and for Europe. The consequence of the German military's independent understanding showed that a state's military means must be in accord with the political demands of strategy. A century earlier, Carl von Clausewitz had argued that 'The political objective is the goal, war is the means of achieving it, and means can never be considered in isolation from their purpose.'[8] However, political policy alone is not sufficient to make strategy, as shown by both world wars escalating out of political control.[9] National strategy requires keeping the political and military demands in tension through a dialectical relationship.[10]

The failure of the United States to win the Vietnam War was a stunning example of the mismatch between the policy aims and military means – the paradox of strategy. George Kennan, the doyen of American diplomacy, observed that the effort to evolve a sound theory of military strategy, and to relate it to other concerns of the national state, has been 'a difficult problem for most great countries; but it is hard to believe that any country has ever been farther from finding satisfactory solutions to it than our own'.[11] Though not fatal, the Vietnam War did considerable damage to the US state. The US is a very fruitful case study of how a state looks at and develops strategy as, after the war, it attempted to reconcile the military means with political aims. The aim of this study is to answer the question of how and why the US changed its military intervention strategy after the Vietnam War.

America after Vietnam is a particularly interesting example, as it developed a clear set of lessons concerning the use of force. Secretary of Defense Caspar Weinberger outlined the resolution of the inherent difficulties of strategy in 1984, with his 'doctrine' outlining six criteria for the use of force.[12] Weinberger has been criticised for providing a 'codification of the Vietnam syndrome'[13] but his speech was a crucial statement of the military's lessons from the Vietnam War experience and outlined the correct way for the US to use military force. The first Gulf War was carried out in accord with his understanding of the relationship between political objectives and military capability, and in 1992 the Chairman of the Joint Chiefs of Staff, Colin Powell, released the *National Military Strategy* that restated Weinberger's views under the rubric 'Decisive Force'. Decisive Force was outlined as a new strategic principle, a change from traditional American strategy.[14] By implication, the lessons of the Vietnam War had been learnt.

The difficulties the US faced in using force after the first Gulf War suggest that the learning was not so clear-cut or consensual. The Clinton administration challenged the Weinberger–Powell understanding of the relationship between political aims and the limitations of the military, and Clinton's first Secretary of Defense, Les Aspin, went so far as to characterise the Weinberger doctrine as an 'All-or-Nothing' approach to war.[15] Once in office, the 'seminal events' of the foreign policy of the Clinton administration were three failed military interventions – Bosnia, Somalia, Haiti – in its first nine months in office.[16] The 1993 failure in Somalia led the White House to release Presidential Decision Directive 25 (PDD 25) on Multilateral Peace Operations, which restated the Weinberger–Powell doctrine,[17] and was contrary to the earlier expressed ideals of the administration. The Clinton administration's strategic practice and understanding were reformulated in line with the revised military thinking but were inadequate for the stated policy of the administration.

Having claimed to have learnt the lessons of Vietnam it is surprising that when faced by the complex environment of Somalia, the political aims unravelled as the military were unable to cope conceptually with the situation and the US effectively ended up going to war. A critical examination of US military intervention strategy is needed, therefore, because the US should have learnt from its extensive experience of using force in a complex socio-political environment when it fought in Vietnam. This failure raises important questions as to the nature of the learning that had gone on since Vietnam, as the military's understanding of strategy, and what was militarily achievable, was a crucial component of US strategic understanding and practice, and shaped US foreign policy. It also raises the question of the extent that the military means inhibit the discretion of the political authorities.[18] Additionally, as Richard Betts asserts,

> confusion continues about what U.S. foreign policy should expect military power to do for less vital interests. What force can accomplish in a specific situation does not follow directly from standard international relations theories or rational choice models. . . . If capacity for informed strategic analysis . . . is not preserved and applied, decisions on the use of force will be uninformed and, therefore, irresponsible.[19]

To highlight how and why the US learnt about relating political aims to military means, four subsidiary questions will be posed and answered in this study: What was new about the strategic understanding? Why was the first Gulf War seen as the vindication of the lessons of Vietnam? Why was it so unable to handle the situation in Somalia? and What is the legacy of this thinking? The sheer scale of the factors that can be covered in these questions requires a further distillation to concentrate on important factors common to all the questions; to answer the questions this study focuses on the learning that went on within the Army prior to Somalia, before addressing the legacy of this thinking on the later interventions in Kosovo, Afghanistan and Iraq.

The Army

The Army is the key subject for three specific reasons. First, the Weinberger doctrine was specifically concerned with committing 'troops to combat' and was an embodiment of particularly Army thinking, therefore it is important to understand the thinking behind it and the consequences of how it was formulated. Second, the broad process of producing strategy is concerned with the structures and constraints involved.[20] The Army is central to US strategy and ultimately its role is fundamental to the use of force. Additionally, its failure to learn from its experience in Vietnam led to the failure of the Somalia intervention. As the First World War German example showed, the strategy and security of the state can rest on how integrated the military's understanding is with the state's policy aims.[21] This raises the final reason, which is the important point of what it means to say that a 'nation' learns.

Where does a state invest its learning, especially, as seen above, as 'strategy' is a dialectical relationship between the political ends and military means as they affect each other in a reciprocal intercourse of structure and agency. The US Army was consistent in its views but different administrations held varying views. As this study will show, it was the understanding of this very relationship between the Army and the various administrations that was deemed an essential component of the strategic lessons of Vietnam. This approach helped to define what was so new about the strategy, and, due to its limitations, made the intervention in Somalia a failure. The Army as a strategic 'structure' was in a transformational relationship with the US government, providing both constraints and abilities[22] for its use of force. The concept of 'structuration' explains this by seeing that the social structure persists only as far as individual actors reproduce the practices that constitute the structures.[23] This model makes it possible to see that the learning was invested in key actors within the Army, and the Army itself was an actor within the nation, making it a vital component of the nation's learning and ensuing strategic practice and thinking. Central to the argument is that the Army's strategic thinking changed, and this is analysed by using the concept of 'identity'.

Identity is an important analytical concept when examining the US Army as it developed a coherent strategic understanding of itself, the nature of war and its utility. Identity brings together the realms of history, practice and ideas, and how they are explained to those who perform them and how they are carried within tradition.[24] The identity developed after the war was of a professional body concerned with the 'Profession of Arms' rather than simply a sociological and generic understanding of being a 'profession'. In the period of this study, the sources of identity moved it from being socially produced, as the nation at war, to one that drew from other militaries and its past. This approach is in contrast to analysts who advocate 'identity' as a sense of difference, in the post-modern sense, as a reaction and relation to 'others'.[25] The contrast to society was one of the very things that it initially wished to avoid. The US Army, in common with militaries generally, has a very strong sense of being rooted in tradition, and uses this in times of adversity. The changes that the US Army made to its thinking and practice in rebuilding itself after the Vietnam War drew on the work of the nineteenth-century analyst Carl von Clausewitz, and on Israeli and Soviet thinking.

The chronological parameters of the study is the period 1973 to 2004, as this takes the analysis from the withdrawal from Vietnam and the institution of the All-Volunteer Army to the new strategic environment after the events of 11 September 2001. It analyses the strategic thinking by examining the doctrine, debate and practice of the Army, before examining the rise and wane of its influence on national policy.

The analysis of the doctrine focuses on the *Field Manual (FM) 100-5*, Operations, and its revisions in the period covered. Doctrine is central to the analysis as the doctrinal changes were the medium of reform of the US Army during this period.[26] Doctrine is 'an expression and awareness of the current state of warfare, an expression of our influence and role as an Army in world affairs and an expression of how we view ourselves in relation to our adversaries'.[27] Theo Farrell takes this further by observing that

> Essentially, service doctrine explains the goals, identifies the tasks, and shapes the tools of the organisation. Furthermore, it does so to three distinct audiences – the members of the organisation, sister military services, and policymakers – and for three distinct reasons. Directed at organisational members, doctrine helps a military organisation to maintain internal coherence in how it prepares for, and prosecutes, military operations. Directed at sister services, doctrine facilitates joint and combined operations. Directed at policymakers, doctrine enables a military organisation to maximise its autonomy and resource-base.[28]

Doctrine thereby articulates how the Army sees itself and war, and importantly how it wants others to see itself.

The debates about doctrine and strategy within the Army are examined through the various journals of the Army. A. J. Bacevich, in his study of the US Army in the 1950s, highlighted the importance of these journals for researchers. He pointed out that they tend to reflect ideas that enjoy official sanction, mirroring rather than determining thought, making them 'ideal for the historian attempting to understand the mind-set of the officer corps at a particular time'.[29] On this basis the journals of the various combat arms of the Army, the Command and General Staff College, and the Army War College are examined. The journals, the Army's own commissioned studies of the lessons of the Vietnam War, writings by influential analysts and confidential interviews are the main sources for the examination of the debates and factors influencing the reforms.[30]

To appreciate the influence of the ideas it is necessary to examine actual interventions. Particular attention is paid to the events in Panama, the first Gulf War and the post-Cold War intervention in Somalia, to see how the thinking influenced the practice of the use of force, and the difficulties the Army faced. Additionally, reference is made to interventions in Lebanon, Grenada, Bosnia, Haiti, Kosovo, Afghanistan and Iraq. Overall, this approach allows an analysis of the military's understanding of why the Vietnam War was lost, the strategic lessons for the military that ensue from this reading, and how it understood 'strategy' itself, before analysing the effect of this new thinking on US intervention strategy more generally.

Methodology

The methodology of this study is broadly from the field of 'strategic studies', a subdiscipline of international studies, as it draws upon the resources of history and political science to understand how politics and war are integrated. Political analysis focuses on the 'distribution, exercise and consequences of power', and stresses the process of power relations.[31] Strategic studies falls under this rubric but 'is different not only because it is more interested in force than in other forms of power, but because it addresses power from the perspective of those wielding it'.[32] This means that it has a critical approach to the strategic decisions of others whilst appreciating their mindset; it does not mean that it identifies with the subject under analysis.[33] This requires critically 'explaining' and 'understanding' the subject under analysis, weaving together external and internal interpretations.[34] The internal logic of an actor is thus taken seriously. Strategic studies lies between security studies (which covers anything that bears on the safety of polity) and military science (which is concerned with how technology, organisation and tactics combine to win battles). It examines how political ends and military means interact under social, economic and other restraints.[35]

Obviously in a study of this kind there is a temptation to veer towards a narrative or descriptive study of the 'history of ideas', a temptation encouraged by the fact that 'new' military history is much broader, paying greater attention to the interaction of war with society, economics, politics and culture.[36] A historical approach has a supreme regard for 'the evidence, the problems it poses and the uses to which it can be put'.[37] For example, Tim Travers, in his classic study of the British Army, clearly identifies his work as 'an attempt to link intellectual history – the history of ideas – with the raw material and events of the war'. He does this through analysing the patterns of thought and the behaviour of senior officers, so that one can understand why events occurred the way they did.[38] However, the aim of this research is much narrower than Travers's, focussing on the particular influence of the Vietnam War on the Army's strategic thinking and its influence.

This study develops previous work on the Army's changes after Vietnam, especially the historical works that have produced detailed chronological accounts of the changes.[39] The first Gulf War reinforced and legitimised many of the changes in the Army outlined in these works, as it had undergone a great change in identity, becoming fundamentally different from the Army that emerged from Vietnam twenty years before.[40] Work with a more conceptual approach looks at the dynamics of political–military understanding within a concept of professionalism,[41] or the broader debate over the use of force,[42] without providing the detail of the conceptual developments and process of innovation in the Army. For example, Shimon Naveh's *In Pursuit of Military Excellence* provides a detailed account and develops a systems theory approach that makes up for many analytical shortcomings in the literature.[43] However, as Naveh is concerned with the development of operational theory within twentieth-century armies he does not place the Army developments, and the strategic consequences, in the broader US foreign policy environment. Carl Builder's *The Masks of War*[44] is important to any analysis of the Army within the strategic environment. Builder self-consciously uses a broad brush to analyse the behaviours of the services and uses the term 'personality' to help explain the Army; but the 'masks' of the title refer to a cover for deeply embedded institutional interests.[45] This study goes beyond simply seeing the Army as a self-interested organisation because after the first Gulf War its behaviour was not bureaucratically maximising, as it was not prepared to undertake many of the new tasks.[46] Obviously, bureaucratic interests were influential due to the sheer size of the Pentagon; as former Secretary of Defense William Perry puts it, 'the Department of Defense may be thought of as the largest company in the world, with more than 3 million employees . . . [and] has an annual budget of a quarter of a trillion dollars'.[47] Ideas and perceptions may be adopted for bureaucratic self-interest, but that does not explain the source of the thinking. Additionally, Builder's approach is limited in its account of changes within the Army's thinking, as is Deborah Avant's analysis, though she correctly highlights the long-term effect of the institutional position on the broader aspects of military innovation.[48] Builder's and Avant's work is important, but this study develops their work by examining the stability and dynamism of the behaviour of the Army.

This study overcomes seeing the important elements of the organisational behaviour, historical practice, doctrine and the conceptual debate in isolation or in pairs, by being interdisciplinary and drawing upon literature covering military innovation and strategic culture. As well as being a focused case study, it will contribute to these literatures.

Innovation

The US Army does not explicitly think strategically, so the subject of this research is to tease out the stated and implicit aspects of the Army's strategic thought in the period after the Vietnam War, and to do this it draws upon theoretical literature on military innovation.

The study of innovation is more than the study of change; it examines the motives, means and extent of change. As Stephen Rosen observes, a 'major innovation' is

> a change that forces one of the primary combat arms of a service to change its concepts of operation and its relation to other combat arms, and to abandon or downgrade traditional missions. Such innovations involve a new way of war, with new ideas of how the components of the organization relate to each other and to the enemy, and new operational procedures conforming to those ideas. They involve changes in the critical military tasks, the tasks around which warplans revolve.[49]

Innovation, therefore, involves a range of ideational and structural changes. The Army will be assessed in terms of the novelty of the reformed 'way of war' after Vietnam and this will be seen in a wider context than its traditional focus upon tactical level, though changes in tactics and standard operating procedures are a crucial aspect of military innovation, as are the mid-level officers who generate them.[50] Innovation makes clear that there has been a change from the historical precedent, or tradition, in the area of key roles and doctrines.

Military innovation literature is used because it is necessary to see what drove the nature of the reform of the Army's thinking after Vietnam. For example, traditionally militaries change, or innovate, as a response to shifts in the strategic environment.[51] This is too limited an approach for this study because it does not explain why the Army's doctrine fundamentally changed from Active Defense (1976) to AirLand Battle doctrine (1982), without there being a corresponding change in the strategic environment.[52] If the changes were actually a case of institutional learning stimulated by the Vietnam War, then why did the US have such a poor strategy, and the Army no doctrine,[53] for the intervention in Somalia, an environment far more similar strategically to Vietnam than the first Gulf War?

Changes in the nature of the Army have commonly been seen as coming from external sources, often generated by the development of new military technology.[54] This approach would help explain why the Army ignored Vietnam scenarios and focused elsewhere, an argument supported by the importance of the Army's development of the new 'Big Five' pieces of equipment.[55] Additionally, 'Active Defense' doctrine was explicitly technologically based, and some critics have gone further and seen AirLand Battle doctrine as primarily technological.[56] What this line of argument does not account for is the changed self-perception of the Army over the whole period after the Vietnam War. As Brigadier General Robert Scales observes, the Army in 1991 was not the same as the one of 1973, and that was due to perceptions of war fighting.

> Army reform centred primarily on ideas and people rather than machines. . . . This new Army would seek to outthink rather than outslug its opponents . . . the Army that met Saddam Hussein was fundamentally different from the Army that emerged from the jungles of Vietnam 20 years before.[57]

The shift from second-generation warfare (dependent on massed firepower) to third-generation (manoeuvre oriented) is in itself a change in innovative drivers from technology to ideas.[58] This study is a critical case study of the importance of ideas to innovation, and bears out the importance of innovation not being simply technology driven. It builds on the work done by Elizabeth Kier on doctrine development after the First World War in Britain and France, as well as broader work, such as Farrell and Terriff's *The Sources of Military Change* on social norms and societal character being a major feature shaping innovation, the military and warfare.[59]

The interwar years have proved a common ground for much of the new research work on military innovation. Implicitly, much of this work addresses the problem of military innovation in the US in the 1980s,[60] and the current post-Cold War difficulties of the US have stimulated a second wave of work on innovation.[61] However, none of the major works on innovation have actually addressed the explicit case of the development of the Army's AirLand Battle doctrine within the context of the American strategic culture. This study emphasises the national sources of the innovation in thinking, and in doing so draws upon work done on the concept of strategic culture.

Strategic culture

Strategic culture focuses on 'those policies which, through persistence, have taken on the character of a tradition or habit or norm'.[62] Strategic refers here to the military dimension of security, and strategic culture is the military dimension of a political culture. As one work on strategic culture expressed it;

> Strategic culture produces tendencies, it creates predispositions, but it does not determine policies. Strategic culture helps to constitute attitudes and behaviour, but cannot on its own fully explain outcomes, since other variables, such as technology, also play a part, and may at any one point dominate.[63]

In emphasising the national context, strategic culture builds upon Michael Howard's observation that: 'Military forces are shaped not only by weapons with which they are armed, but by the social background from which they emerge and the political function for which they are intended.'[64] Historical works such as Russell Weigley's *The American Way of War* and John Shy's *A People Numerous and Armed* have drawn attention to the importance of a particularly American approach to strategy.[65] Weigley's work is particularly important because he outlines a thesis of 'a strategy of annihilation' that, though it blurs the distinction of annihilation and attrition and does not emphasise other approaches, is known as *the* American way of war.[66] It emphasises the destruction of enemy forces and the wearing down of opponents through attrition.[67] Loren Baritz in *Backfire* took this line of analysis further by explicitly identifying American culture as the source of the intervention in Vietnam and determining how the US fought the war.[68] The concept of 'strategic culture' was further developed by political science as it tried to analyse the difference between Soviet and American approaches to strategy, and the consequences of this for defence planning.[69] This work is seen as a 'first generation' of strategic cultural analysis. The main features of the first generation are that the unique variations in history, political culture and geography determine national behaviour.[70] Howard, in a review of one the key texts, summarised the position as: 'Different cultures have different attitudes to war, and these, far more than any rational calculations, will shape their strategy and explain their successes and failures.'[71]

It is the argument of this study that the Army's strategic understanding was initially a product of the broader American strategic culture, but changed to become a dominant influence until 1991. In so doing it altered the nation's strategic culture. Fundamentally, the social alienation that the Army suffered after the Vietnam War meant that its identity could not be mechanistically determined by the broader national culture which had turned against it. The Army developed its own 'professional' identity and emphasis and was clear about what it was, what it could do and how it should be used – its strategic understanding. The Army's changed identity and 'new way of war' was developed within the context of the broader national culture, but was no longer simply determined by it. The Army thus became a significant element within the national strategic culture on its own terms and this altered the US strategic culture.

This development highlights the limitations of first-generation strategic culture analysis, and the problem is addressed by work that sees the organisational culture as an intervening variable between the broader culture and military doctrine.[72] In this case, the US Army moved from reflecting the broad culture to having a separate identity that was based on professional premises, and this became very influential in the use of military force by the US from the end of the Vietnam War to 1991. In other words, the broader culture was no longer a determinant but the context for strategic thinking, and the change in the constitutive norms of the Army (i.e. what made it) altered the regulative norms of intervention (i.e. how it was used). This shift was embodied in the Weinberger doctrine. It is after the Gulf War in 1991 that the influence of the Army waned in defining the strategic culture, though its influence was still great, as will be seen.

Strategic culture aids analysis of the trends within US intervention policy, and has the advantage that these aspects can be tested for their explanatory power. Alistair Johnston's work, in particular, uses the 'ranked set of grand-strategic preferences that is consistent across the objects of analysis' as his test of falsifiability.[73] The Weinberger criteria provide the preferences, and the consequent falsifiability can be tested in the interventions examined.

This research contributes to the broader debate about political–military strategic integration by formulating a hypothesis of the fundamental importance of the US Army's self-understanding as a key source of the nation's strategic thinking and its changing role and influence within that debate. This is particularly important as the implications of the Army's 'new way of war' matched only certain aspects of the broader culture,[74] clearly clashing with the Clinton administration. Also, this study re-reads the effect of the Vietnam War on US foreign policy. Rather than seeing the Army simply blocking interventions to avoid another Vietnam War, it shows that its thinking about the utility of force was more complex and deeply thought out. This is particularly important when analysing the post-Cold War era and the use of force debate in the US. This study furthers that debate, by providing a unique reading of an important aspect of the rebuilding after the Vietnam War. It brings together the historical monographs from within the military, which have stressed the revolutionary changes that were brought about after the war, and those analysts from outside who have stressed the lack of change. It provides a conceptual framework for explaining this anomaly, and furthers the debate on the factors within the US understanding of the use of force and its role in the strategic culture.

This study also develops the literature on military innovation by clarifying the common perception that failure leads to innovation.[75] The case study of the US Army after Vietnam shows that the nature of the learning is in no way predetermined or even self-evident. For example, the Army had the potential to develop great counterinsurgency capabilities in light of its failure, but it chose not to. It actually fought a highly conventional war in 1991 and cited the multidimensional and complex conflict of Vietnam as the root of the learning process. This needs to be explained if the study of innovation after failure is to develop. The role and source of ideas in perceiving the cause of failure and how they are to be redressed is shown to be central to the debate. Innovation is not automatically determined by failure; the nature of the organisational culture is crucial.

This study also highlights the importance of strategic culture for organisational innovation analysis. It develops the institutional theme by showing the importance of the domestic environment of innovation, as in Kier's work, but develops it by looking at the international aspects of military professionalism as a stimulus to innovation. For example, international military professionalism is not simply a response to the intelligence of an opponent's strategy[76] but draws upon new thinking from friendly forces. In the US case this was particularly from Israel. This research also furthers the developments of literature on the domestic role within strategic innovation by highlighting the interplay of this with the role of military professionalism. Using the concept of identity to analyse the Army, and placing it within the broader idea of strategic culture achieves this. It is a check on more universal and deterministic approaches to strategic cultural analysis.

This study is divided into four distinct parts. Chapters 1 and 2 argue that the Vietnam War's nature and loss was a challenge to the US Army because the US Army's constitutional position, and nature as a citizen's army, brought together the political aims and military means of the national strategy. This approach relied upon the application of 'brute force'[77] to accumulate tactical and attritional victories to win wars and has been labelled the 'American way of war'.[78] The loss of the war in Vietnam shattered that strategic relationship and made the Army an all-volunteer force, and by doing so separated the Army's identity from the nation's. It was this change that prescribed how the army saw itself, war and its utility as a political-strategic tool after Vietnam.

Chapters 3 and 4 focus exclusively on the Army and outlines how it rebuilt itself. In addition to developing the Total Force concept to integrate reservists and volunteers to guarantee full support before deployment, the Army developed an understanding of itself as a professional force focused on training and doctrine. The reorientation led to a changed strategic understanding as the reference points for the role of the Army were no longer social – the nation at war – but that of fellow professionals; the Israeli, German and Soviet armed forces were all sources of the new thinking along with the community of US civilian defence theorists. This led to the doctrinal changes of development of AirLand Battle doctrine, examined in Chapter 4. This doctrine was a reconceptualisation of the premises of US Army strategic thinking, replacing simple tactical attrition with 'operational shock' as a new way of war. The new doctrine was the basis for the Army's rebuilding during the Reagan years. The new approach relied on being given clear operational objectives by the executive to allow the tenets of AirLand Battle doctrine to be applied. The strategic understanding was in accord with the broader lessons of the Vietnam War and was the dual source of the thinking that informed the Weinberger doctrine.

Chapters 5 and 6 widen the focus by examining the influence and implications of the Army's thinking on national strategy. They show how the new thinking serendipitously fitted the Reagan and the first Bush administrations' priorities, and how the growth of the defence budget allowed it to be enacted. Importantly, the emphasis on the operational level of analysis provided a template for the Air Force's doctrine, and Congressional reforms enabled the thinking to reach beyond the Army to inform the US military and the management of national security. The Panama invasion and the Gulf War were products of this thinking, and their success a vindication of the developments that had gone on. The failure in Somalia, however, showed the strategic shortcomings of the Weinberger criteria and the operational thinking which lay behind it, whilst the restatement of the Army's thinking by the administration in 1994 showed how influential it had become, due to its roots in the Army's identity and doctrinal capability.

Finally, Chapter 7 takes a much broader perspective and examines the legacy of the Army's thinking and practice on post-1994 interventions in Kosovo,

Afghanistan and Iraq, showing how the thinking was still influential but as a constraining and deforming aspect, rather than the enabling feature it was previously in national strategic culture.

In answering the question of how and why the US changed its military intervention strategy from the Vietnam War, this study argues that strategic co-ordination changed from being based on national mobilisation, to a dependence upon having clear political objectives which were militarily achievable. This formulation and its basis were a product of the Army's reforms and changes in its 'way of war'. The learning of strategic lessons was vested in the Army. The statement of the Army's thinking in the Weinberger doctrine and the practice followed during the first Gulf War show how influential it became. However, the Army's thinking was a self-referential process, as the regulative norms for military intervention strategy, namely what is militarily achievable, are defined by the Army's own sense of professionalism, and this was unsuitable for the new strategic environment. In other words, how the Army saw itself shaped what it could do, and this formed what the nation could do. As a consequence, the failure in Somalia led to the reassertion of the Weinberger doctrine, leaving American strategic culture limited to using troops in interventions which have clear political objectives and are militarily achievable in the Army's own terms. However, as the air campaign in Kosovo showed, without the discipline of troop deployments the administration could ignore the 'strategic' lessons of Vietnam. Kosovo marked the avoidance of the influence of the Army's strategic learning from the Vietnam War, as its constitutive norms no longer provided the positive prescriptive norms for US strategic culture. The response of the G. W. Bush administration to the events of 9/11 has, militarily, been one that has ignored many of the key lessons from the Vietnam War concerning the complexities of political–military strategy. The President is still reliant on his military and its capability, and is constrained by it, however much his Secretary of Defense attempts to transform it.

1

THE US ARMY AND AMERICAN STRATEGIC CULTURE

To understand the US Army's strategic thinking after the Vietnam War, it is first necessary to understand the nature of its social sources. This chapter will outline the main characteristics of the US Army's strategic thought and self-understanding as a product of national culture, establishing its identity and tactics. The constitutional position of the Army provides the basic structure within which the Army's thinking and identity has developed, and this will be examined before going on to see how this legacy changed and evolved over the period to the Second World War. The second section examines how the war was the culmination of a process that saw the Army embodying the militia tradition with an identity as the nation at war. Its tactics and understanding of strategy was a product of this understanding. The final section examines the pressures on the traditional identity which were brought with the start of the Cold War and the development of the first major US standing army, and how this related to the political understanding of strategy in an age which saw the arrival of nuclear weapons. The contradictions between these demands will be seen as the root of the strategic problems the US had in prosecuting the Vietnam War and shaped how the Army perceived the war and its lessons.

The nation's Army

Analyst Carl Builder observes that the Army has 'not shown any particularly strong affinity for strategy'.[1] This is not unique to the US Army. As Ken Booth observed in 1978: 'the study of strategy and participation in strategic-decision making has not been professionally relevant for any military establishment until quite recently.'[2] Additionally, the US has a reputation for not having indigenous strategic thinkers beyond the Navy's Alfred Thayer Mahan and air power advocate Billy Mitchell, which itself is reflective of the fact that the US was primarily a sea power rather than a land power prior to the Second World War.[3] Fundamentally, the United States did not develop and nurture a tradition of excellence in strategy because it did not need one.[4] However, even with the lack of US strategic tradition, the Army has to have some form of strategy so that it can make decisions,[5] and the concept of strategic culture can help to see how thinking is institutionalised, codified and perpetuated.[6] As the military historian John Keegan explains:

> an army is . . . an expression of the society from which it issues. The purposes for which it fights and the way it does so will therefore be determined in large measure by what a society wants from a war and how far it expects its army to go in delivering that outcome.[7]

Keegan, by highlighting the relationship between society and warfare, outlines the importance of the original society for the nature and character of an army and its strategic thinking. For the US Army, the American Constitution, historical legacy and its nature as a citizen's army provided the implicit strategic understanding.

Essential to strategy is the co-ordination of the military means and the political ends, and for the US that relationship is formalised in the Constitution.[8] The kind of armed forces that the US possesses was outlined at the moment of the violent establishment of the United States as it threw off its colonial masters.[9] The Constitutional Convention's outcomes established an 'abiding congruence of purpose' between America and its army.[10] This was seen in the Convention's concern with the Cromwellian 'man on horseback', and they looked to minimise the risk of despotism and a coup. It also reflected the innovative political nature of the Revolutionary War.[11] The Constitution places many checks and balances on the military to avoid the fate of its European forebears, and Dave R. Palmer gives one of the better summaries of the convoluted solution that was developed.

> The United States could maintain armed forces in peacetime, but only if funded by Congress. The president would command the military, but Congress would write the rules. State authorities would command the militia, but would meet standards of readiness set by Congress. The commander in chief would wage war, but only after Congress declared it. The president would end wars, but only with the approval of the Senate. The commander in chief would deploy military forces, but Congress would determine their size and shape. The president would appoint and commission officers, but with the consent of the Senate. The president would command the militia when they might be federalized, but the states would appoint militia officers and oversee the training of the units. The federal government could field regular forces, but the states would retain authority to direct the militia.[12]

The American Constitution broke with the European tradition and placed the Army and its recruitment and training under federal and state chains of command. This gave the Army a distinctive identity compared to its European contemporaries, focused as it was upon the centrality of the Constitution and divided and separated among the executive and legislative powers. The role of commander in chief was symbolically invested in the presidency, rather than in the sovereign, and it is the Constitution itself that is the referent for the identity of the Army. Hence an American officer is commissioned into the Army to 'support and defend the constitution of the United States against all enemies, foreign and domestic: [and] . . . will bear true faith and allegiance to the same'.[13]

The integration of state and federal forces made the involvement of the legislature vital, thereby stopping the Army from simply being the political instrument of the head of state. Additionally, it relied on national support as it is made up of the mobilisation of the nation's citizens. As an Army Chief of Staff put it in 1994:

> The soldiers of America's Army are citizen-volunteers who serve in either the active or reserve components: volunteers who serve the Nation in every state, city and town in the United States. We are the Army of a democratic nation and our institutional core is selfless service to the Nation as prescribed by the Constitution.[14]

The remarkable consistency of thought over the 200 years between 1794 and 1994 concerning the identity of the Army, shows the strength of this tradition and forms the understanding that lies behind the historical development of the US Army.

During the first half of the nineteenth century, the Army's relation to society was one of isolation and neglect. The Army's prime mission during the bulk of this period was securing the frontier and fighting the indigenous population. This era was punctuated by the War of 1812 (1812–14) and the Mexican War (1845–47) in which it was not the regulars but the militia and volunteers respectively who formed the main force.[15] In both cases, non-regulars were quickly demobilised when the conflicts terminated. The small standing army was thus supplementary to the volunteers and state-raised militias. It was the Civil War that brought in the massed armies of the North and South.

The Civil War was a decisive episode for the Army and the nation's strategic culture. It was fought in the Napoleonic tradition, relying on mass armies meeting at decisive points and destroying the opponent's forces at their centres of gravity.[16] As Michael Howard says, in the American Civil War it was the logistical aspect of strategy that was most important, and this has influenced all subsequent US military strategy.[17] US Army General Donn A. Starry supports this logistical/resource basis by observing that in conscript armies there is always a tendency to look on manpower as a virtually free resource, one that, if provided in sufficient numbers and properly supplied, is the best way to win. He argues that 'it is an idea that has dominated US military thought, at least until the advent of nuclear weapons, but which dies hard'.[18]

The Civil War brought the evolution of the massed army idea but it did not bring prestige for the Army.[19] After the war the American Army as a professional body was isolated, reduced and rejected. It was 'unseen, unpopular, or unknown. Northerners were disinterested in it, southerners disliked it, westerners no longer needed it. In 1877 . . . the officers and men of the United States Army went a full year without pay.'[20] Paradoxically, the very isolation of the military after the Civil War was the chief prerequisite for the initial development of army professionalism, as it was withdrawn from civilian society and turned inwards upon itself. It was to bring about the emergence of the first forms of military professionalism.

> The years between 1860 and the First World War saw the emergence of a distinctive American professional ethic, with the American officer regarding himself as a member no longer of a fighting profession only. to which anyone might belong, but as a member of a profession which, if not accepted as learned, could still be intellectually demanding, and whose students were students for life.[21]

The trend to professionalisation was not allowed by the US culture to become an isolated professionalism. For example, the indecisiveness of the Civil War meant that a way to minimise its horror was to emulate the Prussian example and gear the society to war. However, any desire for a 'quasi-military elite' faded after the Civil War in the face of the triumph of the American liberal 'laissez-faire' ideas.[22] The US in 1865, as later in 1918 and 1945, had a hasty demobilisation. It was not to be revived until the excitement of the Spanish–American War of 1898. The primary American concern was civilian, to such an extent that military professionalism itself was questioned, while attempts to transcend societal limitations 'have not usually had happy endings'.[23] The most famous example was Emory Upton, whose book *The Military Policy of the United States*[24] 'was almost a catalogue of mistakes, defeats, wasted expenditures, and unnecessary casualties arising from the voluntaristic, amateurish, civilian-dominated American way of war.'[25]

Upton, after his experience of the Civil War with its purchase of commissions and the civilian interference in the war, prized the Prussian model of military professionalism. He attacked civilian domination of the military, and focused on developing military professionalism, initially by writing and reforming the tactical manual of the Army.[26] Upton's regard for the Prussian model had developed after General Sherman sent him to Europe and a world tour in 1875–76 to study various militaries. His ideas were not adopted in his own time and he committed suicide with his seminal work unpublished, though they were eventually taken up in a revised form by Elihu Root, Theodore Roosevelt's Secretary of War (1899–1904), who published Upton's work in 1904.[27]

Root adopted Upton's institutional reforms, leading to the establishment of a general staff in 1903 and the revision of the militia tradition.[28] This abolished the role of the president as the direct commander in chief, and the authority would be exercised by, or in the name of, the secretary of war, through a chief of staff. Crucially, the nature of the reforms, and the motives for their adoption, were not as Upton originally envisaged. The organisational nature of the reform was not modelled on his Prussian example, as Root utilised large-scale business organisation thinking and adapted it to government, emphasising executive leadership and the efficacy of clear lines of accountability and authority. As Paul Hammond wrote in 1961, the consequences of the 1903 Act 'are still with us',[29] and it was seen as the root of the later business managerialism of Robert McNamara.[30] Additionally, the reforms were not used to develop a separate military caste but to reinvigorate society and foster rugged individualism. President Theodore Roosevelt supported Root's approach, 'not so much interested in its institutional aspects as in its effectiveness in cultivating military "habits" within the American population'.[31] Upton and Uptonianism, therefore, came to stand as a symbol of a military re-invigorating the nation's society, whilst 'pure' Uptonianism, based on the German model, faded with US entry into the First World War. Upton would have been surprised at the ability shown by the democratic government during the war. To American nationalists such as Leonard Wood, the controversial Army Chief of Staff[32] and one of Roosevelt's 'Rough Riders',[33] it was no surprise.

General Wood saw the identity of the Army clearly in relation to the people and the nation. 'You the people make war; the Government declares it; and we, the officers of the Army and Navy, are charged with the responsibility of terminating it with such means and implements as you may give us.'[34] To further this he revived the citizen-army model and established the famous Plattsburg training camps.[35] While they aimed to develop preparedness as part of an interventionist movement against President Wilson's professed reluctance to be involved in the First World War, the camps initiated broad social and political implications, reviving citizen-soldier values within American society.[36] Wood's viewpoint is neatly summarised by the collection of speeches he published in 1915, *The Military Obligation of Citizenship*.[37]

The influence of Wood's movement is shown by one of the recruits to the training camps. Henry Stimson, at the age of 48, enrolled in 1916.[38] As Secretary of War under President Taft (1911–13), Stimson had followed Root's institutional changes based on Upton's ideas and fully backed Wood's views within the Army about the entry of the US into the First World War. It should be remembered that at this time the Secretary of War was effectively America's colonial secretary, and Stimson is seen as the founder of US foreign policy establishment.[39] He symbolised the nationalist movement that went right through to end of the end of the Second World War, and his heirs were the 'Wise Men' of American diplomacy.[40] It was a tradition ended by the Vietnam War. Stimson was a proponent of assertive US foreign policy, and 'a familiar type in American policy-making circles over the previous hundred and fifty years'.[41] The nation's Army, composed of citizens embodying American attributes not simply professionals, underpinned the aspirant and growing US world role.

The spirit of inspired and capable amateurism was to continue in the US Army. General DePuy, commander of Army training (1973–76), wrote in 1976 that:

> we do not train brigade, division, and corps commanders in the U.S. Army. We simply take a chance that an intelligent officer who has survived the promotion system must have some built in intelligence and instincts that will make him an effective commander. This is, of course, mostly nonsense.[42]

The continuity of this tradition shows the strength of feeling against simple professionalism within the Army. However, the nature of the Army as a mobilisation force was to be transformed by the experience of the Second World War and its Cold War aftermath.

The Second World War and the new Army identity

The practice of the Army in the Second World War was rooted in its identity as the nation mobilised, based on a small core outfitted for Mexican border skirmishes and equipped with light tanks to assist the infantry. Going into the war the Army 'had not yet completed the transition that would make it an appropriate instrument of its country's claim to world power'.[43] It had to adapt this approach to fight the war, as it only had two regular divisions that were 'reasonably' ready for combat, one of which was a traditional cavalry division. It adapted by increasing its scale, which was in accord with the expanded political geography of the nation's interests. The Second World War altered the size of the US Army but, crucially, the strategic understanding remained constant. In fact:

> World War II both shaped and revealed American strategic culture as no other war with exception of the Civil War. Two dominant characteristics stand out: the preference for massing a vast array of men and machines and the predilection for direct and violent assault. The war was, at many levels, a war of mass production fought by a country that had used that concept to forge the world's largest and most productive economy. It was neither elegant nor subtle, but it worked.[44]

John Ellis has described this approach as one of 'brute force'. Resources rather than strategy were deployed to defeat Germany and Japan. Ellis criticises the image of the Second World War as a sophisticated armoured war shaped by blitzkrieg thinking. Rather,

> all Allied generals relied in the last analysis on firepower and sheer material superiority to win their battles rather than on any concept of unbalancing the enemy or forcing him to give up ground by threatening moves into his flanks and rear. Time and again the favoured method was simply to bomb him into submission. This point was tersely made by no less a commentator than Patton, who said after the war: 'I do not have to tell you who won the war. You know our artillery did.' General Marshall . . . made it equally clear . . . 'Though our heavy artillery from the 105mm up was generally matched by the Germans, our method of employment of these weapons has been one of the decisive factors of our ground campaigns throughout the world.'[45]

At the operational level this meant reliance upon overwhelming force. For example (albeit an extreme one) at Cassino the defending Germans ran out of shells before the attacking US forces ran out of tanks, and 'commanders seemed unable to impose their will upon the enemy except by slowly and persistently battering him to death with a blunt instrument'.[46] The US Army was not unaware of this. As one US general put it,

> we achieved victory in World War II, generally speaking, without a high degree of professionalism in the fighting units. . . . As far as the fighting aspects, we could win each war by the weight of our effort and the superiority of our weapons, not by the skill of our leaders or the proficiency of our gunners.[47]

However, there was a sense of the nation, through its Army, defeating the enemy, and this was sustained by there being millions in the reserves, a huge draft and a nationally unified resolve. The Second World War brought the Army a prestige that lasted into the 1960s, though it did not have a very sophisticated image.[48] The legacy of the war was later revived after Vietnam, as the 1941 edition of *FM 100-5* 'which helped win World War II' was used in the writing of the 1986 edition.[49]

The victory in the Second World War developed the US's annihilatory approach to war, where the political aim of unconditional surrender was brought about by the decisive defeat of the enemies' military forces. The US achieved this because there was the ability to mobilise the whole nation in the defeat of Nazism, and this gave the Army certain characteristics in its 'way of war'.

Characteristics of the Army

The main characteristic of the US Army at the end of the Second World War was that it was a mobilisation Army. Mobilisation, as with the militia tradition it came from, explicitly linked the use of the Army to the wider society, which meant that the nation's interests had to be at stake for the Army to be used. Therefore, the use of the Army coincided with the activation of the resources and technology of the nation to prosecute the war. The success of this approach in the Second World War meant that the military showed 'a marked predisposition for strategic offensives supported by full national mobilization, employing the economic and technological assets of the nation, to bring to bear a preponderance of power in the most direct and decisive manner possible'.[50] As the contemporary journalist and historian Chester Wilmot put it, during the war Americans 'proceeded on the theory that, if they made their military machine big enough, they could drive it where they willed. Only people with . . . vast resources and vast self-confidence could afford to pursue such a course.'[51] This was a clear perception by the Army of itself. As one future writer of the Army's doctrine, General Donn Starry, wrote: 'it is fair to say that with very, very few, very, very striking exceptions, US military thought to 1945 produced a military system designed to overwhelm by mass in a battle of military and national annihilation, using the production techniques and tools of the industrial revolution.'[52] The mobilisation system was a direct translation of industrial revolution thinking,[53] and its success fed American confidence. The American way of war was truly the nation at war. For the Army this produced two key features of how it prosecuted war.

Direct assault

A mobilised Army has a simple way of war due to its size and training; it is a direct assault focused on the opposing forces. The Army had a tradition going back to the Civil War of fighting in a direct and frontal way. General Grant's strategy for the Union has been characterised as ' eschew[ing] manoeuvre and . . . with head down, seeing red, charg[ing] his enemy again and again like a bull'.[54] This type of strategy has a great reliance on firepower, technology, and logistical ability, underpinned by enormous resources. The opponent is literally overwhelmed on all fronts. The legacy from the Civil War can be seen by the emphasis in the Second World War where 'the Americans envisioned frontal assaults all along the line',[55] by applying overwhelming force, rather than manoeuvre or concentrated and massed forces.

The selection of the enemy's forces as its centre of gravity, and the use of direct attack against it, owes a lot to the tradition of Carl von Clausewitz.[56] Michael Howard has highlighted the importance of this influence, which can be seen in the US Army Field Service Regulation of 1923, where the ultimate objective of all military operations is the destruction of the enemy's armed forces by battle. Decisive defeat in battle breaks the enemy's will to war and forces him to sue for peace.[57] The American military during the Second World War, with the enormous resource of over eight million servicemen, followed this doctrine.[58] General Marshall, for example, massed US forces in north-west Europe as that was the only place the German Wehrmacht could be broken in battle.[59] As Harry Summers has noted, this approach went beyond the Second World War as the *FM 100-5* of 1962 lacked strategic analysis and focused on tactics, it saw that 'the ultimate military objective of war is the destruction of the enemy's armed forces and his will to fight'.[60] This approach, combined with the lack of formal strategy, led to a 'tacticalisation of strategy'.

Firepower

A second consequence of the particular nature of the Army was the aim to annihilate the enemy's forces to obtain its ends quickly. The American forces in the Second World War harnessed enormous resources to generate massive firepower for their attacks.[61] However, American use of firepower is more than simply the attritional approach writ large. The reliance on a mobilisation army, and a reluctance to have a great level of readiness prior to going to war, meant that there was an additional need to use firepower to compensate for the training shortfall. The Army used large amounts of firepower as it 'steeled and coalesced unsteady troops and lessened the harm done by an enemy far out of proportion to its killing effect'.[62] Therefore, firepower supported the mobilised troops, as well as being an effective way of converting the nation's material superiority into destructiveness. Put bluntly, firepower, and especially the artillery, gave the US the edge in battle,[63] and the US was prepared to accommodate the frustration that came with the heavy use of indirect fire that had little regard for accuracy or appropriateness.[64]

American use of firepower is commonly seen as a cultural feature. For example, Major General Robert Scales sees the emphasis on the use of large amounts of firepower coming from the historical legacy of the Civil War, and from the 'essence of American national character', concerned as it is with saving American lives.[65] This approach engenders the idea of 'sending a bullet not a man'. The conversation between General Eisenhower and Marshall Zhukov at the end of the Second World War is an emblematic moment which highlights the American attitude to casualties, in contrast to the Soviet approach. In the conversation Zhukov told Eisenhower that the Soviets attacked through minefields as if they were not there, and were prepared to accept the ensuing casualties. Eisenhower comments that this would not be possible for American or British commanders. Russians assess the cost of war in terms of the overall drain on the nation; Americans judge by the cost in human lives.[66] However, this conversation does not cover the full extent of the American position. Preserving life is not so unambiguous an issue as many analysts portray. This was seen in the Second World War, where

> Their general belief in the direct assault was reinforced by a profound faith in their own men . . . and by their willingness to accept heavy casualties. They had not suffered the terrible losses which had so maimed the British people in the First World War, and they had the advantage of being a nation that was still thriving, and expanding biologically.[67]

Vietnam was to be the US's psychological equivalent of the First World War, as senior officers were to see troops' lives being sacrificed for the 'can do' spirit in the name of career advancement.[68] The importance laid on protecting lives at the cost of operational effectiveness was to become a central issue for the US only during and after the Vietnam War. The use of firepower was more a feature of the historical legacy of the Army's infantry- and artillery-based 'way of war' than simple casualty avoidance, and reflected its identity as a raised Army geared to outright victory. Its strategic understanding was a result of this outlook.

Army strategic understanding

The foremost historian of the US Army, Russell Weigley, outlines its strategic understanding by contrasting it with the thought of Clausewitz.

> Clausewitz's definition of strategy as 'the theory of the use of combats for the object of the war' . . . conveys better than any other concise one what Americans meant by strategy when they thought about the subject

> in its (to them) broadest sense from the beginning of their national history through the Second World War and even through the Korean War. . . . Americans, especially American soldiers, often held to a still narrower definition of strategy than Clausewitz's, the time-worn conventional definition that calls strategy 'the art of bringing forces to the battlefield in a favourable position.' . . . [also meant] military strategists gave little regard to the non-military consequences of what they were doing.[69]

The Army was concerned with the tactical level, producing a strategic outlook that was the accumulation of tactics, the 'tactilisation of strategy' rather than the top-down model of tactics as a result of strategic thinking. Chester Wilmot, in his history of the Second World War, described how this affected officers' understanding of the role of politics in war:

> no political objectives should be given to American commanders in the field. They should be completely free to determine their strategy on military grounds alone, and the supreme military consideration is to bring hostilities to an end. To pursue a political aim is to practice Imperialism.[70]

The criticisms of Eisenhower's policy of focusing his efforts on the rump of the German Army, rather than on the advance of the Red Army, at the close of the Second World War, is a case in point.[71] As Major General Edward Lansdale explained 'the military man's conditioning leads him to see political and military operations as separate, even compartmentalised entities'.[72] Even reformers such as Leonard Wood were far more concerned with the nature of the social identity of the Army as 'America's Army' than with the rather abstract one of political-strategic planning in the First World War. With so much potential power available, Wood's 'interest was not so much in any practical military plan . . . as in the abstract idea of military power, to be realized through the idea of the citizen army'.[73] This highlights the fundamental importance of the citizen army in providing ad hoc strategic guidance. It aimed, with overwhelming force, to lead to cumulative tactical victories, which in themselves would bring strategic success.

New strategic culture, old army

The Second World War and the nuclear Cold War period that followed, changed the political geography of the US strategic tradition, expanding its borders away from Mexico to Europe and onto the rimlands of communism in Korea and Vietnam. With the advent of the Cold War, the US acquired its first major standing conscript Army – a primary constitutional change – which was necessary to the national 'strategy of containment' of communism, especially after its militarisation with National Security Council (NSC) 68.[74] The new Army was a conventionally oriented mobilisation Army, and its strategic understanding was in accord with its nature, primarily concerned with the potential war in Europe and its role on the nuclear battlefield.[75]

The demands of the new strategic view altered the role and utility of military force and brought with it changes in the institutional management of the military. As Eliot Cohen explains;

> The U.S. Constitution was a prime force in shaping American strategic culture between 1920 and 1945. . . . Under the first War Powers Act, passed days after the attack on Pearl Harbor and subsequently renewed, Congress granted Roosevelt virtual carte blanche to reorganize the federal government as he saw fit . . . this extraordinary concentration of power in the executive branch represented an artefact of war rather than a condition of peace.[76]

The Cold War institutionalised the permanent war footing. This was most clearly shown by the National Security Act of 1947 that created a single Department of Defense and the National Security Council, with the aim of enhancing co-ordination between political and military agencies,[77] and of civilian control via the Joint Chiefs of Staff. For the executive the reform was a management rather than strategic issue.[78] For example, where the Second World War showed that armies could no longer be considered independently of air forces or navies,[79] the Army Air Corps was made a separate armed service, the US Air Force.[80] The Army's influence was further weakened by this separation, which also created a deeper strategic split between air and land power that only began to be effectively addressed in the 1980s with AirLand Battle doctrine and the Goldwater–Nichols legislation.[81] As with the Constitutional Convention, political control had a greater priority than military effectiveness. The nature of the American approach to strategy in the post-Second World War environment was shown most clearly by the Korean War.

With the onset of the Cold War in Europe the Truman administration called for an extension of selective service to one of universal military training (UMT) to demonstrate US resolve.[82] General Marshall had earlier called for UMT to foster the citizen-soldier idea, in contrast to the professional military castes of Japan and Germany. By the time Congress began to act on this initiative the Korean War broke out, and the numbers required meant that UMT never materialised. Selective Service, however, drafted 300,000 men prior to Korea, and the Army entered the war as a 'remnant' of the massed armies of the Second World War.[83] The Korean War was thus a mix of massed forces and the narrow draft used during the Vietnam War.

The Korean War 'in its timing, its course, and its outcome' served as a substitute for the Third World War.[84] However, it was fought as a mini-Second World War, with the US showing poor readiness and resultant losses in the early stages with 'Task Force Smith' before it had a massive build-up and successfully counter-attacked. The war reinforced the national mobilisation, resource-based approach to warfare as the US command relied upon tons of munitions 'to compensate for the enemy's superiority in manpower and to hold down its loses'.[85] To counter the entry of the Chinese, and its ability to mobilise more people to fight, the US relied upon its advantage in monies and material to substitute for the lack of numbers. It was an approach that brought the war to a stalemate, but fulfilled its aim of stopping the incursion of communism into the south of the country. The war slightly tarnished the Army's public image.[86] It came away from the fighting in Korea confident in its success, convinced its vastly superior firepower and equipment could always defeat a poorly equipped Asian army, if deployed properly.[87]

The Korean War showed the tensions between civilian demands and Army understanding of the needs of the use of force, as it had raised the perplexing issue for the US of fighting a limited war.[88] The Second World War precept of 'do what you must to achieve victory' was replaced by a set of political–military formulae for planning, waging and ultimately winning the war.[89] The Korean War was a limiting of the American way of war, but in political objectives not military means, as it was geographically contained to the Korean peninsular. This limited the military prosecution of the war. For example, General MacArthur's counter-attack to hit the communist centre of gravity in the north of the country went so close to China that Chinese 'volunteers' poured over the border in support of the north. His concentration on victory by defeating the opposing forces took the war away from the containment policy that had stimulated it. Military dominance of the strategic equation was inadequate and produced the famous clash between the ground commander and the president, which was solved by President Truman sacking MacArthur.[90] MacArthur's understanding of being left to fight as the military needs dictated, meant his 'strategy' was one of compiling tactical victories to defeat enemy forces to achieve victory, the consequences of which were in contradiction to the nation's strategy. Truman's sacking of MacArthur affirmed the subservience of the military to the executive and established clear executive-political control, but exposed the deficiencies of the US command structure which had extended the president's role as commander in chief to one of war management.[91]

The question of deployment was indicative of the debate that was at the heart of US containment policy: the 'Never Again' (or 'all or nothing') and 'Limited War' schools. The Army Chief of Staff, General Ridgeway, and President Eisenhower supported the 'Never Again' school, seeing that the US should be prepared to do everything needed to win, or not to intervene at all.[92] Eisenhower kept the US out of Vietnam after the fall of Dien Bien Phu in 1954 on these grounds. However, the strategy of nuclear 'massive retaliation' underpinned this thinking, but its inflexibility led to the rise of demands for a more malleable response to communism: 'flexible response'. The growing demands of containment policy for tools to address a range of scenarios led to the growth in executive control of the military. This development lessened the influence of the Army's strategic thinking on the broader national strategy.

President Eisenhower continued the trend of increasing executive power over the military when he came into office. In 1953 he replaced the whole of the Joint Chiefs of Staff, so that its members would be part of the administration's team.[93] In 1958 he further weakened the position of the military's Joint Chiefs of Staff (JCS) by reorganising the Defense Department and giving the Defense Secretary the authority to transfer orders directly to field commanders, bypassing the JCS.[94] This gave enormous power to the post of the Defense Secretary and further empowered the executive. The costs of failure in the nuclear age, and the seemingly unique features of weapons, increased the process of civilian control prior to the Vietnam War.

For many, the Korean War was seen as *sui generis*, and the key issue was really that of 'nuclear weapons opening an entirely new historical era'.[95] Nuclear weapons overlay the issues of the growing executive role and the civil–military tensions, as both the Army and US foreign policy focused on military force in an era of nuclear weapons.[96] The administration focused on strategic, i.e. worldwide, nuclear power, whilst the Army saw this as a non-policy and looked to the tactical role of nuclear weapons, placing them within its emphasis on battlefield firepower.[97] The advent of strategic nuclear weapons was to have a greater influence than the tactical battlefield role the Army conceived for them, as they reduced the Army's influence on national strategic thinking

Nuclear weapons enhanced civilian strategic thinking because, as Henry Kissinger explained, 'the vast destructiveness of nuclear weapons made traditional military expertise less relevant; anybody who understood the new technology could play, and the players were, in the main, scientists, joined by a few other academicians'.[98] The specialists' approach was that of theoreticians, not historians,[99] and aimed to resolve what Walter Millis called the great and unresolved dilemma of the age: a 'way in which deployment of military force . . . could be brought rationally to bear upon the decision of any of the political, economic, emotional or philosophical issues by which men still remain divided'.[100] The clash between the theoretical perception of the role of force and the Army's understanding of its utility had been shown in the Korean War but was exacerbated by the need for limited war capability in the nuclear age.

In his best-selling book of the time, Henry Kissinger laid out the key concepts of limited war thinking.

> It is not only that limited war must find a means to prevent the most extreme of violence; it must also seek to slow down the tempo of modern war lest the rapidity with which operations succeed each other prevent the establishment of a relation between political and military objectives. If this relationship is lost, any war is likely to grow by imperceptible stages into an all-out effort. The goal of war can no longer be military victory, strictly speaking, but the attainment of certain specific political conditions which are fully understood by the opponent. . . . Strategic doctrine must never lose sight of the fact that its purpose is to affect the will of the enemy, not to destroy him, and that war can be limited only by presenting the enemy with an unfavourable calculus of risks.[101]

Compellence could be achieved through 'escalating' the cost to the enemy of their rejection of American political signals, by gradually increasing the damage that was done to them. Escalation is a basic dimension of diplomacy and war,[102] and as Richard Smoke explained, a 'special class of civilian military theorists' first used it as a 'concept'.[103] The theory of escalating costs saw that the enemy would be compelled to stop their actions, and the policy would be a success if the political aim had been fulfilled and a nuclear war avoided.

The civilian understanding of the use of force during the early Cold War was in contrast to the Army's. The Army saw itself as a viable political tool to counter the threat of communism, and Korea had confirmed its conventional understanding. With the advent of the Cold War the US acquired its first major standing conscript Army. The influence of the Second World War on the new standing Army was most clearly shown by the fact it 'rubbed out completely the American experience with both insurgency and counter-insurgency with quite negative effects for future US efforts in this area'.[104] For example, the Army's 1954 doctrine manual *FM 100-5, Field Service Regulations: Operations*, still saw limited wars as simply having limited objectives, as in Korea. It was only in 1962 that the Army conceived of it as also involving 'limited means'.[105] The nature of the nation's foundation, and the great utility of the legacy of the Army's history handling small and unconventional wars, was blocked by the evolution of the standing Cold War conscript army.

Prior to the Vietnam War, the new tasks were to lead to the emergence of new understandings of military roles and professionalisation, because the model of the standing Army was in difficulties.[106] As early as 1957 the analyst Samuel Huntington noted that there was a 'Crisis in American civil–military relations'.[107] It was a problematic time within the Army as well, and General Schwarzkopf refers to most captains of the time being 'hard-drinking rogues left over from World War II and Korea. . . . guys just marking time, who had no sense of duty or honor'.[108] Walter Millis captures the mood of the time:

> The future of war was as uncertain as the future of the American military policies which might be adopted to meet its problems. Beginning with farmers who swarmed to Lexington with their flintlocks, we had arrived at a point where we were spending around $40 billion a year . . . on a peacetime military system. We were maintaining nearly 3,000,000 men in uniform at all times; to keep these ranks filled we were continuing an apparently permanent system of peacetime military conscription.[109]

The answer to the uncertainty Millis outlines was to be settled in the crucible of the Vietnam War, at great cost to the nation and its Army.

Conclusion

To understand the Army's thinking after the Vietnam War it is necessary to appreciate the broader context that shaped it. By using the concept of strategic culture the Army's identity has been shown to be a product of initial constitutional position and the historical, geographical and social forces that make up that political culture. The Army was not a devised institution but an outgrowth of the nation's development. It saw itself as embodying the nation and being an expression of its will, not the instrument of the executive.

To understand the role of the US Army within US strategic culture after the Vietnam War it has to be recognised that it was very new as a major military force at that time. While it had a deeply rooted tradition, as a large standing conscript army it was in a novel period.[110] The growing role of the executive in American strategy flew in the face of the Army's understanding of warfare based on the Second World War approach of fighting to victory. The public support for General MacArthur's theme during the Korean War that there was 'no substitute for victory' showed how socially based the Army's emphasis on victory was.

Additionally, the previous experience of war provides the model and lessons for further developments in the military as the learning and understanding of the military is shaped by the fact that for generations it may not be called upon to fight.[111] In the US case this meant that the Second World War and the Korean War were essential elements in the self-understanding that it took to Vietnam. The thinking, which lay behind its self-understanding and its role as an expression of the broader strategic culture, was to fracture under the pressure of fighting the Vietnam War. Fighting a limited war split the institutional and social identity, as the strategic culture of a 'nation at arms' was embodied in the Army. The Army's understanding of the failure of the Vietnam War, and how it rebuilt itself, was to change American strategy and strategic culture.

2

THE VIETNAM WAR AND THE US ARMY

The Vietnam War exposed the fundamental contradictions of the Cold War American strategic culture, confirming that war, as Correlli Barnett says, 'is the great auditor of institutions'.[1] How the war affected the Army, and the ensuing changes in the strategic culture, are a product of how the Army 'audited' the war. The Army saw the war as a product of bad strategy, against the wrong type of enemy and in unsuitable terrain. The mismatch between the Army's perception and the task given to it points to a deeper problem within the unity of American strategic culture, where the executive understanding of the role of military force was instrumental and the Army's was based on mobilisation of the nation. The war was a product of that culture and was to 'traumatise' it.[2]

This chapter focuses on the Army's perception of the war at the time and during the period of rebuilding. The revisions of the Army's thinking on Vietnam will be examined later. This chapter examines the Army's initial perception and how it directly shaped changes in the Army, and does this by examining the nature of the war, the Army's prosecution of it and the assessment of the loss of the Vietnam War. The final section analyses the consequences of the failure for the Army.

US strategic culture and the war in Vietnam[3]

The US involvement in Vietnam was the culmination of the strategic posture and identity of post-Second World War policies.[4] It was the result of the enlarged political geography of the containment policy, a policy that had an inherent contradiction as it provided the need to intervene whilst limiting the means to prosecute it.[5] The tension was most clearly seen by the executive emphasis on developing flexible tools for intervention whilst the Army was based upon mass national mobilisation.

In contrast to the mainstream Army's attitude, successive administrations increased the already enlarged executive role in national strategy.[6] The need was clear to the new Kennedy administration, as the Cuban missile crisis had shown that limited 'shows of force' allowed international crises to be managed.[7] Additionally, President Kennedy had been disturbed by his senior military advisers' inability to look beyond the military field.[8] The administration, therefore, developed the roles and executive management of military force, setting great store by counter-insurgency doctrine and training within the Army.[9] The former Army Chief of Staff, the retired General Maxwell Taylor, who had been advocating a new identity for the Army in the nuclear era and was the chief Army critic of 'massive retaliation', personally advocated a more politicised military policy of 'flexible response'.[10] Kennedy's adoption of a flexible response strategy to address the difficulties of containment was to be tested in Vietnam.[11] It faced opposition from the military, and by 1961 the Joint Chiefs of Staff were opposed to a limited ground war in Asia.[12] Taylor headed a mission to Vietnam and reported the need to raise morale and to show that the US was serious in its intent in resisting a communist takeover.[13] By 1962 the Army had 4,000 advisers in Vietnam, under a new Counter-Insurgency Council chaired by Taylor.[14] Nonetheless, it was not the advocacy of new military options that led the military into the Vietnam War, but containment policy.[15] Kennedy had given new impetus to containment and energised the nation, proposing that the US would 'pay any price, bear any burden'. Like many others, Philip Caputo, veteran of the first combat unit into Vietnam in 1965, was 'seduced into uniform' by Kennedy's appeal of what he could do for his country, full of missionary idealism and the seeming omnipotence of the US. He, like the young Colin Powell and many others, was to be gravely disillusioned.[16]

Vietnam was a test of flexible response, a 'strategy designed to meet just that kind of situation'.[17] However, the complex political and physical nature of the war went against the orientation and strengths of the US Army. Robert Komer provides one of the clearest summaries that the 'war' was in fact three wars,[18] when he says that it

> was a multi-dimensional politico-military conflict encompassing not only out-of-country bombing and a 'main force' war of more or less conventional forces, but a guerrilla struggle, a clandestine terror campaign, and the like. . . . It was . . . a 'war without fronts'.[19]

The frontless war had no defined battle area like the Second World War, which meant that the danger was 'pervasive and chronic' with no secure areas.[20] Not only that, but the physical terrain in which the war was fought was in total contrast to Europe, including, as it did, rainforest, open forest, lowlands, flooding delta, swampland, marshland, grassland and cultivated areas.[21] Additionally, the Army was geared to fighting visible uniformed forces in Europe and not against an enemy who it could hardly see ('low-signature') and who was indistinguishable from the populace.[22] Chronologically, the war proved to be a series of simultaneous wars fought in phases. Each phase shaped the next one.

First phase of the war: prior to 1965

With the fall of French forces after Dien Bien Phu in 1954, the US partially took up the mantle and sent advisers to the country. The initial military advisery effort focused on creating a South Vietnamese military force that was conventional in tactics and equipment and patterned after the standard US organisation.[23] It was geared to be capable of withstanding an invasion from the north. However, it was an Army that was too centralised, and its equipment was too heavy to be capable of coping with an internal insurgency. By 1959–60 the US realised that there was an urgent need for counter-insurgency, and by 1963 it was optimistic of its efforts. However, President Diem's assassination in 1963 led to complete deterioration of the Southern government and a rising credibility issue for the US.[24] The US faced an enormous problem.

> The American image of the enemy as loosely organized groups of bandits or guerillas was not real. The enemy had a plan and worked his plan well, so well in fact that by 1964 he was ready to make the transition to the last phase of the conflict, full-scale mobile war.[25]

By July 1965 the options were seen as leaving the country, maintaining the present force levels and loosing or increasing troop numbers.[26] The decision to introduce US combat forces saved the Republic of Vietnam from total military defeat.

The first advisery phase was followed by an 'Americanisation' of the war and the commitment of half a million US troops from 1965;[27] the policy had led to the US going to war 'in a manner unique in American history. . . . It slunk in on cat's feet.'[28] This meant that there was not a national mobilisation, a key feature of the Army's nature. In 1964, the journalist David Halberstam was already referring to policy in Vietnam as 'The Making of a Quagmire'.[29]

Second phase of the war: 1965–68

President Johnson's policy was to secure the South and increase the pressure on the North to withdraw.[30] As Freedman notes, there was a basic Catch-22 here – 'The South could not be stabilized without pressure on the North: the North could not be pressurized without a more stable South.'[31] The air campaign against the North is the clearest example of the policy of escalation and its weaknesses. It involved dropping graduated amounts of munitions on the North and then stopping to allow the North to consider the costs of their political position.[32] The difficulty for the US was that for the North the war was a war of nationalism, not a limited war, and thus the break in the bombing did not make it reconsider its position and open negotiations. It shored up its position instead. By the time President Nixon launched Linebacker II in 1972, a massive air assault on Hanoi and Haiphong, the North's air defence was rated to be comparable only to NATO's highly sophisticated network in Europe.[33] The US was not able to escalate the costs high enough. It was an approach which provoked the ire of Admiral Sharp, the Commander in Chief, Pacific Command (CINCPAC) and the overall senior commander for the war, leading him to write that the most debilitating aspect of the war was 'the political leadership's naive hope that a major involvement could somehow be avoided by using a "carrot and stick" sort of diplomacy as a means of initiating negotiations with the North Vietnamese'; there was a continual frustration with the 'on again, off again' tinkering with coercive force.[34] However, whilst bargaining with air power the administration had to address the military problems on the ground in the South.

Army tactics

The instrumental understanding of the military by the executive stood in direct contrast to the Army's understanding of strategy being the traditional blending of political and military means through mobilisation. The limitation of the war fitted the administration's policy but left the mobilisation-based Army with the task of actually carrying out the policy. An army that was still reliant on mobilisation thinking fought the ground war.

The incremental change from an advisery role to the introduction of US combat forces brought great difficulties for the Army. A declaration of war by the US has jurisdictional implications, as the military commander becomes pre-eminent in ensuring the unity of effort by the US. With no declaration of war, CIA assets, for example, remained under the Ambassador.[35] The gradual approach also meant, however, that the Army did not change orientation to the fundamentally new tasks of counter-insurgency. The command and control structure, for example, shows this clearly. Previously, US military forces' command and control structures had been tailored to the task at hand. This was not the case in Vietnam. The command and control arrangements evolved from a small military assistance mission, established in 1950, and came to direct a US military force of over 500,000 men. The philosophy of assisting against incursion, rather than commanding the whole war, 'significantly influenced' the development of the organisation.[36] Additionally, the paucity of the command structure was exacerbated by the fact that, as Martin van Creveld shows, the US Forces in 1963 required twenty times as much information as their 1945 counterparts. He concludes that 'To study command as it operated in Vietnam is, indeed, almost enough to make one despair of human reason.'[37] From within the complex and dissipated command structure the Army (with Marine support) fought the land war against the main force enemy.

The Army was responsible for two of the three wars in Vietnam: the main force and guerrilla wars. These roles were under the overloaded command of General Westmoreland at United States Military Assistance Command, Vietnam (USMACV).[38] Westmoreland explained that the US military strategy employed in Vietnam was dictated by political decisions, not military ones, and his approach was shaped by the fact that a ground invasion of North Vietnam was not possible because it was not the policy to conquer North Vietnam, but to eliminate the insurgency in South Vietnam, which could be done 'only by seeking, fighting, and destroying the enemy'.[39] Additionally, if negotiations developed, 'it might compensate for some of the leverage the Viet Cong victories gave the other side'.[40] It was only later in the war that a limited number of troops attacked across the border into Laos and Cambodia.[41] This meant, as Westmoreland stated: 'We will have to grind him down. In effect, we are fighting a war of attrition, and the only alternative is a war of annihilation.'[42]

In Vietnam the political limitation of the war left the Army with the attritional role in the South, importantly without the use of the offensive. This went against the Army's fundamental tradition of the offensive.[43] The national policy meant that it could not fight within its strategic understanding as any initiative, be it political, psychological or military, lay with the enemy.[44] The political limitation of the war thus challenged the strategic coherence of the Second World War model, as the Army then saw no alternative to attrition than by taking the war to the enemy and beating it through battlefield victory 'with such rapidity and thoroughness that Axis military capability would disintegrate'.[45] The Army under Westmoreland, therefore, focused on bringing the North Vietnamese to battle, especially after the success in 1965 of Ia Drang.[46] The focus on the main battle gave a decisive role to artillery and air support.[47] Without having the initiative, the Army relied upon its strength in firepower.

Firepower

The traditional tactical approach in the Vietnam War meant that it was fought as a light infantry war with artillery/air support. The firepower approach to the Vietnam War was affected by its traditional focus on artillery rather than armour.[48] The US Army's approach was more static than other heavy firepower armies that were armoured based, such as the German army. The predominant role of artillery in Vietnam led to the reliance on firebases, which were fixed positions of artillery to generate huge levels of supporting firepower to units on the ground. 'The firebase proved its worth in Vietnam', as it was built quickly, could withstand assault and permitted the field artillery to provide fire support 'of the same high quality as that provided in previous wars'.[49] The artillery was to become very responsive during the war, mainly due to improved communications.[50] However, the fixed nature of the bases meant that their supporting role often changed as they became the seat of the fighting. The most famous example was the siege of Khe Sanh in January 1968, which lasted for 66 days,[51] and was to highlight many of the strengths and weaknesses of the Army's approach to the war in Vietnam.

Khe Sanh 'tested American concepts of defense and demonstrated that good fire support could effectively neutralize a superior force'.[52] The fire support, from land and sky, was truly massive, with 45 B-52 and 300 tactical air sorties a day. Each day 18,000 tons of ordnance was used to lay waste to the surrounding jungle, and the total amount used in the operation – 96,000 tons of bombs – was nearly twice what the Army Air Corps had delivered in the Pacific during the whole of 1942–43. The bombing was not simply indirect saturation but carefully planned boxes of devastating artillery fire round the base, assisted by aircraft. When possible B-52s provided 'arc lights' of supporting bombing in the area.

Militarily, Khe Sanh was a reversal of role as it aimed to be the 'anvil' upon which to hit the enemy. It had a moral purpose to demonstrate US determination. The resulting success in not falling to the assaults on it, turned out as President Johnson's military advisers had predicted; Westmoreland, Wheeler (Chairman of the Joint Chiefs of Staff) and the service chiefs were 'thoroughly vindicated'.[53] The French experience of the overwhelming Vietnamese siege of Dien Bien Phu never materialised. In Khe Sanh's case it was a battle of prestige that the US could not loose but, like so many operations, was ultimately irrelevant. General Giap attacked it to distract the American forces from the upcoming Tet offensive and had no intention of trying to repeat Dien Bien Phu.[54]

Technology

The limitations of fixed firebases were countered by the Army's peacetime innovation of airmobility. The helicopter was to become the symbol of the American approach to the war.[55] Helicopters were used to transport troops, artillery and supplies, providing a 'new' dimension to a commander, as it was a more responsive and flexible means to concentrate combat power.[56] This was necessary as the lack of true strategy meant that troops were 'scattered' all over the country.[57] It was a force multiplier, especially as the strategy moved to one of 'finding, fixing and destroying' the enemy. Fortunately, the Army had developed the First Cavalry Division (Airmobile) to provide a more flexible firepower model.[58] It had developed the idea of integrating helicopters into air assault divisions before the war. with the aim being to have dispersed forces that could be quickly assembled to fight on a nuclear battlefield. However, as Stephen Rosen shows, the peacetime innovation was not the same as the wartime use and later innovations. For example, the helicopters were not permanently integrated into combat units, as the North Vietnamese learned to counter the potential of the helicopters, thus many of the First Cavalry's contacts came from their foot patrols.[59] The technological fix of helicopters became an essential part of the transportation of troops and supplies, reinforcing the emphasis on moving to attack enemy forces rather than occupying territory and developing pacification.

Ironically, the 'technological' approach which could have addressed the difficulty of territorial occupation was underutilised. The armoured forces were to be very effective later in the war, but initial fears that they were not suited to the terrain stopped deployment. By the end of the war, 24 per cent of combat manoeuvre battalions were mechanised or armoured cavalry.[60] Armour was able to provide route protection for troops, especially from anti-personnel mines, and was effective in assisting in destroying enemy numbers through firepower. The attacks on the Cambodian bases in 1970 showed armour's speed of attack, and the US was copied by North Vietnam in 1972 against An Loc.[61] However, the US armoured forces went to Vietnam with little relevant doctrine and could not play a part in the crucial 'finding or fixing' of the enemy, which was an airsupport role.[62] Armoured combat forces were kept dispersed, thereby repeating many of the mistakes of the Second World War.[63]

The propensity of the American Army to fight conventionally was recognised by the North Vietnamese. Some have argued that the Vietnamese commander, General Giap, learnt from the Korean War 'that they must never face a Western army on its own terms'.[64] Giap, therefore, developed a strategy that prevented the Americans from having a target on which they could mass and attack. He dispersed the potential Vietnamese targets.[65] During the 'big-unit' period of 1965–67 the US Army found it difficult to bring the enemy to combat on its terms so it developed the idea of mass sweeps, which was to be known under the blanket term 'search and destroy'. The inadequacy of this approach led to the development of tactics by the 9th Infantry Division and II Field Force in 1968–70 of relying on cumulative rather than mass losses, inflicted through light infantry tactics. The 'constant pressure' concept was to find, encircle and heavily damage the enemy main force and provincial battalions, by losses on small enemy units, thereby denying the enemy sanctuary and effectiveness.[66] The development of 'constant pressure' was an attempt to regain the initiative in a main force war, but was an innovation that was still reliant on 'excruciating direct military pressure'.[67] More generally though, the US response to Giap's strategy was to use its technological and firepower advantage to try and counter his reluctance to join battle; 'helicopter gunships, free-fire zones, defoliants, napalm and bombing were used. This reliance on unrestrained firepower devastated large portions of the nation the United States was ostensibly trying to save.'[68]

The Army's approach of deploying massive firepower reached right down to the tactical level, so that officers in Vietnam were under great pressure to carry out missions, and often to bring in a 'respectable body count', whilst limiting American casualties. As a result firepower from artillery or aircraft was used, rather than men.[69] The consequence of this was that a base of fire could be built up with sufficient power to physically destroy the enemy, rather than merely pin him down. This shifted the tactics away from the infantry to the supporting firepower. rather than overrunning enemy positions whilst still manned, 'they relied upon the firepower of supporting arms to do the job for them. When this assistance turned out to be less than decisive, they would realise belatedly that they had lost the initiative.'[70] As Gibson points out, the 'technowar' production approach was inapplicable to the enemy's strategies.[71] The disheartening nature of this approach, and the deficiencies in the technology which it relied upon, led to a growing frustration with the war.[72]

Public support

Attrition and logistics

The Army's view that the tactical and logistical aspects of the war were being successful increased the frustration, as the war was not won.[73] The inability to achieve decisive victory on the battlefield increased the emphasis on American logistical superiority, which was expensive to run.[74] The reliance on costly resources necessitated a large level of public support to fund and man the war effort, and this made the military vulnerable to Congressional displeasure.[75] The scale of the effort in Vietnam was enormous. The total US Army strength increased between 1965 and 1970 from 966,000 to 1,432,000. This rise certainly represented nowhere near a maximum mobilisation of US manpower. For example, the US Army in 1945 numbered a staggering 8,131,000.[76] It was a huge effort, but ultimately it was fought by a mobilisation force without national mobilisation, or, ultimately, national success. The Army's attritional approach created a dependance on the public for massive logistical support, and this was consistent with its very nature as a public body. The attrition strategy pushed the social aspect of strategy back home, and the war 'nobody won' would also be fought at home.[77]

Mobilisation

The lack of full national mobilisation meant that the Army had a growing problem with the quality and quantity of manpower during the Vietnam War, which critically hindered its ability to 'learn' from its experiences during the war. It had to use those drafted for selective service. The problem was summarised by the Army's Vice Chief of Staff (1968–73):

> Without at least a partial mobilization the Army was denied the use of trained, experienced units and personnel present in the National Guard and organized reserves. This meant that, as the Army expanded from roughly 950,000 in 1964 to about 1,550,000 in 1968 . . . the additional men and women entering the service were mostly very young, untrained, and inexperienced, resulting in the dilution of overall experience in the Army, particularly in the leadership ranks, the officers and non-commissioned officers. The failure to mobilize or to declare an emergency also meant that personnel would flow in and out of the armed forces on a peacetime basis rather than being held in the service for the duration of the emergency.[78]

Non-mobilisation undermined the operational capability of the Army, as it was unable to draw upon the experienced reservists and National Guardsmen, and condemned the Army effectively to keep repeating the learning process as soldiers fulfilled their year-long tour. Furthermore, under this strain the Army was unable to sustain its regular three-year rotations to Europe. The 7th Army, in Europe, effectively became a training and replacement depot.[79] For the Army, the failure to have a national mobilisation had adulterated its nature as it consisted of the Regular Army, the Army Reserve and the National Guard.

For the Army, the lack of mobilisation (prior to the partial one in April 1968) was a fundamental misuse of the Army and its role. It fundamentally challenged its identity. Critics such as Summers see the reason for not calling up troops as a lack of understanding war and the nation's army, and seeing mobilisation as total war in a nuclear age.[80] What Summers fails to recognise is that the administration were thinking far more of the political cost of mobilisation and the fact that it was very conscious of the difficulties and criticism it faced when it had mobilised during the Berlin crisis in 1961. During that period there was an outcry about having careers and families disrupted.[81] The structuring of the Army required mobilisation and the failure to call it up had large repercussions.

One of the major problems the Army had was in leadership.[82] Almost half of the newly commissioned officers in 1967 were the products of officer candidate school (OCS) and were not of a high calibre. Lt Calley (famous as the officer responsible for the My Lai atrocity) would probably not have attained officer rank 'but the demand was such that the Army could not be very selective'. One colonel was quoted as saying that there were two or three thousand more Calleys in the Army.[83] The problem was not only with officer leadership quality. Colin Powell points out that the non-commissioned officers are the backbone of the Army, and they take years of professional training. By not calling up the reserves, the Army was creating instant sergeants, 'shake-and-bake sergeants we called them'.[84] Unprepared officers and non-commissioned officers led to breakdown in morale, discipline and professional judgement, and My Lai was the most famous example. For the Army, the My Lai atrocity was an aberration, but for the public it became indicative of the war, a clear example of the nature of the Army and the regime the US was supporting, a regime that practised summary executions during Tet.[85] Tet was to bring the issue of public support to a head.

Third phase of the war 1968–73

The Tet offensive of 1968, by the Viet Cong against all major cities in the South, was a seminal event in the war and the turning point for public support and perception of the Vietnam War.[86] For the Army, the outcomes of the Tet offensive were a success, as it recaptured all the lost ground and the Viet Cong was finished as a fighting force. It took General Giap till 1972 before he was able to rebuild his forces sufficiently to attack in force again. As Peter MacDonald writes in his biography of General Giap, within a fortnight of its start, except for Hue, the 'Tet offensive was virtually over'. However as MacDonald goes on to say,

> Militarily, both sides claimed they had won. . . . In Vietnam most of its soldiers realised for the first time that they would never win the war, while at home many people turned away from it with revulsion. During Tet, after the complete leveling of one town, Ben Tre, a weary American officer had told a reporter, 'We had to destroy it in order to save it.' For millions of Americans that phrase vividly summed up the futility of the war: nobody was winning, nobody could win.[87]

For the Army, the media had been a crucial weak link in the prosecution of the war.[88] According to General Westmoreland, the policy of escalating the costs of the war was fatally flawed as it was garbled by the voices of dissent at home and the 'sensational news reporting by the mass media'.[89] Television coverage of Tet provided the first live transmissions of war, as a satellite had been placed above the Pacific Ocean just weeks earlier. Before Tet, film footage had been edited and in the process 'most sharp images of injury and death were expunged'.[90] It was the first time that the full horror of fighting came into people's front rooms, and the images of Vietnamese success overwhelmed the public. In a frustrating and perplexing war the role of the media became more important. However, the US media were not as universally critical as is sometimes portrayed.[91] What is beyond doubt is that there was a far closer examination of American actions than of its opponent. As Lewy observes, 'The VC were notoriously uncooperative in allowing Western cameramen to shoot pictures of the disemboweling of village chiefs or other acts of terror, while scenes of South Vietnamese brutality, such as the mistreatment of prisoners, were often seen on American TV screens.'[92]

The media coverage of the fighting after Tet helped to further undermine support for the Army. An example of this was the Battle of 'Hamburger Hill' in 1969. This involved a whole battalion making eight assaults in five days against 'Hamburger Hill'. Eventually the enemy withdrew from their entrenched positions. The American Army, following its usual strategy, soon abandoned the hill. The 'meat grinder' tactics resulted in the battle and hill being given the name 'Hamburger Hill'. 'The seemingly senseless deaths of 241 American soldiers fuelled anti-war protest in America.'[93] It did not make sense to the public that so many lives had been lost, only to then give up the hill. The coverage was combined with Walter Cronkite's practice of having the 'body count' of American casualties displayed on the wall behind the news anchor, 'there every day and every week for years, . . . the stark and riveting altar of collective sacrifice'.[94] Casualties were to become indicative of the failure of the political–military strategy in Vietnam. The stalemated war had become far more like the First World War than the limited war of Korea.[95] There developed a greater national consensus to withdraw from Vietnam.

Even by 1968 the 'war' had spread to the streets of the US with major anti-war demonstrations, especially among potential draftees. As the Chair of the Vietnam Veteran Memorial Fund put it: 'Vietnam was both a war abroad and an interconnected series of traumatic changes at home.'[96] President Johnson announced in a crucial speech to the nation on 21 March 1968, 'Our objective in South Vietnam has never been the annihilation of the enemy. It has been to bring about a recognition in Hanoi that its objective – taking over the South by force – could not be achieved.'[97] Johnson then decided to devote every hour left of his Presidency to the cause of seeking an 'honourable peace' and therefore would not seek or accept nomination for the election.[98] It shocked the nation. The ensuing election saw the Republican challenger, Richard Nixon, running on a ticket promising an end to the war and there was little exploitation of the Vietnam issue in exchanges between candidates;

> in the American public mind . . . by the autumn of 1968 the Vietnam issue had in large measure been de-fused. There was a pervasive sense that the war was on the way out . . . [the candidates] knew that public anxiety, amounting to impatience, for an end to the odious conflict demanded evidence from them of their concern and competence.[99]

Post-Tet

From 1968 the political will to continue the war had gone, but the Army was left to fight on as the US tried to extract itself from the 'quagmire' with some vestige of diplomatic 'face'. However, it was only in 1973 that US forces finally pulled out and 1975 before Saigon fell to the NVA's forces. Therefore, the war was to continue for five more years, a point under-represented by the major histories of the conflict,[100] with more Americans killed in this period than before.[101] It was in the post-Tet period that the Army replaced its commander, Westmoreland, with General Creighton Abrams who had learnt from the war and saw it as a single entity and immediately changed the tactics to population control, used different measures of success and improved the South Vietnamese capability. He also, rather more controversially, attacked bases in Cambodia and Laos – all in a period of diminishing support and resources.[102]

> With the Communists weakened militarily and organizationally by the losses in their repeated offensives, the U.S. and South Vietnam were able for the first time to gain a real measure of control in the countryside. Yet the continued weaknesses of the South Vietnamese regime, the Communist powers of recuperation, and the U.S. decision to begin troop withdrawals in 1969 made this Allied ascendency in the countryside only temporary.[103]

The military successes that the Army began to enjoy, were undercut by the diminishing support at home.

The period after Tet saw the disenchantment that grew with the war imported into the Army.[104] From 1969 the fighting quality of the US Army went into serious decline.[105] The problem was particularly acute because the average age of a conscript was 19, seven years younger than their Second World War forefathers, and making them more vulnerable to stress.[106] The nature of the frontless war was particularly stressful. The Army, dependent on draftees, began to lose effectiveness and started to fall apart. Colin Powell notes in his autobiography that during his tour in mid-1968, 'I was living in a large tent and I moved my cot every night, partly to thwart Viet Cong informants who might be tracking me, but also because I did not rule out attacks on authority from within the battalion itself.'[107] By 1971, Congress was reporting that the Army's drugs and educational problems were so bad that almost 100,000 military men walked away from their military duties in that fiscal year (FY); a field commander in the Army could expect 73 of every 1,000 men to desert.[108] Not only did desertion rise but the public imagination of the dissolution of the Army focused on cases of 'fraggings', where officers were deliberately killed by their own men. Congress confirmed that in the first eleven months of 1971 there were 215 confirmed incidents, leading to 12 deaths.[109] Basic military discipline was fracturing, as was its identity.

VOLAR

Richard Nixon shrewdly looked at the draft issue in light of the domestic crisis that the war was causing and, once elected, established a commission to examine the issue.[110] The appointment of the President's Commission on 'All-Volunteer Armed Force' on 27 March 1969 was 'to develop a plan for eliminating conscription and moving toward an all-volunteer armed force'.[111] The inheritance from the Second World War era of an Army built on selective service was coming to an end. The Gates Commission reported on the all-volunteer force proposals in 1970, and the Army prepared for the development with a series of experiments at selected posts.[112] In April 1970, during student protests, President Nixon announced his goal of achieving an all-volunteer army by June 1973: simultaneously he attempted to make the draft system fairer.[113] With the administration's long-term intention made clear, Congress agreed in July 1971 to extend Nixon's authority to draft for two more years.[114] The introduction of the All-Volunteer Army (the VOLAR) was a symbol of the split between society and the Army. Far from embodying the nation's will, the Army was now alienated from the society it understood itself to embody.

The Army's initial response to the ideational split was a change in recruiting campaign. Since the First World War the Army had recruited to the slogan 'I want you for the U.S. Army' but in 1970 it replaced it with 'We Want To Join You'. Furthermore, the US Army's official magazine changed its name from *Army Digest* to *Soldiers* in June 1971. The change of title was matched by a change of content, reflecting a focus on the individual soldier and moving its readership away from career soldiers to articles about drug addiction and motorcycle trips across country rather than about service bases and the corporate life.[115] Furthermore, technical Army instruction was replaced with a more theoretical/academic education to 'establish a foundation of social, economic and political understanding of the military'.[116] This shift aimed to help make a smoother transition from civilian to military for those joining the Army. There was a clear perception that to remain an Army of the people and express American society then there was a need to 'civilianise' itself to achieve this.[117]

Pertinent critics within the Army saw that it was not only the media who were distorting the image of the Army, the Army was doing so itself with the campaign. As Madigan and Hoy clearly pointed out, the essential dialectic between the nation and its army was threatened by 'The Army Wants To Join You' campaign, because it risked serious misrepresentation. 'The unfortunate consequence is to threaten the dialectic – the dialogue – which was and is essential to civil–military accommodation in the society.'[118] Having attempted to directly express its home society by civilianising itself in such a distorted fashion, the Army displayed how unclear it was about its societal identity, a conundrum made no clearer by the broader social changes.

US strategic culture after the Vietnam War

'Wars transform the future . . . but it is the way a war is brought to an end that has the most decisive long-term impact.'[119] The later stages of the Vietnam War became a period of social fragmentation and the strategic culture faltered. The consensus over containment fell apart and the American social identity split over criticism of the war. The political culture of the US was also wracked by the scandal of Watergate and Congress challenged the power of the executive, especially with the reassertion of Congressional power realised in the War Powers Resolution in 1973. The coherence and consensus behind American strategic culture ruptured under the strain of the adventure in Vietnam.

A direct consequence of the war was that it 'left a deep national skepticism about the overall utility and legitimacy of American military power'.[120] For example, the 1972 bombing escalation 'hastened a transformation of the basic liberal argument against the war, . . . instead of stressing the hopelessness of the war, liberals now began to emphasize its immorality'.[121] As General Westmoreland observed in 1976, 'In recent years, [the veteran of the Vietnam War] has been falsely condemned by some for having fought in a war stamped by propagandists as "illegal and immoral," replete with American atrocities. . . . Nobody has brought forward any legal evidence that the war was in fact immoral.'[122] Legal evidence or not, the image of the war precipitated a growing antagonism towards the Army and the use of military force.[123] This is most clearly seen in the growing influence of the 'dovish' viewpoint during the war, coming as it did during the civil rights movement and the student protests, and with the rise of human rights onto the foreign policy agenda.[124] In the post-Vietnam period, both President Carter and Reagan emphasised the morality of their respective foreign policies.[125] For the Carter administration, negotiating the SALT II Treaty was seen as the primary way forward, rather than using military intervention in areas of conflict, and American military capability was allowed to decline.[126] Others saw that the war made no vital difference to the long-term national security policies of the United States, because it was not a great enough event.[127]

The resultant dovish and hawkish mentalities within post-Vietnam America were particularly clear in the Carter administration, which illustrated the dilemmas of post-Vietnam intervention policy. The Secretary of State and the National Security Adviser, Cyrus Vance and Zbigniew Brzezinski, faced each other with divergent views as the administration focused upon the détente process and on the issue of human rights.[128] Brzezinski saw a fundamental philosophical difference between himself and Vance and Vance's deputy Warren Christopher. For Brzezinski they embodied traditional diplomatic restraint, whilst he was a power politics activist prepared to use force.[129] The Democratic Party itself was divided between the President and the Henry 'Scoop' Jackson wing, which pushed for a stronger and more assertive national security policy, especially on nuclear issues.[130] It was a very post-Vietnam presidential dilemma and agenda. Rather than resolving the dilemmas of using military force, Carter's presidency simply heightened them.

The legacy of the Vietnam War was to become a 'syndrome', deforming and reforming US strategic culture.[131] Before the war the US had had an overly powerful potential,[132] but the result completely reversed this. It led to the reassessment of US foreign policy and the American strategic culture.[133] Richard Nixon saw the war tarnishing American ideals, and affecting American leaders so badly that it had turned the US 'into a military giant and a diplomatic dwarf in a world in which the steadfast exercise of American power was needed more than ever'.[134] Furthermore, Vietnam challenged the question of legitimacy of US military force.[135]

For no institution was the breakdown of strategic consensus more problematical than the US Army. It was, unlike Congress for example, a dependent institution. In Vietnam, even with the withdrawal of public and political support for the war, the Army had been left to carry on fighting. This went against its strategic position as the expression of the national will. Its previous self-image, reflecting its customary behaviour and concerns (norms), was gone.[136] The context and norms provided by the broader culture were no longer available and this left the Army being forced to rely on its own resources to redefine itself. Hence, once it was withdrawn from Vietnam in 1973, its rebuilding relied on developing its own and independent norms within the context of the American culture.[137]

Army lessons

The resentment that built up in the period from 1968 to 1973 is crucial to understanding the priority placed by the Army on having public support and Congressional backing after the war. Public support was necessary to stop the executive leaving the Army isolated from the national consensus and taking the blame for the executive's policies as it did in this period. The growth of political dominance of national military strategy, which containment demanded, had been enhanced by the autocratic management style and focus on systems analysis by Robert McNamara, Secretary of Defense to presidents Kennedy and Johnson.[138] The growth meant, for example, that the JCS were not represented at the White House war planning meetings until late in 1967. Whether this was a deliberate policy of McNamara's or just an act of indifference is unclear.[139] What is clear though is that as Secretary of Defense, Robert McNamara had a 'scarcely concealed disdain for military advice', and therefore the Army, not surprisingly, saw the Vietnam War as McNamara's war.[140] In fact, by 1967 an officer jeopardised his career if he expressed admiration for McNamara.[141] The Army were in practice no longer the expression of the nation through the citizen army model, but simply a tool of the executive – a fundamental change to its identity that reflected, for the Army, a deep misunderstanding of the nature of war by the executive.

Any understanding of the Army's strategic reforms after Vietnam has to appreciate General Westmoreland's comment that, in Vietnam, 'The military quite clearly did the job that the nation asked and expected of it.'[142] Often heavily criticised from within the Army, Westmoreland actually expresses a broad consensus of Army thought on this point and at the time of the initial rebuilding.[143] The failure to win the war and the ignominy of defeat, coupled with the ire that was directed at the military, has to be understood in the context that the Army did its job, did it successfully and did it at the request of the nation.[144] For Westmoreland, the American military man, with few exceptions, performed admirably in Vietnam, and the American military establishment did what the nation's political leadership asked of it. 'The war in Vietnam was in no way lost on the battlefield.'[145] For the Army, the tactical success that it enjoyed in Vietnam did not lead to victory, therefore the loss of the war lay outside of the military and on a more strategic level.[146] For them the strategic defeat was home grown and lost in Washington, DC, not in Vietnam.

Objectives

The Vietnam War was fought as a limited war.[147] and there was Army frustration that the objectives were never 'precisely delineated'.[148]

> In Vietnam, we, the United States, never decided firmly and collectively on operational objectives. And without operational objectives we went on and fought hundreds of successful tactical operations. We inflicted 800,000 KIA [killed in action] on the North Vietnamese and the Viet Cong and wounded a million, to no good end. We never achieved freedom of operational maneuver simply because we never decided which objectives we needed to take, and many of them were in North Vietnam.[149]

In Vietnam the revolutionaries and counter-revolutionaries were engaged in a broader war, whilst the United States was engaged in a self-limiting war, so the dynamic of the conflict moved away from the Americans; the US was the one who was soon counting the cost of involvement, and it could only bear limited, as opposed to total, costs for involvement.[150] For the Army, the nature of warfare itself, the 'Logic of force',[151] works against limiting the means of the military to prosecute the war as conflicts inherently reach for a higher level of conflict.[152] This is particularly true for such a force as the US military, geared as it is to highly destructive assaults and a separatist (demarked military and political realms) view of strategy.[153] The gradualist approach further exacerbated the administration's limited war policy. The Army's reading of the Vietnam War rejected the insight that escalation can, in Eliot Cohen's words, 'ebb and flow'.[154] Where the originators of the concept of 'escalation' were criticised for proceeding as theoreticians not historians,[155] the Army read 'escalation' solely as historians of one failed event.

Gradualism

The Army's entry into the Vietnam War was ragged, reflecting crisis management rather than coercive diplomacy.[156] As one Army Captain, the future SACEUR, General Wesley Clark put it in 1975, 'gradualism represented an unhappy attempt to combine military art and diplomacy'.[157] For conventional critics the war had changed with the escalation of troop levels in 1965, making it a conventional war and policy should have been refocused to reflect that change. For example, Summers sees that, 'In Korea there was a clear break between the advisery phase of our involvement and the war-fighting phase. . . . In Vietnam this clear break did not occur.'[158] The Army's perception of the war as conventional was reinforced by the fact that the Vietnamese response to the US tactics was to escalate its conventional forces. The war being conventional was, therefore, a self-fulfilling prophecy for the Army.[159] This validated and reinforced the Army conventional perception of the requirements of correctly prosecuting the war.

For analysts such as Krepinevich, a critical Army officer of a later generation, the failure of escalation was not conceptual but organisational. As he says, once the war was escalated and Americanised, the Army's primary concern was the deployment of forces 'to execute the same strategy that the ARVN had been failing at for years, only with greater resources and increased intensity'.[160] For him the failure of the escalation policy was that it was simply more of the same policy that had already failed. The strength of Summer's argument about the basic failings in the use of the Army is supported by the fact that its identity was fundamentally unsuitable for the type of war that Krepinevich advocates. For an army tied, in Krepinevich's terms, to the Army concept, with 'a focus on mid-intensity, or conventional, war and a reliance on high volumes of firepower to minimize casualties',[161] it is not surprising that it saw the guerrilla war as, in the main, actually a distraction from the main force war.[162] Additionally, the US Army saw the Malayan example, where the British had focused upon gathering good intelligence as the primary goal in the counter-revolutionary war rather than generating firepower,[163] as an inappropriate analogy of Vietnam because it was a 'soft' communist insurgency. To the Army, Vietnam was a 'real war' against an enemy receiving massive external support, not a 'small war' against irregulars. For them, the Australian Army experience in Vietnam showed that it was not helpful, as Malay-type operations were the Australian's most unsuccessful ones in Vietnam, and its success came through innovation on the ground.[164] The huge commitment of US troops made the intervention a conventional war in practice, and this was not reflected in the executive policy.

Responsibility

Fundamentally, the crisis was a question of how responsible the Army was for the loss of the war.[165] Critics have pointed to the lack of innovation within the Army. They have referred to the changes that the Marines instituted during the war, as evidence that innovation was possible within the constraints of the US strategic culture. The Marines developed 'civic action' programmes to live and work out of villages, and these efforts were a world away from the Army's ideas.[166] The emphasis placed on this by critics of the Army needs to be balanced by the fact that, as innovative as these actions were their scale was minimal. For example, the Combined Action Platoons (CAP) were a key feature of the Marines' more strategically relevant approach. Michael Peterson's study of CAPs shows that:

> At no time did the CAPs have more than 2,500 men. Considering that the peak strength of the Marines in Vietnam was more than 79,000 . . . these numbers are revealing, and demonstrate that even the Marines' response to insurgency warfare was ultimately tokenism.[167]

For Peterson this is not surprising as the Marines are a product of the same culture as Westmoreland.[168] In fact, Shelby Stanton uses the title 'Army' in his history of the war to refer to both the Army and the Marines, because the latter were simply used as ground forces during the war.[169] Innovation was only within the parameters of the traditional viewpoint. As Richard Betts says,

> Resisting civilian unconventional war doctrine, military leaders recognized the military complexity of the war but insisted on dividing the labor, leaving the politics to the civilians and concentrating themselves on actual combat. . . . To these soldiers, mass operations were natural and congenial and could be recommended and pursued with more confidence and energy than the bizarre tactics of the Green Berets.[170]

The clearest proof of this was that counter-insurgency roles were given to Special Forces rather than integrated into general operations.[171] Therefore, the Army's understanding of strategy was at the root of its thinking as it responded to the guerrilla aspects of the war. This difficulty points to a broader strategic problem the US had with the war in Vietnam.

Michael Howard, for one, was damning in his criticism of the West's strategic understanding of counter-insurgencies and the priority that the social aspect of strategy has in these cases, saying that it was,

> the inadequacy of the sociopolitical analysis of the societies with which we were dealing that lay at the root of the failure of Western powers to cope more effectively with the revolutionary and insurgency movements . . . Of the four dimensions of strategy [operational, logistical, social and technological] the social was here incomparably the most significant.[172]

The Kennedy administration's thinking was reflective of this as it had its main emphasis on the military aspects of unconventional warfare, not recognising that 'the centre of gravity of revolution . . . is the political–social milieu of the indigenous system'.[173] During the war, the establishment of the Civil Operations and Rural Development Program (CORDS), headed by Ambassador Robert Komer, would address this limitation.[174] The separation of responsibilities meant after the war there was a growing need for synchronisation of the political and military arms of national strategy,[175] especially as the Communists had had a brilliant strategy during the war.[176] Douglas Pike, in his seminal study of the North Vietnamese Army (PAVN), outlines the strategy, called *dau tranh*: 'In the end victory goes to the side that gets the best organized, stays the best organized, and can most successfully disorganize the other.'[177] The US was unable to match this coherence.

Strategic culture

Gelb and Betts' work, *The Irony of Vietnam*, exactly caught the ambiguity of US policy when they showed that 'the system worked' as there was a consensus over the containment goal of foreign policy, policy stayed near the centre of opinion, and virtually all views and decisions were considered without illusion. As they say, it is a paradox 'that the foreign policy failed, but the domestic decision making system worked'.[178] The mix of policy and force, guided by a purposeful strategy, developed by 'America's overconfident military professionals, clever but arrogant civilian defense intellectuals, and overly ambitious politicians', all failed.[179] As General Starry wrote in 1998, 'the wars in Korea, then Vietnam, made quite clear that, as a nation, the United States simply did not understand the limits of military force as an instrument of national policy. . . . It is a condition that persists to this day.'[180]

Starry was highlighting a fundamental aspect which runs throughout US strategic culture: the mismatch between the Army's understanding of its role and the nature of war, and the political tasks it is given in limited wars.[181] Crucially, therefore, after the war the military's failure to articulate its limitations to the executive would be seen as its crucial weakness.[182] The Army needed to reassert itself to remind America of its role within this understanding of its culture and its limitations.

> The failure to communicate these capabilities and limitations resulted in the military being called upon to perform political, economic, and social tasks beyond its capability while at the same time it was limited in its authority to accomplish those military tasks of which it was capable.[183]

The need to articulate its limitations meant that the emphasis was placed upon communicating what was militarily achievable to the executive, though as Eliot Cohen has pointed out, the military during the war offered the president few alternatives.[184]

The political demands and capabilities did not synchronise in Vietnam, and were not organised to do so as the Army was geared to mobilisation, and the nation was not mobilised during the war. For the Army, the Vietnam War reaffirmed its self-understanding of being part of the American people and not an instrument of the executive. General Weyand, the Army Chief of Staff, summarised this understanding and its consequences for the Army when he wrote in 1976 that,

> Vietnam was a reaffirmation of the peculiar relationship between the American Army and the American people. The American Army really is a people's Army in the sense that it belongs to the American people who take a jealous and propriety interest in its development. When the Army is committed the American people are committed, when the American people lose their commitment it is futile to try to keep the Army commited. In the final analysis, the American Army is not so much an arm of the Executive Branch as it is an arm of the American people. The Army, therefore. cannot be committed lightly. It can only be committed when there is a consensus among the American people that vital interests of such critical importance are involved that the commitment of the Army is warranted.[185]

Army soldiers and leaders returned to America, many of them several times, from a war in which they had won all their battles and found that while they were away the nation had lost the war. This provoked a crisis of confidence in themselves, their leaders, in the Army and in the 'political leadership of the country'.[186]

For the Army it was the failure of the 'national will' that was responsible for losing the war, as public support for the war diminished.[187] Little wonder that Shelby Stanton closed his history of the war by writing that an 'entire American army was sacrificed on the battlefield of Vietnam'.[188] Vietnam, as General Schwarzkopf said, 'remains the worst thing this country has ever done to its soldiers . . . and to itself'.[189] Kennedy's notion of 'pay any price, bear any burden' was too costly for American strategic culture to sustain. The new strategic culture was built on 58,000 deaths, and the demise of the nation's army.[190]

Conclusion

Traditionally the US co-ordinated its strategy through the mobilisation of the Army, and the nature of the Army was determined by the broader cultural context. The growing executive role of the Cold War containment policy changed this. The development of flexible response highlighted the overambitious nature of containment policy: the US strategic culture was not suited to the policy, it did not have a suitable Army for the role and its formulaic response was further exacerbated by the actual nature of the Vietnam War.[191] The Army saw and fought the war within its established understanding, seeing the political and social aspects of the war as the politicians' responsibility. However, the nature and cost of its tactics undermined the very support it was dependent upon. It felt betrayed at home, as it regarded itself as unbeaten on the battlefield; its effectiveness was undermined by the social dissent, and it was left in Vietnam to carry on fighting when the political will had disappeared. The lack of mobilisation of the reserves encapsulated the problem, and the loss of the war shattered the Army's identity as the nation's army, symbolised most clearly with the establishment of the VOLAR.

Strategic rupture had taken place because of the Vietnam War, and the Army's self-identity and strategic understanding was left in tatters. Therefore the rebuilding of the Army focused more on rebuilding its identity, rather than accruing lessons on how to fight counter-insurgencies in the future. When it returned to 'low-intensity conflict' issues it did so with a strategic understanding generated by the new identity, a 'new way of war' and a deep suspicion of the executive, rather than an appreciation of the strategic shortfalls of its operational style in Vietnam.

3

THE ALL-VOLUNTEER ARMY

To understand the development of the Army's strategic thinking after the Vietnam War, it is necessary to examine the nature of the rebuilding it undertook. Essentially, the Army was not able to go on as before because it was now all-volunteer and decimated by the war. The strategic assumption provided by its mobilisation identity was gone, and it had to go back and rebuild from the bottom up. It learnt many lessons from the Vietnam War, but it is essential to recognise how it as an institution actually absorbed and acted upon them. The innovation, and the thinking behind it, was undertaken not simply due to the loss of the war, or technological changes, or changes in the strategic environment; it was shaped by the specific case of the changed identity and nature of the US Army. as that was the aspect which had undergone the greatest change. It was to build itself as an All-Volunteer Force, a standing army that was exclusively professional, and it was aware of the strategic implications. The mobilisation Army that had only been partly mobilised had been decimated and this problem lay at the heart of the innovative changes through the period after the Vietnam War.

The lessons of Vietnam are, therefore, tied up with the consequences that the Army faced after the war. The lessons were not generalisations drawn from a historical analysis, but an attempt to generate principles, or laws, of strategy so that America's trauma in Vietnam would not be repeated.[1] Containment policy had, after all, politicised military professionalism,[2] but how this was addressed after the war was shaped by the experience during it. The approach was to create three new elements: a new Army, a novel American way of war and a revised political understanding of the use of force, which had consequences for the American strategic culture. These three aspects are covered in turn by the following chapters.

The Army's severed social identity

The year 1973 was the turning point for the Army. During that year the Army lost its responsibilities in Vietnam and its nature as a mobilised draft force. On 27 January 1973, three days after his second inauguration (and ironically the day after Lyndon B. Johnson died) President Richard Nixon announced the halting of all hostile acts by US Forces in Vietnam after the signing of the Paris agreements by the North, South and the US.[3] This announcement ended the need for the draft. On 29 March, the Military Assistance Command, Vietnam (MACV) was deactivated and its last commander, General Weyand, flew home.[4] Three months later, on 1 July, Congress finally rescinded the presidential authority to conscript, thereby severing the Army's identity as the 'nation in arms' from its Second World War heritage and ending the era of mobilisation. The public will to fight had disappeared. Little wonder that the Chairman of the Joint Chiefs of Staff saw the will and determination of the people in 1974 as his biggest worry.[5] It left the Army socially isolated, as it was now an All-Volunteer Force (AVF).

The All-Volunteer Army

The All-Volunteer Army moved the Army away from its democratic army/standing army self-image, distorting the nation's capability in the process and undermining support for the professional core of the nation's army. Officers of the period saw the All-Volunteer Army as having a pernicious effect on the nature of the Army and long-term effects on the nation, as it deprived citizens of the experience to serve one's country and the loss of military experience in federal legislative bodies.[6] The damage done to the nation would be further affected by the fact that the All-Volunteer Army deprived the Army of the elite, via the draft, meaning that the Army could not use their skills and, as one General put it, 'the Army needs smart guys'. The loss of the elite in the armed forces also meant that any future war would lead, rather like Vietnam, to the mortal burden falling on underprivileged classes, especially of minority races. Finally, the identity of the Army would be threatened by the fact that it had to find more recruits and would need to be competitive in the marketplace, and having to attract recruits in a competitive environment lessened the attention to making them uniquely 'fighters and combat leaders'.[7] Recruiting campaigns based on the Army wanting 'to join you' were seen as terrible, especially as money or perks are not the traditional motivating drive of a professional soldier. The All-Volunteer Army created a long-term shift in identity, altering the Army's understanding and the nation's perception of it.

Theoretically, the US Army could have taken an isolationist position and rejected the role of expressing society, seeing itself as a separate professional caste. For example, there were concerns that the Army would again withdraw into itself, and could develop into a threat to the democratic system.[8] However, the Army did not do this. Its identity as the nation's army was too resilient. According to Rick Atkinson, 'The officer corps . . . never envinced the kind of bitterness toward the Republic that had poisoned some defeated armies.'[9] The continuance of the ideational basis as expressing the national will was maintained in spite of Vietnam, though there was a keen awareness that the values needed to defend a free society are not necessarily identical to the values of the society it comes from.[10]

The main reason why the Army did not become radically different after the Vietnam War was that the innovations were built on previous practice and traditional thinking.[11] The Army Chiefs of Staff between 1968 and 1976, Generals Westmoreland, Abrams and Weyand, were also the MACV commanders from 1964 till 1973. Vietnam and its lessons was not an abstract problem to them. The direct linkage to the practice in Vietnam provided the Army with the context and stimuli for the changes that took place. The consistency of this approach gave it a structural form, because the individual actors reproduce the range of practices that make up the structures.[12] This helps explain why the post-Vietnam army, staffed by veterans who looked to recover the prestige of the Second World War and reverse the Vietnam experience, did not radically and suddenly make the Army become something different. Unlike a failing company which can buy a new management team in, the Army was reliant on those already in place to bring about the needed reforms. As Stephen Rosen observes, successful innovation requires senior military officers, who were well respected by traditional military standards, to create a new set of operational tasks and a promotion pathway for young officers to follow.[13] This was particularly the case after Vietnam, as Secretary of Defense Laird had re-enfranchised the service chiefs, slapping down civilian units that had grown under McNamara's tenure, by inaugurating 'participatory management'.[14] In this environment the Army needed to regroup and then rebuild, but did so in a context of immediate concerns.

The All-Volunteer Army created a short-term crisis. In Congress fears were expressed that the 'all-volunteer concept is not providing enough good men to meet the nation's recruiting needs'.[15] By June 1972 the Army was 9 per cent under recruiting level for that month alone. The fear was not simply of the shortfall in numbers of volunteers but of their rapidly declining quality. No wonder that one Army Chief of Staff (1968–72), General Westmoreland, later wrote that by 1975,

> Time has . . . demonstrated that the political maneuver by President Nixon of setting aside the draft was not in the national interest. The all-volunteer force has not produced the military posture required by the leader of the free world. Reappraisal of the ill-advised concept is essential.[16]

The effectiveness of the Army was in question because of the All-Volunteer Army. The clear military displeasure with the volunteer concept even led to rumours of the military sabotaging the all-volunteer concept to get the draft reinstated.[17] The Army's new social basis was not working. With the end of the draft the only true social link left was the Reserves.

The citizen-soldiers of the Reserves were in similar ideational crisis. The failure to call them up in 1965 had corrupted the nature and role of the Reserves.

> What had once been clearly defined missions and objectives concerning mobilization were made ill-defined and obscure. The Reserve forces were uncertain as to what was expected of them. Few persons believed that the Reserve forces would be mobilized; as a result, most of the new enlistees signed on not as true volunteers, but to avoid the draft.[18]

During the Vietnam War the Reserves became the repository of those not wishing to be involved.[19] As the President's Commission reported, an incredible 75–90 per cent of enlisted personnel were fulfilling their initial six-year military service obligation in Reserve components because of their fear of the draft.[20] The Reserves had traditionally saved the nation from having a large standing Army, allowing it to rely on mobilisation to augment its numbers. Therefore, the fundamental role of the Reserves had been ruptured by corrosion, and its potential as the link to the nation's citizens, and tying in public responsibility for mobilisation, were to become more important after Vietnam.[21] Creighton Abrams, the Army Chief of Staff in 1972–74, saw a pivotal role for the Reserves in providing a key aspect of the Army's future social identity. As Howard Callaway, the Secretary of the Army (1973–75), saw, 'The Army's obligation to the American people is to field an Army which is both representative of them and acceptable to them.'[22] 'Total Force' was the name given to the idea of using the reserves to create a new American army 'of the people, for the people'.

Total Force

Defense Secretary Laird outlined the initial concept of Total Force, which was to include 'both active and reserve components of the U.S., those of our allies, and the additional military capabilities of our allies and friends that will be made available through local efforts, or through the provision of appropriate security assistance programs'.[23] General Abrams utilised the 'Total War' concept and gained support from the new Secretary of Defense, James Schlesinger, for a new 16-division model of the Army. Schlesinger accepted this understanding of Total Force as it was a cost reduction. As Harry Summers explains;

> In March 1974 Abrams directed that instead of a cut from thirteen to ten divisions, the Army would go from thirteen to sixteen divisions. This would be done by 'rounding out' active Army divisions with combat brigades from the National Guard and by closely affiliating the Army National Guard and Army Reserve with active Army units in what he called the 'total Army.' . . . it would make it very difficult, if not impossible, for the President to deploy . . . without calling up the reserves. . . . The generals have . . . curbed the President's powers, quietly and indirectly, but more efficiently than have all the congressional critics of Executive War.[24]

Abrams's transfer of support missions to the Reserves, and integrating Reserve combat units into active divisions, created 'a total fighting force more reliant on reserves than any other in modern times'.[25] Thus, a Reserve call-up would be needed on practically the first day of any crisis. Abrams had learnt from President Johnson's manoeuvres what was necessary to force a call-up of the Reserves. The Reservists would be responsible for manning the seaports, airports and rail stations to transport

Army units in the first place. Abrams's structure, therefore, automatically obliged the executive to have public and Congressional support for any large-scale intervention policy. As National Guard Colonel George H. Gray put it: 'If the Reserve forces are to be used, the civilian authorities are more apt to be inhibited in undertaking ill-advised and ill-conceived military ventures. . . . [The Reserves] serve as a brake on ill-advised and unwise military ventures conceived by the civilian authority.'[26] Abrams understood this very clearly. Importantly, he was not, as befits a hero of the Battle of the Bulge, altering the American way of war with his Total Force policy. He was clearly only structurally embedding public support for any large-scale deployment. It was a fundamental strategic lesson for the Army from Vietnam; as Abrams said, 'They're never going to take us to war again without calling up the reserves.'[27] Total Force ensured that the Army would not be divorced from society again by executive manoeuvres. It was to be the principle that underlay all other developments in US Army strategic thinking after the war in Vietnam. However, at the heart of Total Forces lies a fundamental contradiction.

The social identity of the Army demands social support for deployments, but the professionalism produced by the All-Volunteer Army gives no place to amateurs. The nature of Total Force was simply to tie in public support, not to actually have amateurs or Reservists as an essential ingredient of ground combat, and the developments that went on during the 1980s only widened this breach. For example, during the Gulf War, when the principle was asserted, the actual role of the Reserves in Abrams's re-conception of the Army was clearly evident. Before the first Gulf War, the Army Reserves were trained in the key aspects of current army doctrine but were not fully operational. So, for example, much of their artillery was not cleared to fire 'live rounds in proximity to actual troops'.[28] Reserve forces therefore require additional training to become fully operational. The key problem here is that Reserve call-ups have a clearly limited timescale. The president could call up a force for up to 90 days with an additional 90 days possible. However, the post-mobilisation training necessary to make them fully operational cuts into this time.[29] Therefore, while the support role triggers the Total Force policy, the professional combat role is left to the All-Volunteer Army. This is clearly shown by Defense Secretary Richard Cheney's implementing the Reserve call-up of support units, but ruling out immediate deployment of National Guard combat brigades meant to augment their under-strength divisions under Total Force. In fact, the combat role for the National Guard was ambitious, as once the 48th Infantry Brigade were activated 'Army trainers would find the brigade so ill-prepared that [the commander, General] Holland was relieved of command.'[30] In practice the Total Force policy meant that the combat role stayed firmly with the professional force and the All-Volunteer Army provisions shifted the Army from being a citizen's army to one of professionals supported, in both senses of the word, by the public. This highlights how far the identity and configuration of the Army shifted from its social identity as the nation at war to one of professionalisation in combat. However, public support only provided a social context for the Army, it no longer provided the norms of how the Army should proceed. The Army, therefore, returned to its historical core identity as a major standing army focused on the potential war in Europe.

Europe

With the end of the Vietnam War, the Army turned its attention exclusively to Europe. For an Army in trauma it is not surprising that it oriented itself as far away as possible from the scene of its own demise. However, the significance of the concentration on the European model of war needs to be seen as more than simply avoiding Vietnam. For example, after Vietnam the whole nation, as the historian George Herring put it, 'experienced a self-conscious, collective amnesia'.[31] While fitting the broader trend of the nation's reticence concerning the use of military force abroad, the exclusively European orientation is significant for its organisational importance in rebuilding the Army and its role, and the fact that when it did return to low-intensity conflict (LIC) issues, it did so from the position of the doctrine and thinking developed for the European theatre. The turn to Europe was not simply a strategic requirement of the nation, but, as Roger Spiller notes, the European defence plan had for years served as 'a kind of de facto doctrine' in the absence of authoritative doctrinal guidance.[32] The reorientation was an organisational necessity to reconstitute an army in critical decline. The complex and sophisticated demands of low-intensity conflict would have to wait until the basic aspects of a military force had been re-established. The Army's exclusive focus on the potential battlefield of Europe was necessary, as it was so utterly run down by 1973.

Europe was the Army's principal mission and in 1972 only four of thirteen active divisions were rated as ready for combat.[33] Not only were divisions unready but, as General Starry a commander of V Corps in Europe in the 1970s observed, 'doctrine, development of equipment, organization and training consistent with the doctrine lies at the heart of an Army' had been allowed to stagnate for the ten years of the Vietnam war.[34] This neglect had been compounded by using the US Army in Europe as the rotational basis for short tours in Vietnam, with the result that it was unable to sustain its regular three-year rotations to Europe. The 7th Army, in Europe, was effectively a depot for forces in Vietnam.[35] This had meant that military proficiency in Europe was unsustainable. The turbulence of the situation within the US Army in Europe was also part of the very broad crisis that was ongoing in the Army.[36] It was to become so bad that

> Forty percent of the Army in Europe confessed to drug use, mostly hashish; a significant minority, 7 percent, was hooked on heroin. Crime and desertion were evident in Germany, with at least 12 percent of soldiers charged with serious offences. In certain units, conditions neared mutiny as soldier gangs established a new order in the barracks through extortion and brutality. . . . Few young men wanted to be among the last to be drafted into an institution that promised to end the draft, and fewer still were

> willing to join voluntarily. As a result, the Army reluctantly accepted markedly lower-quality soldiers. Forty percent had no high school diploma and 41 percent were Category IV soldiers, a mental aptitude grouping of the lowest order. . . . A 1973 Harris Poll revealed that the American public ranked the military only above sanitation workers in relative order of respect.[37]

Consequently the US Army in Europe was in virtual disarray and in rapid need of fundamental and far-reaching reform and a sense of direction to overcome the crisis that permeated every level. For the Army to rebuild itself it had to address its core task.

The European re-emphasis was formally outlined by an Army Chief of Staff study, defining its strategic identity and role. General Creighton Abrams (Army Chief of Staff 1972–74) established the Astarita study group in 1973 to determine the legitimate role for conventional strategy and Army after Vietnam. The group's report advocated a shift to a deterrence and readiness mission in Europe. The report, prepared in 1974 (an unclassified version was published in 1981[38]), shows the consistency of the Army's strategic thinking shifting back to a conventional main force Army focused on deterring the Warsaw Pact in Europe.[39] The Army's role was within the European conventional defence plan, which was based on conventional forces holding the Soviets for a few days or weeks. This holding period would suffice to solve a problem which had led to an essentially accidental war; 'it was a matter of damaging the Soviets badly enough to convince them to stop without risking nuclear war'.[40] In 1981, General John Vessey, the Army Vice Chief of Staff, saw the Astarita report as a turning point in the development of the post-Vietnam Army.[41] The US Army clearly aimed to avoid figuring out how it could have fought its last war better, and aimed to look ahead, not back.[42] General DePuy explicitly stated as much with the release of the 1976 *FM 100-5*; 'this manual takes the Army out of the rice paddies of Vietnam and places it on the Western European battlefield against the Warsaw Pact'.[43]

The Army's turn away from Vietnam and the periphery of containment policy was in accord with the broader turn by the strategic culture away from the periphery of the national policy. Europe was the undisputed core of the political geography of containment, and the 'Vietnamisation' of the war in Vietnam was a recognition that US strategy had to change, drawing American political geography concerns back to Europe and away from Asia.[44] Secretary of Defense Melvin Laird made clear before the Senate Armed Services Committee that,

> Vietnamization is both a means to an end and a beginning: a means to end the American involvement in Vietnam and a means to make a credible beginning on our new policy for peace and increased self-reliance in Asia. . . . Moreover, *success of the Nixon Doctrine can help remove the need for similar American ground combat involvement in future Asian wars, an important objective of our new strategy*.[45] [italics added]

The strategic policy emphasised that involvement in low-intensity conflicts was not to be the role of force in US foreign policy, and accordingly the Army ignored counter-insurgency and ran down its Special Forces, also closing down its military assistance capability, the Military Assistance and Advisory Groups (MAAGs), which were involved in civil projects such as well-boring.[46] The turn from peripheral tasks and regions was matched by a reassertion of the importance of Europe to US defence.

The Army's emphasis on main force threats in Europe was underpinned by the shift in nuclear strategy to a more credible deterrent position, moving away from assured destruction to the development of more flexible options.[47] In 1974 Secretary of Defense James Schlesinger reoriented US nuclear policy towards Europe, 'coupling' nuclear forces to the defence of Europe in the advent of a conventional war. Due to Nixon's domestic political difficulties, Schlesinger had a high degree of independence. One of the 'primary objectives [he] hoped to accomplish during his tenure was to shift the focus of U.S. security efforts back to NATO'.[48] Schlesinger aimed to re-establish European confidence in the American strategic commitment to the defence of Europe.

However, as Henry Kissinger later wrote.

> We for our part, spiritually liberated from the trauma of Vietnam, looked to Europe to share in the regeneration of our purposes: it was after all, that part of the free world with which we had most in common in history, culture, and moral values.[49]

The deep disagreements and difficulties of rebuilding the nation's role in the world were not intellectually resolved until after the 1980 election,[50] and Europe was the site of the regeneration of American strategic culture in the interim.[51] As Robert Johnson points out, 'force deployments justified on the basis of military defence rationales were later seen as being important principally for their psychological–symbolic significance'.[52] For US strategic culture, preparation for war was to mean 'war in Europe'.[53]

The focus on Europe thus blended the Second World War identity of the Army and the strategic orientation of the US after Vietnam. War in Europe was to be the template for later developments, even outside of the European theatre. This was clearly laid out in the 1976 edition of the key doctrine manual, *FM 100-5*:

> Because the US Army is structured primarily for [battle in Central Europe against forces of the Warsaw Pact] and has large forces deployed in that area, this manual is designed mainly to deal with the realities of such operations. *The principles set forth in this manual, however, apply also to military operations anywhere in the world.*[54] [italics added]

Even the development of light battalions and their training at the new Joint Readiness Training Center, established in 1987, had the potential to broaden the

Army's strategic role, but were actually undertaken to increase capability in Europe. Another example of this was the evolution of Central Command to give the US military capability in the Middle East, enacting the Carter doctrine. For the Army this was an outgrowth of its NATO role and capability.[55] The forces made available to Central Command were ones assigned to NATO, and NATO agreed to allow the US to divert forces there, importantly placing European security interests outside its own region.[56] Central Command had 'assigned' combat forces rather than a 'standing' force under day-to-day command, as in Europe. Conceptually, the potential war in that area was deemed the 'half war' of the US contingency planning for one and half wars, and the response to the potential Soviet invasion was to be the same operational concepts as in Europe.[57] The planning for a Soviet invasion through Iran was still in place when General Schwarzkopf took over Central Command in 1988.[58] Europe was the template for the Army's developments and worldwide application in conventional warfare.

The Army justified its exclusively European focus by seeing that a 'Battle in Central Europe against forces of the Warsaw Pact is the most demanding mission the US Army could be assigned'.[59] The Army focused not on most likely conflict but the one with largest consequences. Critics would later see the European positioning by the Army as having more to do with a myth of what the Army is and was, rather than with its strategic role in Europe, especially as the experiences of the two world wars had left the Army with a strong and positive image of itself in the role of defender and liberator of Europe.[60] As A.J. Bacevich observes, although US troops were 'conditioned to view the Soviets as their enemy, American troops instead battled Chinese communists, Vietnamese peasants, Dominican leftists, and Cuban construction workers'.[61] Concerns were also raised that the Army would need to fight in totally different contexts for non-ideological reasons.[62] However, these complaints must be seen in the context of the institutional need to rebuild the Army, essentially from scratch, after the Vietnam War; the retention of a solely European focus was part of a broader cultural reorientation induced by Vietnam, examined below.[63] It must be remembered that the Nixon 'Vietnamization' policy absolved the Army of responsibility for planning for these other types of interventions. Second, Europe provided the key specificity that is needed for successful innovation, by providing a concrete problem for the Army as an institution to address.[64] Europe and the Soviet threat were fundamental to the Army's development of a new identity after the Vietnam War. This was the site for the rebuilding of the Army and its premier concern within the nation's changing strategic culture.

'An inward looking time'

The emphasis upon Europe was in accord with the nation's strategic orientation after the Vietnam War and the requirement for a clear focus from which to rebuild the Army. However, these factors were not sufficient to reconstitute the Army by themselves. The disarray the Army suffered during the war, and the paucity of its management and leadership, created a need to address the actual nature of the

Army as it stood between the disillusionment of Vietnam and the all-professional future. The social alienation it suffered removed the previous guidelines for the Army, and left it to generate its own new nature. What is significant is the independent nature of the reforms. As General Starry told the historian John Romjue, 'for the first time in history, the Army reformed itself from within'.[65] The internal concerns were generated by the Army's organisational problems rather than the analysis of the operational performance in Vietnam. as it had to re-establish itself as a capable force on the potential European theatre. The fact that it achieved it is remarkable, especially considering the low point from which the reforms began.

As the General who spearheaded the rebuilding of the Army's training and doctrine said, the mood of the Army in 1973 was

> in the process of recovering from the numerous effects of the Vietnam war and deep into the challenge of the The All-Volunteer Army. The Army was preoccupied – unavoidably and understandably – with problems of morale, motivation, and directly related problems of attracting and retaining volunteers. It was an inward looking time.[66]

The inward-looking nature of the Army in 1973 did not extend to detailed debate over the nature and lessons of the Vietnam War in the Pentagon. That had become a 'non-subject', and its discussion would bring few promotions. Once South Vietnam fell there was a mood of having 'put the war behind us'.[67] The rejection of the Vietnam experience went so far that the focus was not upon learning doctrine from it, but addressing the rather more basic institutional effects that the war had brought. There were many areas of dispute, among them the self-doubts of the Army, which were due to its internal problems and the nature of the war.[68] Douglas Kinnard's work with Army generals who commanded in Vietnam, for example, highlights the careerism that was endemic in the Army.[69] Additionally, he draws attention to the prevalence of the 'can-do' spirit in the Army, a philosophy carried out at the expense of troops. Within the Army there was a huge level of disillusionment and a chronic need of reform.

One of the most serious legacies for the Army from the war in Vietnam was the question of the quality and nature of leadership.[70] An Army War College report on the views of 450 Lieutenant Colonels had shown what a poor state the Army was in.[71] The Lt. Colonels themselves questioned the integrity of the Army leadership, giving examples of phoney readiness reports, and complaining of rampant careerism, old-boy alignments, inflated awards and fictitious body counts. As General Colin Powell, then a Lt. Colonel, pointed out, the report showed 'the whole facade of illusion and delusion'.[72] The roots of the Army's internal problems were seen as coming from the managerialism within the senior officer corps. The squandering of the national will's support of the fight is also seen in a rather different light when one observes that it was not simply the utilisation of disaffected draftees that made the Army ineffective, but that they themselves were not used efficiently. As the *Congressional Quarterly* put it in 1972,

> One of the recurring causes cited throughout congressional and Pentagon studies of drug abuse, racial tension and discipline problems has been the boredom of the jobs to which many men have been assigned . . . [for example the] misutilization rate of personel in the 8th Army [in Korea] was about 21%.[73]

This shows that not only was popular disaffection being brought into the Army, but that the Army itself had created it. It is not enough to see the disintegration of the Army as the misinformed public reaction to Tet and the failure to call up the Reserves. For example, one of the most contentious issues of the war had been a soldier's one-year tour of duty in Vietnam. It was a policy that was seen to undermine unit cohesion as soldiers were individually moved, and it also led to the accusation that the Vietnam War was a one-year war fought eight times, as troops did not have enough time to learn and build up sufficient experience. The commander of the US ground forces in Vietnam, General Westmoreland, did not justify this controversial approach in terms of military effectiveness, but rather in terms of avoiding the 'hue and cry to bring boys home'.[74] Westmoreland's approach shows why critics inside and outside of the Army felt that it needed to return to its warfighting roots. The senior officer corps was so thoroughly discredited by the Vietnam War that General Westmoreland was booed from the stage in 1972, first at Fort Benning and then later at the Command and General Staff College.[75] This is highly significant as Westmoreland was at the time the Army's most senior officer, the Army Chief of Staff. The divisions and factions that were running through the Army were undermining the whole basis of the Army and were the primary focus of the reformers as they rebuilt it after the war. It had to return to the basic identity of what an army and its soldiers were. The complexities and confusion of Vietnam were not the priority; the need to rebuild was.

The profession of arms

For many soldiers the lesson of the 'inward-looking' emphasis outlined by DePuy, was that the Army must once again become masters of the profession of arms, and for Harry Summers, and many others, this was the 'quintessential "strategic lesson learned" from the Vietnam war'.[76] The nature of professionalism promoted was not simply a generic definition relying on a technical skill base, but a sense of vocation. 'The Regular Commission identifies an officer who has freely entered the vocation of officership.'[77] This understanding stresses the ethical code based on the particular vocation of military professionalism.[78]

The study of war itself was to be the focus, built on the constitutional position of the Army that justified the size and deployment of troops.[79] War was seen as having inherent characteristics, rather than being subject to the excessive rationality seen in McNamara's system analysis.[80] This fitted the Army's traditional approach. As Deborah Avant has argued, the US Army since the Civil War had developed a highly deductive understanding and preparation for war relying on a 'science of war', governed by classic military principles.[81] Huba Wass de Czege, one of the authors of *FM 100-5*, 1982, expressed the ethos behind the new professional identity: 'Had we studied war more seriously before Vietnam, we would have done better. Many of us who fought and won the tactical battles of that war are determined not to lose the next one on the operational and strategic levels.'[82] The Army's professional focus, therefore, turned to the nature of war and its requirements, rather than to the previous priority of being geared to the preparation for the nation's mobilisation for war.[83]

The first stage of the post-Vietnam reform of the Army was organisational. Army Chief of Staff Creighton Abrams established the STEADFAST Reorganisation to address problems within the Army. This was part of a larger reform going on in the Army led by senior officers such as Abrams and Vice Chief of Staff Bruce Palmer.[84] The fundamental change that took place after STEADFAST was the establishment of the Training and Doctrine Command (TRADOC) in 1973.[85] Whilst serving as Assistant Vice Chief of Staff, General William E. DePuy (1969–73) had conceived TRADOC. It was the first basic structural change in the US Army's organisation since the Revolutionary War.[86]

TRADOC

As Assistant Vice Chief of Staff. General DePuy had been tasked to draw down the Army from its peak of 1.6 million men to 800,000. He found that the Continental Army Command (CONARC) was simply too big. He planned taking the training schools out of CONARC and joining them with the Combat Development Command to create TRADOC.[87] DePuy was the architect and, as his commander wrote, 'the articulate proponent' of TRADOC, who obtained the approval of two Chiefs of Staff, Westmoreland and Abrams, the Army Secretary Froehlke, and the Secretary of Defense Melvin Laird.[88] TRADOC was thereby created, with a headquarters controlling 19 separate operating agencies. Simply put, TRADOC's mission, under DePuy, was 'nothing less than to totally rethink the way the Army trained its forces and fought its wars'.[89]

DePuy, TRADOC's first commander, set the direction for the doctrinal reforms within the US Army.[90] Continual training and professional studies are a fundamental feature of the 'profession of arms',[91] and the training and doctrinal focus of DePuy's reforms were to set the shape of the new All-Volunteer Army. He was of the first generation of reformers within the Army, and his emphases would be taken up by the following generation.[92] Reformers relied upon doctrine and training throughout the different levels of seniority to give the Army reforms a focus and a hub around which to rebuild. What is so striking about DePuy is his incredible level of personal influence on the reforms in the Army.

DePuy's personal energy and reforms were the basis for the changes in the Army, and as one of his TRADOC successors put it 'only he could have done it'.[93] He also sponsored many careers in the Army, a very important factor when innovation takes a generation to accomplish its goals because of the time it takes supportive officers to reach senior rank.[94] Under his mentoring seven officers would reach four-star rank, including Colin Powell and the commander of the 1989 Panamanian invasion, Max Thurman.[95] Powell had worked for DePuy when he was the Assistant Army Chief of Staff, a post Thurman would later fill.[96] A Chief of Staff, Vuono, worked for DePuy when he was at TRADOC.[97] DePuy's deputy, Paul Gorman, went on, like Thurman, to be Commander in Chief (CINC) of Southern Command.

DePuy stood firmly in the mainstream of Army thinking and was in many ways the embodiment of much of its approach to the Vietnam War. He was not a dissenter or revolutionary in the traditional sense, but as befitted General Westmoreland's deputy commander, he was a 'true believer' in the cause and potential for success of the Army's practice in Vietnam under Westmoreland.[98] For example, as a commander in Vietnam, he had been aggressive, using great mobility and firepower to close in and destroy the enemy.[99] He was in fact one of the original architects and practitioners of search-and-destroy tactics in Vietnam.[100] For DePuy, visibility was fundamental to land warfare because the most important function of the infantry was to get a forward observer to high ground and then protect him so that he could accurately call in the artillery. DePuy famously stated that this was the infantry's role, as 90 per cent of combat power came from artillery. Unlike in the Second World War, capturing terrain was not the vital issue in Vietnam, because it did not give 'visibility or observation'.[101] DePuy looked to solve the problem by controlling highly mobile ground force attacks from a helicopter in flight. He thus stood in the long tradition of the technological, attritional, force-on-force tactical approach of the US Army. DePuy's aim in Vietnam was to go after the North Vietnamese main force wherever they could be found, and to go after them with as 'many battalions as I could get to fight – what was later called "pile-on"'.[102] The combination of high levels of firepower and mobility was an understanding of the prosecution of war that he brought to his revision of doctrine when he took over the TRADOC command.

DePuy believed that Vietnam was an example of the type of war that the US Army was ill-suited to fight. He saw that 'Regular US Army troop units are peculiarly ill suited for the purpose of "securing" operations where they must be in close contact with the people.' On the other hand, US units could conduct 'clearing' operations and 'are perfectly suited for "search and destroy"'.[103] Therefore, DePuy saw the US Army as geared and capable to fight only main force wars, modelled on a type of tactics that he had developed in Vietnam. It was a reflection of the view that Vietnam was an aberration rather than a fundamental challenge to US understanding of war and the US Army's role.

The October war of 1973

Within months of its establishment, TRADOC was given a clear example of what it had to prepare the Army for as the 1973 Arab–Israeli War broke out. The 1973 war was fundamental to the revisions that TRADOC undertook and provided the guidance and testing ground for the new professional orientation. The analysis of the war, rather than Vietnam, provided the priorities for its future development. As the *FM 100-5* put it, 'The war in the Middle East in 1973 might well portend the nature of modern battle.'[104] General DePuy outlined the fundamental importance of the war in a letter to the Army's Chief of Staff, General Weyand:

> in October of 1973, the Arabs attacked Israel. In 18 days, about two thousand Arab tanks were destroyed along with 4 or 5 hundred Israeli tanks and all sorts of other fascinating consequences became apparent. This was the first large scale confrontation between two forces equipped with modern weapons representative of those found in the hands of NATO and the Warsaw Pact.[105]

The war was significant because it foreshadowed the nature of the war the Army was focusing on in Europe and provided the newly established TRADOC with a plethora of lessons on the nature of conventional war and a test bed for assessing American Army readiness. Measured against the war, US Army doctrine, tactics, techniques and training were found wanting.[106] DePuy saw that the US Army's attention had not been focused on the changing nature and capabilities of modern war, so he had TRADOC concentrate on a fundamental review of all US weapons systems, analysing them against the lessons drawn from the war. This review fitted DePuy's broader concerns with the reform of the Army's professional identity. The analysis concentrated on 'the implication of that war on the tactics, techniques and training of our tank, mechanized infantry and armored cavalry elements and their supporting artillery and air defense. We started at the bottom – squad, platoon, company, battery and troop.'[107] As part of this process General Starry, the Head of the US Army's Armor School, worked closely with the Israeli Army investigating the potential lessons for the US Army. He was sent with the question 'What does the Chief of Staff of the US Army need to know about the Yom Kippur War?'[108] On his return (from many visits) General Starry saw that there were a large number of key lessons, and these were to shape the development of the US Army's doctrine and its later approach to understanding its role and the utility of force in the future.

General Starry outlined the key lessons of the war for the US Army.[109] These were the key pointers for the development of the Army as it focused on the nature of modern warfare. The most striking feature he found was the dramatically increased lethality of the war, on a battlefield of much greater density. He saw that the direct fire lethal battle space was intense.[110] This meant that there was a fundamental increase in the destructiveness of mechanised warfare, a situation that the US Army would have to address. The shift in order of magnitude of material destructiveness was a major resource issue in itself, as the war had used up the equivalent of the entire US tank inventory deployed to the US Army in Europe, in units and war reserves combined. This obviously was a particular concern for Starry as the head of armour.[111] The war was fought at an unsustainable rate for the US Army in

Europe. The fact that this astronomical rate of consumption happened when the American war production plants were being scaled down with the ending of the Vietnam War only increased its significance.[112]

The 1973 war showed that the modern battlefield was 'greatly expanded in size, lethality and complexity',[113] and that the changing technology meant that small nations now had capabilities that had previously only been available to large states.[114] The 1973 war also reinforced the move away from being a mobilisation army. It showed that:

> Time to mobilize behind ocean barriers and deploy to relieve beleaguered forces – both characteristics of our World War I and II experience, was unlikely. . . . This final challenge to the mobilization system spelled for many an urgent need to rethink mass conscription armies, nations in arms, mass industrial mobilization, and battles of military and national annihilation as relevant concepts for the use of military force as an instrument of national policy in our time.[115]

Conceptually, the 1973 war was a watershed for the US Army as it undermined the traditional principles of the US way of war. The war showed that the American tradition and Army orientation towards mobilisation was an anachronism. Not only that, the war itself showed that modern war had undergone an enormous change affecting the nature and role of military forces. The speed and lethality of the Middle Eastern battlefield was such that 'it was starkly obvious that large-scale destruction in a short time was a most likely outcome of first battles in war'.[116] Geared to mobilisation and the slow build-up of resources, the US had traditionally been poor at the initial engagements, such as Task Force Smith in Korea and the Kasserine Pass in the Second World War.[117] Huge resources and a slow lead-in time to achieving combat effectiveness would no longer be possible for the US as a model of how to fight. Potential strength in resources would now have to be translated into prepared equipment and readiness training, which then would be available when needed.

TRADOC in its analytical role, therefore, focused on the question of what equipment lessons were learnt from the war, especially concerning the development of the new M1 Tank.[118] Investment would be made in new technology in the light of the faster and more lethal battlefield that was seen in Israel. Wars would be now fought in a come-as-you-are manner, requiring the Army to focus on the demands of the battlefield rather than on it being an embodiment of the national will and society. It was a challenge to the mobilisation concept of the citizen army and reinforced the need for the focus to be on the exclusively professional army.

General Starry was later to utilise the Toffler's 'third wave' concept to encapsulate the changes in war and its relation to society that had happened, and that the Army had to cope with in establishing its professional focus. The Toffler's 'second wave' model of war relied on a massive national industrial mobilisation for attrition of the enemy. The 1973 war showed that this was now replaced by a new 'third wave' of warfare relying on computerised technology.[119] The war had provided ample evidence of the 'precision revolution in warfare'.[120] The speed and lethality of the battle was greatly increased by technology, enabling the smaller side to win on this dense battlefield. Therefore, the attrition mode was no longer a viable model for the US Army in Europe because of the changed nature and technology of war itself, not simply the political costs of it post-Vietnam. This, of course, only confirmed the lesson from the Vietnam War, where attrition had failed against a smaller opponent, leaving it suspect as an approach against a larger enemy.[121] The 1973 war proved attritional strategy's inefficacy. The focus of the US Army's professionalism was, therefore, on fighting a short and intense war, where the US fought outnumbered, and aimed to fight and win the first battle. The focus of efforts had to be in developing the Army's professionalisation, with a corresponding focus on training, leadership and later doctrine.

Training

General DePuy had a strong reputation in the Army for his stress on the importance of training, which he saw as being a result of his experience in the Second World War, rather than in the Vietnam War. In 1944, in Normandy, DePuy had seen his Division (the 90th) ravaged, even losing replacements so quickly that it lost the equivalent of 100 per cent of its soldiers and 150 per cent of its officers in just six weeks. Not surprisingly this left an indelible mark on his mind.[122] He saw the key reason for this casualty rate as the poor standard of training that soldiers received. They were given 'time-oriented' training, with a set amount of time to be instructed on various aspects of the soldier's craft. There was little obvious concern with how well the individual soldier actually understood this training. DePuy therefore looked to bring about a shift in US Army training.[123]

DePuy's focus on performance training, rather than the more abstract educational or time-oriented training, captures the essence of how TRADOC changed the Army in his time in command. He aimed to rebuild by training troops in tactics and small units and to build up the reformed Army in that manner. General Paul Gorman, Deputy Chief of Staff and Training at TRADOC (1974–77) headed the training reform. DePuy said in an interview in 1979:

> The heart of the Gorman revolution was that no soldier proceeded to Step. 2 until he had demonstrated satisfactory hands-on performance of Step. 1. This same procedure was applied to units. The concept led to the soldiers manuals, Skill Qualification tests, and the Army Training and Evaluation Program. Gorman was also the conceptualizer of the National Training Center and of the advanced simulation and simulator development throughout the Army.[124]

The training reforms focused on establishing realistic training to equip soldiers for warfighting. As DePuy said, 'Morale was low. I . . . asked the major generals running the training centers to stop doing all the dumb things and make whatever changes they wanted to make and then let me know it.'[125] Morale greatly improved, but the irregularity of training was viewed by the Chief of Staff with alarm and stamped out, much to DePuy's frustration: 'I just wonder what kind of an institutional memory we have. It reminds me of the Russian system. I mean, if you got motivation, you got initiative. If you don't got motivation, you don't got nothing! [sic]'[126] DePuy was to build on this opening by looking to revolutionise Army training to move it away from the time-honoured mobilisation-based induction process and hone it to being performance-based and realistic. The self-criticism and the realistic training that was later to be embodied in the Combat Training Centers symbolised the 'training revolution' that he began.[127] The Army was aiming to develop an 'Army of Excellence' based upon its trained skills as warfighters.[128] It was carving out a specific identity in contrast to its previous mobilisation identity; society had designated the military as its 'warrior class',[129] and DePuy aimed to train them as such.

'How to' manuals

General DePuy focused on reorienting the TRADOC schools away from their educational focus and made them concentrate on performance training.[130] Part of the reason for the school's focus on education had been because of the mass mobilisation nature of the Army, as officers were required to operate up to two positions above their present assignment once the army was mobilised. With the end of the draft and the focus on creating an all-volunteer force, this impetus was gone. General DePuy said that he

> reorient[ed] the school system so that it had a larger training as opposed to educational aspect to it . . . there are those who feel that was a mistake, and there are those who feel we should educate officers and train soldiers. I think that is wrong. I think you should train a man for the job he is going to perform, and then you educate him so that the intellectual and moral environment in which he pursues his particular job will be enhanced. . . . I think that the field manuals on the combat operations of a platoon, or a company, or a battalion, are, in fact, the operator's manuals, and the lieutenant colonels, or the captains, or the lieutenants, or the sergeants, need to be trained to get the most out of the mechanisms they have inherited.[131]

As a result of DePuy's rather functional outlook, TRADOC provided the appropriate 'operator's manuals', and training in their use. DePuy's tactical focus meant that TRADOC thus set a goal to produce 40 or more 'How to Fight' manuals, which would instruct everyone in the combat and combat support arms how the Army would fight on the modern battlefield 'at every echelon from the weapons crew through the division'.[132] It is little wonder that manoeuvre critics such as Bill

Lind were scathing about the emphasis on techniques, rather than proper tactical thinking and individual initiative, which is shown in such an approach.[133] DePuy's reforms were aimed at improving the training, but the tactics themselves were not seen as undergoing a fundamental shift in light of Vietnam. However, the concentration on systematic training for war allowed the basics to be established so that the Army could develop a more sophisticated approach over time. For example, it enabled the organisational cultural changes to address the leadership legacy from the Vietnam War.

Leadership

As one commentator explained, General DePuy saw his work based upon a conviction that if one cannot assume mass and technological superiority, then the Army's only remaining advantage was to be found in the quality of its leadership and training.[134] To take the chronology into the 1980s, the training focus developed the concept of profession of arms to include leadership skills. The cultural change in the Army away from time-oriented training for mobilisation to one of realistic practice and evaluation altered the nature of leadership in the Army.[135] As one TRADOC commander put it, 'Our training must be backed up by expert leadership.'[136] The basis of the reformulation was outlined in the capstone manual *FM 100-5, Operations* in 1976: 'weapons, no matter how powerful, are ineffective in the hands of inept, ill-trained, unsure operators. And even proficient crewmen can be rendered impotent if improperly employed by the battle leader.'[137]

The reorientation went all the way to the top ranks of the Army. Training for the future senior leaders was at the 'refocused' US Army Command and General Staff College at Fort Leavenworth, which aimed to cultivate officer leadership skills by engendering an approach of 'how to think rather than what to think'.[138] The Army Chief of Staff (1979–83) Edward C. 'Shy' Meyer saw a clear need for a renaissance in the 'art' of military leadership as the traditional focus for many had slipped 'into the abyss as increasing emphasis was placed on management and specialization'.[139] Meyer personally improved experience-based training for commanders by allowing them to remain in command longer and trying to implement a regimental system.[140] He also aimed to change the Officer Personnel Management Systems (OPMSs) to avoid the Vietnam-era Officer Efficiency Report (OER) culture of management science.[141] The revitalised interest in leadership went in the face of the rampant careerism and institutional focus of the Vietnam era. Meyer further developed the ethos of the Army through the early years of the Reagan administration.

In 1979 General Meyer was faced by a shortfall in troops of 15,400 and the fact that close to half of the serving soldiers were in the lowest mental category allowed.[142] He called it a 'hollow force'. Defence spending had risen from 1977,[143] but Reagan still ran on a ticket of increasing defence spending and fears of a 'hollow army'. Secretary of Defense Caspar Weinberger outlined at his confirmation hearing in front of the Senate Armed Service Committee on 6 January 1981, that defence needed a substantial boost as the armed forces suffered from insufficient manpower and training. He outlined pay and benefit increases to improve the all-volunteer force and give it a better chance of success, with plans for a new GI bill for educational benefits.[144] The Army became more Republican, especially ideologically, in the early 1980s.[145] However, the motive behind the build-up was actually serendipitous to the Army's requirements. As Raymond Garthoff explained, the new Reagan administration was more concerned with spending new defence dollars rather than underwriting existing programmes.

> Less than two weeks after entering office, Reagan approved an immediate increase of $32.6 billion in the defense budget over the $200.3 billion already requested by Jimmy Carter in his last week in office. That Carter request had represented a boost of $26.4 billion above the preceding year. So a massive increase was sought – and approved by Congress virtually intact. The most significant fact about the increase was that it was decided on before obtaining requests from the military services – it was intended to signal the strong resolve of the new administration to build ('rebuild') military strength, and to cash in on the honeymoon with Congress to establish a high baseline for future percentage increases. 'Supply-side' military programming seemed the order of the day.[146]

From within the Pentagon the demand for military spending meant that service chiefs were able to submit their programme 'wish lists', and as these did not absorb enough of the new budget they moved 'from their wish lists to their dream lists, pulling out propositions they never expected to see the light of day'.[147]

The Reagan administration's spending enabled Army initiatives to materialise. A crucial development was when Meyer had appointed General DePuy's protege, General Max Thurman, to the Army Recruiting Command in 1979, and he re-oriented recruiting away from being 'The Army Wants To Join You' to the far more assertive 'Be All You Can Be'.[148] The shift in emphasis to a professional Army promising fulfilment, along with the new GI bill providing the promise of college tuition, meant that Army educational and recruiting standards rose rapidly, reaching a level where 98 per cent of soldiers had high school diplomas. Better recruiting was matched by the funding of new facilities and new standards and emphasis on training. The training revolution and 'Be All You Can Be' campaign were critical to the recruiting and retention of soldiers in the Army and for taking the All-Volunteer Force into a new era.[149] Little wonder that the 1980s Army was seen as one that was 'dynamic, creative, and honest' and a golden period of military thought and debate in the country.[150] It was a period that financed the new training and leadership ideas. However, the doctrinal developments were to be the key change in the Army's professional identity, and this affected the national strategy.

Doctrine

General DePuy's TRADOC rebuilt the Army through a 'training revolution' asserting a new professional identity, furthering its developments in leadership and military values. However, it did not change its strategic thinking, or, initially, the doctrine underlying it. Tackling this issue was to lead to the central importance of doctrine, which itself opened up new vistas for the Army's strategic thinking and changed it.

The reconceptualisation of the Army's doctrine initially was a spin-off from the training revolution. DePuy's concern was with training but

> The toughest issue that we had to face eventually was doctrine. We started out ignoring it; it just was not an issue. One of the basic premises of combining CDC [US Army Combat Developments Command] with the schools was the assumption that it would take care of doctrine. That doctrine then would be disciplined by the necessity of teaching it as well as designing it. And, of course, to some extent, that is correct. But doctrine was not, at the very beginning, much of an issue. It turned out, however, that this business of rubbing the schools together with the CD process did not automatically lead to doctrine nor necessarily to other beneficial results.[151]

The necessity of writing the doctrine manuals led to the 1976 edition of *FM 100-5*, which served as the capstone manual for the 'How to' series, and all the other manuals were derived from it.[152] Doctrine was to become a fundamentally new aspect of the Army's identity. As the 1994 edition of *FM 100-1*, clearly stated, 'The American Army is a doctrine-based, value centered organization committed to serving the Nation.'[153] The first chapter was devoted to 'The Profession of Arms'. Doctrine thus was to become central to the reforms. As the sociologist Morris Janowitz wrote of soldiers: 'Military doctrine is the "logic" of their professional behaviour.'[154] The 'logic' became the focus of reforms once the basic nature of the Army was re-established by DePuy, and he, with his two deputies, personally wrote the 1976 manual, going so far as to actually divide chapters between themselves.[155]

TRADOC and 'Active Defense'

The Army's developments after the Vietnam War were geared to learning to be a professional force geared to the European theatre, rather than drawing down operational lessons from the war. DePuy's reforms focused on professional competence and the release of the 1976 edition of *FM 100-5, Operations*, was to be the culmination of his reform of the Army as the manual was the 'capstone of the Army's system of field manuals'.[156] The manual's aim was to lay down the basic concepts of US Army doctrine, which would in turn form the foundation of what was taught in the service schools, guide training and combat developments throughout the Army.[157] The manual brought together the key concerns of the Army in a didactic manner, based upon a concern with the 1973 war's lessons for the European battlefield.

The combat focus remained 'on the "how-to" of unit-level training, battle drills, and co-ordinating tanks, artillery and infantry',[158] and as a result, thirty nine subsequent 'How to Fight' manuals relevant to FM 100-5 were listed in an appendix.[159] DePuy's concentration on this lower level of management and training meant that the Army worked up from the tactical level to the implicit strategic implications. The strategic thinking was implicitly developed from this basis, whilst the detail was an outcome of the analysis of the potential war in Europe not Vietnam. DePuy rebuilt from the bottom and the doctrine manual was a key motor for the rebuilding process. It was not a document concerned with 'theoretics' but realities and concrete doctrinal specifics.[160]

Purpose

The didactic, 'How to' nature of the manual gave very clear guidance to the Army of TRADOC's thinking on war. This meant, for example, that chapter 3 outlined how generals, colonels and captains were to fight the next war, and this level of instruction clarified and focused the ongoing developments within the Army. The manual aimed to develop a warfighting culture within the Army, stressing the importance of producing 'a unit ready to fight and win now'. For this to happen the manual saw that there must be a rebuilding of confidence, as 'confidence is the cornerstone of success in battle', and 'The US Army must be convinced it will win'.[161] DePuy's 'How to Fight' manuals were the means by which confidence building could take place. The role of the *FM 100-5* was, therefore, to bring these concerns together with the changes that were taking place on the modern battlefield. Thus, for the Army to be effective it must have sound doctrine and this must be derived from 'an accurate assessment of the dynamics of modern battle, and an understanding of all its implications' which then must be communicated throughout all US forces.[162] This was to focus the manual on the technological changes that had taken place on the modern battlefield, its new lethality, and emphasise defence. The doctrine manual brought together the new challenges of the professional focus on training and the challenges of the modern battlefield, and the template for the 'modern battlefield' had been provided by the war in 1973 in the Middle East.

Europe

General DePuy was clear that,

> Soviet forces were recognized as the enemy and Soviet tactical doctrine became the immediate center of attention. . . . Operational and tactical concepts were designed to cope with Soviet strength and the lack of

> maneuver room in West Germany. Those tactics could best be described as an elastic defense combined with counterattacks in order to defend along and close to the border of West Germany.[163]

The manual stressed the importance of understanding the enemy and it then exclusively outlined Soviet history and doctrine. For example, using analysis based on the battles of Kursk and Kharkov, it stated that the Soviet Army 'prefers deep converging penetrations to cut off and destroy large opposing forces'.[164] It went on to outline current Soviet doctrine, stressing offensive breakthrough tactics and the requirements for huge artillery densities that this approach demands and explaining the increased inventories of self-propelled guns being due to the limited mobility of towed artillery to support the Soviet doctrine of fast and deep offensive operations.[165] The high tempo of Soviet offensive doctrine was the key to its success and was the key concern of American doctrine. This concern was enhanced by the fact that the speed of the Soviet offence increased the utility of conventional forces, as 'a high rate of advance reduces the danger of troop destruction by enemy nuclear strikes'.[166]

For the Army the conventional-nuclear pendulum had swung from the conventional war of the Second World War, to the nuclear war models of the Pentomic era, and to the new position of the European battle being a 'concept of conventional–nuclear war'.[167] The massed and outnumbering forces of the Warsaw Pact facing the US Army meant that American doctrine was designed for 'units to fight outnumbered, and to win'[168] on this battlefield. As General Starry wrote;

> The United States Army had to be ready to . . . fight outnumbered, fight and win first and succeeding battles, without sustaining significant or unnecessary casualties, and without having to resort, at tactical or operational levels, to the use of nuclear weapons to overcome disparities in numbers or other capabilities.[169]

The lessons from the 1973 war were to be drawn out for their relevance to the Central European battle, and were the point of convergence of the understanding of the nature of the Soviet threat and the professionalisation lessons of the post-Vietnam army.

All-arms defence

The most significant source of the increased lethality of the battlefield was anti-tank capabilities, which would provide the core for the 1976 doctrine of Active Defense.[170] The manual explicitly stated that the defender now had such an advantage that it was at least a 3:1 ratio, and the attacker only had the initiative to count on.[171] The doctrine in *FM 100-5* was based upon this insight, with tactics using the technical capabilities of anti-tank guided missile systems to make defence more formidable.[172] However, tanks were also shown to have greatly increased killing capability, as they could now hit what they could see and kill what they could hit.[173] Much was made in the manual about the fact that the current US medium tank could penetrate twice the armour at four times the range of the Second World War Sherman tank.[174] However, the increased destructiveness of tanks could not counter anti-tank capabilities alone. For example, the Israelis adopted all-arms combat teams to counter and suppress the effective Egyptian anti-tank weapons. This development helped NATO experts and 'tank protagonists' to deduce that the tank was not an obsolete weapon in this increasingly destructive environment, but that it must be used in conjunction with other arms.[175] *FM 100-5* concurred with this reading and saw tanks as the primary offensive weapon, with all the other elements of combined arms employed to support them.[176] The manual, therefore, saw that modern battles were fought and won by air and land forces working together, centred round mechanised armour. The interaction and co-operation between air and land forces were seen to extend into 'almost every function of combat. . . . The Army cannot win the land battle without the Air Force'.[177] This meant that the importance of combined arms thinking was raised at an embryonic stage of TRADOC's investigations.[178]

First battle

The speed and destructiveness of tanks and the increased capability of anti-tank weaponry not only challenged America's traditional slow build-up and mobilisation but the level of attrition in the initial stages would negate long-term material advantages. The US, as has been seen earlier, was historically unprepared for its first battles. The manual clearly recognised this: 'we are accustomed to victory wrought with the weight of materiel and population brought to bear after the onset of hostilities. Today the US Army must, above all else, *prepare to win the first battle of the next war*' [original emphasis].[179] The reorientation of the US Army away from mobilisation was, therefore, reinforced by the recognition that war, the focus of the profession of arms, had undergone a change which created the need for a new understanding by the Army of the nature of war and how to fight it. TRADOC placed special emphasis in its doctrinal outcomes on the role and impact of modern weaponry on the battlefield. The resultant *FM 100-5* became 'the basic statement of our solutions to the challenge of modern weapons across the whole integrated battlefield'.[180] For example, the whole of chapter 2 was devoted to an analysis of 'Modern Weapons on the Modern Battlefield'.

Technology

DePuy aimed to 'organize the Army to employ and maintain the modern weapons which can drive the outcome on the battlefield', an approach successfully adopted by the German and Israeli armies.[181] His concern was not simply with the current state of technology on the battlefield, but he aspired to design the 1976 edition of *FM 100-5* to cover the period when the next generation of weapons would be absorbed into the Army. He saw this as a necessity as he was conscious of the lengthy process that converted novel technology into new weapons, an operation further lengthened by the time it took to actually procure them. Additionally it took time for the Army to learn how to operate and use them.[182] The effects of technology, and their potential, were therefore a central concern of the new doctrine.[183] The concern with new technology was not simply the traditional American focus on 'high-tec' solutions, but a perception that the changing nature of technology was vital for its effect on the battlefield that the Army was rebuilding for.

For DePuy the concentration on the changed weaponry of the early 1970s was not simply a reinforcement of the traditional attritional/firepower Army practice, because

> Overall battlefield effectiveness depends on weapons capability, the proficiency of teams or crews, and the tactics or techniques of the commander. Thus, the US Army must obtain powerful weapons, develop fully the proficiency of the men who man them, *and train leaders capable of employing weapons and crews to best effect.*[184] [original emphasis]

DePuy was here openly outlining the interrelation between training and weaponry, rather than seeing a simple emphasis on either aspect. For him, the modern battlefield was throwing up new demands and the Army must be equipped and trained to meet them. For example, an Army Training and Evaluation Program (ARTEP) was established which emphasised that 'Training development must provide training standards and techniques *matched closely to the realities of the modern battlefield.*'[185] Rather than looking simply at the professionalisation of the individual the manual recognises that soldiers receive training in units.[186] Thus the corporate identity of the new professionalism was an inherent feature of the training focus, and placed the importance of leadership on the modern battlefield at the centre of concerns. For example, a captain 'must lead and train his men decisively, so that they know he will accomplish the unit mission . . . Soldiers will follow such a leader'.[187] The demands of training were to be a force equaliser in the face of the massed forces of the Soviet Union and Warsaw Pact as 'an outnumbered force must be more effective man-for-man, weapon-for-weapon, and unit-for-unit than the opposition'.[188] Technology was not therefore a be-all and end-all for the doctrinal developments, but played a major role alongside the training emphasis of the initial stages of the professional developments.

In sum, the 1973 war was the focus to bring together the new emphasis on realistic training and the changes in warfare which had gone on whilst the Army was absorbed in Vietnam. As historian Roger Spiller explains, the war brought together the concerns with professionalisation, 'modern war' and the Soviet threat.

> The war . . . supplied the American Army with a new professional reference point, uncontaminated by association with Vietnam. This reference point revealed modern war in its most sophisticated manifestation,

> and in such near-clinical conditions that its lessons were seemingly unambiguous. The war painted a picture of Soviet combined arms doctrine and how much the Soviets had modernised their equipment during the Vietnam years.[189]

The 1973 war provided the US Army with a measure for its professional focus, gave guidance for its developments in weaponry and tactics and helped concentrate it on the nature of the threat in Europe. The lessons it drew were not abstract conceptual points concerned with the evolving nature of war but a very clear model of what the US Army needed to do to fight in Europe against a new generation of weapons.

Tactical focus

The concentration on tank and anti-tank capability was based on the perception that all armies based their land combat power upon the tank.[190] Seeing that the Soviets would overwhelm the US Army with a concentrated mass of tanks, and armoured vehicles with heavy artillery supporting, the manual recognised that

> the success of the defense depends on the destruction of the enemy armor. The problem will be to destroy many targets in a short period of time. Thus the defense must be built around tanks and antitank guided missiles. These are the backbone of the defense.[191]

The defence, aiming to exploit its inherent advantages recognised from the 1973 war, was not to be static: 'the active defense involves the utilization of successive battle positions in depth, to wear down and weaken the enemy, followed by counter-attacks.'[192] In the light of the 1973 war, the defence was predominant in US Army analysis and doctrinal conclusions. It is little wonder that the doctrine outlined in the 1976 manual acquired the informal title of 'Active Defense'.

Active Defense outlined a traditional 'strategy' and, if somewhat revised, US 'way of war', completely ignoring Vietnam and its lessons for the American approach. It advocated a traditional American force-on-force method of using the mechanised arm of the Army to face down the central thrust of the enemy's forces, with the route to strategic victory being through the accumulation of tactical successes. The manual made this very clear:

> The chief mission of these forces must be to fight with sufficient strength and tenacity to force the enemy to disclose the size and direction of his main attack, and to buy time while defending forces concentrate in front of the main thrust. . . . In mounted warfare, armored and mechanized elements (tanks and armored personnel carriers) must be set in motion towards the battle positions in the path of the enemy thrust.[193]

Both the manual and its approach were heavily criticised.[194] For example, writers of the later 1982 manual, saw that the manual's 'active defense' solution to the problem of the Soviet Army's ability to mass at decisive points was to 'take on this center of gravity frontally and directly through gradual attrition and exhaustion'[195] The concern with attritionally grinding down the enemy as the basic orientation of the manual highlighted the amnesia concerning Vietnam. As an Army study of the Vietnam War would point out in 1980, 'Current US strategy, doctrine and tactics still are based primarily on attrition: since such an approach did not work well against a smaller and militarily weaker opponent, it should be highly suspect against a larger and in many ways stronger opponent'.[196]

The reception of *FM 100-5* in 1976 was so hostile that there were nearly 80 essays in *Military Review* criticising one aspect or another, undermining DePuy's intention for the 'Active Defense' manual to be a tactically authoritative and comprehensive treatment of modern warfare.[197] Basically 'Active Defense' was capable of beating the leading Soviet echelons, but the forces following them would have freedom of action and would overrun the US Army. This problem would be axiomatic to the later changes. The analysis developed in light of the 1973 war was not sufficient for Europe therefore. Though 'Active Defense' was able to rebuild pride and confidence in the Army, by 1978 the shortcomings were widely recognised.[198]

Consequently one can see that the first stage of the rebuilding of the Army after the Vietnam War was as significant for what it left out, as to what it contained. The failure to win the war in Vietnam was the stimulus to rebuild the Army but it was not to be the focus of the reforms. The reading of the war as a politicians' war meant that when the time came to develop the unifying doctrine of the new All-Volunteer Army, it looked to its traditional role in Europe and not to Vietnam. This decision was fundamental to the strategic learning that went on from that date. The concepts of the new doctrine and the use of doctrine itself as the means of reform were novel, but only in terms of the traditional concerns of the Central Front in Europe. This approach was given an enormous impetus by the war in Israel, confirming the Army's preferences for conventional war, and setting new conceptual challenges to the professional Army in the light of that conflict. As DePuy wrote in conclusion to his analysis of the lessons of the 1973 war,

> All that we do must relate to these very important lessons, crosswalked to our concepts, and result in the best weapons, the best tactics and the best techniques for the US Army to enable it to win the first battle of the next war while fighting outnumbered.[199]

The *FM 100-5* that was published in 1976 was a result of this process, and showed the clear institutional preference for 'defensive continental warfare dominated by the tank'.[200] The emphasis on speed in a mechanised form of warfare played to US predilections for decisive tactical victory, through direct assault. The novelty lay in the emphasis on the defence, the first battle and the role of doctrine within the Army.

The results of Active Defense

The manual was part of DePuy's overall reforms, but his emphasis on doctrine was used as the method for driving the changes, and eventually opened up the innovation process, leading the US Army to become doctrinally-oriented 'to an extent hitherto unknown in the American military experience'.[201] The emphasis on doctrine would eventually lead to it changing the nature of the Army's approach to war under General Starry's tenure as commander of TRADOC. The process begun by 'Active Defense' took the US Army beyond simply ignoring Vietnam and ensuring that it would 'never again' happen. Later conceptual developments generated the key concepts and concerns that would lead to the doctrine that would fight the Gulf War, announce the Decisive Force strategy and change the 'American way of war'. The parameters and concerns of the second phase of development built upon the base of the reforms in 1976. The concern with doctrine and its role was fundamental to the change in thinking that went on.

The transition to the new concepts was stimulated by dissatisfaction within the Army with the new doctrine, which became apparent soon after its release. As Shimon Naveh observed, the release of the *1976 FM 100-5* produced a cognitive crisis.[202] The crisis was typified as spilled ink and 'dozens of jeep hoods dented' in arguing the merits and faults of the new defensive doctrine; a result, in part, because of how the concept was developed in subsequent manuals as a structured and rigid concept.[203] Resolving this cognitive crisis would be fundamental to the changes that went on, but unlike the first stage of reform the second phase would draw upon much of the work of civilian military reformers who had a different approach and priorities for reform.[204] The Army's professional intellectual base would become broadened, a point not easily recognised by the Army.[205] Civilians would be part of the debate that provided the new concepts that the army could utilise to address its 'cognitive crisis'. The primary figure to recognise this and act upon it was General Donn Starry, General DePuy's replacement as TRADOC Commander.

Conclusion

The initial years of the rebuilding of the Army were crucial to the later nature of US strategy. The dismal state that the Army was in at the conclusion of the Vietnam War was a greater priority to senior officers than drawing specific operational lessons from the war. However, as the conclusion of the war had left the Army isolated from its former position as an expression of the American society, it had to rebuild itself through developing a new professional identity as an all-volunteer force.

With the advent of the All-Volunteer Army in 1973, the mobilisation basis of the Army's identity and practice had been removed and led to the development of the Total Force idea to tie public support in prior to deployment. This set the basic parameters for future developments, but did not provide sufficient guidance to the reforms that were necessary. The context of a more demilitarised foreign policy under President Nixon took away many of the potential focus points of reform, as Nixon's Vietnamisation policy left military force to indigenous troops. This was combined with a renewed emphasis within US policy on Europe. However, the Army's exclusive focus on Europe was also reflective of its own need to return to its basic and primary role to enable it to become a fully functioning armed service again. Rather than the Vietnam War, the 1973 war gave clear indications of the inadequacy of the US Army in any potential war in Europe, and so was the template for the Army to rebuild itself upon.

The internal disarray of the Army was so severe that leadership and morale was seen to be in a state of crisis, and the need for reform was self-evident. The introduction of the All-Volunteer Army and the recognition of leadership failings during the war gave the new identity a particular emphasis on 'the profession of arms'. Training and leadership were placed at the centre of the developments, and a new command, the Training and Doctrine Command (TRADOC) was established to bring this about. Senior officers from the war headed the reforms, lessening the likelihood of radical change, but guaranteeing that the changes they brought in would have support.

The 1973 war was crucial to early years of TRADOC as it provided the criteria to judge the reforms by. Traditional US strategy relied upon mobilisation and the slow build-up of resources, but the 1973 war showed these features to be redundant in a period of rapid and lethal engagements. The technological advancements seen in the war were combined with an emphasis upon the human aspect of war to shape the nature of the realistic training which was the centrepiece of General DePuy's – the first TRADOC commander – reforms. The professional focus was a rejection of mobilisation and the managerialism seen during the Vietnam War.

Rather than looking to Vietnam for strategic lessons, the priority was a rebuilding of the Army from the bottom-up tested against the analysis of the 1973 war. DePuy produced 'How to' manuals to establish the instructional nature of his training reforms. Doctrine thus became important as a driver of institutional training reform rather than an end in itself. The 1976 *FM 100-5* was written mainly by DePuy as an outcome of the training focus and was a restatement of traditional Army concerns with an attritional approach to war. However, its inability to address the primary issue of second echelon Warsaw Pact forces led to it having a critical reception and created a 'cognitive crisis' within the Army. This crisis was to open the Army to a new 'way of war' through the creation of innovative operational ideas.

The reforms immediately after the Vietnam War set the path for the later developments as the Army concentrated on Europe and the development of a new 'professional' identity based on training and leadership rather than the broader American society. What is important here is that the social divisions of the Vietnam War, and the ensuing reforms, pushed the Army onto its own resources of training and leadership as a professional body. The resources and focus for reform had to be found from within the Army rather than simply come from a new strategic concept from the executive.[206] However, the initial reforms of the Army's identity would be given massive impetus by the years of the Weinberger–Reagan build-up, in terms of technology, retention and the quality of soldiers and their lives.[207]

Importantly, the training reforms did not repudiate the previous concentration of tactical destructiveness as the way to fight. Only when it addressed the question of doctrine did the strategic thinking undergo a key change, and later reforms were to be effected through 'the medium of doctrine itself'.[208] These changes were developed from a new basis of the Army being a trained professional force, due in large part to the work of General DePuy. The sophistication and demands of the operational doctrine, which would be developed within TRADOC, could be realised within the Army due to the establishing of basic soldiering skills and concerns. It enabled the new doctrine to be developed, but did not determine it; the initial doctrine was in accord with traditional US strategy but the subsequent one took the professional developments further and was in contrast to the nation's previous strategy. It was the consequences rather than lessons of Vietnam that were to drive the new strategic thinking.

4

INNOVATION IN US ARMY DOCTRINE

The focus of the Army's learning after the Vietnam War had been on the rebuilding of it as a professional force, modelled on the demands of the European theatre and direct lessons drawn from the October War of 1973. These lessons did not change the strategic thinking of the Army. However, by the end of the period 1973–82 the Army's strategic thinking had altered and had done so because of its doctrinal developments. This chapter explains and analyses this process.

The building of the Army's professionally trained identity created a requirement for doctrine, to clearly lay out the Army's thinking and provide a basis for its training. However, the development of doctrine in the period 1973–82 actually brought about a revolution in Army thinking. At the start of the period, doctrine was a result of the training focus but by the end it was the determining stimulus for the later technological developments and force structure of the Army. In the process the Army's identity matured to one of a doctrine-based professional force, founded upon concepts developed by other military professionals and civilian critics and underpinned by a re-examination of the 'principles of war'. The new identity created novel strategic requirements for the US use of military force, and these were to be reflected in intervention policy.

To understand the changes that took place in the period it is necessary to see the stages it went through and the role of civilian critics within it. The first part of this chapter examines the inadequacy of the initial doctrinal approach, released as 'Active Defense' in 1976, and surveys the role of critics in developing new concepts of war for the Army. This is important because the 'cognitive crisis' that the doctrine created was an important motor for innovation in *FM 100-5*, and the use of new civilian concepts to address it. The second part outlines the problems that the revisions aimed to address and the concepts that led to the development of the AirLand Battle doctrine. This advocated a new orientation and criteria for successful warfare, by developing an operational-manoeuvrist approach to war to replace the traditional attritional Army 'way of war'. The final two parts examine the new emphasis and its influence within the rebuilding of the Army and shaping its strategic thinking, showing how the thinking became practice within it. It had large implications for training and how the Army thought of war, thereby defining how the Army saw itself, its role and its utility. The Army's new thinking had changed from being a product of the American strategic culture to one of the variables defining it. The influence and consequences of the new thinking for American polity are examined in subsequent chapters; this chapter deals with its development.

The reform debate

'To understand any description of war and the proposed fighting of it . . . it is . . . necessary to understand the circumstances under which the liturgy was laid down.'[1] As two of the authors of the 1982 *FM 100-5*, Huba Wass de Czege and L.D. Holder, made very clear:

> The basic question of *why* doctrine was changed can be answered simply: Army commanders became convinced as a result of their field training and war games that they would be unable to defeat the Soviets using the doctrine of 1976. These commanders believed that they could beat the leading Soviet echelons using the 'active defense' but that the initial battles would render our units ineffective while leaving Soviet follow-on forces intact with complete freedom of action.[2]

Addressing this crucial problem would be the drive for the reforms. It was a development of DePuy's reforms carried on by his successor General Donn Starry.

General Starry

The Army and civilian critics were clear that there was a need for reform, but organisational change also requires the necessary resources and managerial commitment to provide the innovation.[3] Additionally, the timings of the reforms meant there were no major conflict demands made on the Army in the midst of its changes. In this context, the key organisational aspects of Army reform were to be provided by General Donn A. Starry. Starry had been General DePuy's deputy at TRADOC and it was his appointment as TRADOC Commander in 1977 that led to the development of AirLand Battle doctrine.[4] Between his TRADOC appointments he had commanded V Corps in Europe, where he focused on leadership within the Corps, 'walking the battlefield' with his officers, seeing evidence of the new 1976 doctrine and of the rebuilt confidence to defend against the first wave of Soviet attacks. Starry's open exercise with his officers was enhanced because he was in the unusual position of being so close to the changes at TRADOC that he could bring about needed alterations.

A keen student of military history, Starry looked to return the US Army to a more professional orientation geared to warfighting and drawing upon the historical principles of war, a failing of the 1976 manual he had highlighted.[5] Additionally, he saw that support for the 1976 doctrine had been weakened by there having been too little organisational consensus building behind it.[6] The development of doctrine could not therefore be done in isolation. As Huba Wass de Czege wrote, it was

> impossible to separate a discussion of doctrine from other matters central to how an army fights. These include the purposes of the army, its equipment, its soldiers, the existence of external threats, the nature of modern combat, society at large, technological advances, and so on.[7]

Therefore, on his return to TRADOC he broadened the base of the culture from which DePuy had pulled ideas together, with the recognition that the new doctrinal thinking must incorporate the strengths of current thought and improvements urged by constructive critics.[8] Spearheading this process made Starry a 'doctrinal revolutionary'.[9]

General Starry was conscious that reforms required a consensus, as they took time to implement and no one lasts long enough in post to stop the system zig-zagging with each new appointment.[10] To generate support from within the Army, he and his doctrine writers stressed that the *FM 100-5* revisions were very much the progeny of DePuy's work.[11] Not only that but he saw the ideas he promoted as pulling together existing ideas, rather than seeing them as totally innovative.[12] However, the trend of the Army being the sole author of its new doctrine is over-emphasised in later accounts. For example, in its official account of the first Gulf War, the Army's narrative of the changes that took place after Vietnam only mentions civilians increasing Congressional funding and does not mention their role in the development of new doctrine with the infusion of new ideas, even though the change in the Army's thinking was fundamental to the victory in the Gulf War.[13] Starry actually broadened the professional basis of the Army.

As Starry undertook his reforms critics were clear that 'The US Army is currently pursuing a general warfare doctrine which is bankrupt.'[14] To generate support and to develop the new doctrinal concepts, Starry had a briefing containing his key ideas ('a bunch of slides I used to talk about war') and took them to many audiences who commented upon them.[15] The ideas behind AirLand Battle

> changed based on comments, observations and questions from audiences ranging from Congressional hearings to lectures at war and staff colleges in this country, in the United Kingdom, Canada, Germany, France and Israel.
>
> When we finally cleared Leavenworth of the disappointed doctrine writers, got [then Lieutenant General] Bill Richardson in office there and [General] Shy Meyer in office as chief of staff, we were ready to write – at Leavenworth – what became the 1982 book. . . . Many people heard the briefing – whatever its name – and more than once. Most noted it was never quite the same – the second and third times they

> heard it, it may have included something someone in a past had suggested. Soon, many came to believe it made sense; further, they came to believe it was their idea. Armed with those two things, you can change a world. And we did.[16]

It was from this basis and with the consensual approach that General Starry addressed the problems of 'Active Defense' and the potential battlefield of Central Europe. The published doctrine, AirLand Battle was the result of 'The efforts of many high-level military and civilian experts, doctrine writers, and army and air force agencies.'[17]

General Starry and his team deliberately engaged with civilian critics as he generated support for his doctrinal changes, even going so far as to nominate General Don Morelli in a liaison role.[18] The openness was extended to critics, such as John Boyd and William Lind, who were invited to lecture at the Army Command and General Staff College.[19] Contemporary accounts show that the debate was generated and sustained by a small group of 'outsider' critics, 'a dogged knot of dissenters poised against the Pentagon and its allies', which captured media attention and cultivated support in Congress.[20] As Colonel John C. Studt (USMC) observed in 1985, 'the entire movement for military reform is driven largely by civilian intellectuals, not military officers – one noteable exception being retired Air Force Colonel John Boyd'.[21] During the period of the debate the civilian thinkers were accorded a central position in the Army's debate.[22] Starry's approach was, therefore, a 'systems approach' to changing the US Army.[23] He saw the developments as part of an ongoing evolutionary process, and the most important civilian contribution was the discussion on manoeuvre warfare.

Civilian reform movement

The reform movement had a broad and disparate agenda, concerned with a wider effort to bring about changes in US military doctrine, strategy, weapons and organisation; and it particularly targeted the failures and shortcomings of the Pentagon.[24] The reformers played an important role in the broader defence debate from the end of the Vietnam War into the second term of the Reagan administration, but were not a heterogeneous group.[25] They had two primary concerns: changing US warfighting from its attritional basis, and moving procurement from a small number of highly sophisticated weapons to a large number of cheaper and proven weapons.[26] To address these concerns the reformers advocated the adoption of a manoeuvre-oriented defence posture.[27] The two concerns were linked in reformers' analysis,[28] especially as it was manifested in NATO strategy.[29] The concepts which the civilian thinkers highlighted were that of a manoeuvrist approach to war, with its associated understanding of the nature of conflict, and the need for an 'operational' level of analysis within doctrine, which operated at the 'campaign' level rather than the single battlefield level. The broader Congressional role is examined later below.

The seminal article in the doctrinal reform was published, controversially, in the Army's own professional journal, *Military Review*,[30] in 1977 by William S. Lind, who was an aide to Senator Gary Hart. He eventually published his ideas as *Maneuver Warfare Handbook*.[31] His article, 'Some Doctrinal Questions for the United States Army' laid out many of the key aspects of the debate about 'Active Defense' and US Army doctrinal developments, and provided the mechanism for the debate to address the necessary changes.[32] Lind questioned the doctrine of 'Active Defense' and challenged three interrelated features of Army strategic thinking: the direct assault, attritional thinking and the concentration on tactics.

The direct assault

Lind was the primary architect of 'manoeuvre' as defined by the military reform movement.[33] At the deepest roots of manoeuvrist thinking lay J.F.C. Fuller's work on mobile mechanised forces[34] and the writings of Basil Liddell Hart on the 'indirect approach'. Liddell Hart had greatly influenced Israeli thinking in the 1973 war and the German Army's earlier development of 'blitzkrieg'.[35] Lind advocated the continued viability of the 'indirect approach', as it successfully created unexpected situations for the opponent as attacks were not direct but came from surprising directions. Lind's concept of manoeuvre was to develop Liddell Hart's terrain-based idea, as he emphasised disorienting the enemy through the medium of time as well as place and for this he drew on another writer on military affairs, John Boyd.

Lind championed the 'Boyd cycle' model of conflict. John Boyd's views were based on his considerable personal success as a combat fighter pilot, but he only gave a series of briefings and never published his ideas as a book.[36] Lind summarised Boyd's work as seeing conflict 'as time-competitive observation–orientation–decision–action cycles'.[37] For Boyd, each party to the conflict begins by observing his enemy and surroundings. Having done this, he then orients himself on the basis of his observations. From his assessment of his orientation he makes a decision and then puts it into action. As the action changes the situation, he again observes his enemy and surroundings and repeats the process. This model of conflict became known as the 'Boyd Cycle' or 'OODA Loop' (Observation–Orientation–Decision–Action). If one side goes through the process faster than his opponent he then gains an enormous advantage, as the faster combatant will soon be acting differently to the slower combatant's last observation. This forces the slower party to act inappropriately, till he is disoriented and ineffective in the conflict.

Lind used this conceptualisation as the basis of his understanding of the manoeuvrist approach. 'Maneuver means Boyd cycling the enemy, being consistently faster through however many OODA Loops it takes until the enemy loses his cohesion – until he can no longer fight as an effective, organized force.'[38] Boyd's model saw the winning edge coming from being the faster party through the cycle, and in the original air combat scenario this was dependent upon the pilot's visibility and quality of his controls.[39] Boyd's ideas, therefore, rested on good intelligence and command and control. For the US Army to utilise Boyd's ideas, Lind saw that it would be necessary for it to become more decentralised, able to cope with confusion, and to avoid formulaic responses to situations – a direct contrast to traditional US approaches.[40]

Lind also challenged traditional methods as he advocated an approach where the stress lay on movement and intellectual agility, rather than on simple attrition. In his article Lind takes the term 'manoeuvre' beyond the traditional military understanding of movement, by contrasting it with attrition/firepower doctrine. Essentially, 'Attritional doctrine uses manoeuvre to bring firepower to bear to physically reduce the opposing force.'[41] Analysts such as Bruce Gudmundsson saw the traditional US use of firepower as standing in the tradition of French attrition rather than in the German manoeuvrist approach,[42] which many manoeuvre critics advocated.[43] For Lind, the difference was that firepower was used in blitz attacks to enable friendly forces to manoeuvre, by stopping the enemy massing its forces, rather than being used simply to destroy them; the idea being that they fired to manoeuvre rather than manoeuvring to fire.[44] Lind saw the 1976 *FM 100-5* as an example of continued adherence to the attritional tradition.[45]

Tactics

Furthermore, Lind went on to criticise the first battle concerns of *FM 100-5*, 1976 seeing it as a tactical approach to war, and one that failed adequately to cope with Soviet second echelon forces, which provided the Warsaw Pact with the capability to lose the first battles but still win the 'war'. Lind saw that it was necessary to look beyond simple linear tactical engagements as the way of winning. As part of his broader reform agenda, he looked to change the understanding of the nature of tactics and operations, outlining that the manoeuvrist approach relies on three key reference points: 'mission-type orders, the focus of effort or *Schwerpunkt*, and the search for enemy surfaces and gaps.'[46]

Mission-type orders are key to the necessary decentralisation for rapid Boyd cycling, as the order tells the subordinate commander what his superior's intent is for the mission, but leaves how to carry it out to the subordinate. As the situation changes the subordinate does what he needs still to fulfil the superior's intention, informing him of the changes but not waiting for permission to act. Understanding the intent of the senior commander is the key contractual relationship between officers here, requiring a clear 'focus of effort'. The focus of effort is the unit designated to strike at the enemy's weak point, supported by all the other units, to overthrow the usually larger opponent. Placing the *schwerpunkt* is more than simply finding an enemy weakness, but aims at tactical gaps in the line of defence, and throwing all the weight against the weakness. The gaps themselves are found by 'reconnaissance pull', where the reconnaissance on the ground, rather than commanders above, determine the gaps and the necessary response, pulling other forces behind it into gaps seeking the line of least resistance.

Tactically, manoeuvre places a crucial emphasis on the aim and intention of the senior commander and devolves responsibility for achieving it down the chain of command. This shifts command culture from 'command push' to that of 'reconnaissance pull', which is the responsibility of all units, though there are obvious occasions when specific and detailed initial orders concerning timing and initial objectives are needed.[47] The aim is a more flexible and faster passage through the Boyd cycle. As Lind outlined it, attrition aimed to reduce the opposition physically, whilst manoeuvre aimed to break an opponent's mind and will by a sequence of dislocating surprises at all levels of war. As Lind wrote:

> In the maneuver doctrine, maneuver is the ultimate tactical, operational and strategic goal while firepower is used primarily to create opportunities to maneuver. The primary objective is to break the spirit and will of the opposing high command by creating unexpected and unfavorable operational or strategic conditions, not to kill enemy troops or destroy enemy equipment.[48]

Importantly, manoeuvrist thinking utilises operational and strategic-level analysis, rather than relying on simple tactical agility: for example, blitzkrieg was focused on the operational level.[49] Other civilian critics were to take Lind's initial concept further. Edward Luttwak, for instance, addressed the problem of the exclusively tactical focus by bemoaning the lack of terminology in Anglo-Saxon military language for the operational level of warfare. He outlined the need for an operational level of analysis and was an articulate advocate of a 'relational-maneuver' concept.[50] Luttwak conceived of the operational level as coming between tactics and theatre strategy, a level of analysis that had been lacking in the US conduct in Vietnam. As he pointed out, the Vietnam War had been conducted almost exclusively at the tactical level, and at the theatre level above that, with almost no operational level in between.[51] The development of operational thought came from the Russian 'school' of manoeuvre thinking.[52]

Historically, the need for operational-level thinking arose because of the size of forces fielded in twentieth-century warfare, as compared to earlier armies where a single figure could combine the strategic and battlefield responsibilities in the manner of a Napoleon or Marlborough. The days of a decisive battle where the strategic victory could be sealed by a single destructive battle ended at the Battle of Waterloo in 1815.[53] The sheer scale and complexity of twentieth-century militaries meant that the management and control of the vast force was itself a vulnerability that could be used to bring about defeat. One can draw an analogy from sport, where in boxing size and weight can allow a boxer to dominate a smaller opponent and dispatch them with attritional blows; whereas in judo the size of a larger opponent can be used against them to destabilise them and bring about their defeat by throwing them whilst off balance. In essence, the increased size of modern militaries brings additional vulnerabilities for them. Shimon Naveh, in his study of the operational concept, expresses very clearly what this meant for military thinking.

> The basic proposition . . . is that the way to defeat a modern military system is not by aiming at its destruction, as was claimed by Clausewitzian philosophy for more than a hundred and twenty years, but rather through the notion of operational shock, defined in Russian as *udar* . . . operational shock implied, first and foremost, the neutralization of the rival system's rationale, i.e. its operational ability to attain the aim or objectives assigned to it by the strategic authority.[54]

It was an influential idea in Soviet thinking. General Tukhachevskii, the seminal thinker on the issue, removed the idea of destruction and replaced it with the idea of operational shock, or system disruption, and the later Soviet concerns with 'simultaneity, momentum and fragmentation' rather than simple attrition opened up new conceptual vistas for US Army doctrine.[55] By engaging with the civilian critics, and studying Soviet doctrine, the whole concept of operational-level thinking became more important.[56]

Civilian criticism and the Army

Army critics were often scathing of the manoeuvrists, especially over whether they offered an alternative to attrition. Daniel Bolger, a major, saw that 'This maneuver/attrition split is a bogus one, invented with an eye to avoiding Vietnam-era body counts. It cannot be found in any of the great works on war.'[57] Critics who lumped attritional thinking with technology and firepower also frustrated General DePuy – he thought that this caused analytical confusion.[58] For example, he noted that new technology has a complex relationship with doctrinal thinking, and does not automatically lead to new tactics or vice versa; in fact

> Inventions often open up new possibilities within the doctrinal context – e.g. smart munitions. Some inventions move outside the doctrinal envelope – e.g. nuclear and directed-energy weapons. Others greatly complicate the execution of preferred doctrine – e.g. electronic warfare and chemical warfare.[59]

The doctrine writers did not want 'maneuver for maneuver's sake, but its proper balance with firepower'.[60] The need for it to be a practical scheme was also drawn out by John Mearsheimer, who tried to put into practice the ideas that the manoeuvrists were advocating for Europe.[61] He wrote:

> A close examination of the prescribed maneuver-orientated defense, . . . reveals a fundamentally flawed idea. At best, it is a vague prescription so lacking in substance that its impact on future policy will be negligible. At worst, it is a formula for disaster.[62]

Mearsheimer saw that they were really prescribing an inadequate mobile defence.[63] His conclusion was that 'NATO simply cannot escape a war of attrition with the

Soviets, unless the Pact wins a quick and decisive victory'.[64] As Wass de Czege said, the concentration on the decision cycle ignored 'the impact of numbers in warfare. At some point, numbers do count'.[65]

Different approaches

The differences in concerns between the reformers and the Army captured a broader clash of cultures, as the actual reforms to be implemented relied to a large degree on those inside working via the limitations and concerns of the institution. Richard Betts caught the mood of reformers' strategic thinking when he wrote that Edward Luttwak seemed to see strategy as 'an autonomous art, a genie that should drive defense planning, unhobbled by managerialists'.[66] For example, Lind displayed the trait of abstraction over political constraints when he questioned whether German demands for forward defence sacrificed militarily correct principles.[67] The contrasting methods, with their different points of references and limitations, have been typified as rational, natural, and open systems approaches.[68] Civilian reformers looked at strategy in a 'rational' manner. For example, Lind saw that 'Preparing to win in combat must be the highest priority in the allocation of time, dollars, and rewards, at every level and under all circumstances.'[69] The civilian strategists worked from the outside with a clean sheet, aiming to achieve a strategic end-point. An 'open' approach emphasises the nature of the broader environment in which an organisation operates, as this constitutes how they function.

An example of an 'open' organisation was provided by the US Marine Corps (USMC). The Marines' reactions to manoeuvrist thinking give an indication of the identity concerns of the Army after Vietnam, and the manner of the Army's innovation. The USMC were far more open to Lind's ideas, and his book *Maneuver Warfare Handbook* contained a 64-page appendix of five lectures on manoeuvrist thinking delivered at the Amphibious Warfare School by the USMC Head of Tactics, Colonel Michael D. Wyly.[70] Manoeuvrist thinking was officially adopted by the USMC, and underpins its first formal doctrine manual, *FMFM 1, Warfighting*, and its supplementary *FMFM 1-1, Campaigning*.[71] This can be explained in terms of the identity of the USMC. Unlike the Army, the USMC was not tied to a particular theatre of war as it had a more generic role and uniquely had its three-divisional size dictated by law to ensure that it was not disbanded.[72] However, it was tied to amphibious warfare, which, after the invasion of Korea at Inchon, was not a major factor in the history of containment policy. The Marine Corps therefore conceived of itself as a flexible policy tool, the 'first to fight'. Poorly funded and insecure in its strategic role, it advocated its strengths as a smaller combined arms service developing from its tradition of small wars fighting.[73] Thus, it developed a maritime force projection role of a combined nature, with air-ground teams focusing on mid- and high-intensity wars with close air support.[74] This gave it a forcible entry capability, and it had pre-positioned ships to take on the roles the Army did not cover with its concern with sustained land campaigns.[75] The Marine Corps was ideally suited to the adoption of manoeuvrist thinking as it looked at war from a position of first principles, rather than addressing the particular difficulties that the Army faced in Europe. Additionally, as the USMC worked on campaigns it was not large enough to be simply attritional in its approach to combat. The fact that the Army was not so explicitly manoeuvrist shows that it was constrained far more than the Marine Corps and utilised manoeuvrist thinking to address the particular concerns it had in Europe.

The Army actually pursued a 'natural' approach, where groups within the organisation are crucial to the process, producing shifting hierarchies of interests, generating the resultant strategies. In other words, the existing organisation adapts the ideas to its own requirements through a key reforming group within it, rather than taking on the critics' ideas wholesale. General DePuy and later Starry were working from the inside, looking at doctrinal analysis in a 'natural manner', having to take into account the living organisation characteristics and how they could be taken into new realms. As Michael Messe explains, champions of innovation have a dual focus of advancing doctrine and the needs of the Army.[76] For example, Westmoreland, as Chief of Staff, had emphasised evolutionary change over revolutionary ideas to stop the Army ripping itself apart.[77] To be successful the development of doctrine had to account for the nature of the organisation that was to enact it; it could not happen in isolation. General DePuy was clear that

> Doctrine is a somewhat circular enterprise. It must inform and instruct the Army on how to operate, but it is not really doctrine unless it also expresses the manner in which the Army actually goes about its business. In short, to be doctrine it must 'take'.[78]

This captures some of the elements as to why the reformers' agenda and Army reformers had a tangential relationship, with the Army commenting that critics were being pure strategists.[79] The civilian critics were looking to first principles, whilst the Army reformers were very conscious of the nature of the organisation. General DePuy saw virtue in the criticisms but felt the critics did not understand the Army. He wrote:

> The manoeuvre enthusiasts are, of course, entirely right in favoring a war of aggressive movement as the key to success. . . . Who could disagree with such sound thinking? Where the outside critics err is in their assertion that the U.S. Army does not understand all this.[80]

For example, the 1976 manual's chapter 4, 'Offense', advocated the aim to shock, overwhelm and destroy the enemy.

> The pace of new attacks delivered on the enemy should exceed his ability to react, so as the offensive progresses, teamwork among enemy forces deteriorates, his defense disintegrate, and his units lose cohesion.

> Foremost, advancing units must bypass points of resistance, striking deep and fast.[81]

The lessons of 1973 oriented the Army towards these concepts.[82] However, the concepts were still rudimentary as the *FM 100-5*'s 1976 release had been premature; the timing of its publication had been set by DePuy as he came to the end of his time as TRADOC commander, rather than when the doctrinal developments were fully worked out.[83] Additionally, the ideas were masked by the manual's emphasis on defence, and the doctrine's extension into other manuals and application in the field as a 'highly structured and rigid conception' of how to defend.[84] It was only once the emphasis turned to the predominance of the offensive that the concepts became fully developed and ascendant.

For the likes of Bolger, the contribution of manoeuvre critics, however flawed, was important:

> maneuverists have consistently challenged the American defense establishment to look at itself. The results might not be maneuver warfare, but they are unquestionably an improvement over the dejected wreck of a military that emerged from Southeast Asia.[85]

Reformers were aware of this and, as Lind conceded, civilians provided ideas and concepts but ultimately it was up to the military to reform itself.[86] Not only had it to reform itself, it had to meet current commitments with the forces at hand, developed under different criteria,[87] while these forces were going through an evolutionary period. The evolutionary rather than revolutionary nature of the changes that were going on in the Army does not diminish the huge changes that the evolutionary process brought about. Civilian analysts contributed important conceptual criticisms challenging traditional emphasis on the tactical focus of direct assault, and the new manual was to emphasise speed, manoeuvre and surprise far more.[88] The US Army was to move away from the traditional strategic culture posture of attrition. Attrition was typical of materially rich states,[89] but ultimately it was a 'non-strategy'[90] and the new doctrinal developments would provide the US with a 'strategy'. However, the new thinking would come from addressing clear practical problems, rather than abstract reflection on the nature of war, though the reconceptualisation of the terms of the debate was crucial.

AirLand Battle doctrine

The primary practical difficulty Starry faced with the battle in Central Europe was the lack of 'depth' in 'Active Defense'. As Lind had observed, the focus on 'winning the first battle' left the US Army vulnerable to the following echelons of Soviet forces. By not addressing this particular problem in 1976, a conceptual evolution was stimulated which led to the key tenets of AirLand Battle doctrine.[91] The changing title of Starry's presentation to address this problem shows the emphasis on this issue: Corps Battle, the Central Battle, the Integrated Battle, the Extended Battle, and finally AirLand Battle.[92] As Starry laid out, the need for deep attack emerged from the nature of the potential enemies,[93] and as one of his doctrine writing team explained, the deep battle may ultimately determine success or failure.[94] Additionally, some critics saw it embodying the criticisms made about the prosecution of the war in Vietnam, with the failure to be offensive enough and the underuse of the role of interdiction in Vietnam.[95] However, much of the specifics of the Soviet style of echeloning stimulated the development of AirLand Battle, even though the consequences of it were for universal application. As one of the authors explained, 'Almost all armies echelon forces in depth whether attacking or defending.'[96] The solution to the problem of depth provoked new doctrinal concepts, and a brief examination of NATO's solution to the problem will highlight the different emphases that TRADOC doctrinal reforms had.

Follow-On Forces Attack

AirLand Battle doctrine (ALB) grew out of the concern with the European Central Front. Like the NATO concept of 'Follow-On Forces Attack' (FOFA) AirLand Battle doctrine was concerned with 'Deep Attack' concepts because of the Soviet conventional build-up, the US Army's reactive defence doctrine and the development of emerging technologies.[97] General Rogers, the SACEUR and former US Army Chief of Staff, was clear that 'Follow-On Forces Attack' improved NATO conventional capability as part of the deterrence policy of 'flexible response'.[98] He was equally clear that 'Follow-On Forces Attack' was not AirLand Battle doctrine. For Rogers,

> the historical record shows the ACE [Allied Command Europe] has been developing and pursuing its FOFA sub-concept since 1980. It is not the product of any one nation; it is a wholly ACE product tailored to the European environment.[99]

Rogers had instigated a study in 1979 to improve NATO air interdiction capabilities to address Soviet second echelon forces and Operational Manoeuvre Groups (OMGs).[100] All Warsaw Pact forces 'not committed to the initial attack' were referred to as 'follow-on forces'.[101] 'Follow-On Forces Attack' was a concept aiming to restrict the size of opposition forces taking part in active operations in Central Europe,[102] and was 'designed to attack with conventional weapons those enemy forces which stretch . . . as far into the enemy's rear as [the] target acquisition and conventional weapons systems will permit'.[103] To fulfil its aim to prevent or reduce follow-on forces' influence at the battle front required the exploitation of western technological superiority.[104] Final 'Follow-On Forces Attack' proposals were submitted to NATO's Military Committee in October 1981, whilst AirLand Battle doctrine was formally released nearly a year later, in August 1982.[105]

The independent development was shown by the key differences between 'Follow-On Forces Attack' and AirLand Battle doctrine, where AirLand Battle doctrine 'carries . . . features that do not apply to the deterrent and defensive missions assigned to ACE'.[106] Crucially, AirLand Battle doctrine was conceived of as a model of universal application, a point reinforced by the revision of the doctrine in 1986 where AirLand would be adapted to the needs of the Allied Command Europe.[107] Additionally, American forces assigned to Europe would also deal with emergencies in the Persian Gulf.[108] AirLand Battle doctrine was initially a briefing pamphlet on doctrine and force design, commonly known as *The AirLand Battle and Corps 86*,[109] showing it was a US Army product to address its difficulties as well as NATO's. Studies showed that the differences between 'Follow-On Forces Attack' and AirLand Battle doctrine were crucial. as AirLand Battle doctrine focused on 'near-term' impact of forces rather than the longer time frame of 'Follow-On Forces Attack'; and AirLand Battle doctrine was a 'doctrinal encroachment' on the procedures of other national corps due to differences in the control and application of airpower.[110] Vitally, as Rogers made clear, AirLand Battle doctrine integrated the use of conventional, nuclear and chemical weapons, planned pre-emptive strikes, and attacked across the border with ground forces – all of which did not fit NATO strategy and its demands.[111] It was a different solution to the problem of 'Deep Battle' and had different roots.

Depth

With the publication of the AirLand Battle doctrine, the understanding of 'depth' became far more sophisticated. 'Active Defense' had an interdictory understanding of depth, as a place behind the forward line of troops.[112] The 1976 manual had raised the 'depth' issue seeing that the offence was most decisive when it 'strikes with overwhelming force into the enemy's rear, and destroys or captures his service support, combat support, and command and control'.[113] In AirLand Battle doctrine the threat of Soviet echelons meant that the entire depth of the battlefield was to be used

> to strike the enemy and to prevent him from concentrating his firepower or maneuvering his forces to a point of his choice. . . . The battle in depth should delay, disrupt, or destroy the enemy's uncommitted forces and isolate his committed forces so that they may be destroyed. The deep battle is closely linked with the close in fight.[114]

The objective of AirLand Battle doctrine was therefore oriented to the opposing force rather than just terrain.[115] Importantly, the role of interdiction was to create time and space gaps, not to relieve manoeuvre forces of having to face second echelon elements.[116] By conceptually pulling together the rear and forward battles, 'depth' referred not only to terrain behind the front line but 'to time, distance, and resources'.[117] This was important as this understanding of depth provided much of the momentum for the attack and elasticity in the defensive.[118]

Prior to the release of the new doctrine in 1982, General Starry's seminal presentation (his 'bunch of slides') was published in 1981, his last year as TRADOC commander. The article, 'Extending the Battlefield',[119] placed the conception of depth and the subsequent developments in a broad perspective. Fundamentally he saw the solution to the problem to be 'by merging active defense and deep attack of follow-on echelons into one battle. It embraces the need to seize and hold the initiative through maneuver of forces and fires.'[120] This was the basis of AirLand, and was geared to moderating the force ratios of the NATO and Soviet forces at the forward line of troops (FLOT) via active defence and interdicting rear echelons before they came to the FLOT. The focus was the traditional force on force, with a high concern for attrition of opponent's forces, but the consequences would lead to fundamental change away from traditional concerns, utilising concepts outlined within the manoeuvrist and operational debate.

The development of the basic pairing of the ideas of 'Active Defense' and deep attacks was the key part of the change in the US approach to war. By extending the battlefield deeper in terms of space and in time, Starry also saw 'depth' as extending the range of assets figuring in the battle 'towards more emphasis on higher level Army and sister service acquisition means and attack resources'.[121] The 1986 manual followed in this pattern and saw that the developments in deep reconnaissance, air mobility, long-range fires and special operations forces (SOF) 'will blur the distinction between front and rear and will impose a requirement for all around defense and self sufficiency on all units'.[122] The 'deep' battle therefore generated demands to reconceive the battlefield in terms of a holistic concept of the whole battlefield, rather than simply at the initial line of engagement.

'Depth' built upon Starry's lessons of the 1973 war, where the intensity of the battlefield prevented a single weapons system dominating, which in turn generated a clear need to employ 'all tactical battlefield systems in closely synchronized all-arms action'.[123] The need to fight deep against the follow-on echelons thereby required the need to 'see deep' and so Starry shifted the relationship between technology and Army doctrine to one where the doctrine dictated the technological requirements, unlike DePuy's reaction to the 1973 war. Starry saw that the 'extended battlefield' was not a new concept but that it was 'a more descriptive term for indicating the full potential we must realise from our acquisition, targeting and weapons systems'.[124] Fundamentally,

> the extended battlefield is not a futuristic dream to remain on the shelf until all new systems are fielded . . . implementing the concept today means that we are building the receptacle into which every new system can be plugged immediately.[125]

Starry was reversing the dynamic so that weapon system development, or 'technology', would be developed in response to doctrinal needs, a position which, in the words of General Paul Gorman, 'No responsible leader of any service would disagree with.'[126] AirLand Battle doctrine allowed this thinking to have substance, to such an extent that critics saw that the intelligence demands generated by the doctrine outstripped the capabilities of the technology of the time.[127] The conception of depth saw that the key in the co-ordinated deep battle was not technology, but the seizing and holding of the initiative to disrupt the following echelons.

Starry's fundamental shift to the concept of the deep battle was to provide the basis for the key tenets of AirLand Battle doctrine, and as such was the source of the new strategic requirements. By addressing the key practical problem of the second echelon forces in Europe the new professional identity opened up the Army to a more sophisticated understanding of doctrine that was to generate a new 'way of war'. Rather than being simply a product of the mobilised nation, the developments under Starry highlight the centrality of an independent professional force developing strategic criteria based upon its own analysis, rather than on the demands of the broader society. The key tenets that were developed from this process were to provide the governing principles for the correct use of military force.

Initiative

US strategy had traditionally relied upon a slow build-up for its combat and attritional strategy. However, the deep battle relied on seizing and holding the initiative, which was also a clear difference to Lind. The AirLand Battle saw that the side that retains the initiative can, 'with deep attack and decisive maneuver', destroy the opposition's ability to fight and organise in depth.[128] The 1973 war had clearly shown that the side holding the initiative on the modern battlefield won.[129] This meant that the defensive must be more than denying victory, but must take the offensive to seize the initiative.

> Initiative implies an offensive spirit in the conduct of all operations. The underlying purpose of every encounter with the enemy is to seize or retain independence of action. To do this we must make decisions and act more quickly than the enemy to disorganize his forces and to keep him off balance.[130]

Surrendering, or failing to seize, the initiative led to defeat on the deep battlefield. However, for this to happen the Army had to think beyond tactical engagements and a 'strategy' of wars won by accumulated battlefield victories. Starry saw the conceptual significance of this for the traditional way of war.

> AirLand Battle is a grand offensive defense. . . . That is why, realize it or not, the concept is dramatically at odds with our historic perceptions of what is necessary to win, drawn from our Napoleonic heritage, our obsession with the mass concepts of the industrial revolution and our fixation on substituting technology for numbers.[131]

The contrast with the traditional approach was clear to the reformers, but for the Army to enact the new approach it had to change its strategic conceptualisation of war. It had to shift its thinking from tactical attrition to understanding combat in terms of the operational level, as critics such as Edward Luttwak had advocated. The move to the operational level changed the focus of US military effort from the level of the battle, and the accumulation of victories to win the war, to the campaign and thereby placing the battle in a broader context. Where critics of the prosecution of the Vietnam War had already highlighted this failing in the US Army, the reformers came to it via the route of reconceptualising the battle in Europe. The result of this was to change how the Army fought its campaigns and the demands this placed on the higher command levels of the nation's strategy.

Operational level

The *FM 100-5, Operations*, 1982, explicitly stated that an Army's operational concept was the core of its doctrine. 'Operational' meant attaining strategic goals within a theatre of war, combining battles in a campaign.[132] The significance of the degree of change that this symbolised can be seen by the second chapter of the manual which was concerned with operational-level thinking rather than, as in 1976, the effect of weapons on the modern battlefield. The continuous analysis of the lessons of the 1973 war, which had provoked the chapter in 1976, had been dependent on the Israeli Army's analysis and accounts of the fighting, which lacked operational thinking.[133] Starry harnessed the resources of the civilian debate to bring together the depth and initiative ideas so that the 'operational concept of *FM 100-5* is the central idea of the manual. It stresses the importance of the initiative' and of throwing the enemy off balance.[134] The use of operational thinking opened the door to developing a more complex understanding of the way to fight and win wars, utilising the concepts of the civilian critics and the broader understanding of the nature of the professional US Army.[135] The manual succinctly stated its operational concepts at the opening of chapter 2, stressing the role of the initiative and how to achieve it, and saw that the best way was initially to degrade the coherence of the enemy by striking critical units from unexpected directions, rather than hitting the enemy's leading formations.[136] The emphasis was therefore on a broader understanding of the role of the Army on the battlefield, expanding its understanding of space, time and resources available, in the context of the campaign rather than the battle.

The change in emphasis meant that US Army conceptual thinking developed greatly in sophistication.

> Army units will fight in all types of operations to preserve and to exploit the initiative. They will attack the enemy in depth with fire and maneuver and synchronize all efforts to attain the objective. They will maintain the agility necessary to shift forces and fires to the points of enemy weakness. Our operations must be rapid, unpredictable, violent, and disorientating the

> enemy. The pace must be fast enough to prevent him from taking effective counteractions. Operational planning must be precise enough to preserve combined arms cooperation throughout the battle. . . . This requires that the entire force thoroughly understands the commander's intent. Subordinate leaders must align their operations with the overall mission. . . . Success on the modern battlefield will depend on the basic tenets of AirLand Battle doctrine: *initiative, depth, agility, and synchronization.* [original emphasis][137]

Before analysing the concepts in more detail, it is necessary to note again that the doctrine outlined here was a radical reorientation of US Army thinking away from the prescriptive Jominian tradition to a more dynamic and complex understanding of war.[138] The nature of the reforms helped generate this change. The training orientation had created a demand for doctrine to focus the new ideas, whilst the inadequacy of the subsequent doctrine to address the second echelon forces created a demand for a novel approach. Its method was analogous to a shopping trip, as TRADOC drew upon other thinkers to help it solve the primary difficulty of the depth of the Soviet attack. This was combined with the need to create a consensus behind the reforms. TRADOC thus engaged with a broad range of professionals and interested civilian critics, many of whom had concerns that were different to the main task of TRADOC, but whose ideas were utilised if appropriate. The process was not simply an academic exercise, in a pejorative sense, but a sophisticated progression of problem solving.

Manoeuvre critics' ideas, and the Soviet conception of manoeuvre and firepower, were adapted to the US Army's thinking. Soviet thinking was closely examined because it belonged to the 'enemy' and was a potential model for the Army's problems. The change in orientation owed more intellectually to the professional examination of fellow professionals' ideas and practice rather than to its social identity as a mobilisation force. In fact, the Soviet work on 'deep battle' was the source of many of the concepts. As the Soviet military historian John Erickson says, the 1982 *FM 100-5*, by adopting the principle of the equal importance of firepower and manoeuvre and by distinguishing tactics and operations, along with its later move to the operational art, was clearly indebted to Soviet thinking, to such an extent that 'General Svechin, G. Isserson and Marshal Tukhachevskii would at once be impressed and flattered, sufficiently so even to overlook the protracted intrusion upon their copyright'.[139] The sources of US Army thinking about war were thus being oriented to fellow professionals rather than fellow American citizens.

The sophistication of the doctrinal process and its conclusions enabled the Army to take its thinking further. By advocating examining warfare at the operational level the Army was moving away from thinking in terms of tactical engagements alone. By placing their thinking at the operational level (the level of the campaign), issues such as national purpose, the scale of effort, the relative tempo of the campaign, as well as depth and space, became crucial. However, rather than stay with this as a level of analysis, which was vulnerable to being seen as 'grand tactics', the Army's thinking moved to functioning at the operational level – the operational art. In other words, rather than thinking up to the operational level from the tactical, the thinking, the planning assumptions and understanding of the battlefield should now come from above, through the operational level further down to the tactical level. It aimed to stop war being seen as a series of unconnected engagements, with attrition as the only measure of success, and more as the achievement of strategic goals.

The 1986 manual explained in detail what was meant by the operational art and showed how the Army's thinking had developed.

> Operational art is the employment of military forces to attain strategic goals in a theater of war or theater of operations through the design, organization, and conduct of campaigns and major operations. A campaign is a series of joint actions designed to attain a strategic objective in a theater of war. . . .
>
> Operational art thus involves fundamental decisions about when and where to fight and whether to accept or decline battle. Its essence is the identification of the enemy's operational center-of-gravity – his source of strength or balance – and the concentration of superior combat power against that point to achieve a decisive success. . . .
>
> Operational art requires broad vision, the ability to anticipate, a careful understanding of the relationship of means to ends, and effective joint and combined operations.[140]

The development of operational thinking, therefore, moved the Army from its tactical concerns to the much more strategic thinking that required addressing what military conditions needed to be produced to achieve the strategic goal, the sequence of actions that would produce it, and the application of the resources to accomplish the sequence.[141] This was a fundamental point. The strategic thinking was brought about by the concern with the 'deep' battlefield, and the adoption of the principles of the initiative and operational thinking, a move from attrition to manoeuvre. The process of developing a new professional identity after Vietnam therefore opened up the Army to a new approach, a 'new way of war' that was a repudiation of the practice in Vietnam but, importantly, was not a product of the analysis of the Vietnam War. Vietnam gave the Army the impetus and crisis necessary to develop the changes in thinking, and those changes came out of manoeuvre thinking.

Manoeuvre

General Starry moved the US Army's thinking further away from attrition, aiming to disorient the enemy by strategically pitting weakness against strength, and tactically dispersing forces to 'place the enemy at a disadvantage' in a less costly manner.[142] Facing an outnumbering force, Starry regarded it as necessary to look again at some long-held convictions of the US Army that were drawn from a time when the US was the outnumbering force. This approach opened up the new doctrine to manoeuvrist critics' thinking. The transition from attrition by technology and tactics, to operational manoeuvre, was the vital shift in the doctrinal process.[143]

Manoeuvre or movement has a long military tradition. In the AirLand Battle doctrine it was not conceived of in the exclusive terms laid down by the civilian critics, where it was the opposite of attrition. For *FM 100-5* manoeuvre was the dynamic element of combat, allowing the concentration of forces to use surprise, psychological shock, position and momentum to enable smaller forces to defeat larger ones. It was seen as 'the employment of forces through movement supported by fire to achieve a position of advantage' from which it could then destroy or threaten to destroy the enemy.[144] In operational terms, manoeuvre meant the focus of effort moved away from the traditional centre of enemy forces to its weakest point. As the manual outlined:

> The object of maneuver at the operational level is to focus maximum strength against the enemy's weakest point, thereby gaining strategic advantage. At this level, successful maneuver is achieved through skillful coordination of fire in depth with movement of large units. At the tactical level, maneuver contributes significantly to sustaining the initiative, to exploiting success, to preserving freedom of action, and to reduce vulnerability. Successful maneuver at this level depends upon skillful movement along indirect approaches supported by direct and indirect fires.[145]

The source of the new thinking was made explicit, recognising the classic rather than contemporary sources.

> The ideal attack should resemble Liddell Hart's concept of the expanding torrent. It should move fast, follow reconnaisance units or successful probes through gaps in enemy defenses, and shift its strength quickly to widen penetrations and to reinforce its successes, thereby carrying the battle deep into the enemy rear. It should destroy or bring under control the forces or areas critical to the enemy's overall defensive organization before the enemy can react.[146]

The utilisation of manoeuvre to bring about operational success relied very heavily on a skilled force which could adapt and shift focus quickly, and AirLand Battle referred to 'agility' as one of its key tenets, requiring a flexible organisation and quick-minded leaders. Army manoeuvre advocates saw that this utilised the national characteristics of flexibility, adaptability and the ingenuity of the 'American soldier'.[147] This was in accord with DePuy's concern with 'output orientated' training, and AirLand Battle was taking this further. This was necessary as manoeuvre demanded an Army and commanders '*who can act faster than the enemy*. They must know of critical events as they occur and act to avoid enemy strengths and attack enemy vulnerabilities' [original emphasis].[148] However, as manoeuvre was not simply taking place at the tactical level, but operationally, there was a requirement for this process to be repeated across the area of the campaign. In terms that are absolutely reminiscent of John Boyd and the OODA loop, *FM 100-5* outlined the nature of the manoeuvrist battle at the operational level. Commanders must act faster than the enemy, seeking his weaknesses and

> This must be done repeatedly, so that every time the enemy begins to counter one action, another immediately upsets his plan. This will lead to ineffective, uncoordinated, and piecemeal enemy responses and eventually to his defeat.[149]

The essence of Boyd's thinking and the root of Lind's criticisms were absorbed into the fundamental core of AirLand Battle's thinking of how to fight and win wars. The tactical approach was replaced by a focus on the operational level and the attritional tradition was superseded by a concern with firepower and manoeuvre combined, defeating the opponent through the tempo of the application of these principles.[150]

The adoption of the 'indirect approach' was a conceptual breakthrough that placed an enormous burden on the requirements of the Army's training, further pushing forward the reforms brought about by General Gorman at TRADOC. AirLand Battle doctrine thus reinforced the training emphasis of the first stage of the reforms. As General Sir John Hackett explained, the indirect approach lay at the heart of Blitz warfare and 'is only for bold and highly skilled professionals'.[151] It was here that the new thinking was so effective for the US Army, as it focused US training and stressed the importance of training for the future of the Army. The tempo of the war that AirLand envisaged stressed the high quality of leadership that was needed, even at the lower command levels.[152] The publication in 1982 stated that 'The AirLand Battle doctrine . . . outlines an approach to fighting intended to develop the full potential of US forces.'[153] As the 1986 manual reconfirmed, the Army's outlook was that 'Training is the cornerstone of success.'[154] However, operations based on a doctrine of non-linear battles, attacking enemy forces throughout their depth with fire and manoeuvre, have requirements that go beyond being flexible: they must be co-ordinated and be provided with a single, clear objective to pursue.

'Mission orders'

AirLand Battle's operational understanding placed enormous stress on the role of command and control. The stress on developing leadership, training skills and the technological requirements to 'see deep' was matched by the emphasis on the commander's management of the tempo of the command cycle.[155] As Starry wrote,

> He needs to turn that information–decision cycle in time inside the enemy's information–decision cycle so that, instead of simply reacting to what the enemy does, he can seize the initiative. In order to win the battle, holding the initiative is essential.[156]

The emphasis on the relative tempo of the decision cycle has implications for the commander in terms of handling the incoming information and then distributing his orders. Starry saw the problem as threefold: the sheer volume to be assimilated, the non-prioritisation of the truly important, and sequential reporting, which slowed and mixed information.[157] The gathering and analysis of tactical intelligence was central.[158] Hence the commander must first set out the elements of information he needs to run the battle, and then task the communications system to bring him that information.[159] Having laid out what he needs to receive from his communications system, the commander then must lay out to his subordinates what he wants to happen to the enemy. With such a flexible understanding of the battlefield he is unable to give exact instructional orders, so he is reliant on making clear his intent to his subordinates, requiring 'the use of mission orders and the application of mission-orientated tactics'.[160] This means that the commander must determine what exactly his intent towards the enemy is, and that it is consistent with his superior's intent, and that it is communicated clearly to his subordinates.[161] This requires that the entire force thoroughly understands the senior commander's intent and that all subordinate leaders align their operations with the overall mission.[162] Therefore, the shift to 'mission-type' orders that the civilian critics advocated increased the demands and furthered the professionalisation of the Army, but also placed an obvious emphasis on the political leadership to provide an exact outline of its intent towards the enemy so that the 'mission-type' orders could be devolved down the chain of command. The command and control model inherent within AirLand Battle doctrine therefore demanded unambiguous political aims to be outlined prior to engagement; without it the conceptual model of a faster Boyd cycle would not work and the US Army would be the ones disoriented and overrun first. The manual explained this as a need for synchronisation.

Synchronicity

Sychronisation was a central tenet of AirLand Battle doctrine and brought together the concerns of combined-arms operations with the Boyd cycling command model of warfare. Synchronised combined arms complement and reinforce each other, greatly magnifying their effects so that they become more than the sum of their parts. This perception was taken to involve conventional forces and nuclear and chemical ones, along with American allies' forces.[163] Achieving maximum combat power meant more than combined arms doctrine though, as the Boyd cycling requirement meant that the combined arms had to be synchronised to the commander's aim, allowing him to go through the cycle faster than the enemy. Synchronisation 'results from an all-pervading unity of effort throughout the force.

There can be no waste. Every action of every element must flow from understanding the higher commander's concept'.[164]

Synchronisation is both a process and a result, working together the elements of time, space and purpose.[165] It was the culmination of the conceptual development of AirLand Battle doctrine, bringing together the concern with seeing and fighting deep by seizing the initiative and retaining it through an agile and flexible force, which could only happen if all aspects were synchronised. This was summarised by the near credal statement: 'Success on the modern battlefield will depend on the basic tenets of AirLand Battle doctrine: *initiative, depth, agility, and synchronization.*'[166]

Synchronicity was an ambitious aim, one that could easily negate the advances in agility and initiative that the reforms looked for. The understanding of the concept of synchronicity in AirLand Battle doctrine was not alignment or simply co-ordination but an emphasis on the unity of effort of all forces towards a single aim via a clear intent. Naveh interprets the concept of synchronisation as implying a synergy of effort.

> The planned action should be *synergetic*, i.e. throughout its entirety. represented by the initial aim, the system should yield a general product that is significantly greater than the linear arithmetic sum of its components' accomplishments. Moreover, in order to be regarded as operational, the matter must reflect the notion of *synthesis*, through the aspects of combined arms combat, amalgamation of the various forms of warfare, and the integration of the various forms and formations within several geographical units and different dimensions of time.[167]

The synchronisation requires a synthesis of effort, but as the manual made clear, the doctrine required that commanders 'must ensure a unified, aggressive, quick, precise, agile, and synchronized effort throughout the force'.[168] The aggression in application, the tempo, was the essential ingredient that moved AirLand from being a co-ordinated action to a synchronised one. As the manual went on to explain, the concepts required

> effective leadership and an effective command and control system through which the commander-
>
> - Learns what is going on.
> - Decides what to do about it.
> - Issues the necessary orders.
> - Keeps track of how the battle is going.[169]

The effectiveness of the unity of effort was built on the speed of command and aggression of the implementation and, therefore, the leadership and training given to the troops were central. At heart the change in 'way of war' was conceptual and relied on out-thinking the opponent, not on technological improvements or formulaic response to battle; it was a revolution in ideas.[170]

Underpinning the revolution was a 'unity of effort' and, as the 1982 manual said, 'Unity of effort *depends on motivation*'.[171] The motivation to fight pulled together the disparate elements within combat, co-ordinating them under one command and towards one object, as the fight is between two systems aiming to defeat each other, and to frustrate the opposition's attempts to defeat it.[172] It is a holistic approach to warfighting, and the aim is central and is the 'cognitive compass' which provides the manoeuvre with its positive direction.

AirLand Battle doctrine's emphasis on the aim, motivation and synchronisation of effort, therefore, was conceived in terms of the nature of war and the Army's professional focus. It provided the basis for the reforms of the Army and the later criteria for the executive.

The influence of AirLand Battle doctrine

The military reformers' ideas became influential as they were supported at the Chief of Staff level and underpinned by the 'status' they had within the Army. DePuy and Starry had made sure of the Chiefs of Staff's support, from the initial 1973 reforms, where General Creighton W. Abrams had supported the direction of the changes. through to Generals Weyand, Rogers and Meyer who continued it.[173] The consensus building that Starry initiated and the reputation that he, DePuy and Richardson had within the Army meant that 'they were trusted' by their contemporaries and senior officers.[174] By broadening the base of professionalism and organisationally embedding it, Starry was able to set the course of the doctrinal developments. The 1982 AirLand Battle doctrine was actually published after he had left TRADOC. The next edition of *FM 100-5*, in 1986, was a reassertion of the doctrine published by his former number two at TRADOC, General Bill Richardson. The Army reorganisation was essentially complete by the first Gulf War in 1991 and, importantly for the reformers, 'proved effective in battle'.[175] The subsequent revision of *FM 100-5* was to wait until 1993, after the first Gulf War.

Influence

AirLand Battle doctrine dominated US Army doctrine, thinking and force structure up to the first Gulf War in 1991. It redefined the Army's identity and understanding of its role, nature and political utility, as 'It furnishes the authoritative foundation for subordinates doctrine, force design, materiel acquisition, professional education, and individual and unit training.'[176] AirLand Battle doctrine thinking was tied to the future developments of the structure of the Army.[177] The organisational studies into the future development of heavy divisions of the Army, with 1986 as the marker point, called 'Division 86', and the later work on light infantry divisions, 'The Army of Excellence', gave organizational structure to AirLand Battle doctrine.[178]

The doctrine also shaped the Army's light divisions. It had two light divisions, the 101st Air Assault and 82nd Airborne, but in the mid-1980s it planned the creation of five new light infantry divisions for roles outside Europe, with an emphasis on getting to places under six days in a pre-crisis and low-intensity role. There was a worry that this might encourage the greater use of military force and ensnare the US in undesirable conflicts.[179] Reformers pushed through the institutional changes in the divisions in the face of opposition, and AirLand Battle thinking and its principles gave it the conceptual tools to address the tasks. As the light infantry manual, *FM 7-20*, 1992, said:

> AirLand Battle is the doctrinal basis for meeting these challenges. It involves maneuver at all levels and tries to use the full potential of US forces. It is offensively orientated. . . . The thrust of AirLand Battle is to disrupt the enemy's synchronization, preventing him from applying combat power at a decisive point; and to create opportunities for US forces to destroy his force.[180]

AirLand Battle doctrine provided the concepts for the light infantry battalions that were deployed in the complex emergencies undertaken after the Cold War.

However, the range of reform focused by AirLand Battle doctrine was not just at this level. The deliberate promotion of the reformers' ideas was to open up allied forces to manoeuvrist thinking. This was especially true for the UK.[181] NATO, in its 1983 review, regarded manoeuvre as a key principle of defence and rejected a passive approach and aimed to seize the initiative.[182]

Key to the development and propagation of the new thinking was the fact that it was a deliberate move to generate a professional critical culture to effect change within the Army, rather than having change forced on the army from outside.[183] The emphasis on changing the culture of the Army to the reformers' thinking was promoted in TRADOC's area of responsibility, by using the US Army Command and General Staff College (USACGSC) and its Combined Arms and Service School (CAS) to develop a common culture within the Army,[184] a move enhanced by the development of the Advanced Military Studies course at Fort Leavenworth.[185] The brightest students from the Command and General Staff College were given an additional year to look at strategic and operational aspects of war, and acquired the nickname 'Jedi knights'.[186] They were

> trained up in US Army doctrine, covering every aspect of operational art and the land/air battle . . . their mission is to spread the word at US headquarters around the world . . . and American generals were soon seen arriving at Nato conferences flanked by their pair of Jedis.[187]

For the doctrine writers, the professionalisation of the Army meant that it needed to operate at a higher 'threshold of theoretical and practical understanding of war',[188] and the theoretical content of the manual was 'drawn from the lessons of history, the writings of the great military theorists and the Army's historic approach to operations'.[189] For example, one of the authors of *FM 100-5*, Huba Wass de Czege, outlined the importance of Clausewitz to the doctrine writers, even though critics saw the dynamism of Clausewitz's thought being fossilised within the 'principles of war', reinforcing perceptions that Jomini not Clausewitz was the true parent of American thinking.[190] Nevertheless, a bibliography of classic works was appended to the 1982 manual.[191]

Training

Fundamental to the promotion of the ideas was the model of the Army which the reformers were developing, which took the reforms initiated by the Army Chief of Staff (1972–74), Creighton Abrams, to a further professional level, reversing the process whereby the Army repeatedly paid in blood for its lack of preparedness.[192] The US Army established a trilogy of 'train, fight, lead', which was the realisation of the thinking it had developed since the end of the Vietnam War, based on AirLand Battle doctrine.[193] The jewel in the crown of this movement was to be the establishment of the National Training Center, at Fort Irwin in the Mojave Desert in California, which was opened in 1981.[194] It was the first reactivation of a military base in twenty years, at an estimated cost of $299.4 million in facility repairs and construction alone.[195] As the official historian explained, the National Training Center 'offered the best sort of training short of war' and developed the spirit and will to win in a heavy force environment.[196] Crucially, the need for the training centre was driven by the recognition that AirLand battle doctrine, and the associated new weaponry, meant that existing ranges and training land were inadequate. With its opening and the first exercises there in 1984, the commander of TRADOC looked to counter the lack of 'manoeuvre' practised by the Army and to feed this back into the later doctrine manuals.[197] It also aimed to integrate the Air Force into the exercises in the near future.

The National Training Center provided a live firing area and two force-on-force practice areas, covering 1,000 square miles. Within the National Training Center a specialised Opposing Force (OPFOR) was developed to fight using Soviet doctrine and materiel. This enabled training for the European theatre to be as realistic as possible. The training was greatly aided by the development of the laser-based MILES system, which allowed the hits, misses and kills of soldiers and equipment to be monitored electronically by the observer/controllers. The establishment of the Joint Readiness Training Centre in 1987 (which was moved to Louisiana in 1993), further developed realistic training for the army's light infantry and airborne brigades.[198] The aim of the training centres was to develop warfighting capability, and essential to the process was the making of honest after action reports (AARs).[199] The process was described by one participant as 'self-critical sessions' where the observer/controllers: 'insisted on taking time to discuss what happened, why, and how to fix things for the next round. Accordingly, every major episode of mock combat concluded with several hours for AARs at all levels.'[200]

The learning that these exercises produced was co-ordinated through a Center for Army Lessons Learned (CALL) set up in 1985.[201] The institutionalisation of the self-critical process and its emphasis within training and officer leadership was the clearest evidence of how far the Army's internal identity and culture had changed. It was in direct contrast to the business managerial culture that was so evident during the Vietnam War era. The legacy of Elihu Root's reforms at the turn of the century, where business practice was instituted to reform the Army and take it into the earliest stages of professionalisation, was being overturned by the training reforms built on the AirLand Battle doctrine understanding of warfare. The requirements of AirLand Battle doctrine and the leadership legacy of the Vietnam War meant that the Army developed its own criteria of 'warfighting' as the orientation for itself. Independent of society, the Army initiated and institutionalised its understanding of professionalism and how the Army should be, thereby exhibiting a new professional identity built on the lessons and legacy of Vietnam. With the establishment of the National Training Center the Army learnt its lessons through realistic training so that it was prepared for the 'first battles' of future wars. The historical legacy of learning through failing in the initial engagements was overturned, replaced by realistic training in the tenets of AirLand Battle doctrine.

The new way of war and strategy

The Army's doctrine was actually an espousal of a new 'way of war' compared to the established American strategic tradition. Where mobilisation had provided the key continuity between the political aims and military means, the institution of the VOLAR principle had severed this link and professional developments had led to a new set of criteria. Concentration on the first battle replaced the slow build-up of mobilisation; the direct assault was superseded by the requirement to manoeuvre; and rather than a tactical and direct approach, AirLand Battle doctrine looked to the operational level and thinking in terms of depth. The thinking was a marked change in the US Army thinking about war, how to fight it and how to win. It now aimed to collapse the enemy rather than simply annihilate it. As the manual said, 'Effective manoeuvre . . . keeps the enemy off balance. It continually poses new problems for him, renders his reactions ineffective, and eventually leads to his defeat.'[202] Finally, AirLand Battle doctrine specifically shifted the emphasis from the defence to seizing and holding the initiative, thinking operationally, and taking a synchronised approach to the use of military power. The operational and synchronised focus provided the means for joint doctrine with the Air Force, and shaped the Army's revived Low-Intensity Conflict (LIC) developments.

Air Force

The Air Force had become independent from the Army in 1947, which created inter-service rivalry and a fractured and uncoordinated national strategy, as the Vietnam War clearly showed.[203] The separation was reinforced by the Air Force's emphasis on strategic (namely long-range) bombing during the early Cold War period. Strategic Air Command (SAC) had a long-range nuclear role as part of the nation's Single Integrated Operational Plan for Nuclear War (SIOP), and by 1959 the Army and Navy budgets were being reduced and the savings were going to the Air Forces' SAC.[204] The lack of ground support emphasis in Air Force thinking is clearly shown by the fact that the A-10 aircraft, designed in the early 1970s, was a historical anomaly, as it was the first and only Air Force plane designed to attack ground targets and provide direct support to ground troops.[205] As Mike Worden's study of the Air Force after the Vietnam War shows, there was a shift in Air Force leadership away from bomber to fighter generals, which he saw as part of the broader process initiated by Secretary of Defense Laird to bring younger officers through the ranks and to stimulate new thinking in the upper echelons of the Air Force.[206] The shift from strategic bombing was to be significant because the Air Force generals who became Chairman of the Joint Chiefs of Staff, George S. Brown and David C. Jones, were both generalists,[207] rather than SAC officers in the model of the Vietnam-era Curtis LeMay. SAC's loss of prestige and dominance within the Air Force[208] meant that the Army's emphasis could be accommodated, to such an extent that in 1993 one officer wrote that 'Official and unofficial US Air Force and Army thinking about airpower have converged since the end of the Vietnam War.'[209]

From 1973 onwards, Tactical Air Command (TAC) and TRADOC commanders had met regularly to discuss offensive air support issues,[210] but the convergence of the two services' thinking was provided by the development of AirLand Battle doctrine, developed independently of the Air Force and wholly configured to land warfare.[211] This was part of the process that shifted airpower thinking away from tactical interdiction to theatre-wide operational campaigning, in line with Army thinking about how to prosecute war. The Air Force was redefining itself away from its strategic/nuclear role. As Robert Hamilton explains,

> The Army's promulgation of ALB [AirLand Battle] doctrine had a major impact on USAF thinking. . . . ALB's central concepts of deep attack, second echelon interdiction and joint air–land operations were readily accepted by air power thinkers hungry for an expanded role for conventional airpower and a common conceptual framework to analyze Air Force doctrine.[212]

This signalled a clear shift of emphasis from strategic bombing to tactical support: 'The analogue of SAC's SIOP focus became the TAF's [Tactical Air Force] obsession with AirLand Battle.'[213] By the mid-1980s the US and NATO forces acquired the beginnings of a coherent body of thought on tactical air support, stressing an independent second echelon strategic role in AirLand Battle doctrine and 'Follow-On Forces Attack'.[214] These developments brought together the emergent technology and a traditional concept of interdiction,[215] utilising the Joint Surveillance Target Attack Radar System (JSTARS), the NAVSTAR Global

Positioning System, the new Apache helicopter and a new range of Precision Guided Munitions (PGMs).[216] As one Deputy Chief of Staff explained, the 'Big 5' programmes initiated prior to AirLand Battle doctrine provided firepower and mobility, but the doctrine depended on exploiting emerging technologies to see deep, strike deep, process data and manage communications, and these guided the programmes.[217] The inter-service improvements were part of a larger post-Vietnam movement to bring together the services, and AirLand Battle doctrine provided a point of convergence for the tactical and operational thinking of the two services, enabling the development of the early stages of jointery and national synchronised fighting.[218]

Low-Intensity Conflict

The Army's emphasis on a synchronised approach to combat was to shape its developments of Low-Intensity Combat (LIC) when interest in it was revived. Low-Intensity Conflict had always been a problem area for it.[219] However, after Vietnam the Army purged itself of the skills it acquired there,[220] and instead used the strategic thinking within AirLand Battle doctrine to provide the template of the nature and role of the Army in these types of conflicts. While the Army did not simply ignore Low-Intensity Conflict, it clearly had a low priority within Army doctrinal development.[221] This is an important point to recognise.

The Army's rebuilding after the Vietnam War concentrated upon the establishment of professional criteria within it and it focused its efforts on the European theatre, as that was the role for which its could garner support inside and outside the organisation. This did not mean that it only concentrated on Europe. Its importance lies in the fact that once the Army returned to Low-Intensity Conflict it did so having established the new identity of doctrinal professionalism outlined by DePuy and Starry. It was these criteria that provided the Army's approach, rather than operational lessons drawn from Vietnam. This again was for consensual reasons, as the Army did not draw upon its Low-Intensity Conflict experience in Vietnam to develop this new doctrine because, as Richard Downie's study shows, it was unable to develop a consensus as to what the lessons were.[222] AirLand Battle doctrine was able to provide a consensual strategic model for the Army as it revived its Low-Intensity Conflict concerns. As *FM 100-5*, 1986 said: 'While AirLand Battle doctrine focuses primarily on mid- to high-intensity warfare, the tenets of AirLand Battle doctrine apply equally to the military operations characteristic of low-intensity war.'[223] AirLand Battle doctrine provided the strategic understanding of Low-Intensity Conflict and the tenets for the Army's doctrine in this type of combat, as the developments in the 1980s show.

General Meyer in his 1980 White Paper had argued for increased capability to meet threats from outside the European theatre.[224] The Army had established the 1st Special Operations Command (SOCOM) in 1982, under the operational control of the theatre Commander in Chief (CINC), who was responsible for developing the means to respond to various threats. The mindset of the new command was made clear by its attempt to rid itself of Psyops (Psychological operations) and the Civil Affairs unit, and to include the Ranger battalions,[225] which were doctrinally based on AirLand Battle doctrine.[226] AirLand Battle's requirement for operations behind the enemy's lines in Europe led to the resurgence of Special Forces, and in the Reagan period they were to be mainly military trainers and advisers.[227] In July 1985, following its early work together, TRADOC joined the Air Force Plans Directorate in beginning to develop joint low-intensity doctrine,[228] which was eventually published in 1990 and mainly devoted to insurgency and counter-insurgency situations and focused on the indirect application of US military power.[229]

Strategically, Low-Intensity Conflict was conceived of in synergistic terms, with the Army only providing a supporting role for the broader national policy. The nation was to use the Army in the way it was configured as a professional force-on-force (Clausewitzian) army, and its place in policy was only to provide this capability. AirLand Battle doctrine was the model for the Army's nature and role and placed demands on the national strategy rather than forcing changes on the Army's doctrine. For example, in 1984 Brigadier General Donald Morelli, one of the key figures in the development of AirLand Battle, wrote that the development of light infantry divisions and Special Forces capability were not a route to victory in Low-Intensity Conflict as success 'does not rest upon the commitment of US ground forces in a combat role'. He saw that the Army's potential role was not in advocating new ways to fight but in developing the conviction 'that such conflicts cannot be won through force of arms alone'.[230] For Low-Intensity Conflict operations the conclusion was that success did not rest on the commitment of ground forces. Therefore, the Army did not have to develop new ways of fighting, as there was a need to synchronise 'all elements of national power', using the logic and basic tenets of AirLand Battle doctrine.[231] Even later criticisms of Army counter-insurgency saw the need to build on the 'core logic' of the doctrine.[232]

The broad 'synergistic' understanding of Low-Intensity Conflict gave the Army a specifically 'military' role, which was defined in terms of the AirLand Battle identity as a force geared to the initiative and the aggressive use of firepower to destroy the enemy's forces.[233] Thus the influence of politics at the tactical level was not understood as inherent to the conflicts or the responsibility of the Army. Instead, the influence of politics was conceived of as the 'political imposition of restrictions of movement, in the use of force, in engagement criteria, and possibly in the sizes and types of forces used'.[234] By seeing politics as an external constraint, rather than an inherent feature of conflict, the Army's capabilities in this key aspect were poor. For example, the key role of civilian affairs was only at battalion strength, plus reservists, and psychological affairs were a separate operations group, rather than an inherent aspect of all operations.[235] However, AirLand Battle doctrine provided a 'strategic' approach to the use of force.

Operational thinking as strategy

The AirLand Battle doctrine conception of operational 'synchronicity' provided a coherent strategy through the development of the operational-level thinking.[236] The focus on a synchronised use of national power through the application of AirLand Battle doctrine provided the formula for the use of the Army as a tool of national policy. The development of operational-level thinking had clear strategic consequences, as all efforts were to be focused on a common goal of the commander's intent. For the US this meant that at the strategic level the President, as the Commander in Chief of the Armed Forces, determines the political aim.[237] However, the Army, being focused on the operational level and looking to fight in campaigns, required the executive to translate the strategic aim into political objectives. Not only that, but the objectives had to be militarily achievable. 'Strategy' was, therefore, understood to be the establishment of the political objectives of a militarily achievable campaign. As *FM 100-5*, 1982 made clear, the 'strategy' required

> that the political purpose be clearly defined and attainable by the considered application of the various elements of the nation's power. Not until the political purpose has been determined and defined by the President and Congress can strategic and tactical objectives be clearly identified and developed. Once developed the strategic objectives must constantly be subjected to rigorous analysis and review to insure that they continue to reflect accurately not only the ultimate political end desired, but also any political constraints imposed on the application of military force.[238]

The operational doctrine of AirLand Battle demanded clear political aims and objectives, making achievable operational objectives the foundation of the relationship between military means and political aims. Political and military objectives and operations must therefore be presented in clear, concise, understandable terms, as 'simple and direct plans and orders cannot compensate for ambiguous and cloudy objectives'.[239] The strategic aim was to be the hub around which the synchronised operational manoeuvre rotated and this reinforced the Army's perception of the lack of strategic guidance during the Vietnam War.

The objectives were therefore to be handed down. As Zvi Laniar points out, *FM 100-5*'s understanding of 'objective' reflects a hierarchical order aligning the political purpose and military aims of the war 'despite all the evidence for the complex, reciprocal relations between the two, and the high price armies pay for ignoring their interplay'.[240] Moreover, manoeuvre reformers' exclusive focus on the operational level was vulnerable to the same criticism of broader political blindness.[241] The Army's thinking under AirLand Battle was the 'operationalisation of strategy' therefore, unlike the earlier 'tacticalisation of strategy'. However, neither model had an understanding of a fluid and dialectical political–military relationship.

Crucially, as the development of Low-Intensity Conflict thinking showed, what was militarily achievable was defined by the Army's professional identity, rather than the demands of policy. Thus a viable 'militarily achievable' political object was set by the nature and capability of the Army. The development of this thinking was in accord with the broad strategic lessons that the Army had drawn from Vietnam, and the lessons drawn could only be enacted because the Army began to be structured in this manner, as abstract 'lessons' only have substance once they are enacted and embodied. In this context the Army did not see a need to develop new ways of strategic understanding and doctrine; national policy needed to recognise the nature and role of the Army and use it accordingly. This position would become the espoused policy outlined by the 'Weinberger Doctrine' in 1984, a doctrine influenced by Harry Summers's *On Strategy*, and by the then Commander of Readiness Command, General Donn A. Starry.

Conclusion

The reform of the nature of the US Army's doctrine after the Vietnam War was the crucial change in its 'way of war' and the nation's strategy. The driving force behind the changes was a product of the internal developments that had gone on with the professionalisation of the Army. The rebuilding of it from a mobilisation basis to being a professionally focused one, created the requirement for it to be well trained and led. The reforms were given a clear focus by the concentration on the European battlefront and the lessons of the 1973 war gave it a template upon which to test its changes. The reforms accorded with the broader institutional concerns with being a main-force European mechanised Army.[242] Doctrine only became important as a tool to bring together the changes in training. However, the inadequacy of the initial doctrine led to a revolution in the nature of US Army doctrine, as it developed the AirLand Battle concepts to counter the second echelon forces of the Soviet Army. The consequences of the new doctrine were revolutionary as it was used to change the nature of the Army[243] and its tactics and provided it with a new way of war.[244] In the process the Army's professional reference point had shifted from its social role, to that of fellow professionals and interested civilian critics. Doctrine thus helped generate a new identity and 'way of war'.

The change in doctrine was innovative as the adoption of the operational-manoeuvrist provided the Army with a new theory of victory.[245] This change was crucial for the understanding of the national strategy as it created new political requirements for the national authority. The replacement of attritional warfare with firepower and manoeuvre, through AirLand Battle doctrine, provided a set of clear strategic needs to be fulfilled for the synchronisation of national power. This changed the national orientation. As Luttwak himself observed in 1987, 'national styles' are products of stability, and during periods of transition they become less homogenous, and the lack of determined homogeneity was clearly shown by the changes in the American Army with its adoption of the 'relational-maneuver operational method'.[246] No longer did the broader culture define the criteria for the use of the Army and its 'way of war'. In fact, the central importance of doctrine was to take on the nature of being an interest to be defended,[247] rather than even being simply an outcome of the training reforms.

The importance accorded to doctrine in the reform process altered the nature of the strategic culture. Previously mobilisation had shaped the nation's strategy and the Army's approach to war, but the independent development of the professional identity led to doctrine which had fellow professionals and the demands of warfare as its reference points. Thus, once Low-Intensity Conflict again became an issue the Army referred back to AirLand Battle doctrine, rather than society's demands. In fact, it reversed the relationship as it outlined its capabilities and the potential role it could play in policy rather than developing new tactics for the new demands. It limited the demands that could be made upon it. This was important because it highlighted the nature of the strategic learning that had gone on since the end of the Vietnam War. The concentration on the internal rebuilding and the establishment of a new professional identity was the premier concern of the Army rather than the operational lessons from Vietnam.

The criteria that the Army developed were, therefore, an outcome of its reformed nature. The response to Vietnam was far more than 'never again' and a simple process of concentrating on Europe to the exclusion of all other theatres. It developed a strategic formula, based on its training and doctrine, of what it could achieve and how it was to be applied. AirLand Battle created the need for the national command authority to provide clear aims and objectives for the Army so that it was able to act in accord with its nature. It needed to be able to take the initiative with overwhelming force, so that the new 'way of war' could disrupt, disorient and destroy the enemy forces. Following these criteria would allow the nation to synchronise its military power. There was a need to follow this approach as the Army thought, and was structured, in this manner. The legacy of the strategic failings in Vietnam was thus more than 'never again', rather it included fundamental positive lessons of how to successfully deploy the Army and prosecute military interventions. The basis for this thinking was the new social identity of the Army and its operational doctrine. The irony was that the issue of politics pervading all levels of war was not accommodated in either the fighting in Vietnam or in AirLand Battle doctrine. How these internal changes related to and influenced the national culture and strategy is considered in the following chapter.

5

THE INFLUENCE OF ARMY THINKING

The US Army's strategic thinking directly shaped American strategic culture from the end of the Vietnam War to the conclusion of the first Gulf War in 1991. The developments by TRADOC reformed the nature of the Army (its constitutive norms) as it allowed the development of the AirLand Battle doctrine. This doctrine and the strategic lessons from the Vietnam War produced the priorities or, in Alistair Johnson's terms, a 'ranked set of preferences' for the use of force by the US. The 'preferences' shaped the strategic culture and became the criteria (the regulative norms) for the use of military force by the US. The position of the Army in relation to the culture was thus reversed because it was no longer the nation mobilised but an assertive agent within that very culture, setting the terms for its use. Whilst the Army focused on tactical and operational-level planning, its requirement for national-level political co-ordination was enacted by the Congressional reforms and embodied in the Goldwater–Nichols Act.

The following chapter outlines the growing influence and impact of Army thinking on US strategic culture and the criteria or regulative norms of intervention policy. It examines the changes in the strategic thinking after the Vietnam War and how the Army's thinking became part of the process, by examining the administration's adoption of the Weinberger doctrine and the institutional changes in the strategic culture brought about by growing Congressional assertiveness.

US strategic culture post-Vietnam

The Vietnam War shattered the consensus behind the containment policy and its associated intervention strategy.[1] President Carter aimed to develop a foreign policy based on human rights, which have been part of American policy since.[2] However, as noted in Chapter 2, the Carter administration embodied the nation's tensions with the clashes between the hawkish National Security Advisor Zbigniew Brzezinski and the dovish Secretary of State Cyrus Vance.[3] The issue of military intervention came to the fore again in 1979 with the invasion of Afghanistan by the Soviet Union. President Carter was outraged by this action because it showed a 'broad readiness' of the Soviet Union to use their own forces rather than proxy ones.[4] The invasion killed what remained of the détente process and led to a much stronger posture by Carter.[5] The more hawkish position taken by him included the famous hostage rescue fiasco in Iran, Desert One. Brzezinski and Harold Brown, Secretary of Defense, were the only principals to support the use of force, and after the fiasco Vance resigned. Desert One was a turning point as there was a 'discernible shift in public mood . . . [suggesting] that the "Vietnam syndrome" of general opposition to military preparedness and action is now largely muted'.[6]

Ronald Reagan was elected on the tide of the more assertive mood, embodying an optimism in America and a mastery of public symbolism.[7] His election was a turning point in US foreign and domestic politics.[8] Reagan saw that whilst the US had been debating the utility of military power, the Soviets had embarked on a vigorous military modernisation programme.[9] In response to this, he increased defence spending by 40 per cent in real terms in his first three years in office.[10] Reagan's remilitarisation was crucial to rebuilding the national image and 'Americans' sense of their own needs'.[11]

A crucial part of the rebuilding addressed the morality of the war itself. The polarisation over Vietnam was so extreme that it took Guenter Lewy to open up the debate in 1978, with his revisionist account of the war that countered the arguments about the immorality of the war.[12] President Reagan led the political counter-attack aiming to restore pride in America and its Army. He used his inaugural speech to refer to Bellau Wood (First World War), Omaha Beach (Second World War) and Vietnam as sites of heroic American deaths.[13] A month later he personally awarded the Medal of Honor to Sergeant Benadez, a Vietnam veteran.[14] This was a very important step in the process of rehabilitating the social position of the Army and not seeing all soldiers as 'baby-killers'. The Reagan administration endorsed this, and as Secretary of State George Shultz explained in a speech on the tenth anniversary of the fall of Saigon:

> Whatever mistakes in how the war was fought, whatever one's view of the strategic rationale for our intervention, the morality of our effort must now be clear. Those Americans who served, or who grieve for their loved ones lost or missing, can hold their heads high: our sacrifice was in the service of noble ideals – to save innocent people from brutal tyranny.[15]

The 'revision' of the war was in accord with deeper understanding of the US itself, as national myths embody a version of the past and the future. As Robert McKeever explained, 'since the tension between the Vietnam experience and controlling national myths could not be borne indefinitely, entailing as it did a paralysis of will and action, the time soon came when Vietnam, rather than the national myths, had to be reinvented'.[16] However, Reagan's

> resuscitation of a Wilsonian internationalist grand design . . . achieved both normative and cognitive legitimacy. But he proved less successful in legitimating his strategy, especially in regard to the critical issue of the use of US military power abroad – the primary cause, after all, of the breakdown of the Cold War consensus.[17]

The support for the Reagan administration's more vigorous approach did not stretch to a more aggressive 'roll-back' policy against Soviet influence in Central America, and neither did it accord with the Army's perception of its role. How policy came into accord with the Army's thinking is related to the broader changes that had gone on within American strategic culture with the end of the Vietnam War.

The role of Congress

The foreign policy consensus prior to Vietnam had favoured a strong executive lead, the 'Imperial Presidency', and presidents from Eisenhower to Nixon had seen the sharing of power with Congress in foreign policy as a degradation of the Presidency.[18] The shattering of the consensus brought a readjustment of the executive role, and at a time of weakened presidency with the Watergate scandal, the legislature restricted the Presidency's powers. The War Powers Resolution of 1973 formally attempted to restrict the Executive Branch's prerogative in foreign policy after the Vietnam War.[19] The resolution stated that

> The President in every possible instance shall consult with Congress before introducing United States Armed Forces into hostilities or into situations where imminent hostilities is clearly indicated . . . and . . . shall consult regularly with Congress until United States Armed Forces are no longer engaged in hostilities.[20]

The Resolution required Congressional approval for troop deployments overseas, and to terminate involvement within 60 days of reporting to Congress. However, neither Congress nor presidents enforced the legislation, as it was unable to accommodate both sets of interests.[21] For example, both the Senate and the House invoked it after the Grenada invasion, not as a criticism of the invasion, but to ensure the withdrawal of American troops once the US nationals' safety had been assured.[22] The War Powers Resolution was really symbolic, reflecting a new determination in Congress.[23] Its importance lay in its emphasis on Congressional micro-managing of foreign and defence policy; the clearest example being Reagan's military policy in Central America.

Congress blocked the administration's aims in Central America, and with the Boland Amendments prohibited the CIA and Department of Defense from furnishing any military equipment, training, or support to anyone to overthrow the government of Nicaragua.[24] Importantly, the checks on the Presidency were able to keep combat troops out of Central America. However, the institutional limits were unable to stop the Iran–Contra affair.[25] The Iran–Contra scandal showed that the executive had to resort to a 'private army', with the CIA Director William Casey ignoring the law and having a 'private terrorist army raised and equipped and supported from the White House and CIA Headquarters'[26] to fulfil his aims. Reagan's public reluctance to reassert his claims of presidential supremacy in foreign affairs demonstrated the continuing influence of the Vietnam legacy as he appreciated the limits that the memory of Vietnam imposed on the office of the president.[27] By the Spring of 1986 he was able to get Congress to lift the ban on aid to the Contras, and it rescinded the Boland Amendment and supported sending lethal aid to the Contras in Nicaragua.[28]

Congressional use of the purse was the most powerful tool of constraint on the executive. The War Powers Resolution was the clearest symbol limiting executive policy, but its passing had been followed in a matter of days by the important Department of Defense Appropriation Authorization Act, 1974. This outlined that 'No funds may be appropriated for any fiscal year to or for the use of any armed service . . . unless funds have been specifically authorized by law.'[29] This act gave still greater control to Congress and, as General Westmoreland observed, the Case–Church Amendments to it overrode the president's authority to react to the breaking of the Peace Treaty in Vietnam.[30] The willingness that Congress showed for micro-management was one that the Secretary of Defense, in particular, had to take seriously.[31] He had to do this because resources allocated by elected officials were critical for the increasingly expensive military technology.[32] Congressional power and support are crucial for the executive and the Pentagon to implement programmes, especially as, in the words of one former Assistant Secretary of Defense, the 'DOD's major internal functions are to produce an annual budget for submission to the President . . . to the Congress and to acquire weapons systems for which funding has been obtained'.[33] The Congressional analysis of the Presidential budgetary proposals via the two-stage process of authorising the substantive proposals and appropriating the itemised requests in the bill, was a key tool in limiting the executive.[34]

Legislative assertiveness was coupled with an enhanced role for Congressional staffers. As Adam Garfinkle pointed out, 'Less noted but equally consequential, the Budget Reform Act 1974 allowed the Congress expanded power over the purse and facilitated the explosive expansion of its own staffs.'[35] The strength of Congress's reasserted power was shown by the assessment of the position after the Reagan administration had left office.

> Congress was able to maintain, even expand, its role in defence policy against the wishes of the most popular president in modern history and in the throes of a strongly conservative tide in U.S. politics. . . . The new balance between the branches of government clearly reflects fundamental alterations in the nation's perceptions of the international system and of the U.S. role in that system. The American people have extended the system of checks and balances, always prevalent in domestic policy, to the realm of foreign and defense policy. This is a new development in U.S. government.[36]

This forced the executive to pay close attention to Congressional and public concerns, and brought to fruition a more coherent expression of the nation's strategic culture in terms of the interrelationship between the strategic 'trinity' of the president, the public and the military that was the fundamental distress of the Army after Vietnam. It did this by weakening the executive and simultaneously taking onto itself new powers, reinforcing Congressional authorisation for action. This approach stood clearly in the constitutional framers' intentions 'which represented a radical break from monarchical rule in England, and . . . [a] commitment to republican principles in the conduct of foreign policy'.[37] The growth of Congressional power helped to rebalance American strategic culture, as it has a crucial role in articulating public concerns.[38]

Defence Issues

Congress developed as an alternative source of policy in its own right in matters of foreign policy and defence. It was not always a benign influence and was to be a subject of intense debate in the Reagan years.[39] The newly found power enabled positive strategic developments to take place at the institutional level, the highlight of which was the Goldwater–Nichols Act of 1986. The movement away from the executive prerogative in defence issues to a more dialectic relationship between Congress and the White House reduced the potential for another Vietnam, but also gave room for groups such as the Military Reform Caucus to influence policy in the name of building defence 'consensus'.[40] James Fallows's 1979 article in the *Atlantic Monthly*[41] was one of the first shots of the reformers to bring public attention to defence issues, particularly about overly complex weapons systems and the loss of the 'military art'.[42] They asked what US interests were, what strategy was best for these interests and therefore what the ensuing doctrine and strategy should be.[43]

Critics also came from within the services. For example, to promote the reform of the management of national strategy, Air Force General David C. Jones, as Chairman of the Joint Chiefs of Staff, and General Meyer, as the Army Chief of Staff, appealed for changes to the Joint Chiefs of Staff system by appearing before Congress whilst in office.[44] General Jones articulately outlined the fundamental problems, from a position where

> after serving on the Joint Chiefs of Staff longer than anyone else in history and under more Presidents and Secretaries of Defense (four of each), and being a student of military history and organizations, I am convinced that fundamental defense deficiencies cannot be solved with dollars alone – no matter how much they are needed. . . . By the summer of 1980, after serving as Chairman . . . for two years, I had become convinced that we could not begin to overcome our defence problems without a basic restructuring of military responsibility.[45]

Jones saw that the Vietnam War was fought by each service on its own and that there was a clear need to get things right on the battlefield first time.[46] These public criticisms of the Joint Chiefs of Staff system gave great impetus to the JCS

Reorganization Act of 1982, but the legislation died in the Senate due to John Tower, chairman of the Senate Armed Services Committee. However, 'It would be less than a year before . . . the waning months of 1983 proved Jones tragically prescient.'[47] It was after the events in Lebanon and Grenada that the will was developed to bring in the Goldwater–Nichols Act of 1986 to reorganise the armed services, enabling an institutional 'synchronicity' of political purpose and military means.

Failure to learn

The use of military force by the Reagan administration in 1983, in Lebanon and Grenada, was to provide the impetus that led to the administration's adoption of the Army's thinking, as laid out in the Weinberger doctrine. The reforms undertaken by Congress broadened the influence of the Army's thinking in the management of national strategy. The crucial events took place two days apart in October 1983. On the 23rd, a suicide bomber killed 241 US Marines in Beirut, shocking the nation. Two days later the US successfully invaded the island of Grenada. Both events, and their interrelationship were absolutely crucial to the later direction of US military intervention policy.

Grenada

The invasion of Grenada was important because it re-legitimised the use and utility of the use of force for the administration. As George Shultz the Secretary of State made clear, the Falklands War had been an important part of the process of rehabilitation of the utility of military force after Vietnam.

> The British decision to go to war for these desolate, wind-scoured, scarcely populated rocky islets 8,000 miles from London was the first marker laid down by a democratic power in the post-Vietnam era to state unambiguously that a free world nation was willing to fight for a principle. The world paid attention to this – and not just the Third World either; it was noted by the Soviets too. Attitudes everywhere were significantly affected.[48]

On the 25 October 1983, the US invaded Grenada, a small Caribbean island, where there were 784 Cuban personnel, the majority of which were part of the Point Salines airport development.[49] Its significance lies in the fact that it was the first serious use of offensive force by the US since Vietnam, even though it was ostensibly a rescue mission of American medical students, and the US forces were to evacuate 740 Americans from the island. It was supposed to be a simple operation that, in the words of the Deputy Commander, General H. Norman Schwarzkopf, was conceived as a 'one-punch knockout'.[50] US forces overran all opposition on the island.

Politically the Grenada intervention was a success, reinforcing the Reagan administration's challenge to the absolute prohibition against using force.[51] However, the fragility of the renewed utility was shown by the fact that the administration was dependent upon retrospective public support. As Shultz wrote of the mood in the White House at the close of the intervention:

> We were all aware that how those students behaved and what they said to the media would greatly affect how the intervention in Grenada would be perceived in the United States. . . . Finally, one student came out and went down the front stairs. At the bottom of the stairway, he fell to his knees and kissed the tarmac. . . . Suddenly I could sense the country's emotional turn around. Our effort in Grenada wasn't an immoral imperialistic intervention: it was an essential rescue and a job well done.[52]

The low-risk military operation was politically high risk, but the gamble paid off. The fact that the public legitimacy of such a large operation should be dependent on the reaction of one student shows just how significant Grenada was for rebuilding American intervention policy. For the US, force was re-legitimised, as its virtue was based on success.[53] As David Horowitz put it, 'To Americans who cherish their own rich heritage . . . "No More Vietnams" can mean only this: no more American Defeats.'[54] Grenada was a further step in the public rehabilitation of the Army's position in society, and though it was more reminiscent of the Dominican invasion of 1965 than the Vietnam War,[55] it showed that force could be used acceptably.

The insecurity of the administration and the Army during the operation was shown by the way the media was managed. The invasion was the subject of a news blackout, and television pictures put out by stations carried the notice that they were 'censored'. Dan Rather of CBS went so far as to tell viewers that the film that they watched was 'shot by the Army and censored by the Army'.[56] Admiral Metcalfe, the commanding officer, held to the view that the 'no press' policy was a logistical extension of the tight security that covered the early planning and diversion of the amphibious force to the Caribbean.[57] The outcome, however one sided, was fundamental to the Army's self-perception. As Rick Atkinson explained,

> In the wake of Grenada, the United States Army . . . awarded nearly nine thousand medals for valor and achievement, far more than the number of soldiers actually on Grenada. . . . Therein lay the crux of Urgent Fury. For all its shortcomings, for all the derisive commentary about the pathetic nature of the enemy against which American power was hurled, the invasion of Grenada was a victory. Armies fight with morale and espirit as much as they fight with tanks and bullets; after Grenada, soldiers walked a little taller, not because of their battlefield exploits but because of the huzzahs from the rescued students and an appreciative citizenry at

> home. The United States Army, its self-esteem battered in Southeast Asia, needed to win a war, any war.[58]

However, the confidence that the invasion brought was tempered by the difficulties that had been experienced in Lebanon.

Lebanon

The events in Lebanon in 1982–84 clearly showed the lack of institutional learning that had gone on since the Vietnam War, and the Reagan administration was to learn a crucial strategic lesson there. Initially, the US troops had a non-offensive role in the country but soon became the target of various factions. The US had then taken sides and backed President Gamayel.[59] This made them direct combatants in the conflict, changing the situation, especially as they were monitors to withdrawal agreements.[60] As the DOD report later explained, 'By the end of September 1983, the situation in Lebanon had changed to the extent that not one of the initial conditions upon which the mission statement was premised was still valid.'[61] Eventually, in October 1983, a suicide bomber killed 241 Marines and led to the US withdrawal from Lebanon.[62]

The deployment was a mistake and could have embroiled the administration in another Vietnam-style conflict, as it did the Israelis who stayed.[63] With the Beirut bombing the military were again seen as victims of government policy and the inappropriate use of military power.[64] It was significantly to affect later interventions. For example, in the Panama invasion the military showed a continuing suspicion of the State Department, because the military saw that it had been embroiled in Lebanon,[65] and the advice that the Pentagon put forward concerning the political commitment to, and force levels necessary, in Bosnia were a product of both Vietnam and Beirut.[66] However, Lebanon had more immediate repercussions.

Secretary of Defense Weinberger had not been against the use of 'any' military forces in Lebanon, but was concerned about the specific missions they had once they had been sent.[67] He judged the first Multi-National Force (MNF) deployment to Lebanon a success, as it had virtually no losses and had supervised the removal of the PLO from Beirut.[68] The difficulties began after that, when the National Security Council staff pushed for another mission to 'force the withdrawal' of the Syrian and Israeli forces from Lebanon.[69] Weinberger objected because the mission had 'fuzzy' objectives, and once they were defined they were unobtainable. The Joint Chiefs of Staff also objected to the lack of clear objectives, because the proper size, armaments and ROEs (Rules of Engagement) were difficult to define. However, the mission went ahead and US troops were landed without a final agreement by the opposing Syrian and Israeli forces to withdrawal. Weinberger and the Joint Chiefs of Staff continually urged the dissolution and withdrawal of the second Multi-National Force.[70] After the 241 deaths, an investigating commission report placed in the public arena many of the arguments about 'presence' that Weinberger had been making privately.

The Department of Defense report, the 'Long Commission', published after the bombing, highlighted the problem of providing a 'presence' in Lebanon.[71] The key difficulty was that each level of command understood it in a different manner. For example, the Rules of Engagements given to servicemen were seen as detracting them from their readiness, as there was one set for the embassy detail and one for the rest.[72] The Beirut Rules of Engagement would become emblematic of dangerousness of ambiguity, as 'the suicide-truck bomber . . . was able to run past a guarded gate because officials were so worried about accidentally shooting a civilian that Marine sentries were ordered to keep their weapons unloaded'.[73] Weinberger quickly established a single set of ROEs and a shortened chain of command.[74]

Weinberger was deeply affected by the Beirut bombing. It was seen as showing that the military had again be forced to operate without the necessary clarity of purpose. This actually ignores that the Pentagon had defined too narrow a mission for the Marines, whilst the National Security Council had not developed a military strategy that could provide sufficient time to generate a viable Lebanese government. As F. G. Hoffman says, the mission actually fell between the stools of inevitable failure and being poorly defined – there were too few for peace, and too many to die.[75] In the aftermath, however, Weinberger heavily promoted his views about the use of force within the administration, though he delayed their public release until after the November 1984 elections.[76] The ensuing debate within the administration between the State and Defense Secretaries[77] concerning the use of force were a turning point for the adoption of Army strategic thinking about the use of force. However, the interventions were also to provoke Congressional interest in the reform of the management of national strategy.

Interest in the reform of the military was fuelled by the events in Lebanon because, as Edward Luttwak observed, the closing months of 1983 'revealed once again the deep structural defects of the military institutions'.[78] In other words, not only was the policy at fault but so were the military. There was a clear inadequacy of counter-terror training, organisation and staffing. For example, in Lebanon the command structure was seen as ill-equipped to handle the mission, with the entire USCINCEUR chain of command seen to be at fault. The Secretary of the Navy John Lehman observed: 'it is ironic that the uniformed military always blames McNamara for what is in fact a hallmark of its own peacetime bureaucratic mindset.'[79] Lehman highlighted a second key factor of the failure to learn. President Reagan had left the timing and operational specifics to the military, which had repeated the old practice of tit-for-tat airstrikes, the nature of which were 'classic twenty year old Vietnam "aluminum cloud" daylight alpha strike. No surprise, no deception, no countermeasures by the aircraft.' Just fly in, drop your bombs and fly out at medium altitude.[80] The military targeted militarily useless sites, with confused objectives, and did not use precision night attacks, as would later happen in Libya in 1986.[81] Lebanon exposed weaknesses in policy and practice and highlighted the need for reform.

Later examination of the Grenada operation raised many of the same issues for the US. Analysts outlined failings of a muddled chain of command, control and communications; the inability of the separate services to work together: not using special operations forces properly; poor intelligence and equipment failures.[82] The Navy also questioned the emphasis on jointness, which it felt cost efficiency, and that its self-sufficiency with carrier group and air support were being overlooked.[83] Criticisms of the Grenada operation were to give impetus and substance to the reformers, within and especially without the Army. The thinking that had been developing from within TRADOC was shown by Grenada to be both necessary and appropriate, and the criticisms of the invasion by civilians were to help push the reforms through. This happened once Weinberger had made his famous speech.

The Weinberger doctrine

Shultz–Weinberger

Shultz and Weinberger clashed over the proper use of military force by the US.[84] David Twining has explained the difference as one of 'prudent force' versus 'cautious force'.[85] George Shultz looked to integrate military and diplomatic power far more closely, in particular to have political tools to address the problem of terrorism. His concern was to have the tools for coercive diplomacy, because he saw that inaction, like appeasement, was worse, and the murkiness of many politico-military situations made a clear need to subordinate military effectiveness to political objectives. As Christopher Gacek noted, Shultz's critique was the first cabinet-level criticism of the 'Never Again or All-or-Nothing' philosophy – it was not a question of force being a last resort, but that force must be used decisively and overwhelmingly.[86] He was not arguing for a return to the Limited War ideas of the Vietnam era, though he did see Weinberger's speech as 'the Vietnam syndrome in spades'.[87] Weinberger's perspective was of the department responsible for carrying out the tasks. Armies are traditionally reluctant to get involved in war, especially as they bear the brunt of the cost of the involvement,[88] but the criteria Weinberger laid out was reflective of more than this; it was a public posting of how the military saw their role after Vietnam.

Lessons of Vietnam

To understand Weinberger's thinking it is important to recognise what influenced him.[89] The most obvious influence was the Army's reading of the lessons of the Vietnam War. As one critic pointed out: 'Weinberger's speech may be read as almost a summary of conclusions of official military summaries of the lessons of Vietnam.'[90] Weinberger's Military Assistant, General Colin Powell, was an advocate of the 'official' line, though neither publicly acknowledged his influence on the writing of the speech. However, Powell's published views were in accord with the doctrine and his position in Weinberger's office was significant. For example, Army Chief of Staff General Wickham said that Weinberger relied so heavily on Powell that he could not let him go after two years, so he stayed an extra year in office, being rewarded with a 'third star' and commanding a corps in 1986, even though he had never commanded a division.[91] Powell was, as his authorised biography says, a disciple of Clausewitz from his days at National War College in 1973.[92] The 'Army' perception of the Vietnam War and Clausewitz had been outlined in Harry Summers's *On Strategy*, and Weinberger's speech writers were greatly influenced by it.[93]

Summers

Summers' book *On Strategy*, an analysis of the Vietnam War, was written for the Army under the auspices of the Army Vice Chief of Staff, General Kerwin, as part of the Army War College's examination of the conflict.[94] Summers's thinking on the Vietnam War was important, particularly as he had already co-authored an article on Vietnam with the previous Chief of Staff, General Weyand.[95] Using materials provided by the BDM study of *Strategic Lessons of Vietnam*[96] and other secondary material, he argued that the war was lost strategically, i.e. that the Army won its battles but the country had lost the war. This conclusion was actually a rejection of the BDM study, which had criticised the conventional attrition strategy. Summers saw the Vietnam War in conventional terms, and some Army critics saw his book as using a flawed understanding of the nature of the war to absolve the military of responsibility for failure.[97] However, General Meyer endorsed Summers's analysis by ordering its publication in 1981 and distributing copies to all Army general officers (whilst reformer Newt Gingrich sent copies to all members of the US Senate and Congress).[98] It provided a template for the Army's broad understanding of strategy. For example, the 1981 report of the commander of 193rd Infantry Brigade in El Salvador, General Frederick Woerner, was derived from *On Strategy*.[99] Woerner saw that defeating the rebels needed a broad national policy and would cost $300 million in military aid and take nearly five years to complete, which Reagan administration officials saw as unnecessarily bleak.[100] The Army went on to provide mainly trainers, most of whom were conventionally oriented.[101] *On Strategy* was still on the Command and General Staff College, Army War College and the Chairman, Joint Chiefs of Staff reading lists through the 1990s,[102] and it is still on the Chief of Staff of the Army's reading list, because it an 'excellent tool for educating the future commander. More important, the work can serve as a guide for self-education about a critical period in American military, political, and social history.'[103]

Summers made explicit the previously implicit understanding of strategy and the nature of the US Army, and he did so by drawing on the work of Clausewitz's *On War*. He made much of Clausewitz's dictum that 'war was the continuation of politics by other means' prosecuted by a trinity of 'people, army, and government'. Villacres and Bassford have pointed out that the 'trinity' was 'an alteration of the concept expressed in *On War*'.[104] Clausewitz actually said that war was a combination of irrational elements (i.e. violent emotion), non-rational factors (e.g. chance) and rationality (an instrument of policy), and Summers was using only an illustration of the concept.[105] However, when one refers to Army strategic thinking and the influence of Clausewitz on it, one is really referring to the key aspects of Summers's reading of him and his reading of Vietnam. Summers's book helped stimulate a revival in interest in Clausewitz and articulate the Army's understanding of the key failures in the past. As Michael Handel (Professor of Strategy at the US Naval War College) explained, Summers's 'important and timely book' meant that a 'stab in the back' mentality did not develop within the Army, as he outlined that successful strategy depends not only upon the military but also on the government and people.[106]

Weinberger took this theme up and placed public support at the heart of the doctrine. Public support, not reference to UN or international legal norms, was to be the authoritative basis for Weinberger's doctrine.[107] As Cori Dauber has argued, the doctrine is an argumentative device for shaping the public debate on the use of military force.[108] Public support was the key difference between him and Shultz.[109]

Weinberger's speech

Caspar Weinberger gave his famous speech on the uses of military power to the National Press Club on 28 November 1984.[110] In it he outlined what was to become known as the 'Weinberger Doctrine'. He aimed to define 'Under what circumstances, and by what means, does a great democracy such as ours reach the painful decision that the use of military force is necessary to protect our interests or to carry out our national policy?'[111] He 'developed six major tests to be applied when we are weighing the use of U.S. combat forces abroad'.[112] The criteria can be summarised as follows:

1 The US should not commit forces to combat unless it was vital to its national interest or that of its allies.
2 If it was necessary to put combat troops into a situation,

> we should do so wholeheartedly, and with the clear intention of winning. If we are unwilling to commit the forces or resources necessary to achieve our objectives, we should not commit them at all. Of course if the particular situation requires only limited forces to win our objective, then we should not hesitate to commit forces sized accordingly.[113]

3 If the US committed forces to overseas combat

> we should have clearly defined political and military objectives. And we should know precisely how our forces can accomplish those clearly defined objectives. And we should know precisely how our forces can accomplish those clearly defined objectives. And we should have and send the forces needed to do just that. As Clausewitz wrote, 'Noone

> starts a war – or rather, no one in his senses ought to do so – without first being clear in his mind what he intends to achieve by that war, and how he intends to conduct it.'[114]

Weinberger was clear that war may now be different from Clausewitz's era but well-defined objectives and consistent strategy were still essential.

4 The relationship between objectives and the forces committed must be continually reassessed and adjusted.

> We must continuously keep as a beacon light before us the basic questions: '*Is this conflict in our national interest?*' 'Does our national interest require us to fight, to use force of arms?' If the answers are 'yes,' then we *must* win. If the answers are 'no,' then we should not be in combat.[115]

5 Before committing US combat forces abroad there must be reasonable assurance that it has the support of the American people and Congress. 'We cannot fight a battle with the Congress at home while asking out troops to win a war overseas or, as in the case of Vietnam, in effect asking our troops not to win, but just be there.'[116]
6 'Finally, the commitment of U.S. forces to combat should be a last resort.'[117]

The importance of the doctrine to Weinberger is shown by the fact that he reiterated it in an article in *Foreign Affairs* and made it one of the pillars of his defence policy, along with the strategic defence initiative, arms control and competitive strategies.[118] However, the criteria are not as straightforward as they would at first seem as, ironically, Weinberger's own use of military force interpreted the criteria in a liberal manner – they need to be critically examined.[119]

Weinberger made clear the political context and the influence of Vietnam on his thinking:

> The President will not allow our military forces to creep – or to be drawn gradually – into a combat role in Central America or any other place in the world. . . . I believe that the tests I have enunciated here today can, if applied carefully, avoid the danger of this gradualist incremental approach which almost always means the use of insufficient force. These tests can help us to avoid being drawn inexorably into an endless morass, where it is not vital to our national interest to fight.[120]

The concern was essentially with the use of troops in combat, rather than with non-combatant signalling for diplomatic crisis management. For example, the crisis over Poland in 1980–81 showed that troops could be used as a political 'signal'. This was acceptable because of Europe's importance to US interests and the policy was affected by the prominent memory of the 1968 invasion of Czechoslovakia, rather than by Vietnam.[121] In regions outside of Europe, however, signalling was seen as a dangerous route into war so, in the case of Libya for example, troops were kept out of the mission.[122] If force was to be used then it was applied in overwhelming quantities against small states,[123] because it was the most effective way for the American military to prosecute war, and thus to achieve the intended political results of intervention.

Weinberger placed militarily achievable political objectives as the centre of his doctrine, as policies need clear objectives to use the Army properly and be able to work; 'Policies formed without a clear understanding of what we hope to achieve will never work.'[124] This reflected the influence of the third key source for his speech.

Readiness Command

Summers's influence was the embodiment of the broader strategic understanding of the Vietnam War, but Weinberger was faced by the practicalities of deploying troops as they were equipped and trained at the time. The Army's new published doctrine of *FM 100-5* laid out that the principles of war called for clear objectives. However, the commander of Readiness Command (responsible for providing the Army force for deployments) was General Donn Starry, the man behind the development of the AirLand Battle doctrine. Starry had kept repeating to the Secretary the same criteria as the published 'doctrine', to such an extent that he finally flew down to see Weinberger to lay out his concerns. Weinberger was therefore receiving advice that brought together the strategic lessons from Vietnam and the strategic lessons that resulted from the rebuilding of the Army at TRADOC. In consequence, Weinberger was advocating the Army's viewpoint by accepting that military missions should have clear objectives and, crucially, that they were militarily achievable. More importantly, what was militarily achievable was defined by the reforms and training which the Army undertook, therefore making its self-understanding the criteria for military intervention policy. In other words, how the Army had rebuilt itself after the war shaped the tasks that could be undertaken. The significance of this can be seen when Secretary of State Shultz referred to the political aim of the broader policy, AirLand Battle doctrine looked to the executive to refine the aim into a series of militarily achievable objectives. Crucially, objectives that were not militarily achievable were illegitimate, even if they were part of the broader policy aim. This was a key difference of view as it meant that how the Army saw itself dictated the policy. This trend can be most clearly seen by examining the demand for 'clear objectives' by Weinberger.

To support the demand for clear objectives, Weinberger cites Clausewitz directly to advocate a swift and decisive approach, rather than a prolonged one. As Michael Handel shows, this is a contradiction inherent in Clausewitz, where the 'momentum of offensive' (or principle of continuity) meets with 'the culminating point', the mark of the end of the momentum.[125] The culminating point is where the offensive peaks and the force risks counterattack and defeat. It always recurs when the destruction of the enemy cannot be the military aim.[126] Clausewitz leaves the resolution of the problem of the balance between the offensive and the culminating point to the commander.[127] Thus Clausewitz and Weinberger make the military responsible for defining the resolution of conflict and setting the nature of the objectives to be achieved. Importantly, Clausewitz was using the term 'strategy' in the modern sense of 'operations',[128] as he pays little attention to important factors at the national strategic level; for example, the importance of alliances, public opinion and domestic stability.[129]

This highlights a key gap in the modern application of his analysis, and this is carried over into Weinberger's thinking, especially as Weinberger's emphasis on the militarily achievable renders obsolete the Clausewitzian emphasis on the priority of political aims, rather than objectives, in setting military strategy. Clausewitz's emphasis was on war being a continuation of policy, but this was read as operational objectives and termination points rather than understanding 'strategy' in a manner appropriate to a later age of warfare. Liddell Hart's reading of Clausewitz's dictum was very acute: seeing that the object of war is to obtain a 'better peace', and that the prolongation of policy in war must extend beyond the termination of fighting.[130] The overall political aim of the policy is the crucial aspect, rather than the overemphasis on the objectives at the operational level. However, the US Army's model of warfighting was in accord with this narrower reading. What this means in practice is that post-operational concerns were relegated to other agencies, co-ordinated by the national executive not the Army. They were not the Army's area of concern. The primary concern for Weinberger, therefore, was not with the efficacy of the Army as a useful diplomatic tool, but with establishing clear operational and achievable objectives. This was a crucial aspect of the nature of the debate, and of the learning that had gone on since the Vietnam War. Weinberger went beyond challenging the executive to use the military with proper regard for its nature, to advocating that the military should not be used at all unless it was fully in accord with its own self-understanding of what was militarily efficient; and that was far more restrictive. This advocacy, rather bizarrely, reversed Clausewitz's intention as it made policy a continuation of the nation's operational tools of war, rather than a continuation of strategic policy. It was the 'operationalisation' of strategy. Weinberger's doctrine has distorted missions.[131]

Influence

The level of importance accorded 'military efficacy' in policy considerations was the issue at the crux of the Weinberger–Shultz debate. Shultz saw that Americans want foreign policy to reflect the nation's values, as well as wanting foreign policy to be effective. Traditionally, of course, this was achieved by the mobilisation of the nation behind a cause. For Weinberger, in the post-Vietnam era of the professional Army, the criteria for effective policy was seen as synonymous with what was militarily effective, and that was produced by the Army. The broader dilemma of 'morality against practicality' echoes the differences that would be repeated in the post-Cold War debate.[132]

With the development of a separate professional identity for the Army, US society was no longer the reference point, and military effectiveness could actually be in opposition to espoused national moral views. Operational requirements were key to the Army. The Army's development of AirLand Battle gave it a clear list of military requirements of seizing the initiative and aiming to disrupt and destroy the enemy through mass and manoeuvre, as part of a synergistic strategic approach at the national level. Moral policies that did not fit these requirements were not practical, and so failed. The Army as the tool of intervention was clearly capable of defining intervention policy, rather than have policy requirements define it.

This point was caught by Andrew Krepinevich, the premier critic of the Army's lack of learning, who saw the Army erecting barriers to avoid fighting another Vietnam War:

> The result has been that instead of gaining a better understanding of how to wage counterinsurgency warfare within the unique social, political, and military dimensions comprising that form of conflict, the Army is trying, through the six tests enunciated by Secretary Weinberger, to transform it into something it can handle.[133]

This highlights an important aspect of the learning and the conclusions that were drawn from the Vietnam War – rather than having the wrong Army, the nation fought the wrong war. Krepinevich's book, *The Army and Vietnam*, was highly critical of the Army's organisational learning during the Vietnam War and its lack of doctrinal development for the unconventional war it fought there. It was influential in the attempt to increase later US special operations capability during the 1980s.[134] The book was 'the flip side of Summers' book',[135] as it stressed that the US Army fought the wrong type of war in Vietnam by ignoring counter-insurgency. Summers had made his views on the nature of warfare clear when he wrote, in response to Senator Cohen's admonitions concerning Low-Intensity Conflict that it was actually war, as 'A War Is a War Is a War Is a War'.[136] However, Krepinevich's critique of the 'wrong' Army was rebuffed, as the Army and the administration understood the American defeat in the same terms. They both blamed 'a lack of will, too much democracy, betrayal by the press, and the political constraints on the military'.[137] In fact, as D. Michael Shafer's classic study *Deadly Paradigms* showed, the administration in the 1980s was repeating many of the features of the earlier approach by being concerned simply with the 'Soviet threat', and promoting a formulaic Low-Intensity Conflict response, rather than one geared to the specific complexity of each situation.[138] The concentration on generic armed forces providing only military capability as part of a broader national policy was in accord with Weinberger's criteria and reflected the learning that had gone on.[139] The alternative advocated by Krepinevich that there was a need to have a broad understanding of the nature of Low-Intensity Conflict and the Army's potential response, was lost in the broader consensus on the correct lessons drawn from the war.

The six tests, however limited they were as lessons of Vietnam, were actually reflective of the Army's professional learning and the nature of the American polity. For David Twinning. Weinberger's doctrine 'represents a maturation and sophistication of our strategic judgement'.[140] As Michael Handel says, the Weinberger doctrine is a utilitarian, realistic yardstick not much concerned with moral questions; it cannot provide specific advice but

> its contemplation can raise many valid questions and caveats before a decision to commit forces is made. From this perspective, and given the unique nature of the American political system, the Weinberger Doctrine has made and will continue to make an important contribution to U.S. national security policy.[141]

Weinberger's speech provided the template for the use of military force by the post-Vietnam American strategic culture. Presidents Reagan and Bush endorsed the key tenets.[142] As Craig and George said, Weinberger's emphasis that the 'use of force in support of foreign policy must give way, if necessary, to military requirements for the effective, efficient use of force', faced no significant challenge as the new political–military doctrine for the US until the Bosnian war.[143] However, to move Army thinking from acceptance by the administration and make it sustained national policy, the management and structure of national security had to be reformed. The experience in Grenada and Beirut provided the impetus.

Rebalancing the strategic culture

By the 1980s the primary leadership for change was Congress,[144] and this was most clearly seen in the passage of the Goldwater-Nichols Act of 1986.[145]

Goldwater–Nichols

As we have seen, there was a wide military concern with the need to reform the Joint Chiefs of Staff structure,[146] but the success of the reform measures was mainly due to Congressional dissatisfaction with Pentagon internal management.[147] As reformer Air Force Colonel James Burton explained in 1993:

> Defeat in Vietnam, disaster at Desert One, unbridled ambition and rampant careerism in the officer corps of all services, the incestuous revolving door between the defense industry and Pentagon officials, the almost daily revelation of horror stories about $600 toilet seats and $400 hammers, a steady stream of weapons systems either inadequately tested or purchased regardless of poor test results, and a regular diet of senior military

> and civilian officials lying to the public and Congress to cover up embarrassments were only a few of the symptoms of a corrupt business that cried out for reform.[148]

The Goldwater–Nichols Act provided the vital organisational coherence to the post-Vietnam 'intervention strategy' because it addressed the key weakness of the national strategy, namely the command and control issues and inter-service rivalry. Army reformers such as General Paul Gorman saw that the unreformed Joint Chiefs of Staff was useful for justifying force structure and procurement funds but 'patently not useful for prosecuting war'.[149] As reformers pointed out, the US had never won a war since the creation of the Department of Defense and the Joint Chiefs of Staff.[150] The focus on warfighting that Gorman helped to engender through his training reforms, and the conceptual developments which built on this basis, gave substance to the ideas behind the proposed jointness, developing a more synchronised strategy by the US.

The Goldwater–Nichols Act had many aims, among them formulating strategy and improving advice to the President.[151] To do this it obliged the President to write a national security strategy report and made the Chairman of the Joint Chiefs of Staff the principal military adviser to the President, the National Security Council, and the Secretary of Defense.[152] The Act also clarified the chain of command, outlining that it ran from the President to the Secretary of Defense down, but importantly 'transmitted through the Chairman of the Joint Chiefs of Staff'.[153] The Act aimed to aid the President rather than establish a separate body with responsibility for the use of military force. It explicitly stated that the reforms of the Joint Chiefs of Staff were not to make it, or allow it to operate as, a General Staff.[154]

The reforms placed influential power in the singular position of the Chairman of the Joint Chiefs of Staff, thereby avoiding Upton's ideas after the Civil War of creating a General Staff. The Chairman was responsible for strategic planning and providing the strategic direction of the United States, subject to the President and Secretary of Defense, which gave him enormous power, as he was no longer the expression of the collective views of the other Chiefs of Staff but singularly responsible and placed over them in seniority.[155] This made him, in Vincent Davis's words, the 'chief strategic thinker for the United States'.[156] It formalised and integrated the position of the military, in the shape of the Chairman of the Joint Chiefs of Staff, within the defence process. This process had previously been so weak that it was perceived as one of the key failures of the prosecution of the Vietnam War. As General Bruce Palmer wrote in his reflections on the war, strategic guidance must 'emanate from the civilian leadership . . . although they should be approved only after views of JCS have been fully taken into account'.[157] The Chairman's position and views were made influential in the planning process, especially at National Security Council level.

The level of influence of the Chairman of the Joint Chiefs of Staff has attracted criticism, as Goldwater-Nichols made him the de facto commander of the American forces, and therefore reduced the sources of military advice for the civilian authority.[158] This development has led to a unitary nature of advice from the 'military' being proffered to the administration, but at least it was advice integrated into the political process, unlike that of the Chiefs of Staff under Robert McNamara during the Vietnam War. For example, the military intervention in the Philippines by the US in November 1989 shows how successful the chain of command was after the Goldwater–Nichols Act. The intervention was in response to a coup attempt against President Corazon Aquino, and the US expressed 'extreme hostile intent' against the coup with a display of airpower by F-4 Phantoms overflying the rebel-held airbase and threatening to shoot down aircraft that took off. It worked. After the intervention Colin Powell wrote:

> The night the coup ended, I left the Pentagon feeling good. I had applied Clausewitz's teachings, or Weinberger's Maxim No. 3, and my own rule in forming military advice: take no action until you have a clear objective. We had applied restrained, proportionate, calibrated force, linked to a specific goal. And it had worked.[159]

The coup failed and the American intervention was managed with 'a clear line of authority for graduated military action, commander-in-chief to Secretary of Defense through [the Chairman of the JCS] to the appropriate military units'.[160]

Joint

The act not only aimed to improve the management and development of defence policy, it also aimed to make the forces work together in a 'joint' manner – to 'purple' the forces (the supposed colour of the blended services). The idea built on Army and Air Force developments, as they had signed the *Memorandum of Agreement on US Army–US Air Force Joint Force Development Process* in May 1984, widely known as the '31 initiatives'.[161] Goldwater–Nichols established unified combatant commands, rather than single service commands, under the control of a Commander in Chief (CINC) who is responsible for what he thinks is best for the command's task requirement.[162] The job of the Chief of Staffs was to provide the CINCs with the appropriate tools to do their jobs, but they were not in the line of command. The jointery was to reach down the ranks, so that an officer had to serve in a joint duty assignment to be promoted above brigadier general or rear admiral.[163] Although the aim to develop jointery was complicated by there being no new joint doctrine, especially tactical doctrine, in the Goldwater–Nichols reforms,[164] the tactical unity and operational thinking engendered by AirLand Battle doctrine provided de facto joint doctrine for the two services. It did not resolve the long-term strategic/tactical debate on the role of airpower within national strategy, focusing as it did on the operational level, and from 1985 the Air Force questioned the division of tactical and strategic and emphasised that they were really indivisible.[165] However, the emphasis on strategic effect being the prime rationale for the individual services existence was clear – whether that was to be mediated through the other services was another issue.

Army thinking

The Goldwater–Nichols Act was seen as a triumph for the Army's thinking. as the debate took on a 'strongly anti-Navy cast'.[166] Least affected by the developments in the Army's thinking was the Navy, a service that was the most strategically independent of them all,[167] and one that did not undergo the soul-searching the Army did after the end of the Vietnam War.[168] Additionally, the potential war in Europe was the concern, primarily, of the Army and the Air Force and the Navy's strategy relied on NATO holding the European Central front.[169] Naval opposition to Goldwater–Nichols was tied to the concern that naval assets would not be used with the most efficiency as many of the new commands would be under Army officers and ground forces think and act differently.[170] Putting naval operations under a centralised CINC 'was a victory for the rigid organization desired by the Army and Air Force for a war on the central front, and a defeat for the mobile, opportunistic use of naval force as expressed in the maritime strategy'.[171] The act rejected the Navy's global thinking and stress on independence and the Navy felt that it lost the argument due to 'intense pressure for greater centralization and coordination. That was for the most part an argument about U.S. strategy in the theater of greatest concern, Europe.'[172]

The Navy was also fearful of the great concentration on the role of the Chairman, who could stifle debate and establish a second centre of power to rival that of the Secretary of Defense's, muting criticisms by service chiefs of staff, especially that of Chief of Naval Operations; this fear was also expressed by some inside the Army.[173] The increased significance of the Chairman of the Joint Chiefs of Staff was developed by the personality and personal influence of Colin Powell, the first Chairman to be appointed after the Goldwater–Nichols Act. His views were influential because he had served in the previous Reagan administration as Caspar Weinberger's Military Assistant, been President Reagan's last National Security Advisor, and the first Gulf War raised his profile to such an extent that he was seen as a potential presidential candidate, eventually becoming Secretary of State.[174] Powell was prepared to push his discretionary power as 'far as it could legally go'.[175] As Lorna Jaffe, of the Joint History Office, explained, General Powell did not see his position as Chairman as one of simply responding to Presidential initiatives.

> Rather than waiting for the President to enunciate a new national security strategy, which he and the Secretary [of Defense] would then be charged with implementing, General Powell believed that it was his responsibility to press for a change in strategy in response to the changes in the strategic environment.[176]

Powell therefore had a fundamental influence on the ensuing force structure, defence planning and national strategy that culminated in the 1992 National Military Strategy; he 'successfully shaped that guidance'.[177] The views that formed his outlook on military power and statecraft, which Powell consistently put forward from his influential position, have been described as the 'standard view of officers of his generation'.[178] It should be remembered that both of the Chairmen of the Joint Chiefs of Staff (CJCS) in this period, Powell and Shalikashvili, were Army Vietnam veterans, and their generation had drawn clear lessons about the use of American force that meant that there should be clear political objectives established prior to risking any US casualties. Powell also clearly understood AirLand Battle doctrine and its implications.[179] However, the influential new position of Chairman of the JCS relied, due to its nature, on the personality of the Chairman himself,[180] and neither of Powell's successors were able to shape the intervention debate as much as he did. Ultimately, however, the post gave more power to a single US military officer than ever before. As Robert Buzzanco has written in his book on the Vietnam War, 'American military leaders may never have mastered Vietnam but they have gained influence, power, and appropriations since then – all after losing a war.'[181] Buzzanco's ironic criticism does not recognise that for the military, and the Army in particular, one of the key strategic lessons of the war was precisely to be more influential in the process, and Congress with the Goldwater–Nichols Act made that happen, bringing together the Clausewitzian 'trinity' outlined by Summers. However, as MacKubin Thomas Owen warned in 1985,

> Anyone who suggests that restructuring the JCS will cure all the security problems of the nation is simply irresponsible. The current [i.e. unreformed] structure is the result of the interaction of political–ideological, economic, and strategic–military forces that reflect the American political tradition.[182]

What was clear in hindsight was that the political tradition was greatly affected by Vietnam, and the reforms were reasserting the cultural strategic balance in light of this reading of the war, a reading in tune with Harry Summers's *On Strategy*. However, the limitations of Congressional reform to bring substantive change, without the balance of elements outlined by Owens, was most clearly shown with its concern with forcing the Department of Defense to develop greater special operations capability. The difficulties associated with this reveal the ability of the military, and the Pentagon in particular, to limit the growing role of Congress in defence issues. Successful innovations had to appeal to each of the constituencies involved – the White House, Congress and the Pentagon. Goldwater–Nichols was able to do this, driven by Congress, whilst Low-Intensity Conflict was a far more ambiguous issue.

Special operations

Developing Low-Intensity Conflict capability faced much opposition from within the Department of Defense and the administration.[183] Congressional frustration with the slow speed of the Army's approach[184] led it to force legislation through, culminating in the passing on 14 November 1986, the Nunn–Cohen Amendment to Fiscal Year 1987 National Defense Authorization Act.[185] It was specific in detail, and established the US Special Operations Command (USSOCOM) and the Office of the Assistant Secretary of Defense, Special Operations and Low-Intensity Conflict (SOLIC) and gave them a major funding source.[186] Eventually this and subsequent legislation provided a list of nine 'special operations activities' plus a tenth of 'such other activities as may be specified by the President or Secretary of Defense'.[187] There were two key problems with the thinking.

As James Scott's study of the 'Reagan Doctrine' shows, internal wrangling bedevils the nature of US foreign policy making:

> the process by which this strategy was formulated and applied was complex, messy, and laden with individual, organizational, and institutional conflict, compromise, and cooperation. Policy emerged from the shifting interactions between the White House, Congress, bureaucratic agencies, and groups and individuals from the private sector.[188]

When the new National Security Council level board established to address the issue first met at the end of Reagan's administration, it was actually more 'like a new armed service than a unified command'.[189] This added to the complexity. By establishing a separate three-star (Lieutenant General or equivalent) command, rather than placing them within the four-star (General or equivalent) combatant commands, the reforms cut across the integration and synchronising of armed capabilities that Goldwater–Nichols aimed to produce. This was borne out during the Gulf War, when General Schwarzkopf removed Psyops and Civilian Affairs from SOCCENT (Special Operations Command Central) and placed them under theatre headquarters, and forbade special operations units entering Iraq. It was a tense relationship.[190] Second, in the context of facing 'irregular' forces, as Eliot Cohen noted, the reluctance to interfere in internal politics and the military desire to operate autonomously runs counter to the 'requirements of small war'.[191] However, creating a Special Forces capability does not address this. For example, with the one exception of the prison rescue, conventional forces could have done every special operations mission in the Panama intervention.[192] In addition, the limitations of a high-risk, high-reward capability to end hostilities through a single, decisive, special operations action was shown to drastic effect in Panama and Somalia.[193] The crucial requirement for a developed 'small war' doctrine should not lie with a separate Special Forces command, but within light infantry doctrine, especially as they were geared to AirLand Battle doctrine. New Special Forces may avoid another Tehran rescue fiasco but would not address the problems that Vietnam had clearly shown.

For all that, the difficulties of isolated civilian imposition of innovation are shown by the problems faced with the Nunn–Cohen legislation. By not having administration support, or the backing of the Pentagon, the legislators could force structural change but not alter the culture of the Army. AirLand Battle reformers had appealed to all three constituencies as they rebuilt the Army's identity. As one of the key Low-Intensity Conflict reformers, Noel Koch, explained in 1989, the US has not developed effective counter-insurgency because military resistance to it was 'abetted by civilian leadership'.[194] The scars of Vietnam, and the associated social betrayal the Army experienced there, were too deep to develop Low-Intensity Conflict without the Army having first redeveloped its core identity. and confidence in the support from the nation. For the Army the civilian reformers were too premature in their aspirations. The Army matched the broader strategic culture on this point, and the Panamanian intervention showed this clearly.

Conclusion

The Army's strategic thinking shaped US strategic conceptions of the use of force. The Army's emphasis upon having public and Congressional support for the use of military force was in accord with the broader culture's attempts to limit the power of the executive. Congress became more assertive after the Vietnam War, most clearly shown by the passing of the War Powers Resolution, and it took a larger role in foreign policy and defence reform issues. This was combined with the Reagan administration emphasis on restoring pride in America. which included understanding the war in the same manner as the Army and being prepared to use military force again. The Reagan build-up allowed the reformers' ideas to be implemented in the Army. However, the rehabilitation of the use military force by the administration was not initially conceived of in the same terms as the Army's.

The failures of the Lebanese intervention and the military performance in Grenada brought intervention issues back into the public debate and highlighted the need for changes in the manner in which the US used military force. The Weinberger doctrine and the debate with the Secretary of State brought the administration's thinking in line with the Army's ideas. The Secretary of Defense drew upon the ideas contained in Harry Summers's *On Strategy* and the arguments of Readiness Command's CINC General Donn Starry, the developer of AirLand Battle doctrine. The strategic ideas contained within the Army's thinking were further developed by Congressional concerns with the management of the use of force and the Goldwater–Nichols reforms based on Army priorities. The changed institutional context of American strategic culture therefore brought Army strategic concerns to the fore, both formally and informally, by realigning the relations of Congress and the White House, thus integrating the Clausewitzian trinity as outlined by Summers.

The influence and impact on the culture went beyond this. AirLand Battle doctrine gave the trends substance by providing the motive and means for service jointery, and an emphasis on national-level strategy. AirLand Battle doctrine, however, limited the acceptance and management of broader Low-Intensity Conflict roles with their emphasis on political–military concerns at the operational and tactical levels, as conceived in Summers–Clausewitzian terms. However, Low-Intensity Conflict developments were themselves not subjects of total consensus within the culture, a key feature of the post-Vietnam strategic culture and a division that would re-emerge under the Clinton presidency.

The period after the Carter administration showed that the Army provided the framework and substance for the reform of the strategic culture. Congress brought in needed reforms of the management of national strategy but it was in line with the Army's thinking, and its doctrinal changes gave many of the key emphases substance. In other words, Congress could not reform national strategy in isolation from the military as the machinations of the Low-Intensity Conflict reforms showed. The Weinberger doctrine was therefore a sophisticated strategic model for American use of force, with the Army providing the substance and the broader culture the parameters. It was a remarkable new model of military intervention strategy, but reflected the limitations within the US strategic culture. The next chapter examines the strengths and weaknesses of the approach in practice.

6

INTERVENTIONS

Panama, the Gulf, Somalia

This chapter examines the use of force by the US in the context of the end of the Cold War, and how the Army's thinking influenced the nation's adaptation to the new strategic environment. It examines the interventions into Panama, Somalia and the first Gulf War. Panama was a precursor of the first Gulf War, which was a large-scale test of the Army's thinking and practice. The first Gulf War was seen as the cathartic vindication of the developments that went on in the Army and proof that it and the nation had learnt the lessons of Vietnam. However, the confidence generated by the success in the first Gulf War provided an impetus to use force far more readily in the new strategic environment, and the Clinton administration very quickly undertook a series of new roles in the world. Somalia was the test of this approach and the limitations of the Army's strategic thinking were soon apparent, and the fragility of the strategic coherence was quickly exposed. The failure of the mission to Somalia led to a reassessment of US military intervention policy and a reassertion of the Weinberger doctrine with Presidential Decision Directive 25. This left the US in a greatly weakened position in relation to humanitarian interventions and coercive diplomacy. Army thinking had become embedded in US thinking and shaped the strategic culture but no longer provided a utilisable tool of policy. The strategic thinking and practice therefore began to move away from the Army's priorities by avoiding using them, a dynamic that will be examined in the final chapter.

Panama

During a period in which seismic political changes were going on in the heartland of Europe, the US was distracted by a drug dealer (and 'chief of government'[1]) in Panama, and was unable to coerce him. The conflict with Noriega was to escalate from crisis to crisis, the US having to resort to tougher measures each time. President Bush eventually responded with military force, and on 20 December 1989 he ordered an attack on Panama to 'safeguard the lives of Americans, to defend democracy in Panama, to combat drug trafficking, and to protect the integrity of the Panama Canal Treaty . . . and to bring General Noriega to justice in the United States'.[2] It was the largest military action since Vietnam, but as one former US ambassador put it, it had all the characteristics of the last US colonial invasion brought on by an employee/employer spat.[3] The Panamanian intervention showed the influence of the Weinberger thinking and that of the reformers on the Army. It also made clear the limitations of US crisis management.

Crisis management

The use of force against Noriega was a result of failed policies to get him to comply with US wishes. The US was unable to make its intentions clear to Noriega because the bureaucratic infighting and the resultant mixed signals reinforced Noriega's misperceptions of US intentions, meaning that its threats lacked credibility.[4] However, as Eytan Gilboa has explained.

> The way in which the United States handled the Noriega affair was not an isolated case in how the United States has handled international crises in recent years. Several critical issues and mistakes made in this confrontation reappeared in subsequent international crises, most noticeably in the 1990–1991 Gulf crisis and war.[5]

The Bush administration resorted to force due to the failure of policy, not as an advancement of it. As Rebecca Grant's RAND report on the policy process during the Panamanian crisis put it, 'the decision to intervene was a last-resort option stemming from a sequence of errors and mismanagement'.[6]

The use of force as a last resort is a long way from a true coercive policy. Alexander George showed that 'if force is used at all it is not part of conventional military strategy but rather a component of a more complex political-diplomatic strategy for resolving a conflict of interests'.[7] The handling of Noriega did not place force as part of a larger strategy, and the speed of its use stopped it from being part of the coercive policy. As Lawrence Freedman explained, coercion deals with the role of threats, and the target must weigh the choice between compliance and non-compliance. Coercion is not about denying choice by threatening force, which means that coercion is not 'simply about the design of efficient threats' but bargaining, based on the assumptions of how the actors construct reality.[8] This has been a perennial problem for the US.

Critics have seen the failure to understand the 'key differences in the perceptions, values, and motivations of both allies and opponents' as a feature of American strategy.[9] Even Robert McNamara has retrospectively accepted that the failure to understand the difference in cultural perception was a key weakness of the American prosecution of the Vietnam War.[10] The Army has been seen as a primary factor in the generation of this approach to American use of force, where in-depth knowledge of an environment was substituted for technical solutions (such as statistics and computer simulation), converting genuine military and political problems, as in Vietnam, into technical ones. This does not allow a proper evaluation of the crucial intangibles in a conflict.[11] The handling of the problems in Panama is an important example of where the ignorance of the culture lay in Washington, so was not simply Army-led but reinforced by it. Panama is an important case study because it portrays this combination clearly.

Cultural considerations

The cultural 'blindness' of US handling of crises is shown, in the case of Panama, to be a product of the nature of the national strategic management rather than simply due to formulaic approaches taken by Army CINCs. It is possible to see this in the case of Panama because, as a regional responsibility, it was a backwater in terms of spending and equipment and only came to prominence because the Cold War ended.[12] General Woerner, the Southern Command CINC, was a strategic thinker outside the Army mainstream, and was concerned with the broad nature of US policy throughout South America and had published to this effect.[13] He was worried that the concentration of policy on Noriega meant that Panama would become the whole of US Southern American policy, and that partisan political objectives could jeopardise the attainment of US policy.[14] Additionally, Woerner was unknown in Washington circles and had lost the confidence of visiting congressmen and State Department officials because he recognised the sovereign status of Panama and wished to deal with the Panamanian Defense Force accordingly. His in-depth knowledge and experience in Panama led him to aim to create 'fissures' in the regime to bring a Panamanian solution to the problem of Noriega.[15] This was not popular in Washington. As Bob Woodward made clear, Woerner was seen as a 'wimp' and was pushed hard by the Chairman of the JCS, Admiral Crowe, to be more aggressive.[16] The tension came to a head with General Woerner's comment to a public meeting in Panama that there was a policy vacuum in Washington towards the region because there still was no Assistant Secretary of State in charge of the Americas. This statement angered the White House and led to Woerner's removal from his post.[17] However, the administration waited until Crowe was out of the country before firing General Woerner. As Secretary of Defense Dick Cheney explained 'it was purely a political decision'.[18] Cheney then blamed the White House, especially National Security Adviser Brent Scowcroft.[19] Admiral Crowe was concerned that the administration was trying to change policy but found it easier to blame a general and slide round him as the Chairman of the JCS.[20] The irony was that the Army did not have anyone to replace Woerner, and he had recently been asked to extend his tour there. Thus a general due to retire was asked to take over; the DePuy protégé, General Max Thurman, known affectionately as 'Mad Max'. This move altered the handling of the crisis in Panama and the assumptions behind the invasion, bringing them in line with the nature of Washington's internal priorities.

General Woerner's staff recognised that the Army core was happy to replace Woerner with Thurman (the former Army Vice Chief of Staff), because he was not a 'Washington pro' and Thurman was, even though Thurman did not have any local knowledge and did not speak Spanish.[21] Dick Cheney had recognised that

General Woerner was an expert on Panama, but felt that he had gone native.[22] In fact Thurman

> made no secret of his belief that Woerner and many Spanish-speaking officers on his staff suffered from 'clientitis,' or too much knowledge, and therefore sympathy, with the place and its personalities. Thurman seemed to regard his predecessor's expertise as a contributing factor to the crisis.[23]

Thurman's distrust of Woerner's staff and his lack of personal knowledge would prove decisive, as an attempted coup took place against Noriega on 3 October, the first Tuesday after he took office.[24] Thurman failed to support it because he distrusted the advice proffered by Woerner's staff. This was crucial as the removal of Noriega was the primary concern of the Bush administration.[25] The 3 October coup happened at an awkward time for the US policy machine, as Bush had severed diplomatic relations on 1 September; Thurman only formally took office on 30 September; Powell was appointed CJCS on 1 October and the NSC's Senior Director for Latin American Affairs, former Ambassador Everett Briggs, resigned on 29 September over policy in Panama.[26] At no time was there a greater need for a culturally informed CINC, but the administration had sacked him and left the national security bureaucracy to handle the situation.[27] Planning for a military intervention was accelerated, as the failure of the coup generated the political consensus needed for direct US military action.[28]

General Woerner had started writing contingency plans for the invasion of Panama, but Thurman did his planning in an altered context. Both planned to use overwhelming force but interpreted it differently, as Woerner aimed to use the military build-up to force Noriega out and, if this failed, to approach senior Panamanian commanders to get them to push him out. Mass was to be used to protect the 50,000 US citizens in the country.[29] He also had planned a much greater concentration on the state of governance in Panama after the invasion, stating 'I determined that Civil Affairs and civic action were critical assets in the execution of my strategy.'[30] General Stiner, who was the operational commander under Thurman, had no interest in this aspect of the intervention at all.[31] His plan was exclusively military. Whilst Woerner called for controls on the use of firepower, especially near the wooded neighbourhood around the Comandancia, and looked to take over executive power for the transition period,[32] Thurman and Stiner focused on the main war aspects of Panama and did not, for example, anticipate the massive looting and destruction of downtown Panama that took place after the intervention.

Weinberger enacted

The use of force by the Bush administration fulfilled the key Weinberger criteria. The motives for the invasion were clear and the objectives for the invasion were obtainable, and there was no risk of a foreign power escalating the intervention. The giving of clear guidance, and the Secretary of Defense not meddling in the operation itself, was attributed to Dick Cheney's views on these very failings in the Grenada and Mayagüez incidents.[33] It was also his first 'war' as Secretary of Defense.

The problem of public support was countered, as it had been in Grenada, by the intervention being undertaken quickly without a clear indication of popular or Congressional support (which was in recess). Dick Cheney deliberately delayed the press pool, which had been set up after Grenada.[34] The success of the intervention, along with the swift withdrawal of troops, meant that it proved extremely popular in the United States, with 'public opinion polls show[ing] that about 90 percent of Americans . . . approved of it'.[35] Fears that the media would weaken support were somewhat justified, as the coverage given to Noriega's flight to the Papal Nunciature and General Thurman's antics outside to try and frighten him out showed.[36] The coverage was further tarnished by reports of 4,000 Panamanians being killed and that two of the 23 US troops which had been killed had died from 'friendly fire'.[37]

The political objectives of overwhelming the Panamanian state to remove Noriega, to secure the canal and to protect US servicemen, matched the Army's capability, and it achieved them. A key factor for the success of the intervention was the management of it. 'Operation Just Cause', as it was called, provided the first field test of the new command structure of the Armed Forces and 'showed improved readiness, training and co-operation'.[38] The ground commander, General Stiner, was given clear mission command to run the operation by General Thurman, the CINC. The success of the intervention was due to force being used decisively, quickly and in overwhelming quantities; there was no gradual build up of force which then attritionally drove through the country. The Americans assembled a force of 26,000 troops, and faced the ill-equipped Panamanian Defense Force (PDF), who were unable to fight a prolonged war against such odds, leaving it with little chance of survival after the capture of Noriega.[39] The massed US force was able to achieve 'simultaneity and tempo in a spectacular way. Overwhelming force secured a quick victory at minimum cost.'[40] The intervention was not an example of AirLand Battle doctrine in practice, but showed the clear grasp of the manoeuvrist thinking which lay behind it. It hit 27 targets simultaneously in Panama. By militarily decapitating Noriega's grasp on power and rendering him powerless, by using overwhelming force, fighting at night and catching the Panamanian Defense Force in its barracks, it defeated rather than destroyed it. The centre of gravity had been identified and the pitched battles were not fought at each set of barracks.[41] The use of overwhelming force, as Powell continually advocated, matched the clear political objectives.[42] Mass and manoeuvre were combined to create an effective application of military force, rather than simply swamping the enemy and defeating it through attrition and escalating costs.

The coherence of the political–military co-ordination revolved round the operational focus of the intervention, where the national command provided clear objectives and soldiers planned the mission.[43] The success of Panama was a reinforcement of the model of national strategic guidance working synergistically to provide operational and achievable military objectives. As one US Army officer explained soon afterwards:

> Viewed from the operational perspective the invasion of Panama reflects some of the recent changes the United States has made in its methods of controlling military power. . . . In this invasion the strategic objective given to the operational military commander was about as clear, precise, and militarily achievable as a strategic objective can be. . . . This short decisive war consisted of one campaign which had only one battle and attained one specific military strategic objective, which was also the desired political objective. . . . In Panama the United States used sufficient force to resolve the issue quickly and favorably before public support waned. Public support hinges on success in war.[44]

The fact that some commentators saw the American intervention acting like 'an overly-militarised federal posse' did not get round the idea that it also showed that there was a consistency and effectiveness to the revised intervention strategy.[45] The military means were fulfilling the policy ends, and so the intervention was a 'coherent' strategy of the application of military force, using mass as a means to victory rather than for simple attrition or avoidance of failure.

Military limitations

Panama, however, showed the weaknesses as well as the strengths of the rebuilt Army. As one young Lieutenant pointed out, the training he had undergone had brought about the unit cohesion and effectiveness in Panama.[46] However, he and his men had five roles between the beginning and end of the intervention, each with a new set of Rules of Engagement, and the lack of 'cross-training' for roles other than closing and killing the enemy was missing. There was a need for specific guides and 'plenty of good training to go with it'.[47]

This point was borne out by a Lieutenant Colonel who saw Panama exposing the lack of appropriate doctrine in the US Army:

> Planners were guided by capstone Army doctrine relying on overwhelming speed and firepower. Although the soldiers showed great restraint in the use of force, many Panamanian civilians died needlessly because of such excessive application of force. If there had been proper doctrine to guide these soldiers then these casualties might have been reduced.[48]

Still not in place were the key criticisms of the 'Army concept' applied to the Vietnam War by Andrew Krepinevich, concerning the counter-productive effects of firepower on the psychology of the population. The political responsibility still lay at the national level, rather than within the domain of the Army at the operational or tactical level.

The focus on the exclusively military problem of the Panamanian Defense Force meant that there was little account taken of the aftermath of the war, but this characterised the whole policy. The intervention carried out short-term political objectives, rather than fulfilling long-term political aims, and critics have highlighted a weighty list of failings, among them the fact that civilians were kept out of the planning process, the reconstruction plans were disconnected, there was an unclear chain of command for the rebuilding, and a basic lack of clarity concerning what Panama would be like in the immediate, medium and long term.[49] The lack of conception of the long-term role and purpose of the military intervention in Panama was a clear failing, and the lack of provision for basic policing showed the gaps in the political–military planning.

The scale of the intervening force in Panama, and the costs in blood and treasure of failing to capture Noriega, raised a key political question of whether so much destructiveness for the arrest of one man was worth it.[50] However, the limited understanding of strategy outlined as 'the applying of military means to fulfil the ends of policy', would see the Panamanian intervention as a successful and coherent application of military force, made possible by the acceptance by the different branches of the polity of the Army's thinking as the way to intervene.

Colin Powell's assessment of the Panama intervention made clear how important an episode it was for the military, and for his term as Chairman of the Joint Chiefs of Staff.

> The lessons I absorbed from Panama confirmed all my convictions over the preceding twenty years, since the days of doubt over Vietnam. Have a clear political objective and stick to it. Use all the force necessary, and do not apologise for going big if that is what it takes. Decisive force ends wars quickly and in the long run saves lives. Whatever threats we faced in the future, I intended to make these rules the bedrock of my military counsel.[51]

The fact that this military thinking had gained general acceptance allowed the revised intervention strategy to develop; the executive used the Army in the way that it thought that it should be used. It was a synergy of political aims and military means controlled by setting militarily achievable objectives. As F.G. Hoffman says:

> the Pentagon's preferred paradigm was tested in Panama and found satisfactory by the military. [It] walked away feeling good about its planning and execution in this battle laboratory. On the whole, the operation was a huge tactical success and achieved its major operational objectives. Yet the professed claims of clear objectives, use of overwhelming force, and oversimplified civilian–military policy making reflects the limitations of relying upon force to achieve lasting political outcomes.[52]

The sacking of the less than bullish Woerner was to affect other commanders later when dealing with Dick Cheney,[53] and was a great fillip to the main war planners. The Army had the potential to develop broader concepts as the Cold War ended, as it moved emphasis from heavy to light divisions. But Panama set this back. For example, immediately after the Panama intervention the US military clarified that it no longer directed the political side of the post-war reconstruction process, reinforcing the separatist model of its role. Thus in Haiti in 1993 the Army only provided security rather than reconstruction, going for limited and attainable aims.[54] The critical civil–military tasks that did come within the Army's domain at the tactical level were delegated to the new Special Operations Command, and General Stiner became its CINC. He saw it as having a key role in the achievement of decisive victory in Panama, but analysts have questioned this.[55] The Panama intervention helped keep tactical political issues out of the Army's ken and reinforced the emphasis on 'going in big' rather than rapid and selective operations.[56] This was in line with the strategic thinking on Low-Intensity Conflict which had developed after the establishment of AirLand Battle doctrine, seeing the military providing an exclusively main-force military tool only as part of a broader national policy.

Panama was, therefore, a combination of the Pentagon's traditional emphasis on mass and the evolving use of manoeuvre, and its success was vitally important for lessons of the application of force, especially as the shadow of Vietnam still hung over the operation. US intervention was still only possible in the most restricted conditions, against opponents who had no serious prospects of winning or retaliating in kind. At a time when the president was looking to make budgetary cutbacks and was soon to announce a commission to examine base closures for the draw-down after the Cold War,[57] there was more than a little irony in analysts saying that the US needed to become more manoeuvrist because 'In the future even the US will be unable to rely on mass to overwhelm the opposition in all but special circumstances'.[58] The approach employed in Panama was to be repeated on a much larger scale two years later; Panama had proved the Army was now a force capable of carrying out the will of the commander in chief: 'Just Cause proved it: Desert Shield and Desert Storm would further validate it.'[59] For the Army, the Panamanian operation showed that its 'post-Vietnam doldrums were over' and that it was a highly trained, superbly equipped army of 'disciplined and dedicated professionals who knew their business – the business of war'.[60] It was a cathartic operation.

The Gulf War

On 2 August 1990 Iraq invaded Kuwait.[61] The US-led UN coalition raised against this incursion of sovereign territory was unable to remove Iraq from the conquered territory through diplomatic means and so began, on 16 January 1991, an air campaign as the first stage in the effort to convince Hussein to withdraw.[62] His failure to do so led to the ground offensive beginning on 24 February to drive out the invading forces. This was done with such effectiveness that the ceasefire was called four days later. The speed and manner of the defeat undermined Hussein's ability to test US staying power, a key aspect of his policy.[63] The coalition inflicted a decisive military defeat on the Iraqis.

For Americans, the victory was a restoration of national pride after Vietnam. As President George Bush announced afterwards, 'It's a proud day for America. And, by God, we've kicked the Vietnam syndrome once and for all.'[64] In fact, the war strengthened it because the result reinforced the post-Vietnam beliefs.[65] The Gulf War was the culmination of the process of rebuilding the strategic culture after the trauma of the Vietnam War, and was a test of the professional developments that had gone on within the Army. The role that the Army was given, its own performance and the huge public support it received made it a deeply cathartic experience. The war and its management were in accord with the Army's thinking and showed how influential it had become. The Gulf War vindicated the lessons the Army had learnt from the Vietnam War.[66]

With the success of the campaign the shadow of Vietnam was lifted as the lessons of the proper management of strategy and of a professional force geared to war-fighting had been learnt. However, as Freedman and Karsh say, the Vietnam analogy to the Gulf War, in terms of political cause, geographic conditions, historical context and military circumstance, is misleading.[67] The Gulf War played to America's military strengths to a remarkable degree, even to the extent of using the Mojave desert as their primary training ground for tank warfare. Many critics have pointed out there were many unique political and military features of the Gulf War, which makes it a poor test of future types of warfare.[68] For example, the lead-in time alone was significant as this greatly increased readiness because, in strategy, time is capability in the same way that in economics 'time is money'.[69] A different scenario would have been more testing, and leading critics such as Jeffrey Record see it as a 'hollow victory'.[70] This is not to degrade the achievement in the Gulf, only to point out that a different type of war, as Vietnam was, would have posed a different set of tests of the US's strategic thinking and military capabilities than Saddam Hussein and the first Gulf War did. A conventional desert war with a long lead-in time may confirm the rebuilding of the Army that took place, but the focus of this analysis will turn to the strategic conclusions drawn from it and their bearing on the Vietnam experience.

The Gulf War certainly showed the US's 'unsurpassed ability to move and supply major military forces to almost any shore'.[71] However, for the Army the war was a vindication of far more than the traditional US strengths in logistics and technology. In the opening chapter of the US Army's official account of the first Gulf War the author, Robert Scales, makes an illuminating statement concerning the importance of the war to the Army after Vietnam. He refers to

> the transformation of the American Army from disillusionment and anguish in Vietnam to confidence and certain victory in Desert Storm. Only 100 ground combat hours were necessary for the Army to reestablish itself convincingly as a successful land combat force. During that brief period, mechanized forces moved more combat power faster and further

> than any similar force in history. They averaged 95 kilometers per day, more than twice as many as the Wehrmacht's best blitzkrieg effort. Helicopter-borne forces conducted history's greatest aerial envelopment by placing the combat elements of an entire division 160 miles deep behind enemy lines. As part of the Coalition, the American Army decisively defeated the fourth largest field army in the world. It did so at the lowest cost in human life ever recorded for a conflict of such magnitude.[72]

As Roger Spiller notes, Scales' whole account is seen as a 'proof of the thesis . . . that the Gulf War was the validating event for virtually all Army's interwar efforts to rebuild itself'.[73] The Army had rebuilt itself from the devastation of the Vietnam War, so the officers who took the Iraqi surrender

> had stayed the course after Vietnam, vowing to restore honor and competence to the American profession of arms and, most important, to renew the bond between the Republic and its soldiery. This – Safwan, March 3, 1991 – was their vindication. . . . the war had lasted not six weeks, but twenty years.[74]

The war also confirmed the doctrinal reforms, training and procurement policies. So, for example, when questioned as to whether the Army would have lost fewer lives or taken less risk and still accomplished Desert Storm if it had used Active Defense not AirLand Battle doctrine,[75] the answer was clear.

> By 1991, the United States, but not its allies, had wholeheartedly accepted AirLand battle. That proved a most fortunate decision; much of the low cost of the ground phase of the war can be attributed to the sheer speed and depth of the U.S. advance. That speed was attained because the U.S. Army had equipped itself specifically to execute an AirLand offensive.[76]

AirLand Battle doctrine with its 'combined and coordinated assault, maneuver, deception, deep strike' was practised in the Gulf on a grand scale.[77] Thus TRADOC's historian wrote, 'TRADOC was able to witness the fruits of twenty years of concept, doctrine, and training development.'[78] Due to the realistic training, Army units entered the war battle-wise and hardened. Not only that, but as the creator of AirLand Battle observed, the Gulf War showed that for the first time the US Army had a coherent concept of modern battle at both tactical and operational levels.[79] The Army had overcome the failures in Vietnam and had proven itself a professional warfighting force. It was a vindication of its development and showed that AirLand Battle was not simply an academic exercise but attended to the problems of morale, discipline and professionalism; namely, it was an organizational and procurement strategy.[80] The first Gulf War was also a vindication of its strategic thinking, as victory was achieved by the fulfilment of its demands, mediated through the organisation created by the Goldwater–Nichols reforms.

Weinberger enacted

In the months leading up to hostilities, US military leaders had gone on record as to what they saw as the lessons of Vietnam and how the experience there had shaped their understanding of how to prosecute war.[81] In the event the use of military force in the first Gulf War was the closest the US came to fulfilling all six principles outlined in Weinberger's speech.[82] President Bush had internalised the strategic lessons from Vietnam; as he says in his memoirs,

> Colin Powell . . . sought to ensure that there were sufficient troops for whatever option I wanted, and then freedom of action to do the job once the political decision had been made. I was determined that our military would have both. I did not want to repeat the problems of the Vietnam War . . . where the political leadership meddled with military operations. I would avoid micromanaging the military.[83]

The use of clear objectives, the necessary forces to win and no micro-management of the war therefore governed the campaign.[84] Finally, the success of AirLand Battle doctrine in providing a conceptual basis for a coherent strategic application of force reinforced the Weinberger model for the US.

First, President Bush clearly outlined the nature of the objectives of the use of force: 'Saddam Hussein's forces will leave Kuwait. The legitimate government of Kuwait will be restored to its rightful place, and Kuwait will once again be free. Iraq will eventually comply with all relevant United Nations resolutions.'[85] With a clear objective established early, President Bush then authorised the deployment of sufficient forces to allow a decisive victory, crucially doubling the forces in theatre to defend Saudi Arabia and moving from a one corps to two corps attack.[86] It was a clear rejection of the incremental approach of the Vietnam era, and the shift allowed planners to avoid a frontal assault and to undertake an enormous flanking manoeuvre.[87] The management of the strategy was as envisaged by the Goldwater–Nichols reforms, with the force requirements being set by the CINC, General Schwarzkopf, mediated through the Chairman of the Joint Chiefs of Staff, General Powell, to Secretary of Defense Dick Cheney. Victory in the Gulf War was a proof of the efficacy of the reforms and 'at the highest level the goals of the DOD Reorganization Act were largely achieved'.[88] Finally, President Bush undertook to have clear public support for the use of force.

President Bush pulled the strategic 'trinity' together by undertaking to generate public support prior to the use of force and to provide careful management of it during hostilities. Having doubled the forces in the Gulf, Bush went to Congress and the UN for approval of the use of force, knowing that he had to convince the public that he could prosecute the war effectively and bring it to a decisive conclusion. As the President reported, one senator told him:

> 'Mr. President, do what you have to do. If it is quick and successful everyone can take the credit. If it is drawn out, then be prepared for some

> in Congress to file impeachment papers against you.' . . . and he's 100% correct.[89]

Bush had studied Johnson's handling of Congress.[90] The Gulf War was not 'slunk in on cat's feet'.[91] Bush received substantial support from the House and a narrow backing from the Senate (52 to 47) four days before hostilities began, though to achieve this he had to broaden the war aims to include stopping Saddam developing nuclear weapons – rather ironic in the light of his son's endeavours.[92]

The media policy carried out during the first Gulf War was based on the feeling that 'a prolonged war on television could become impossible, unsupportable at home'.[93] The first Gulf War showed the development of a policy that learned to use the media as part of the overall campaign,[94] and built on the lessons from the Panamanian invasion. The need to use the media was generated by the nature of the war, as there was great sensitivity on both sides to its domestic and international political context, which for Bush meant minimising casualties and careful leadership of the alliance.[95] The use and control of media coverage to enhance public support was an immense success. As one commentator observed immediately after the war,

> One still marvels at the news coverage of the war, in that its scope, depth, and length were overwhelming. . . . The result was a packaged, clean war, where smart weapons surgically destroyed bridges, and military equipment and installations. We were overawed with these precision weapons, and the whole thing appeared so clean and precise one could forget that people were dying. . . . the public's sense of euphoria was maintained.[96]

In the aftermath of the war analysts saw that the Vietnam War had become an anachronistic model of military/media relations, as the nature of both elements of the relationship were now very different. Changes in the media's satellite technology, combined with the extended battlefield and lethality of AirLand Battle concepts, raise new challenges for the media in the future.[97] Media coverage was entering a post-Gulf rather than post-Vietnam age, leading to concerns that the 'CNN effect' was driving foreign policy, though this was disputed.[98] The change in media relationship was nowhere more clearly shown than during the air campaign against Serbia in 1999, where the media was integral to the campaign[99] and 'psyops' troops were on 'work experience' at CNN.[100] The media were no longer a distraction to the prosecution of war but a fundamental aspect of it.

The success of the Gulf War showed that the Vietnam syndrome was essentially about American defeat, and casualties were important mainly as an index of failure.[101] The establishment of clear achievable objects prior to war, and fulfilling them, classified the war as a success; as President Bush announced at its conclusion, 'Kuwait is liberated. Iraq's army is defeated. Our military objectives are met. Kuwait is once more in the hands of Kuwaitis, in control of their own destiny.'[102]

However, the definition of success was criticised because Saddam Hussein was left in power and the rhetoric used prior to the war seemed unfulfilled. As Brian Bond argues, it is victory rather than decisiveness that is key.[103] The decisiveness of the Weinberger doctrine, based on Army thinking, was able to provide the nation with a coherent approach to strategy, but concentrated upon its military nature, rather than its political one. The military's dominance of the whole termination period shows how far the Bush administration gave the military autonomy. General Schwarzkopf was given great leeway, to such an extent that, as Eliot Cohen said, a 'Roosevelt or Churchill would not have . . . allowed a Schwarzkopf to negotiate an armistice without guidance on the peace terms to be exacted at the end'.[104] In other words, the dialectic of civil–military relations was resolved by political deference to the military, in the manner of the Army's very own lessons. Cohen is correctly and articulately critical of this approach to strategy.[105] It is ironic that General Schwarzkopf himself later criticised the formula of victory advocated. On television one month after the war he raised questions about the conclusion of the war, but backed away from this in his memoirs.[106] As Freedman and Karsh note, whilst the war was terminated on military advice and agreed because of the images of destruction on the 'highway of death', ultimately it was due to the fact that the Iraqis ran for it that the war stopped so quickly.[107] The strategic management lessons of clear objectives and public support learnt from the Vietnam War were enacted by the administration, but ultimately it was the perception of success that was crucial. However, the strategy and success in the first Gulf War was a vindication of the Army and its Clausewitzian understanding of itself. Thomas Dubois observed that US policy and strategy in the Persian Gulf crisis 'should certainly earn the approval of Weinberger and Clausewitz alike'.[108]

Synergy of nation's power

For analysts such as Shimon Naveh the war showed the systemic change in the nation's approach to warfare. As he says, the Gulf conflict

> witnessed a vigorous encounter between two military cultures: the first based its professional ethos and strategic credo on a system logic, which exemplified the complexities of the post-modern reality; the second derived its rationale from the dynamics of the industrial era. It was a confrontation between a military system which had undergone a conceptual transformation accomplished through the application of the innovative paradigm of operational manoeuvre, and a system locked in the archaic conventions of the nineteenth-century . . . paradigm.[109]

The strategic synergy achieved by the US was seen as being provided by the Army's approach to jointery, and 'in an age of unprecedented technological advances, land combat is now, more than ever, the strategic core of joint war fighting'.[110] This perception was based on a reading of the war where

> The presence of soldiers on the ground during Desert Shield and the decisive joint air and ground operations that ultimately ejected Saddam from Kuwait during Desert Storm again demonstrated that determined enemies can only be defeated with certainty by decisive ground action. Nevertheless, the success of any manuever depends on the ability of land, sea, and air forces to make conditions favorable for the ground soldier as possible. The more an enemy is battered, blinded, and deceived, the more surely a groundforce can end the conflict at the lowest possible cost. The Gulf War again demonstrated that wars can be ended decisively by occupying our enemy's territory.[111]

Jointery had been a key lesson of the Vietnam War, and the Army's doctrinal emphasis on the operational level gave it substance during the 1980s. However, it 'worked' to the extent that it was in the organisation's interest and fitted their doctrine. Goldwater–Nichols had been opposed by all the services after all, and had taken five years to bring to pass.[112]

As noted, the 1980s saw the start of genuine joint thinking with the Army's reforms and the relationship with the Air Force at the tactical level. However, one can see how much they were based on the Air Force's acceptance of the Army's doctrine and the role given them by it. AirLand Battle doctrine had thus been the tool of jointery and the first Gulf War brought a shift in the relationship between air and land power in the nation's strategic culture – they separated again.

AirLand Battle doctrine was the assertion of the primacy of land power over air power.[113] However, the static rather than offensively mobile nature of Iraqi forces during the first Gulf War meant that the application of firepower was not 'executed completely in the spirit or letter of AirLand Battle',[114] and this highlighted the limitations of jointery that AirLand Battle doctrine provided. In it's reading of the first Gulf War the Army underestimated the role of air power; for example, seeing that ground casualties were kept low because the Americans owned the night.[115] This ignored the weeks of air assaults prior to the use of ground forces. The Army understanding of jointery built on the operational-level focus was proven to be too limited in its understanding of the application of air power.

The provision of a tactical and operational role for air power provided by AirLand Battle doctrine meant that there was no provision for an independent air campaign plan, which was to be needed in the first Gulf War.[116] This was a key issue during the war, because the tasking of the air campaign split between targeting the Iraqi ground forces prior to the ground attack by the coalition, or whether 'strategic' targets in Iraq should be hit.[117] Lt General Charles Horner was the CENTCOM (Central Command) Air Commander during the Gulf War under General Schwarzkopf, and he stressed 'the integration of air with ground forces', though the initial plan owed more to the strategic conventional bombing ideas of Colonel John A. Warden.[118] For example, during the first two weeks of the war, of the 1,185 targets nominated by the Army, only 137 were actually hit.[119] The reforms in the management of the forces meant that the conceptual difficulty could be addressed through the 'joint' chain of command and the central control of air assets, but with the conclusion of the war air power was able to reassert its dominance over land power.

The Gulf War revitalised air power's strategic emphasis and reduced the role of foot soldiers,[120] though the author of the Gulf War Airpower survey urged caution about over-optimism of air power's achievement. Eliot Cohen saw that airpower was a commanding and innovative but seductive asset, because it offered 'gratification without commitment'. However, as he goes on to point out, even though signposts existed before the war that a revolution in air power is to occur, someone would still have to make it happen'.[121] As the architect of the Gulf air campaign advocated, air power and precision technology had moved beyond the previous ideas of conflict being action, reaction and uncertainty, and given birth to 'parallel warfare'.[122] Airpower analysts saw that 'Airpower proved it could substitute for land power . . . even if it could not hold ground it could deny it to hostile ground forces.'[123] By the mid-1990s the Air Force was advocating that it could fight 'deep' even before the ground forces were in place, thus highlighting what AirLand Battle doctrine had not resolved – namely, authority of the joint forces air component commander over corps commanders, campaign priorities and what to do when the battle plan might not follow synchronised joint force employment.[124]

Before the Army's post-Gulf developments began to be implemented, the legacy of the professional rebuilding during the 1970s and 1980s and its strategic and operational thinking was still in place. This was to be very significant as the victory in the Gulf and the renewed confidence it brought turned the US thinking on the utility of war upside down. The convergence of national interest, international morality, military prowess and low casualties all fed popular expectations about the shape of the post-Cold War world.[125] President Bush captured this mood when he said, 'We must build on the successes of Desert Storm to give new shape and momentum to this new world order, to use force wisely and extend the hand of compassion whenever we can.'[126] The military success in the Gulf meant that the post-Cold War period was, in Charles Krauthammer's words, America's unipolar moment with the Gulf War marking the beginning of an era of 'Pax Americana'.[127] The Bush and the early Clinton administrations used the rhetoric of American exceptionalism to articulate America's role.[128] The optimism of the nation was based on the military victory managed by a strategy developed after the Vietnam War. The nature and legacy of that approach, and its basis in the Army's identity and strategic understanding, was soon apparent.

A new national approach

The Army's view of the Gulf War, embodying its self-identity and understanding of its role and utility, was formally adopted as the national military strategy in the *1992 National Military Strategy* (NMS).[129] It gave substance to the military's developments and outlined the strategic direction of the armed forces, providing a rationale and capability for 'the remainder of the 1990s'.[130] The document's conclusion states that among the elements that have 'really changed' in the 1992 strategy is the principle of 'Decisive Force'.[131] Although the term also refers to theatre-level operations,[132] 'Decisive Force' is one of the essential elements of the national military strategy, and is defined as: 'the ability to rapidly assemble the forces needed to win – the concept of applying decisive force to overwhelm our adversaries and thereby terminate conflicts swiftly with a minimum loss of life.'[133]

When put so bluntly the only thing surprising about it as an American strategy is the claim that it was new or that it shows a real change in US strategic thinking. Arguably it can be read as a summary of 'the American Way of War' reaching back to the Second World War.[134] Samuel Huntington in 1985, for example, had advocated a rapid, offensive, decisive use of force, with overwhelming force, because it was appropriate to US history, its political and military institutions, and represented a shift back to traditional ways of thinking underpinned by principles of war.[135] For some critics, the novelty of Decisive Force was the change from a slow build-up and mobilisation to fast application of force, and was really a revival of the old military concern with absolutism and autonomy, plus new limited ends and brief public support.[136] However, if one returns to the Truman–MacArthur debate, one sees that the emphasis is not simply on the application of fast massed forces, but on establishing clear objectives and defining victory as the fulfilling of the political objectives rather than simply annihilating the enemy's fielded forces.[137]

General MacArthur provided a dichotomous model of civil–military relations, with the politicians handing over responsibility to the military to prosecute the war to victory whatever the political cost. Truman correctly rejected this. The Vietnam War was perceived as the opposite of this, where the executive had taken responsibility for much of the detail of the military campaign. Decisive Force, and the AirLand Battle thinking behind it, remodelled the political–military relationship, placing clear strategic responsibility on the executive to provide the political aims and also, crucially, the objectives which could be carried out at the military operational level. The operational and tactical level were the responsibility of the military but, rather than having a 'tacticalisation of strategy', Decisive Force was an 'operationalisation' of strategy, with the operational-level objectives set by the executive and the tactics meeting those needs. Overwhelming force was needed to fulfil these clear objectives, rather than simply to wear down the opposition through the accumulation of tactical victories, as had happened in the past. The emphasis on 'objective setting' was the real novelty.

General Powell had consistently tied together the need for clear objectives and the need to amass an overwhelming force – the Powell doctrine. He saw it as vital that the objectives for the use of force were clear.

> Is the political objective we seek to achieve important, clearly defined and understood? Have all other nonviolent policy means failed? Will military force achieve the objective? At what cost? Have the gains and risks been analyzed? How might the situation that we seek to alter, once it is altered by force, develop further and what might be the consequences?[138]

Not only must one have a clear objective, but this must be combined with using all the force necessary to end the war quickly and to save lives.[139] The political objectives had to be militarily achievable, and what was achievable was defined by how the Army understood itself as a professional force. As Kenneth Campbell laid out clearly

> The military's reluctance to use force in the post-Cold War era is the culmination of an organisational process that began with the military's near-death experience in Vietnam, triggered the imperative of organization preservation, and provoked a process of learning and dramatic change. . . . There have been no new Vietnams.[140]

The criteria set the terms of the intervention debate in the early 1990s. The pervasiveness of the criteria is shown by the fact that the Bush administration's Andrew Natsios (the official responsible for man-made and natural disasters outside the US, 1991–93) supported the Powell doctrine and saw a need for defined and achievable missions.[141] The Army's main criterion was therefore establishing the terms of the debate, a criterion established upon its understanding of its identity. The influence went far beyond the internalisation of the principles of the Weinberger doctrine by Bush and his administration,[142] and had become the formal military policy of the nation. The acceptance was beyond the simple criteria but shaped how the whole issue was examined. For example, James McDonough noted that, 'Nowhere in former Secretary of Defense Caspar Weinberger's six principles does it read that the U.S. military must agree to its commitment.'[143] What McDonough fails to see is that the Weinberger doctrine does not need to require explicit military agreement as the nature of the six criteria are already acceptable to the military and shape the debate concerning the use of military force in its terms; the military's concerns are built into Weinberger's doctrine.

Limits of the approach

The self-referential nature of the thinking advocated in the *National Military Strategy* was effective as long as the professional preparation was for roles that the executive requested. The difficulty would come with missions that did not match the Army's identity, and these would expose the nature of the understanding of the relationship between the political aim and military means of strategy. Martin van Creveld's book, ironically published in 1991, *The Transformation of War*, is clear on the point that 'Clausewitzian trinitarian' war is only one of many types of war, particularly the types of war which affect US interests. These are the types of wars the government needed to deal with but the Army disliked.

> Trinitarian war is not war with a capital W but merely one of the many forms that war has assumed. . . . Based on the idea of the state and on the

> distinction between government, army, and people, trinitarian war was unknown to most societies during most of history. . . . The news that present-day armed violence does not distinguish between governments, armies, and peoples will scarcely surprise the inhabitants of Ethiopia. the Spanish Sahara, or . . . those of Northern Ireland . . . the *locus classicus* of nontrinitarian war, have as their populations approximately four fifths of all people living on this planet. If anybody should be startled at all it [should be] . . . the members of the defense establishments who for decades on end have prepared for the wrong kind of war.[144]

A vocal critic of the US Army, Ralph Peters (a former US Army officer himself) makes the same point.[145] Furthermore, as Mary Kaldor explained, these 'new' wars reflect a social revolution in military affairs, as the strategies used by the parties draw on and develop the experiences of guerrilla and counter-insurgency wars, creating a requirement for peacekeepers to be 'a mixture of soldiers and policemen' to address the mix of war, crime and human rights violations that make up these types of wars.[146] As van Creveld says 'Given that one's understanding of the nature of war necessarily underlies the way it is conducted, the problem is anything but academic.'[147] This is particularly the case for the US as it faced a plethora of cases of this nature in Africa, southern Europe and the Caribbean. The US Army had extensive experience of complex political–military warfare in Vietnam, so it and the national strategy should, potentially, have been well prepared for conflicts of this nature. However, the Army has avoided the broader cultural aspects of war, even though it has been advocated since the 1980s as fourth generation warfare.[148]

Basically, the strategic lessons drawn from the Vietnam War and embodied in the Weinberger doctrine, and expressed in the *National Military Strategy*, do not fit these situations.[149] First, the rationale underpinning the Clausewitzian approach, national interest, does not match so-called 'second tier' conflicts, because they are not justified in those terms.[150] Weinberger therefore gives insufficient policy guidance as how to approach these conflicts. This is particularly important as liberal interventionism is faced by a potential contradiction: the principle committing states to military intervention also forbids the ruthlessness necessary for it to succeed.[151] Second, the quick, decisive military interventions advocated do not fit the requirements of complex emergencies. For example, in challenging ethnic cleansing there is a need for an armed commitment to be maintained until trust is built and elections held, or states will be carved into smaller ethnically pure pieces, thereby sanctifying the ethnic cleansing.[152]

It would be wrong to make a bald comparison with the war in Vietnam, but the situation in Somalia had important characteristics that the Army could have used their experience in Asia to help them address. The intervention into Somalia was unlike Vietnam in that there were no ostensible national interests at stake, there was no unified population, or single commander; rather, it was a power vacuum. But the Army showed the weakness of a purely 'military solution' by ignoring any idea of nation-building, and avoiding the fact that the sheer size of the force altered the situation and committed the US.[153] Army critics such as Krepinevich had stated that lessons needed to be learnt to integrate pacification within the Army's application of force, but this was still not in place, highlighting that the 'lessons' that were drawn were of a particular rather than self-evident nature. The Somalia intervention shows the nature of the lessons drawn from the Vietnam War and how the Weinberger doctrine was based upon the operational doctrine of the Army and the nature of the Army's identity and civil–military relations. Somalia exposed the nature of the strategic learning that the US undertook after the Vietnam War.

The coherence of the national strategy was built upon the operational–level focus of the Army's thinking but this faced difficulties in the new environment. The term 'complex emergency' is utilised to capture the new environment of post-Gulf tasks, addressing humanitarian disasters marked by intra-communal violence and exacerbated by the collapse of government and state security. As John Mackinlay says, success in this context is both a conceptual and operational problem.[154] The operational-level thinking was unable to address the requirements of 'complex emergencies' after the first Gulf War. The US Army, by understanding Low-Intensity Conflict as a problem at the national strategic rather than tactical level, had considerable difficulty coming to grips with operational and tactical aspects endemic to unconventional war (or 'ragged wars'[155]). As one journalist covering the Haiti intervention wrote, 'operations other than war' were 'an empty space in an army's traditional reality, where there are no friends and no enemies, no front or rear, no victories and, likewise, no defeats and no true endings'.[156] This was the type of difficulty faced in Vietnam, and Somalia proved the limitations of the Army's strategic lessons from Vietnam.

Somalia

The American intervention in Somalia broke new ground for the UN and the US. Rather than being the revitalisation of a pre-existing Cold War-era approach it was a new type, a 'second generation', of peacekeeping.[157] The UNOSOM II (United Nations Operations in Somalia) mission was the high-water mark of the UN's attempt at collective humanitarian enforcement and rehabilitation, matched by the Clinton administration's optimism about 'assertive multilateralism'.[158] The mission to Somalia was very important in assessing US learning because force was deployed into an ongoing conflict, rather than into post-conflict situations as happened later in Haiti and Bosnia.

The first Gulf War saw the return of the 'can-do' spirit and confidence within the Army, and the Pentagon accepted the mission on the understanding that the Department of State and the UN kept out of the way.[159] The US handling of the mission highlighted two of the key limitations of the doctrinal thinking, namely, the operational understanding of strategy and the applicability of AirLand Battle doctrine tenets to the conflicts the Army had to face after the first Gulf War. As the US would find, seeing the military as part of a broader national strategy, and understanding the co-ordination of political and military matters as an issue at the national level rather than also at the tactical and operational level, would be undercut by the non-cooperative and aggressive nature of the operations on the ground.

The deployment was conceived of as a military mission to enable the delivery of humanitarian aid, and the Weinberger doctrine was in place in the early stages of the mission.[160] As the US CINC later wrote, 'Great care was taken to develop an approved, well-defined mission with attainable, measurable objectives prior to the operation commencing.'[161] The US provided 28,000 troops of a 30,000-strong UNITAF (United Task Force) under the rubric of 'Operation Restore Hope'. The mission was deemed clear and successful as it: secured food distribution; was limited in geographical scope, to be completed near the date of the inauguration; and it relied on sheer numbers, technical superiority and aggressive patrolling for authority.

The Army kept to explicitly military tasks according to the Weinberger doctrine. It kept out of politico-military roles and did not protect non-governmental organisations (NGOs) or get involved in plans such as the Australian military were carrying out with civil-affairs work, building a relationship with the community and rebuilding the police and justice system. These activities were seen as mission creep.[162] Mission creep is when 'new or shifting political guidance requires military operations different from what the intervening force initially planned'. This is not the same as 'mission swing' where 'the mission changes in response to a quick deterioration or improvement of the operational environment that occurs irrespective of the intervening force's presence or efforts'.[163] This conceptualisation, fitting neatly the primacy of national political objective setting, says little of operational environments that develop and differ from what was initially planned due to the very presence of the intervening force. This gap in conceptualisation became clear in Somalia.

The Weinberger doctrine proved insufficient for the task in Somalia. This was because 'it soon became clear that establishing a secure environment meant doing more than getting food to distribution centers, deterring gangs, and returning fire when fired upon'.[164] The mission moved away from having clear objectives as the situation on the ground changed, requiring the development of a second mission to assist the rebuilding of the Somali political system and government. This was necessary for the development of a 'secure' environment, and was a product of the previous policy, rather than simply Clinton administration overreach. James Woods, Deputy Assistant Secretary of Defense for African Affairs in both administrations (1986–94), makes a key point when he says that:

> Those who argue that the Somalia operation under guidance from the Bush team was sound and successful, whereas the operation under the Clinton team was unsound and disastrous, seem . . . unwilling to confront the main point: The policy stream was continuous and the complete seeds of disaster were put in place by decisions and guiding principles and assumptions hanging over from the beginning of the operation.[165]

The assumption that militarily achievable political objectives were able to provide sufficient national political guidance in such a complex situation as Somalia was fundamentally at fault. There was a requirement to provide a level of military security so that political objectives could be established as part of an integrated policy. This is a key issue and shows the limitations of relying on a top-down model of objective setting.

The US approach meant that the operation that had begun as a humanitarian one became highly militarised, with ten times more funds spent on the military than on humanitarian assistance.[166] The deteriorating situation led to a more aggressive stance and UNITAF managed to kill hundreds of Somalis in its first three months.[167] However, unlike the Canadian airborne, the US was not to be haunted by images of 'unprofessional' soldiering that included torture killings.[168] American professional discipline held.

The mismatch between political aims and the military means were to lead to a stunning failure. There is no doubt that 'The United Nations' unique multinational character and institutional constraints made it inherently dysfunctional for managing such complex military operations in dangerous environments.'[169] However, the US, and the US military in particular, had carved out an independent role making it and not the UN responsible. The problem came from the mismatch between the demands on the ground and the US's approach. As James Mayall noted, 'The problem with the American approach was that the strategic doctrine did not easily translate into tactical principles for containing the conflict on a day-to-day basis.'[170] This is most clearly seen during the period of UNOSOM II.

With the advent of UNOSOM II the US went to war. US forces were reduced to a Quick Reaction Force, based on Tenth Mountain Division, and were later joined by a Delta Force Team. These units were used by the US against Aideed and not to support the UNOSOM II mission. Jon Howe, a retired US admiral and former deputy national security adviser, was appointed the UN Secretary General's Special Representative. As Howe later observed, 'The presence of specially trained troops and the real possibility that Aideed would be captured provided new leverage.'[171] The independence of contingents of US troops meant that the UNOSOM II had three de facto chains of command: the UN, US Central Command, and US Special Operations Command.[172] The command arrangements were American, and the UN Secretary General, Boutros Boutros-Ghali, worried about the independent chain of US command.[173] UNOSOM II was also marked by a decreasing restraint on use of force. Following a crucial attack on Pakistani peacekeepers on 5 June, which saw the death of 24 Pakistani soldiers, Howe directed a very aggressive response causing large casualties. The turning point for UNOSOM II was on 12 July when

> helicopter gunships from the QRF [Quick Reaction Force] staged a no warning attack on a SNA [Somali National Army] headquarters where a meeting of top Aideed lieutenants was believed to be underway. Eleven TOW antitank missiles were launched at the so-called 'Abdi house,' first demolishing stairways, then the meeting area. The helicopter attack was

> followed up by QRF troops. The estimated number of Somali casualties in the raid varies from 20 (UNOSOM) to 215 (International Committee of the Red Cross [ICRC]).[174]

By this point in the operation, as one Deputy Assistant Secretary of Defense wrote, 'in effect, and regrettably for the operation and Somalia, UNOSOM and Aideed were now at war'.[175] The Weinberger doctrine was insufficient to guide intervention policy in the complex environment, as it was premised on doctrine that aggravated rather than addressed the situation.

Army doctrine

The Army's tactical doctrine was a product of the AirLand Battle doctrine developments. The lack of development of relevant doctrine and training, especially urban warfare capability, had been noted in the Panama intervention and the lack of this was of concern to Army analysts.[176] Prior to 1993 the Army had only two relevant doctrine manuals on Operations Other Than War (OOTW): the 1990 joint manual *FM 100-20/AFP 3-20, Military Operations in Low Intensity Conflict* and *FM 7-98, Operations in Low Intensity Conflict.*[177] As *FM 100-20* said, 'The term low intensity conflict reflects an American experience.'[178] These manuals were conceptually confusing as Low-Intensity Conflict was used to refer to the environment, the set of operations, and the low end of conflict spectrum, and by late 1992 the manuals were outdated as they focused on counter-insurgency (COIN), internal defence and development (IDAD) and counter-narcotics.[179] Specific doctrinal guidance was therefore absent. However, the doctrine that the light infantry in Somalia relied on was the *FM 100-5, Operations*, 1986 edition, and the resultant *FM 7-20, The Infantry Battalion*, 1992 manual. The Army operated to AirLand Battle tenets.

The *FM 7-20*, 1992 saw that infantry forces can operate in low-, mid- or high-intensity environments and 'The AirLand Battle is the doctrinal basis for meeting these challenges.'[180] It placed Low-Intensity Conflict in a broader strategic context, seeing that 'US policy recognizes that indirect, rather than direct, application of US military power is the most appropriate and cost-effective way to achieve national goals and to protect US interests in a LIC environment.'[181] The consequence of the marginalisation of the political–military aspects at the tactical level meant, for example, that light infantry battalions did not integrate psyops (psychological operations) and civilian-affairs roles. Additionally, it had no S5 officer (civil–military relations) at battalion level. In fact, the status of civil–military affairs teams was so low during the Somalia mission that deployment kept being put back till it was weeks behind the rest of the mission, negating its effect; much to the frustration of the officers charged with the role.[182]

As Theo Farrell explained, 'The US Army's existing beliefs about how wars ought to be fought, together with flawed thinking about peacekeeping, lay behind the disastrous military escalation under UNOSOM II.'[183] The use of the offensive to try and seize the initiative was the mode of operations, based as it was on AirLand

Battle tenets and using technology, such as the Cobra helicopter and Blackhawks, to manoeuvre.[184] In addition, the US approach of trying to force co-operation was in clear contrast to European and Commonwealth commanders who relied on persuasion.[185] General Sir Michael Rose later referred to crossing the line from peacekeeping to war as the 'Mogadishu line'. He saw that one could use force but it had to be at the minimum level, with due warning and impartial application.[186] Sudden attacks by massive force against a particular party, such as the attack on SNA headquarters on 12 July, broke all three of these criteria. At fault was the fact that US doctrine did not divide operational-level consent from the tactical level.[187] For example, independent breaches of consent at particular locales (the tactical level) were seen as indicative of a broader (operational level) lack of consent, and they were thus treated aggressively. The failure to recognise the specific dynamics of a particular area was very expensive for the US.

The problems of the aggressive American approach were to come to a head with the US Special Forces raid on two of Aideed's lieutenants on 3 October 1993, which ended with the death of 18 US troops.[188] The limitations of a single, decisive and aggressive action to end hostilities was clearly shown.[189] The special forces actions revealed not only a proclivity for the quick fix, but some very basic training errors, which included repetition of assault procedures which lost the element of surprise, and a soldier falling 70 feet as he left a helicopter because he failed to hold onto the rope.[190] The initial US response to the capture had been the massive use of firepower that had killed up to a thousand Africans.[191] President Clinton quickly announced the plans for US withdrawal.[192]

US Army tactics were thus counter-productive to establishing an impartial role and developing a secure environment. Furthermore, seeing itself as a part of the national strategy in the region in a separate manner, undermined the broader aspects required to establish the humanitarian relief. Operations Other Than War (OOTW) have a clear need for adaptive force packages, with flexible troop leading practice, utilising good intelligence. This requires training time to adapt to the new roles.[193] The US Army's approach was counter-productive to the needs of the situation and it was unable to provide the appropriate strategic tools for the mission. This was the cost of the Army not addressing the distinctiveness of small wars by the time of the deployment to Somalia in 1993, and instead relying on its strategic model developed from AirLand Battle.

Strategic lessons

Many of the lessons concerning the interrelation of political and social issues at the operational and tactical levels,[194] were available if the Army had drawn separate lessons from the Vietnam War. For example, Stephen Rosen, whilst at the DOD, wrote an influential article in 1982 which clearly pointed out that 'The general problem of limited war is not only the *diplomatic* one . . . but the *military* one of how to adapt, quickly and successfully, to the peculiar and unfamiliar *battlefield* conditions in which our armed forces are fighting.'[195] Colin Gray made a similar point in 1999: 'Armed forces that decline to take small wars seriously as a military art form with their own tactical, operational, and political – though not strategic – rules invite defeat.'[196] Which is what happened in Somalia. Thus clear and overdue strategic lessons on the use of force, that could have been learnt from the Vietnam War,[197] were entering US Army doctrine and training too late for the rapidly changing strategic environment. The political will for this type of operation collapsed after Somalia.

The experience in Somalia appears to have provided the US military with valuable lessons. The 'capstone' doctrine *FM 100-5* began to address 'Operations Other Than War' (OOTW) in the 1993 edition.[198] The principles of *legitimacy*, *perseverance* and *restraint* joined the classic ones of *objective*, *unity of effort* and *security* in *FM 100-5*.[199] Restraint had not previously even been an 'imperative' of Low-Intensity Conflict.[200] The principles behind Operations Other Than War (OOTW) doctrine were thus a second set of principles, which caused confusion.[201] For example, the same planning process is used for war and Operations Other Than War (OOTW), thereby failing to recognise that there are different principles applied to each.[202] The particular American problems with conceptualising its own missions were captured by John Fishel in the title of his article 'Little Wars, Small Wars, LIC, OOTW, The GAP, and Things That Go Bump in the Night'.[203] Sceptics questioned whether the military culture could accept the new doctrine, rejecting as it does the aggressive and Weinberger-based approach.[204] More importantly, it was too late to be applicable in the period; as Boutros Boutros-Ghali saw clearly, the October attack had dealt Aideed a huge blow, but the psychological blow to the US was far greater.[205]

At the heart of the US's problem was the development of new concepts that were in line with the nature of its Army. Analysts such as Peter Viggo Jakobsen have called for the development of new doctrine to help states handle the complex coercive and peace enforcement environment that now faces western states.[206] The problem is the self-understanding of militaries,[207] and the US Army in particular. The concept of diplomat warriors,[208] integrating strategic and operational concerns, clashed with the professional soldier developments focusing on AirLand Battle and its concern with decisive victory. As Thomas K. Adams pointed out in a provocatively titled article 'LIC (Low-Intensity Clausewitz)', US Army Low-Intensity Conflict doctrine was a misapplication of understanding of military means being separated from political goals at the operational level, and only linked at the national-strategy level. As he says,

> the fundamental tenets of US Army LIC doctrine, heavily influenced and directed by flawed efforts to apply Clausewitzian principles, have not led to effective structuring, equipping, training and operating of LIC forces. Consequently, US Army efforts at unconventional war-fighting have been less than successful. . . . To expect a conventional army to conduct political operations is to expect it to perform the impossible: it is not . . . equipped for such missions.[209]

The conceptual understanding of the utility of force was thus a self-referential cycle, where what is 'militarily achievable' (a key aspect of Weinberger's doctrine) is determined by the nature and choices made by the military – in this case the Army. Post-positivist critics have highlighted the trend whereby arrangements are 'created' and conceptualised as 'choice posing as truth'. These 'arrangements' have a propensity to be self-fulfilling prophetic norms.[210] This is what the Army has done. Simply put, the Army's earlier choices had become self-fulfilling truths. and part of the Clinton administration's problem was that it moved too fast for the institution to undertake the new roles. The institution understood things in a particular way and this was difficult because 'the changes in the security environment are still recent and the institution and its members have not had time to adjust their professional expectations, behaviour, and self-images in response to them'.[211] The Army's view of itself was founded on the confident post-Gulf War self-perception of professionalism developed since the 1970s, not the post-Cold War era. As the Army's Chief of Staff wrote:

> The U.S. Army is a doctrine-based organization in a values centered profession. . . . From our doctrine flows how we think about the world and how we train, equip, and organize our forces to serve the nation. . . . While the professional basis of the Army is unchanged, our professional knowledge continues to evolve to account for modern challenges. . . . Our tradition of delivering success at whatever the nation asks of us is strengthened through our understanding and articulation of the modern principles of war.[212]

In consequence the civil–military tensions concerning the nature and role of the Army would again come to the fore and shape US policy.

The debate between the Clausewitzian model of the Army and the broader Creveldian viewpoint is part of a much larger debate on the policy of the US in the world. The roles given to military force are reflective of different national policy strategies, and the US interventionism debate was part of a much larger debate on the role of the country post-Cold War.[213] It is understandable for the US Army as a military arm of the state to think in terms of Clausewitz's criteria, especially as many western governments and militaries were nervous of 'ethnic' and 'intra-state' violence.[214] However, it is necessary to understand how this viewpoint was so influential when it was so 'inappropriate' for the nature of the conflicts which the US faced. It had large consequences for US foreign policy and the nature of the international system.

Conclusion

The Panama intervention clearly showed the influence of the Army's thinking on the administration's policy. The success of the intervention made it a model for later uses of force for the Bush administration. The intervention was also important for making clear how the Army's practice had changed, combining mass and manoeuvre effectively to prosecute a quick and decisive campaign. The Panama intervention also showed coherence between the management and execution of the use of force in accordance with the development of the strategic culture and Army lessons. However, the limitations of the use of force concerning the long-term political policy towards Panama was clearly a political failure, and the Bush administration's handling of the episode outlines how the Army was actually used in interventions as a 'hit and split' force.[215] Panama's success entrenched the emphasis on the Army's separatist identity and curtailed broader developments in the Army.

The first Gulf War showed the influence and effectiveness of US Army thinking on the American strategic culture. The war was a vindication of the learning that it had undertaken since the end of the Vietnam War. The setting of clear militarily achievable objectives for the military, providing it with the resources necessary to carry out the policy and garnering and sustaining support for the campaign was clear evidence of the absorption of the strategic lessons of Vietnam. Additionally, the war showed the Army's new 'way of war' and the fruits of its emphasis on realistic and doctrine-based training. It achieved a clear outcome fulfilling the President's objectives. The strategic lessons of Vietnam had been learnt and applied, with the political aims and military means used effectively in a synergistic manner. The Weinberger doctrine and the Army thinking which lay behind it provided the basis for a coherent approach to the use of force by the US. However, the first Gulf War changed perceptions of warfighting and brought an end to the reforms that the failure in Vietnam had engendered, bringing a rise in the influence of air power in the strategic culture.

The intervention into Somalia showed the inadequacy of the Weinberger doctrine for coping with 'complex emergencies', whilst the doctrine which underpinned it led the US virtually into a state of war against the Aideed faction. The focus on politics being the concern of national strategy rather than integral to the tactical level meant that the US Army was unable to cope with the demands of the intervention. The Army was simply not doctrinally equipped for the intervention showing that the strategic lessons from the Vietnam War were less to do with the operational failure there and more to do with the rebuilding of the Army's identity and its proper use by the nation as a professional force.

However, the legacy was influential in shaping the US's role in international affairs through the 1990s and in shaping the response to the events of 9/11. Why the views were so influential and how that affected policy is the subject of the final chapter.

7

RETURN TO THE GULF

The final chapter has a much wider focus and takes a broader perspective to examine how the Army's thinking influenced the nation's adaptation to the new strategic environment. It examines the new roles undertaken by the Clinton administration before considering the subsequent interventions in Afghanistan and Iraq, following the attacks of 11 September 2001. During this period the strategic understanding generated by the military was of prime importance to the US because the foreign policy after the Cold War was a highly militarised one. As Bacevich notes, one of the key premises of post-Cold War policy was to maximise the utility of US military 'by pursuing an ambitious, activist agenda'.[1] In basic terms the US under President Clinton was a pragmatic promoter of democracy (rather than a Wilsonian idealist) and used force to improve the world.[2] The later Bush administration used military force more directly, in a realist's sense, against states to make the US more secure. There were two different perspectives of 'security' operating in the period between 1993 and 2005 but both relied heavily on military force; the 1990s saw 108 foreign operations in 53 countries, compared to 19 in 14 in the 1980s.[3] The recourse to 'coercive diplomacy' was used with varying success.[4]

The limitations of the Army's strategic thinking were apparent in this period, and the fragility of the strategic coherence it had generated was quickly exposed. The responses to the first Gulf War and the intervention in Somalia showed the key trends of the Army understanding itself in a narrow sense of being professional – in a technically proficient manner – with a limited role in interventions. The limited utility of this approach meant the strategic thinking and practice of the nation began to move away from the Army's priorities by avoiding using them, until the revived use of the Army after the events of 9/11. To examine this, first the chapter analyses the technical perspective, civil–military relations and intervention policy, before examining the intervention practice of the period and the reaction to 9/11 and the interventions in Afghanistan and Iraq.

Revolution in Military Affairs

The Gulf War of 1991 convinced many that the nature of warfare had undergone a change comparable in nature to changes brought by the Napoleonic Wars or industrialisation.[5] The first Gulf War experience did not provide a final vision of a revolution, but strongly hinted at greater things that could come, and the 1990s saw the US military focusing on realising many of these aspects. The Army in particular focused in this period on the technical aspects of war rather than the social and political features of the changing nature of warfare and international relations.

Leaders of the Revolution in Military Affairs (RMA) such as William Owens, Vice Chairman of the Joint Chiefs of Staff (1994–95), write that

> We now have a pretty good idea that the American RMA stems from the way several particular technologies will interact. . . . We have decided to build . . . the *system of systems*; namely, interactions that will give us dominant battlespace knowledge and the ability to take full military advantage of it.[6]

The aspiration is to lift the 'fog of war' and ease the 'friction' of conducting war – two key bugbears of military commanders as they operate in a complex and fluid environment with imperfect knowledge and impedimenta. For advocates like Owens, the Revolution in Military Affairs allows greater 'battlespace awareness' where the senior commander's comprehension of his forces, the enemy, terrain and other factors such as logistics are hugely improved.[7] The improvement will be due to sensors and reporting systems. Second, it will create a central nervous system of command, control, communications, computers and intelligence (C^4I). This will allow the organisation to gather data, create information and convert it into knowledge, an awareness that can then be communicated to the organisation. The novelty lies in the sheer speed and power of the emerging technologies that will be available to commanders. The third and final key concept, is the use of precision force allowing pinpoint strikes and a range of destructive capability that does not rely solely on weight of munitions. Together these aspects lead to the military forces being transformed by technology. As Owens says

> There have been other Revolutions in Military Affairs in this century and in centuries past, and the thing they share in common is how national leaders and military commanders properly exploited technology to change the course of history.[8]

However, even enthusiasts for the changes that information warfare can bring realise that it is not a silver bullet, and there is still a need for philosophy and leadership.[9] This is especially true as the narrow view isolates allies and leads to a separation between the military strategy, capabilities and technology of the United States, and those of its closest military partners. The US needs to extend an offer of partnership to make its Revolution in Military Affairs a transatlantic endeavour.[10] However, due to the complexity and sophistication of US forces, and the difficulty of effective operational blending with foreign forces, the US still aims to retain fighting self-sufficiency.[11]

The shift in the intellectual basis of American strategic thinking from the 1980s was shown most clearly with the publication in 1995 of *Joint Vision 2010*. It outlined that doctrine was derived from technology, and not from the strategic environment which was 'uncertain'.[12] The 1997 national policy document *Quadrennial Defense Review* was based on this document and was heavily criticised for being self-referential and immaculate; as war was seen as synonymous with the Revolution in Military Affairs and the US achieving full-spectrum dominance; 'adversaries, it seems, will not benefit from the information revolution or field capabilities that could allow them to counter U.S. forces'.[13] The *Quadrennial Defense Review* showed little organisational or conceptual change in military thinking with the end of the Cold War, demonstrating a 'blockage' in the Army's learning cycle.[14]

The separate professional identity had shifted from invigorating Army thinking to being a parochial interest to defend, with the lessons of history having little influence. This is not unique, of course.[15] For the Army, the broader trends of the Revolution in Military Affairs fed various aspects of its self-understanding, in particular an understanding of professional that focused on the technical rather than on the social aspects.

1990s development

The first Gulf War showed clearly how the nature of professionalism had changed since the end of the Vietnam War and how it closed down the social and political aspects of its thinking. This was most clearly seen with the issue of calling up the Reserves.[16] The failure to call up the Reserves during the Vietnam War was one of the key criticisms of the prosecution of the war there, as it undermined the quality and morale of the soldiers who did the fighting. After the war General Abrams (Army Chief of Staf, 1972–74) had instituted the Total Force concept in such a manner that the Reserves had to be called up to provide the logistical back-up, thereby limiting the executive. However, as General Abrams's biographer says, the lack of combat Reserves in the first Gulf War in 1991 was highly ironic, because it was not the civilians who refused to call up the Reserves but 'it was the *military* leadership that did not want the combat reserves'.[17] It showed how the Army's identity had shifted, so that the combatant role was vested only in the active duty forces, and Reserves were only to provide support; it was a question of combat readiness.[18] The nature of Reserve call-up was to support the professionals, and they focused on the operational concerns of combat. The Army's identity referred to the demands of war and the needs of AirLand Battle; the public role was to support the Army, but not to constitute it. The Army's success confirmed this division and led to the perception of what the key lessons of the first Gulf War were.

For the Army the first Gulf War 'closed' the Vietnam chapter but in fact it left many of the lessons behind. As Jeffrey Record pointed out, the lesson for potential American enemies from the war was not to challenge the US on its own terms and, also, to hope that Americans will 'conclude that the Gulf War is a model for the future'.[19] The US military did. Two factors came together to realise Record's fears. First, major regional contingencies are by far the most 'comfortable' security challenges for the US military, and it is for these that they plan.[20] For example, many saw the lessons of the war as a vindication of the main force and anti-gradualist approach, and this fitted their perception of the post-Cold War world. 'Establishing the battlefield conditions necessary for winning big, winning quick, and without casualties is one of the primary lessons from the war', even though the future battlefield will be different and the war itself had changed the nature and preparation for future warfare.[21] In this period, this trend was reinforced by the fears of the peace dividend as the Army was drawn down after the Cold War. Second, the 'techno-euphoria' and the image of it as 'computers at war,' reinforced an exclusively technological approach to the lessons of the war.[22] General Fred Franks was the new TRADOC commander and had been VII Corps commander in the first Gulf War and for him, VII Corps' experience was 'an indicator of what the whole Army would have to be able to do'.[23] He placed a decisive stamp on the Army's post-Gulf doctrine and the war gave 'glimmerings' of significant changes in warfare, especially concerning new weapons systems, which allowed simultaneous attack on the enemy in depth.

General Sullivan, the Army Chief of Staff (1991–95), argued that the US needed a different model of its armed forces and saw the changes in technology as dramatic as those in international politics, with the trends of lethality and dispersion, volume and precision of fire, integrative technology, mass and effects and invisibility and 'detectability' (*sic*) as key aspects of this change.[24] The emphasis was shown by the development of the Army XXI test brigade at Fort Hood, Texas, which aimed to capitalise on the new information available from emerging technology. As General Sullivan observed, 'we woke up in the early 90's to a powerful, ongoing trend and in turn made a virtue out of an inexorable movement'. Sullivan championed the development of Force XXI to take the Army from the industrial to the information age.[25] Force XXI became TRADOC's main effort.[26]

TRADOC Pamphlet 525–5, Force XXI Operations set the intellectual foundations for the next century – 'an Army that will leverage the power of information-based warfare and organizations to decisive advantage'.[27] It aimed for a greater increase in capability through focusing combat power by the integration of the battlefield. rather than simply developing new artillery pieces or tanks, and had a clear aim of internal efficiency.[28] Fundamental to the efficiency was the digitisation of the Army. Digitisation would enhance the tempo of operations, and increase the 'lethality and survivability' that Force XXI envisioned.

Force XXI was part of a very much broader developmental aspiration. where the Army aimed to develop Army XXI, which would then lead via 'Army Vision 2010' onto the 'Army after Next' for the years 2020–25. General Reimer, Army Chief of Staff (1995–99) saw that the best way to describe the 'Army after Next' was to look at it in terms of the principles of knowledge, speed and power.[29] The idea was to force the enemy to give in to 'our will' by shaping the battlespace, enhanced by precision fires, information and detection and engagement.[30]

What was less clear was the Army's strategic purpose. The new doctrine published after the first Gulf War, *Field Manual 100-5*, 1993, saw the Army coping with the new strategic environment that was bereft of the specific geography of Europe and an Army struggling to clarify its purpose.[31] The new doctrine manual showed a marked shift from operational to strategic-level concerns.[32]

Though the publication of *Field Manual 100-5*, 1993, actually marked the end of the formal era of AirLand Battle doctrine,[33] the need to maintain organisational coherence is shown by the four key tenets of AirLand Battle doctrine (initiative, agility, depth and synchronisation) being kept in the manual, whilst adding 'versatility'.[34] Versatility was required for a range of potential scenarios and was a 'prerequisite for a strategic Army'.[35] General Fred Franks, who had worked with General Starry on AirLand Battle doctrine, saw a new strategic environment for which the Army had to adapt. The Army looked to demonstrate its ability to be 'rapidly alert, mobilize, deploy, and operate anywhere in the world'.[36] The context was now understood as the Army fighting as part of a joint, combined, UN or interagency force. To this end the emphasis moved to the Army being deployable and responding rapidly to crises with a mixed force, whilst still be capable of achieving a decisive victory.[37] The Army was thus moving to being an offensive force looking to project military power across the world, but the emphasis was still on main force warfare. The manual was a retraction into the technical aspects of the profession, rather than a direct address of the huge proliferation of issues that the Army might, on behalf of the nation, have to undertake.[38]

The strategic thinking of the AirLand Battle doctrine-era still underpinned the new manual. For example, General Fred Franks still maintained that military forces 'should only be committed when the end state is clearly defined'.[39] Victory was still the aim of campaigns, whilst achieving political objectives was the key in other military operations. Crucially, though operations were still conceived in terms of deep, close and rear,[40] depth (space, time and resources) now included purpose.[41] The role of purpose was still only seen as an issue for Operations Other Than War, however, not for main force conventional warfare itself.[42] In addition, the actual inclusion of a chapter on 'Operations Other Than War' itself was the subject of much debate at the four-star generals conference considering the manual. For example, General Joulwan was a firm advocate of moving the Army and the doctrine away from a conventional warfare focus, with its emphasis on mechanised infantry and tank battles, towards the interagency-type operations that had been conducted by Southern Command against drugs.[43] Generals Franks and Sullivan, who believed in the key role of doctrine as an engine of change for the Army, supported the inclusion of Operations Other Than War in the manual.[44] However, it showed that purpose was understood as handed down in main force war, rather than being integral to each level. The abstract and highly technological understanding of warfare that the Army's doctrine in this period outlined further supported the trend.

The revised 2001 *Operations* manual, named *FM 3-0*, which formally superseded the 1993 manual, had a more abstract understanding of the concept of 'battle'.[45] The new 2001 manual was seen as the product of joint doctrine and moved further away from the distinctions of 'war' and 'Operations Other Than War', rolling them into one term – 'operations'.[46] It advocated a full-spectrum understanding that worked with concepts of offence, defence, stability and support.[47] The idea was that a commander 'combine and sequence' these four aspects to accomplish the mission, with the nature of the mission dictating the proportion and relationship of the different aspects. It was the Army's way of addressing the ambiguity that lies between war and other operations, but the designation of 'stability' operations (covering peacekeeping to counter-terrorism operations) hardly equips the Army conceptually to cope with the scenarios that 'can be more challenging than in situations requiring offensive and defensive operations'.[48]

The abstract understanding of 'battlespace', rather than war, lay at the heart of the understanding of 'operations'. With the planned battles and campaigns no longer in Europe against a known force, the manual had to refer to a generic understanding of it. 'Battlespace' was a crucial conceptual issue, and was defined as 'a physical volume that expands or contracts in relation to the ability to acquire and engage the enemy. It includes the breadth, depth, and height in which the commander positions and moves assets over time.'[49] The 2001 manual saw it as the environment, the factors and the conditions commanders must understand to complete the mission – it was an enormous list: air, land, sea, space, the 'included' enemy, friendly forces, facilities, weather, terrain, electromagnetic spectrum and the information environment.[50] Not only had the battlespace changed, it was to be dealt with in non-linear terms and operations looked at in terms of decisive, shaping and sustaining – basically, directly accomplishing the task, creating and preserving conditions for success, and enabling the operations by support and security.[51] The other great move away from linear thinking was the understanding of non-contiguous battlefields, where the boundaries between areas of operations were not shared.[52] Operations were, potentially, to take place in pockets. The Army had moved a long way, doctrinally, from the linear world of 'Active Defense', towards a dominant, flexible and highly technological Army doctrine with a strong emphasis on battle command in a fluid, complex and multi-dimensional 'battlespace'.

The conceptual innovation undertaken in this period generated the need for an organisational change and critics noted the dilemma of this and how ambitious it was.[53] *FM 3-0* was written to serve three armies: the existing force, the modernised digitised force and the Interim force.[54] Beyond all these was the futuristic aim of developing the 'Objective Force', which the manual does not address.[55]

The Army's doctrinal developments are obviously part of the much larger cultural shift of emphasis in strategy to technology after the success of the first Gulf War, encapsulated as the Revolution in Military Affairs debate. However, the emphasis on technology driving doctrinal change missed the fact that from the mid-1970s it was *social* and technological forces that eventually brought industrialised warfare to an end and initiated the revolutionary process, replacing mass destruction with 'precision destruction'.[56] The innovation was thus not only in technology but in the ideology which produced a new theory of victory.[57] For example, William Lind highlighted that the changes in the US Army were a revolution in ideas that goes back to 1918, whilst Andrew Krepinevich's model of revolutions in warfare ties technology, organisational change and operational concepts together.[58] The exclusively technological focus fostered by the Army was a corruption of the AirLand Battle evolution and was indicative of how far the basis of the Army's thinking was dependent on a referent which ignored the social and political aspects of its nature – namely, a professional focusing on the technical aspects of war.

The avoidance of the social and political aspects of the Revolution in Military Affairs are part of a broader divergence between social and military values.[59] A.J. Bacevich has been one of the most severe critics of the US Army's model of professionalism and sees the continued limited utility of the Army arising from the 'persistent limitations of professional orthodoxy'.[60] He sees it as embodying the ideas that: politicians are kept at some remove; people observe appreciatively; there are neatly defined campaigns and battles, and tolerable cost victories. It is a corruption of the genuine strategic thought that AirLand Battle doctrine tried to engender but 'It is a vision of the Persian Gulf War replayed over and over again', where technology replaces political, social and cultural aspects of changes.[61]

As Lawrence Freedman observed, the Revolution in Military Affairs after the first Gulf War was most critically affected by the end of Cold War limits on the prosecution of war being lifted.[62] Therefore, any model of technological change has to be placed in its social and political context to understand its relevance. As Freedman went on to say

> The RMA does not offer the prospect of a virtual war by creating a situation in which only information matters so that there is never any point in fighting about anything other than information. Territory, prosperity, identity, order, values – they all still matter, and provide the ultimate tests of a war's success.[63]

Nowhere was this borne out more clearly than in the intervention into Somalia, which showed the key limitations of looking at military problems as technical ones, fought with 'stand-off' politicians. Desert Storm showed the US was still better at battles than wars, and that the military still needed to understand military victory as political victory.[64] Technology alone cannot provide victory and Somalia was important for highlighting the limits of the strategic understanding that had been developed after the Vietnam War. Whilst the Army was developing a greater concentration on the technological aspects of its profession, the broader national strategic requirements were rebuffed by it in the name of its professional identity.

Civil–military relations

Where the first Gulf War reinforced the professional aspects of the Army's understanding, Somalia revived the Army's Vietnam-era fears that soldiers' lives would be lost as the result of the executive misusing the Army. This perception was reinforced by the 'draw down' of the Army from 18 divisions to 12, whilst still retaining a two 'major regional scenario' capability. As a salutary warning of the dangers during this period, the Army Chief of Staff, General Sullivan, often invoked the memory of the 'Task Force Smith' during the Korean War, where a poorly equipped and under-funded US Army performed badly.[65] The 'draw down' reinforced the Army's focus on main force war rather than complex emergencies. However, unlike the immediate post-Vietnam period, the Army now had a clearly articulated sense of itself and a set of criteria of how the Army should be used, and this was to be a major inhibitor of the broader use of the military post-Cold War. Namely, it possessed convictions and intended to act upon them.[66] This brought it into conflict with the administration, which heightened already poor civil–military relations, and ultimately this led to a diminution of influence of the Army as the prime shaper of the strategic culture – the administration looked to other national tools to further its policies.

The 'Vietmali' syndrome

The White House had reacted quickly to the failure in Somalia and looked to place the blame outside itself.[67] Admiral Howe and his interpretation of his mandate was particularly targeted.[68] Many in the military blamed the administration and saw it as the root of the problem. Secretary of Defense Les Aspin was singled out, particularly for not sending sufficient armoured support to the troops on the ground.[69] The administration's reaction to the Somalia failure sent shock waves through the Pentagon, especially in the Office of the Joint Chiefs, bringing greater distrust of the White House and pushing to the fore deeper civil–military problems.[70] The administration reacted by sacking Les Aspin and putting forward a former military officer, Bobby Ray Inman, as his replacement, though Senator William Cohen eventually became the new Secretary.[71] The distrust engendered by the administration led to the rise of many problems from the Vietnam era in the perception of the executive by the military, and Richard Holbrooke caught this mood by referring to the 'Vietmali' syndrome.[72]

For the Army, the nature of the domestic relationship between the White House and the military was a greater cause for concern than that of a potential external enemy; in particular it was fearful of being seen as an abstract 'instrument' of power. An instrumental approach had very clear consequences for the Army and the tension was caught by General Powell, who, when asked by Madeline Albright, the Ambassador to the UN and later Secretary of State, 'What's the point of having this superb military that you're always talking about if we can't use it?' thought he'd have an aneurysm. As he said, 'American GIs were not toy soldiers to be moved around on some sort of global board game.'[73] Another senior Army officer saw the continued use of military force by the administration as covering for a lack of policy and not understanding what force could and could not do, referring to Secretary Albright as 'Half Bright'.[74]

The clashes gave a clear indication that in the eyes of the military the new administration understood neither the nature of force nor the services that would be tasked to undertake the missions. This was in direct contrast to the previous Secretary of Defense, Dick Cheney, who for Powell had

> learned that we are not a thing. We are not a bureaucracy. We are not a system. Instead . . . a human organism that must be cared for, that hurts. that must be trained, that bleeds, and that must always be tended to.[75]

President Bush had understood this aspect of the military, and said so repeatedly.[76] Seeing the Army as a tool of diplomacy, rather than seeing what the Army was and what it could or could not do, was a fundamental culture clash with the Clinton administration, which caused great fears for the nature of civil–military relations in the US.[77] The clearly articulated understanding of professionalism and the shadow of Vietnam hung over the relations. For example, the Chairman of the Joint Chiefs General Shalikashvili (1993–97) used the privilege of his position to wear the insignia of the disbanded MACV (Military Assistance Command, Vietnam) as a tribute to those who had died in the war.[78] It was a vivid reminder of the lessons and relevance of the Vietnam War to the new administration.

The new administration's understanding of force was based on a different regard for the military and a more critical reading of the Vietnam War. There were well-reported incidents of White House staffers not employing former military service people, and saying that 'they don't talk to the military'.[79] Clinton's personal record during the Vietnam War,[80] and his confrontation and backing down from advocating gays in the military weakened his stance against the military as his administration challenged the Army's understanding of professionalisation. Having an unpopular Secretary of Defense, Les Aspin, who was seen as 'too academic', exacerbated the problem.[81] The 'first two years of the Clinton administration were marked by an extraordinary display of open disdain and hostility by the military for the new president'.[82]

The clearest expression of the military's fears was the fictional story that won the Chairman of the Joint Chiefs of Staff's essay competition, 'The Origins of the American Military Coup of 2012'.[83] The essay by Charles Dunlap Jr, an Air Force Lieutenant Colonel, was published in the Army War College journal *Parameters*, and portrayed a scenario of how civil–military relations could break down so critically in the US that a military coup could take place. The reason was the misuse of the military in too many and too broad a series of roles. It portrayed an identity for the Army in line with Summers's reading of Clausewitz, which also reflected the outlook of the Chairman of the Joint Chiefs of Staff at the time, General Colin Powell.[84] The debate continued even after Clinton was out of office. On leaving his White House appointment as Presidential military aide Lt. Col Patterson noted

> There was no sadness. There was only the sense that the man in the Oval Office had sown a whirlwind of destruction upon the integrity of our government, endangered our national security, and done enormous harm to the American military in which I served.[85]

The issues of personal integrity were a particularly galling issue for military officers, as well as the cutbacks and deployments of the military forces. The military perspective had a very different view of the world and the military culture was divorcing from society.[86]

The separate sense of professionalism was reinforced by the reaction of the administration to potential casualties and a revival of the 'zero defects' culture within the Army due to the cutbacks. The Army's perception, rather than public intolerance,[87] was to be the predominant factor in US use of force policy after Somalia. This was shown by an incident within eight days of the Rangers' deaths in Somalia. In Haiti the administration aimed to restore the presidency of Jean-Baptiste Aristide, stem the flow of refugees to the US and respond to the calls of the Black American caucus who had done so much to elect the President.[88] The *Harlan County*, a ship flying the UN flag and carrying US Special Forces and Canadian soldiers, was about to dock in Haiti when an angry crowd chanting 'Somalia! Dead American soldiers' greeted it, and, ignoring the views of the US diplomats on the ground, the ship turned round.[89] It was a decisive moment for US policy. The President made clear that when sending in troops

> My first concern, and the most important one, obviously, is for the safety and security of our troops. General Shalikashvili and Lieutenant General Hugh Shelton, our commander in Haiti, have made it clear to all involved that the protection of American lives is our first order of business.[90]

This is remarkable because the concept of the professional soldier is founded on an understanding of unlimited liability.[91] The conception of the professional soldier advocated by the Army ruled out its use as a combat force in complex emergencies. In Haiti, for example, the mission was limited 'in time and scope', and aimed to facilitate a 'quick-hand off to the United Nations'.[92] As the former US Army officer Ralph Peters complained, this undercuts the nature of the Army 'as they maneuver to avoid roles in "nonmilitary" problems, they betray the trust placed in them by the citizens they are pledged to protect. A military's reason for being is to do the nation's dirty work.'[93] Politically a 'risk-free' approach severely constrains the type of mission that can be undertaken and the policy of handling risk and the emphasis placed on force protection in Somalia, Haiti and Bosnia, undermined the reputation acquired in Grenada, Panama and the first Gulf War.[94] The administration was adopting the Army's agenda of poor civil–military relations, the technical understanding of warfare and the political aspects of war being a national rather than also being a tactical issue.

Thus one can see that Weinberger's doctrine was not simply an abstract list of criteria for the use of force, but articulated how the Army saw itself, its role and utility as a tool of American foreign policy, and the impetus behind the administration's use of force was in direct contrast to the Army's thinking. In the light of the civil–military relations and problems that the Clinton administration faced over the use of force, Weinberger's prediction in 1990 was very prescient.

> Policies formed without a clear understanding of what we hope to achieve would also earn us the scorn of our troops, who would have an understandable opposition to being *used* – in every sense of the word – casually and without intent to support them fully. Ultimately this course would reduce their morale and their effectiveness for engagements we *must* win.[95]

The failure in Somalia was to bring the reassertion of his criteria, again establishing them as the norms of US strategic culture, even though they severely constrained US policy towards 'complex emergencies'. Thus it was the Army lessons and the nature it developed, not simply the historical or demographic nature of US strategic culture,[96] which limited the US as it met the post-Cold War world. The professionalism developed after the Vietnam War opened the Army to new vistas of thought and practice but its legacy was to restrict its further development and hinder the strategic culture's response to the new strategic environment.

Weinberger reinstated

The outcome of the administration's domestic troubles was to alter US policy in regard to UN and NATO as it staved off criticism by reasserting the Weinberger doctrine to avoid a repeat of Somalia. The norms of the strategic culture were therefore reasserted to be in accord with the doctrinal limitations of the Army, its identity and the fears of the administration. The administration had to rebuild a consensus within the strategic institutions over the issue of peacekeeping and, as after Vietnam, congressional assertiveness was to be a major factor for the administration.[97] As Deborah Avant observes, the military's influence is greatly increased when there is a lack of civilian consensus, due to the delegated power given to the military.[98]

The Army and the JCS were articulate about its concerns and their influence was greatly increased because of the structural changes of the Goldwater–Nichols Act and the delegated power given to the military through the creation of the joint Commanders in Chief (CINCs). The weight of the CINCs' budgets, and the political authority given them by the White House and the Pentagon, meant that they were actually more powerful than ambassadors who formally outranked them. Whilst in Washington 'their wings were clipped' but it was in their theatres and during operations that they were most powerful.[99] Their headquarters had grown to more than twice the size of their Cold War predecessors', and their budget of $380 million a year was lavish compared to the budget-strapped State Department.[100] The CINCs became the 'Proconsuls to the Empire' and, as Dana Priest says, 'had acquired a power unheard of in the military in the course of America's history'[101] (Rumsfeld later reasserted the fact that the president was the Commander in Chief, and the CINCs were re-branded as Combatant Commanders to address the growing perception of their power.)[102] It was recognition of their growing importance as the US became more dependent upon the military, as it filled the vacuum left by 'the indecisive White House, an atrophied State Department, and a distracted

Congress'.[103] The military were therefore a direct and key player in foreign policy when force was planned and used.

Richard Holbrooke's personal account of driving US policy in Bosnia places the military's influence in a broader context when he notes that White House policy had to get military agreement because, 'their backing was needed to get congressional and public support for the mission, which meant they had the upper hand in the debate over what their mission would be'.[104] Congressional developments, therefore, increased the military influence through its own developed role in foreign and defence policy. The compromise that was reached between the White House and Congress on the approach to using military force in peacekeeping issues, was President Clinton's Presidential Decision Directive 25 (PDD 25).[105] PDD 25 was a clear revival of the tenets of the Weinberger doctrine, along with additional checks on the UN to avoid a repeat of the Somalia problems.

PDD 25 established standards to assess whether US personnel should participate in peace operations and the list included:

- Participation advances US interests
- US participation is necessary for operation's success
- The role of US forces is tied to clear objectives and an endpoint for US participation can be identified
- Domestic and Congressional support exists or can be marshalled
- Command and control arrangements are acceptable
- There exists a determination to commit sufficient forces to achieve clearly defined objectives
- There exists a plan to achieve those objectives decisively
- There exists a commitment to reassess and adjust, as necessary, the size, composition, and disposition of our forces to achieve our objectives.[106]

As the National Security Adviser, Tony Lake, said at the time, PDD 25 aimed not only to improve peacekeeping but also 'to enhance the cooperation between the Congress and the executive'.[107] Congress kept a tight control on the funding of missions by retaining a case-by-case approach, forcing the administration to establish an end point and exit strategy for each mission.[108] Lieutenant General Wesley Clark, as Director for Strategic Plans and Policy for the Joint Chiefs of Staff, was on hand at the press release to show that the 'military has played a major role in defining the command and control aspects of this PDD'.[109] However, it was clear that military thinking lay behind the concepts and the DOD gained the most; as one Deputy Assistant Secretary of Defense for Peacekeeping and Peace Enforcement Policy put it, 'Self interest, not foggy idealism, makes the DOD an advocate of selective and effective peace operations.'[110] Criticism of the administration policy was clear.

The revival of the Weinberger doctrine was reaffirmed in policy statements such as the 1995 Secretary of Defense's Report,[111] and 1995 *The National Military Strategy* (NMS). *The National Military Strategy* released under General John M. Shalikashvili's name, reasserted the principle of 'Clear Objectives: Decisive Force'.

The principle was explained as: 'In any application of force, military objectives will be clearly defined to support our national political aims in the conflict. We intend to commit sufficient force to achieve these objectives in a prompt and decisive manner.'[112] The strategy prescribes the use of 'decisive military force in war'[113] and in major peace enforcement operations, incorporating the lessons learned

> in Iraq, Somalia, and the former Yugoslavia . . . our guidelines will continue to be to: Commit sufficient forces to achieve clearly defined objectives; Plan to achieve those objectives decisively; Reassess and adjust, as necessary, the size, composition, and disposition of our forces to achieve these objectives.[114]

The strategic principle of Decisive Force, as outlined in the 1992 *National Military Strategy*, was not therefore a principle tied to General Colin Powell alone with the 'Powell doctrine', but reflected a consistency within the Joint Chiefs of Staff in their approach to issues concerning military interventions and the use of force. Decisive Force has become a constant of US military strategy, and is one of the four concepts that govern the uses of force in General Shalikashvili's later 1997 *National Military Strategy*.[115] The strategy reflected the priorities of the Army.

The administration's acceptance of the criteria was in reality a massive shift in position by the president, as PDD 25 undermined not only peacekeeping efforts but also the overall capacity of the UN for the foreseeable future.[116] The White House had the initiative but in the face of Congressional and bureaucratic pressures, and executive disagreement, the need to achieve consensus sealed the fate of 'assertive multilateralism'.[117] For example, Rwanda was the first case considered under the PDD 25 rubric, and the administration saw its policy there as a success, because it brought the number and cost of missions down.[118] As Madeline Albright, the then US Ambassador to the UN, says in her memoirs, the military were opposed to intervention, as there were no security guarantees, no co-operation between parties and no readily achievable mandates. The possible option of 'large and heavily armed coalition led by a major power' was not actually possible 'because of Somalia'.[119] Although the complexities of military intervention in this context were profound,[120] the US reaction to the genocide in Rwanda has been accurately described as, 'as little as possible, as late as possible, along with – but after – as many others as possible, and for as short a time as possible'.[121] The administration went so far as to refuse to refer to it as genocide for legal reasons, and its lack of response did huge damage to its reputation – it was seen as a case of western indifference to African suffering and blatant double standards at the time of Yugoslavia; 800,000 Rwandans died.[122] (Five years after the massacre President Clinton visited Kigali airport for three and a half hours and referred to 'genocide' eleven times.[123]) A US official at the time noted in his diary

> A military that wants to go nowhere to do anything – or let go their toys so someone else can do it. A White House cowed by the brass (and are we to give lessons on how the armed forces take orders from civilians?).[124]

Albright stands squarely in the historic American liberal tradition[125] and continued to advocate a liberal agenda as Secretary of State. However, the administration's response to Rwanda was an extreme reaction to learning the limits of military power, especially as the administration had many options it chose not to exercise.[126] Rwanda signalled the end of a brief period of liberal internationalist hope that had opened up in 1989.[127] The nation compensated for the inflexibility of its conventional forces by developing separate tools of statecraft, the prime one being the Special Forces.

Special Forces

The challenges that the Army wished to avoid in this period did not go away. At the forefront was the particularly difficult issue of facing a physical enemy configured unconventionally. The challenges of asymmetric warfare, as it is now called, were a continuous feature of warfare in the twentieth century. The Army has bypassed it by establishing the Special Forces as a separate branch within the Army, and shifting its emphasis from a combat role to that of being trainers.[128] The explosion of Special Operations Forces (SOF) to fill the strategic need to address these issues, coupled with the rise of airpower, has diminished the Army's role in the strategic culture.

The Special Operations Command (USSOCOM) had been activated in 1987, and by 1999 it was averaging 5,141 personnel deployed away per week, and from 1998–2001 SOF had deployed to an average of 150 countries per year.[129] The 2004 financial year request had a budget for Special Operations Command of $6.8 billion and 49,484 personnel (one-third in reserve components).[130] It was a 47 per cent budget increase as USSOCOM shifted from being a 'supporting' to becoming a 'supported' command.

Special Forces give the nation the ability to address a broad spectrum of missions and give the CINCs broad capabilities within their commands. The CINCs have used them as part of a much broader attempt to use military force to engage in other countries, especially in preparation for times of crisis. Special Forces develop a knowledge and influence in areas that are potential trouble spots.[131] They gave the CINCs the ability to influence situations. This is quite ironic as they had been created by the civilian reformers in face of military opposition. Therefore, thirty years after the Army disbanded its Special Forces, and nearly twenty after an acrimonious fight concerning its establishment, the necessary strategic tool the nation needed grew enormously. It was a reflection of the changing strategic culture. In the war against terrorism it has the key mission to disrupt, defeat and destroy terror networks.[132] The growth of Special Forces meant that the recalcitrance of the Army led to it being bypassed by the strategic culture.

One can thus see that the Army's self-understanding generated a series of constraints that meant it had a clear lack of utility for the Clinton administration's intervention policy. The wide-ranging and limiting effect of the Army's narrowed thinking on the strategic use of military force for this agenda can be seen clearly in intervention policy, particularly that in the former Yugoslavia.

Intervention practice

The initial Clinton decisions on Bosnia showed the influence of the Army's thinking. as it primarily reflected military thinking, both in terms of the issues to be covered and the outcome recommended.[133] Clinton's major initiative in 1995 was in accord with the military criteria. even though his Bosnia policy brought NATO to a state of crisis.[134] The failing policy meant that, as Anthony Lake is reported to have said to the president, 'Bosnia has become and is the symbol of U.S. foreign policy.'[135] Clinton, on 27 November 1995, implemented the Dayton agreement by deploying troops to Bosnia, but he made very clear that it was on the military's terms. He said the military mission was 'precisely defined, with clear, realistic goals that can be achieved in a definite period of time', and that troops have authority, training and equipment to respond to threats or violations with 'overwhelming force'.[136] The Army was deployed according to its own terms, with clear political aims and objectives that were militarily achievable.

The administration's rhetoric and aspirations could not be matched by Army deployments and the West's failure to intervene was due to the US's refusal to put troops on the ground.[137] The reluctance of the US to put troops on the ground in such conflicts led Edward Luttwak to distinguish between theoretically available troops, and those that are actually 'politically useable' in real-life confrontations.[138] The campaign in Kosovo showed the trends and difficulties most markedly.

Fearing the start of a fourth war in the Former Yugoslavia by President Milosovic, NATO undertook an air war against him to stop the ethnic cleansing his government was carrying out in the previously autonomous region of Kosovo. It was NATO's first war. However, it was the low point for the US military strategy, as the problems of a coalition war[139] combined with the Clinton administration's dilemmas concerning the use of military force.[140] The professional model of what troops should do, along with the administration's fear of casualties, meant that at the start of hostilities in Kosovo in 1999, President Clinton said 'I do not intend to put our troops in Kosovo to fight a war.'[141] US troops were shown to have little political utility because, as with Bosnia and Haiti, soldiers would not be deployed until the conflict was finished.

The declining utility of US ground forces fed the broader strategic lessons of the first Gulf War, whereby air power became the strategic tool of choice over land power, leading to conflicting understandings of 'joint' doctrine.[142] The events in Kosovo highlighted the continual tension between ground and air thinking as the disagreements about targeting issues between the Allied Force Air Commander, Lt General Michael Short and the overall Commander, General Wesley Clark, made clear. As Clark said, it was

> the classic struggle between Army leaders, who want the Air Force to make a difference in the fight on the ground, and some adherents of airpower, who saw airpower as strategically decisive, without the recourse to the dirty business of ground combat.[143]

Where AirLand Battle doctrine, combined with the Army and Air Force agreements, had helped alleviate some of this, the developments in the post-AirLand Battle doctrine age did not. For example, air advocates saw the air campaign in Kosovo as 'deep' battle, as NATO hit strategic targets and attacked the ground forces.[144] The primacy of the air role was a culmination of the Air Force's growing influence and utility. The Air Force reasserted its importance to US strategy throughout the 1990s, seeing that it could provide 'a war winning strategy' through 'aerospace control with precision weapons'[145] and became predominant within the strategic culture, especially as the reluctance to be involved on the ground grew. A key term of strategic analysis became Effects Based Operations, air power thinking institutionalised nationally. It aspired to be 'A process for obtaining a desired strategic outcome or "effect" on the enemy, through the synergistic, multiplicative, and cumulative application of the full range of military and non-military capabilities at the tactical, operational, and strategic levels'.[146] The Army had been talking about this as 'strategy' for years, but the first Gulf War had ended the learning cycle which the Army had undertaken since the Vietnam War concerning air power, weakened its relationship to air power, and ultimately altered its status within the strategic culture. Thus in the 1990s the US's 'New Way of War' was based on the routine use of precision weaponry, and the ability to go against an adversary with near virtual invulnerability. As Eliot Cohen notes, these two factors make air power overwhelmingly attractive for medium and small-scale uses of force.[147] By the time of Kosovo the US had entered an era of 'virtual war' where it dominates the sky and space but not the ground.[148]

But Kosovo was not only indicative of the declining utility of US ground forces and the attractiveness of air power to the administration, but also that it was a war that showed the tensions between political aims and military means,[149] and was fought within a new understanding of the aims of policy. The Weinberger doctrine was revised and bypassed, whilst coalition partners outlined a doctrine of international community rather than self-interest for interventions.[150]

The Kosovo War clearly showed that strategic lessons could be ignored when troops were not to be deployed; the very strategic lessons of Vietnam that the Army had generated. As Wesley Clark, the Supreme Allied Commander Europe (SACEUR) had written twenty-five years earlier,

> military action must be constrained by political aims, but, where these constraints signal an unwillingness to employ military means fully to obtain the object of the intervention, the political aims themselves will be jeopardized. . . . [thus] Military actions which might generate incremental but diffused pressure against the enemy should be avoided.[151]

The risk-free approach towards the deployment of military force shown in Kosovo is a rejection of the basic lessons learnt in Vietnam about the executive facing the costs of using military force correctly. For example, the air power campaign against Serbia shifted objectives within days, escalated the use of force and eventually took

78 days to bring to a conclusion. The Clinton administration's policy clearly ran in the face of the Weinberger criteria and suggested that the lessons of the Vietnam War on the use of force were embodied in the Army. The norms of having clear objectives, a defined end state, using overwhelming force and being militarily achievable, which it had developed after the Vietnam War and which became national policy, were shown to belong to the strategic culture only when it was concerned with the deployment of troops. Kosovo rejected the strategic learning from the Vietnam War era. The final legacy of the war was a parody of strategy; suffer no casualties. It was the low point of the post-Gulf War developments but reflective of broader trends in international relations.

War, like most social concepts, has become far more 'fluid' in a period of globalisation. The nature of globalisation has shifted the emphasis of military force from occupying territory to that of controlling space and time. As Zygmunt Bauman notes concerning Kosovo,

> Engaging in ground combat was resented not just for its possible adverse effect on domestic politics but also . . . for its total uselessness and even counter-productivity as far as the goals of the war are concerned . . . the conquest of territory with all its administrative and managerial consequences . . . [were] meant to be by all means avoided.[152]

Thus one can see that the nature of air power fits the broader developments within the national culture, with its emphasis on flexibility, the reluctance to suffer casualties for civil–military reasons and the national emphasis on technological solutions. The organisations that bring these trends to bear have also changed in the period under examination, meaning that the historical anomaly of the Army as the predominant organisation shaping US policy was replaced by the Air Force. The model of US warfare thus shifted to being a philosophy of virtual war, backed by the Revolution in Military Affairs. Kosovo was to prove to be the nadir for the main trends in the Army's developments of the 1990s and showed that there was a clear need for the Army to reform itself; it showed there was a need for the Army to 'transform'.

Transformation

The shift of the strategic culture to air power and Special Forces, over conventional ground forces, had a lot to do with the limits of the Army rather than simply the requirements of the administration's strategy. The demands of peacekeeping, humanitarian aid and quasi-imperial policing do not resemble war against peer competitors which the Army concentrated upon. A key event during the Kosovo conflict showed the mis-directed nature of Army developments, when General Wesley Clark, the CINC, tried to increase Army influence on the ground and it proved a fiasco.

The basic idea was to protect victims of ethnic cleansing, with the deployment of Task Force Hawk – 24 AH-64 Apaches attack helicopters. Instead, the Army showed how far it was from being a utilisable strategic force.[153] The Army determined that to deploy this force it needed to send 6,200 troops and 26,000 tons of equipment (by flying 550 C-17 sorties) including 12 MIAI tanks and 42 Bradley Fighting vehicles, at the cost of $480 million. Other issues, such as the rebuilding of the airfield at Rina, Albania to house them, the 12 days it took the helicopters to deploy to theatre, the fact that when they arrived they were not ready for combat (as the pilots were not proficient in night flying goggles and 65 per cent had less than 500 flying hours on them), completely undermined it. The massive, and massively expensive, Task Force was never used. For $480 million no utilisable military capability was generated to protect the victims of ethnic cleansing; they were thus ‘protected’ by reception into refugee camps.

As Michael Vickers puts it

> coming out of Kosovo, the United States Army found itself face-to-face with irrelevance and declared it had ‘gotten the message.’ In short order, the Army jettisoned its ill-advised Army XXI project – little more than an effort to add a gloss of information technology to a conception of mechanised warfare dating back to the 1930s – and embarked on a new initiative to create a lighter, more-mobile forces.[154]

The lessons of Task Force Hawk and Kosovo reverberated throughout Congress and the Pentagon. Due to the fiasco, General Shinseki, the Chief of Staff, launched the Army onto the path of transformation, aiming to make the Army a deployable force capable of meeting the strategic challenges.[155] The Army began to field the new ‘Stryker brigades’ as part of the effort to bridge its light and heavy forces in line with the developing Army ideas.[156]

However, the Army process was indicative of broader failings of the Pentagon reform and the long-term need to address strategic, technological and military structure problems.[157] The drive to ‘transform’ the military was an issue that became a part of the broader defence debate of the 2000 presidential elections.[158]

Donald Rumsfeld, the new Secretary of Defense (2001–), aimed for rapidly deployable, fully integrated joint forces that were capable of reaching distant theatres quickly, striking them swiftly and with devastating effect. As he said, in addition to building new capabilities, transformation also required rebalancing existing forces and capabilities.[159] Rumsfeld was also clear that ‘transforming the military is not an event; it is an ongoing process. There will be no point at which we can declare that U.S. forces have been “transformed”.’[160]

Rumsfeld aimed to reassert civilian control of the military in an abrasive manner. In addition his ideas clashed with the Army’s vision. For example, General Eric Shinseki had announced his version of transformation a year before Rumsfeld’s arrival.[161] As such he, not Rumsfeld, was the initiator of the theme in public debate. From Rumsfeld’s viewpoint, however, Shinseki’s vision of transformation was not fast enough and was tied to Cold War systems such as Crusader and Comanche (artillery and helicopter programmes). Basically Rumsfeld saw that some units would get lighter but the basic mainframe would stay as it was and he wanted new ideas. The two spoke across each other.[162] Rumsfeld nominated Shinseki's replacement 15 months before the due date, thereby making him a lame duck and undercutting his transformation plans.[163] A number of senior Army generals turned down the post as Shinseki's replacement, and eventually General Schoomaker was brought out of retirement to become Chief of Staff in 2003. He was an anomaly because he was the first Combatant Commander to take up the post and he came from a Special Forces background. Secretary Rumsfeld did not attend Shinseki's retirement ceremony.

Transformation has become a key aspect of the military debate in the US. However, Rumsfeld has been criticised for not radically rethinking defence, as the administration's future defence plans actually conform to pre-administration thinking, whilst radically increasing the spending on it.[164] For example, only $25bn of the $400bn budget is transformational, and $10bn of that is on Star Wars.[165] Rumsfeld has also been critiqued for his emphasis on technology rather than troops.[166] The Pentagon has an Office of Defense Transformation and they have determined that 'Network Centric Warfare (NCW) is the core concept that guides the transformation of the U.S. military. NCW is the embodiment of Information Age warfare.'[167] This takes the debate back full circle to the emphasis on technology after the first Gulf War and the lessons that were generated by it. The veracity of this thinking was soon tested with the administration's response to the events of 9/11.

9/11

After the traumatic events of 11 September 2001 the United States' change in strategy led them to war. The declared 'war on terrorism' brought many of the examined themes into broad relief.

The Bush administration came into office with a very different rhetoric to its predecessors, and a different understanding of security and the use of military force. Hard power, as opposed to Nye's concept of 'soft power', was advocated, along with a clear unilateral emphasis on freeing the US from the constraints that tied them internationally.[168] For example, National Security Advisor Condoleezza Rice dismissed the broad internationalist agenda of the outgoing administration before coming to office. The new administration would be international 'but it will also proceed from the firm ground of the national interests, not from the interests of an illusory international community'.[169] Realist thinking underpinned the administration's thinking and this was a part of the revolution in American foreign policy that the president drove.[170] The scale of the tragedy of 9/11 soon swamped the nuances of the unilateral emphasis and led to a more Neo-conservative perspective, with emphases on raw unilateral military power, moral ideals and the Middle East.[171] Ironically, at the very moment when international support and sympathy for the US was at its greatest, the president asked the world 'are you with us or against us?'

The militarised response to terrorism, announced by the president with the 'War on Terrorism', and the state-centric emphasis of the neo-conservative and realist agenda, gave the Army a much clearer and defined strategic role. The premise was that the challenges were 'essentially military in character and that military power alone can deliver victory'.[172] The use of force by the US would thus, when the Army was involved, be by default based on the developments that had taken place within the Army. These criteria set the priorities for their use. For example, as Bob Woodward observed, General Tommy Franks's briefing to the President in December 2001 concerning an invasion of Iraq had a list of needs that 'put the president on notice that the military had certain expectations, that the success of any operation would be contingent on others meeting those stated conditions. At the same time it could be seen as a list of demands.'[173]

Having declared a 'war on terrorism',[174] the first strategic requirement was to harass and attack the bases of Al Qaeda and capture Osama Bin Laden. It was a situation ironically reminiscent of the Schultz–Weinberger debate of the early 1980s, when the State Department had called for US military forces to be used against terrorist training camps in the face of Pentagon criticism and rejection of this role. It was also a repudiation of the more careful approach of the Reagan era and the Clinton administration's use of cruise missiles. However, Bin Laden slipped through the net and the war rapidly shifted from being one against terrorists to one aiming to bring down the Taliban regime that hosted them. The war against terrorism thus became far more conventional and fought as an issue of regime change. This trend was soon extended to the rogue regime of Saddam Hussein in Iraq. Each will be examined in turn.

Afghanistan

'Operation Enduring Freedom' in Afghanistan focused on the destruction of terrorist training camps and associated infrastructure, the capture of Al Qaeda's leadership and ending all terrorist activity in Afghanistan. It also aimed to bring down the Taliban regime and establish a government capable of providing peace and stability. Military expediency determined strategy as the nature of the terrain made the operation a difficult military task, as did running operations in a land-locked country – technology was thus a key force multiplier, run from the Central Command's Headquarters back in Tampa, Florida.[175] Special Forces' teams liaised with Northern Alliance warlords for an offensive against the Taliban. Kabul fell without a fight on 11 November 2001 and Konduz later in the month. Many Al Qaeda defenders fled into Pakistan. In March 2002 'Operation Anaconda' was launched against a concentration of hideouts. This aggressive clearing operation used large amounts of firepower and dispersed Al Qaeda resistance sufficiently to bring the main combat operations to a close. It had been a very rapid and highly successful operation.

The intervention in Afghanistan continued the trend towards the use of air power and aimed to avoid the use of heavy ground forces.[176] Much to Rumsfeld's annoyance, the initial planning was deeply conventional.[177] The actual operation looked to have a 'light footprint'. However, it was a conventional air campaign, combined with the extensive use of Special Forces, though never in huge numbers. Allies within Afghanistan provided much of the ground support capability. As Stephen Biddle says, this combination of Precision Guided Munitions (PGMs), Special Force and indigenous allies is not a revolution, but actually a typical twentieth-century mid-intensity conflict, with unusually heavy firepower.[178] What is noteworthy is the fact that in Afghanistan the Special Forces initially worked for the CIA, building support among the population and co-ordinating local forces. However, once it was returned to Army control the priority became hunting the Taliban and Al Qaeda; even though the intelligence was so bad it was not a very effective reallocation of role. Basically, Special Forces were re-conventionalised, for example, having to shave off their beards. Like Vietnam, the Army moved them from working with and protecting the population, towards hunting and engaging the enemy.[179]

Operation 'Enduring Freedom' in Afghanistan is a good case study to evaluate American conventional military power, but it is hardly a watershed as it was so one-sided and took place in a failed state that had been riven by civil war for 23 years – though of course the Soviets had come to grief there.[180] Though the terrain made identification of targets very difficult, for advocates of the Revolution in Military Affairs the war was a significant fillip for the use of technology.[181] The operations in Afghanistan were seen as a successfully applied Network-Centric understanding of warfare. The Taliban collapsed so quickly because

> Air attacks also made it very difficult for the Taliban to move around within Afghanistan, thus preventing them from concentrating to meet attacks. Another is that the speed of advance, once it got going, made it impossible for Taliban leaders to react in time. This would be the OODA-loop theory of victory for network-centric warfare.[182]

However, as Warren Chin has shown, the factors that led to the Taliban's defeat had a lot to do with its vulnerability due to the prevailing political conditions within Afghanistan, rather than simply US military reforms or Taliban incompetence.[183]

Three years on, elections have been held in Afghanistan and there is a multi-national operation stabilising the country. However, the security situation is still allowing terrorist groups to regroup and plan attacks, and the drug trade has actually increased. Military forces in Afghanistan 'are dealing with threats posed by foreign fighters and the remnants of the Taliban, by "warlords", and by standing militias, exacerbated by a lack of capacity in the Afghan army and police'.[184] The situation is particularly critical on the eastern border with Pakistan and the south around Kandahar. The serious security gap outside Kabul is a continual problem because the US-led military has focused exclusively on 'anti-terrorist' operations, rather than securing the country through peace enforcement and peacekeeping operations.[185] However, a few US units have changed tactics and moved to 40-soldier platoons living in villages to tie themselves in better with the local communities.[186] However, the Taliban are slowly rebuilding, and Afghanistan's future as either a floundering state or narco-mafia state of opium producers and warlords is still in the balance.[187] Obviously, Afghanistan now has far less potential to generate a direct threat to the US and in this regard the intervention has worked, for now. The US is slowly internationalising the security problem as it shifts the emphasis from a unilateral approach to warfighting to a multilateral peace-building approach. Kabul has a 6,500-strong UN peacekeeping force, and a small 1,800-strong NATO force.

The US military strategy in Afghanistan had lasting political ramifications that have made it difficult to establish effective governing institutions. The 'light footprint' ideal of relying on local forces has meant the US is in a pact with the warlords and militia leaders whose very survival depends on continuing insecurity.[188] This has been at the root of all other problems in reconstruction efforts in Afghanistan, especially as the focus has been on anti-terrorism activities rather than rebuilding. In addition, US authority in Afghanistan continues to rely on 'awe as much as force'. The awe is maintained, not by a sizeable presence, but by timely and destructive air power. The issue for the US, as anthropologists have long pointed out, is that the legitimacy of violent force is based on its moral acceptance, and once that acceptance begins to diminish a downward spiral of greater uses of physical force is generated, until there is no difference between good or bad, legitimate or illegitimate, uses of violence.[189] In Afghanistan, for example, as Michael Ignatieff observed, mistakes such as the bombing of a wedding party in summer 2002 may be deemed military 'mistakes', but it reduces awe and awakens more resistance to American power.[190] It is an example of the fact that war is a social activity, rather than simply a technical problem, and there is a clear and intimate linkage between social, political and economic reconstruction, along with the security and governance issues that inherently lie within it. This aspect of conflict has been avoided in the name of 'technical' professionalism.

The strategic failure to capture Osama Bin Laden does not undermine the fact that there is now a reduced threat from Afghanistan but it was achieved through 'regime change' rather than decapitation of Al Qaeda – it became a conventionalised war against a new and asymmetric threat. A broader view is needed.

The Bush doctrine

The administration developed a new doctrine governing the use of military force based on broad principles, which addressed the national fears generated after 9/11.[191] As David Dunn rightly shows, it was a coming together of ideas of realist anti-appeasement, American exceptionalism, assertive unilateralism and threat inflation. It was also shaped by the US understanding of force – the use of force is not a failure of policy, and when fighting you fight to win.[192]

The concepts evolved in speeches from September 2001 and became formal policy in September 2002 in *The National Security Strategy of the United States of America* (NSS, 2002).[193] The threat is seen as the combination of religious and political extremism with the availability of weapons of mass destruction – radicalism and technology combined. The key threats are seen as terrorist organisations, weak states that harbour terrorist organisations and rogue states. The US looked to counter this with strong military forces and with a policy based on combining American values and interests. The Bush doctrine outlines an imminent, multifaceted, undeterrable and potentially calamitous threat to the United States that demands an unprecedented response because the threat has no precedent in American history.[194] Fundamental to the thinking was that the US would act against emerging threats 'before they are fully formed'.[195] The *National Security Strategy* aimed to prevent a threat developing and the emphasis was not on the immediacy of the threat, but on the necessity of acting when an attack can still be forestalled.[196]

Tied to the emphasis on pre-emption, the administration had outlined in the 2001 *Quadrennial Defense Review* a policy of regime change.[197] The weakness of the chosen opponents and their potential future capability meant the policy was actually more preventive than pre-emptive. The contentious issue of the US wanting to enforce one code of international conduct whilst following a permissive one itself is a crucial issue surrounding the controversial doctrine.[198] The controversy was embodied in the debate, especially with European allies, concerning the invasion of Iraq.[199]

Iraq

In the 2002 State of the Union speech President Bush outlined an 'axis of evil' where certain states and their terrorist allies threaten the peace of the world, especially through weapons of mass destruction.[200] It had deliberate echoes of fighting the 'reckless' Axis powers of the Second World War.[201] Iraq was listed as one of the key players in this and the source of the main terrorist threat, so it was seen as the site for the changing of US policy to a revisionist position towards the Middle East. Like his father before him, the president was invoking the Second World War and the threat of weapons of mass destruction (WMD) to garner public support for an attack on Iraq. Designating Iraq a 'rogue state' also fitted a mainstay of US foreign policy since the end of the Cold War. A 'rogue state', rather than being a specific kind of country, can actually be seen as denoting a political instrument to mobilise support for hard-line policies of isolation, comprehensive containment and rollback.[202] The Bush doctrine followed this line. Bush had Iraq at the top of his list of security issues, whilst Clinton told him that he had it last on his list of five.[203] This was ironic because 'by disregarding the success of inspections and sanctions, Washington discarded an effective system of containment and deterrence and, on the basis of faulty intelligence and wrong assumptions, launched a preventive war in its place'.[204] How the invasion serves US long-term security is still in question, as are the bases for the intervention.[205]

Three imperatives guided planning and conduct of the campaign: find and neutralise weapons of mass destruction, prevent Saddam setting fire to the oil wells or dumping it in the Gulf and isolate and destroy the leadership, whilst keeping the casualties to a minimum.[206] Associated with these was the aspiration to deliver humanitarian aid as quickly as possible.

Unlike the 1991 war, the emphasis was on 'overmatching power' rather than 'overwhelming force'. The air and land campaign was to be run synchronistically and to strike many targets simultaneously in an effort to overload the Iraq defence command and control. It was based on the use of precision munitions from a position of air supremacy throughout the war. After 12 years of No Fly Zones Iraq's capability was seriously eroded. The 2003 campaign looked to address the issues thrown up by the 1991 campaign, which had run the air and land campaigns sequentially rather than integrated them, and the strategic air effort had remained separate from the effort in Kuwait and the political infrastructure was not targeted. 'Shock and Awe' was the moniker given to the approach.

The basic idea was to 'shock' the Iraqis into surrendering by controlling rather than seizing territory south of Baghdad, before establishing points for a final attack on the capital city and home of the regime. An initial air strike failed to kill Saddam Hussein but the raid showed very clearly that the war was about decapitating and removing the Hussein regime. It was to be a rolling attack generating constant overwhelming pressure along several lines of operation. It was the embodiment of OODA-loop thinking, as it looked to create multiple crises for the regime to deal with and then collapse as it tried to cope with the overload. There was thus stress by the US on operational fires, manoeuvre, sabotage, disarray in the inner circle and supporting the opposition.[207] The emphasis was on tempo: the relative speed of the US over its adversaries. The vote in Turkey not to allow its territory to be used as a base for a ground force invasion eliminated the northern front as an approach for ground forces. This left the US Fourth Division, literally, at sea. This strategic turn of events was particularly galling for the Army because they were a fully digitised division with the most up-to-date equipment. The plan thus had V Corps swinging up along the western side of the Euphrates, whilst the Marines (1 MEF) would push through the heavily populated Tigris and Euphrates valleys to the east. The British division was to take Basra in the south. North of Baghdad the ground-force role was to be taken up by Special Forces – they were given responsibility for almost two-thirds of Iraq, having to protect the western flank of the Coalition and open a second front in the north, using Kurdish support but not enough to trigger a Turkish intervention in the region.

In less than a week US forces had made a huge advance into enemy territory, to such an extent that supply levels were becoming critical. The final advance on Baghdad ran from 30 March to 12 April, in a series of concurrent operations where the Third Infantry Division drove through the Karbala Gap and the First Marine Division crossed the Tigris at An Numaniyah.[208] The Marines used armour to destroy Fedayeen resistance in the cities with light infantry support. On the western side V Corps had a five-pronged assault. By 3 April the outskirts of Baghdad were being probed, and the combined air and ground attacks had rendered most of the Republican Guard units defending the city very ineffective. The US used 'thunder runs' of high-speed armoured sorties with A-10 support and attack helicopters, to capture the city, first taking the airport, then into the centre of the city, and finally the Marines driving in from the east. The Abrams tank, developed for a totally different environment, gave enormous confidence to the psychological task of imposing America's will on the capital. By the 6th, members of the regime were fighting their way out of the city. A mere 44 days after operations began, the president declared on 2 May 2003, 'Major combat operations are over.'[209] Unlike Bin Laden, Saddam Hussein was eventually caught some months later. For the Army it was a clear victory and it planned to start pulling out of Iraq within 60 days.

The speed of victory was stunning and the potential costs, in terms of casualties. the use of WMD, an Iraqi scorched earth policy and the like. were far lower than planned. Advocates of the Revolution in Military Affairs and transformation see this as due to the speed, precision and situational awareness of the Coalition. However, as initial post-action studies by the Army are making very clear. the inherent weakness of the Iraqi forces was as much a contributory factory as the use of technology.[210] Iraq's weaknesses created a permissive environment for US forces. The Iraqi military failings were so basic and so extensive that they are unlikely to ever be duplicated. For example, the training levels were so poor some Iraqi divisions had not had a live firing exercise in the previous 12 months, whilst some divisions had only shot four rounds in the previous year. The US equivalent would have fired around 2,500 rounds. Iraqi marksmanship was thus very poor. Their tactics were also amateurish and terrible, as they went for frontal assaults in civilian vehicles against armoured vehicles. They seemed to deliberately avoid soft-skinned vehicles. On top of this, the use of static positions failed to combine cover, concealment and fields of fire. However, the main surprise was the total failure to exploit the urban terrain. At least eight major cities could have been the scene of very prolonged fighting and the Iraqi High Command seems to have deliberately deployed Republican Guard and regular forces in rural areas and in the suburbs of key cities. It is puzzling why the Iraqis, like the Taliban before them, made themselves so vulnerable to air power by being caught in the open, and why they did not fight a protracted guerrilla war against the US high-tech offensive, particularly in the cities. The difficulties of the siege in Falluja in 2004 show how much could have been made of this, especially as the aim of rebuilding Iraq would not be compatible with levelling the city.

For all the speed of the high-tempo invasion, over a year later the fighting was continuing and the US casualty count went beyond 1,000. The most conservative estimates number the civilian casualties of the war at between 14,000 and 17,000. Over 7,000 were killed in the main phase of the fighting.[211] There has been continued resistance in Baghdad, the 'Sunni triangle' north and west of Baghdad, in the south in Basra and in the Shi'a cities of Najaf and Karbala, and the Kurdish city of Mosul and other northern cities. In the Spring of 2004 there was a serious insurgency in Najaf led by the Shi'a cleric Moqtada al-Sadr and was only quelled, despite the heavy fighting, by the intervention of the Grand Ayatollah Ali al-Sistani.[212] Falluja was controlled by anti-coalition forces for a long time. Earlier the US had withdrawn from Sadr city in Baghdad and handed over much of the patrolling to Iraqi forces, as the aggressive tactics in the city had not defeated the insurgents.[213] Like Afghanistan, the need to thus rely on indigenous 'friendly' forces in areas has weakened and complicated the attempted stabilisation of the country. Concerns have also been raised about the numbers of troops in the country being insufficient for the tasks given them.[214] On top of this Ambassador Jay Bremer's decision to disarm the 400,000 former members of the military has received rightful criticism for making the security situation much worse.

The Army's reluctance to be involved in 'nation building' haunts the post-invasion situation. For example, there was an underestimation of the post-war security challenges, leading to a lack of constabulary forces.[215] As with Panama, there was extensive looting after the regime had fallen, which in the case of Iraq stripped it of any viable infrastructure from which to rebuild. As one recent study put it 'The strategic plan for the military aspects of the 2003 war in Iraq have been lauded as brilliant. But neither the U.S. military nor U.S. civilian agencies have a corresponding capacity to plan for postwar reconstruction.'[216] Basically, the poor reading of the likely outcome complicated the situation in Iraq, as it was hoped the Coalition would be seen as liberators. It was also assumed the Iraqi police and military forces would remain intact. These misperceptions, coupled with the lack of security for reconstruction firms, means that the rebuilding of Iraq as a viable country and state is a long way off. Not only that, but there is also a growing awareness that foreign terrorists are being drawn into Iraq to engage in insurgency,[217] thereby drawing terrorism away from the US but making the invasion begin to have the opposite effect to the one intended of pacifying Iraq. The mismatch of national aspiration and action on the ground has, again, worked against each other. It is a situation akin to the nature of warfare outlined by van Creveld, Kaldor, Peters and others[218] – all rejected in the name of technical proficiency.

Colonel Charles Callwell pointed out in 1896 that 'small wars' ('operations of regular armies against irregular, or comparatively speaking irregular, forces . . . where organised armies are struggling against opponents who will not meet them in the open field'[219]) are different to wars against regular forces. He noted that beating the hostile armies is not necessarily the main aim, and that 'moral effect is often far more important than material success'.[220] Principles governing regular warfare may be wholly inapplicable in this environment. For example, the demands to use minimum force are a crucial component, and the responsibility for this lies within the organisation's culture.[221] Marine Commandant General Krulak gives a clear example of the changing nature of warfare that the Army needs to address. He called it the 'strategic corporal' and the 'three bloc' war.[222] Basically, land forces have to cope simultaneously with warfighting, peacekeeping and humanitarian aid, happening concurrently and within blocks of each other. Not only that, the 'strategic' consequences of actions, and the responsibility for the decisions that have a strategic effect, are moving much further down the chain of command. Being fast and decisive with full spectrum dominance did not resolve this problem, and neither does a centralised digitised command. After the Vietnam War, the rebuilding meant blindness to many of these aspects. Little wonder the Army is having huge problems even understanding the dynamics of the conflict in Iraq. For example, at the most basic level the Army has yet, for all the huge technical developments, to establish a dedicated training centre or specialised organisation to prepare and train its forces to conduct peacekeeping operations. It is thus still down to individual units to prepare itself for the operation.[223] The Pentagon has no single organisation to co-ordinate its response to asymmetric threats. It was only in 1998 the US military created programmes specifically for urban capabilities, though now the emphasis is on asymmetric warfare.[224] The lack of conceptual understanding is shown by the Army's creation in 2004 of an 'Asymmetric Warfare Group' to assess the tactics used to exploit US vulnerabilities, especially on how to deal with the threat of IEDs (improvised explosive devices) which are a particular problem in Iraq and are driving the changes.[225] The Pentagon is drawing upon Israeli practice.[226]

As Iraq shows, these broader skills are necessary in modern main force war as well as in the more humanitarian work. The accusations and trials for torture of US forces raise very large questions concerning the professionalism of some small parts of the Army in these circumstances. Young men and women in this very stressful environment need to be trained, physically and mentally, for its rigours. The culture of winning wars, strategic thinking premised on achievable objectives, a highly conventionalised Army face huge problems with the intractableness of urban conflicts and cultural wars.[227] The cost of not training for this and avoiding the issue of the social and cultural aspects of warfare is seen clearly in Iraq. The heavy reliance on officers at the platoon and company level challenges the traditional hierarchical thinking. Though the US military has been criticised for having a 'pathological resistance' to guerrilla warfare, some isolated units are attempting to work closely with the local culture and structures to provide a greater degree of security.[228] However, this should not be an optional extra but is inherent to the nature of war and strategy.

The lack of utility of the post-conflict US policy is partially due to the lack of utility of the Army, which is itself due to a gap in capability and concepts, and that is a product of a particular self-understanding. As Douglas Macgregor, a retired colonel, notes, in terms of logistics and force design the Army's deployment to Iraq showed that it still thinks in terms of Second World War models. In fact, as the leading critic and advocate of Army transformation, he notes that the limits of the self-understanding are very far reaching.

> More and more questions are being raised regarding the need for a transformed army because of the conventional army's repeated inability to make its presence felt in joint operations from Kosovo to Afghanistan. In contrast to the air force, the navy, the Marine Corps, and special operations forces, the conventional army is not seen as being interested in or as capable of 'riding to the sound of the guns' on the new battlefields.

> . . . The hastily assembled and largely unready task forces sent to Somalia, Haiti, Bosnia, Kosovo and Afghanistan point to structural and institutional weaknesses in the army that have persisted for fifty years.[229]

Legacy

Where Starry's reforms and Richardson's developments in the 1970s and 1980s focused on the priority of doctrine and training, the post-Gulf developments looked to the dominance of technology. One can see that by 1997 the trend was in full flow and reached fruition in Iraq. The 1997 *National Military Strategy* clearly reverted to the traditional US approach to strategy by seeing advanced technologies as providing 'new Operational Concepts and Doctrine' which in turn stimulates organisational change; 'information superiority is at the heart of full spectrum dominance'.[230] Robert Scales, the former Major General who led the Army after Next project, is clear the US Army will continue to replace manpower with technology for the foreseeable future.[231] The shadows of the techno-war thinking that were seen so clearly in the Vietnam War had returned. As Gibson said of Vietnam, instrumental action does not pre-empt social reality – the world of values, norms and traditions – and the Vietnam War had a deep structural logic of how it was conceptualised and fought: 'Vietnam represents the perfect functioning of this closed, self referential universe. Vietnam was *The Perfect War*.'[232] As the post-Vietnam reformers, and many in the Army, challenged this thinking, they showed that people and ideas come before hardware; what you are trying to do comes *before* what you can do. As Robert McNamara observed in 1995 of the prosecution of the Vietnam War,

> We failed then – as we have since – to recognize the limitations of modern, high-technology military equipment, forces, and doctrine in confronting unconventional, highly motivated people's movements. We failed as well to adapt our military tactics to the task of winning the hearts and minds of people from a totally different culture.[233]

As Iraq shows, the US and its Army is still better at winning battles than wars and it still struggles to win the peace. It has an over-reliance on one operational concept regardless of the strategic situation. The prevalent theme of this weakness in all the interventions examined can be seen to be shaped by the fact that the Army does not provide the capability to do otherwise, and does not sufficiently include the broader social and political aspects of conflict in its doctrine, training and planning. This is then exacerbated by the poor interagency process and the directions from the National Security Council.[234] At a more conceptual level, the terms and concepts provided by the Army's 'lessons of Vietnam' shape how the practice of strategy is perceived and the options on offer to the administration – the tools of the policy – shape the policy. As Hannah Arendt noted, 'the means used to achieve political goals are more often than not of greater relevance to the future world than intended goals'.[235] This makes the nature of Army reform a very important issue. As the final section of a book on the development of the US Army and its effect on US intervention policy, the Iraqi experience holds many depressing and frustrating features.

Conclusion

The first Gulf War showed the influence and effectiveness of US Army thinking on the American strategic culture. The war was a vindication of the learning that it had undertaken since the end of the Vietnam War. The setting of clear militarily achievable objectives for the military, providing it with the resources necessary to carry out the policy and garnering and sustaining support for the campaign was clear evidence of the absorption of the strategic lessons of Vietnam. Additionally, the war showed the Army's new 'way of war' and the fruits of its emphasis on realistic and doctrine-based training. It achieved a clear outcome fulfilling the president's objectives. The strategic lessons of Vietnam had been learnt and applied, with the political aims and military means used effectively in a synergistic manner. The Weinberger doctrine and the Army thinking which lay behind it provided the basis for a coherent approach to the use of force by the US.

However, the first Gulf War changed perceptions of warfighting and brought an end to the reforms that the failure in Vietnam had engendered, bringing a rise in the influence of air power in the strategic culture. The Army's understanding of professional as a technical proficiency, its avoidance of broader roles in interventions and a position enhanced by White House fears, reinforced this trend and crippled policy.

The intervention into Somalia showed the inadequacy of the Weinberger doctrine for coping with 'complex emergencies' – the doctrine that underpinned it virtually led the US into a state of war against the Aideed faction. The focus on politics being the concern of national strategy rather than integral to the tactical level meant that the US Army was unable to cope with the demands of the intervention. The Army was simply not doctrinally equipped for the intervention showing that the strategic lessons from the Vietnam War were less to do with the operational failure there and more to do with the rebuilding of the Army's identity and its proper use by the nation as a professional force.

The Army's professional focus, in terms of the roles it would undertake and the emphasis on technology in light of this learning and avoidance of a 'new' Vietnam, meant that it had to 'reinvent the wheel' when it came to the lessons of military interventions at the end of the Cold War.[236] This is ironic as the US had a strong tradition of Low-Intensity Conflict prior to the Second World War; it was a fundamental feature of the founding of America and its rise as a world power.[237] Weinberger had placed its concerns with 'effectiveness' at the centre of the debate and it provided, in Peter May's terms, a 'perceptual map' for the US on intervention issues.[238] By the time of the intervention into Kosovo the constitutive norms of the Army no longer provided a 'synchronised' and coherent strategy for the nation;

rather, it fragmented it. The Army was no longer the key driver shaping US strategic culture. As Kosovo showed, the Weinberger doctrine could be ignored and the tools of military intervention could be drawn from the other service far more readily – however, this reinforced the national emphasis on technological solutions.

The response to 9/11 shows the persuasive influence of the Army's thinking. The Bush administration has a highly militarised foreign policy, and the Combatant Commanders are key players in the nation's policy. The focus on winning battles and campaigns rather than on the peace that the nation wishes to win may address the immediate problem but leaves an enormous number of highly volatile situations that have to be continually addressed.

A coherent strategic criteria requires the Army to develop a more dialectic civil–military understanding, a 'post-modern'[239] professional identity, rather than retaining its post-Gulf model. It needs to integrate political and military aspects of conflicts far more to see the ambiguity that lies at the heart of strategy and modern warfare. Constitutionally the formal responsibility for this lies at the Combatant Commander level, as enshrined in law by the Goldwater–Nichols Act, but the practice of the Army, its doctrine and its Standard Operating Procedures need to enact this. It needs to see that politics informs all levels of warfare, and this includes the effect of force protection measures such as the use of tanks to patrol. The Army needs to be far more open and engaging with the population, and to recognise that issues such as cultural insensitivity and wearing reflector sunglasses has a political effect when dealing with the populous. The Army needs to be able to deal with the whole spectrum of warfare. The Army cannot split the political away from its responsibilities, and its thinking needs to reflect this. It also needs to demand of the nation's politicians what 'the peace should look like' and not rely on providing victory. The Army needs to use its influence to stop forcing the successive administrations and Combatant Commanders to think and work in terms of victories. After all, *strategy* is a method of thought.[240] The thought needs to broaden. As Liddell Hart says

> The object in war is to attain a better peace – even if only from your own point of view. Hence it is essential to conduct war with constant regard to the peace you desire. . . . If you concentrate exclusively on victory, with no thought for the after-effect . . . it is almost certain that the peace will be a bad one, containing the germs of another war.[241]

Whilst hostilities continued in Iraq, the Vietnam War again became an electoral issue in 2004.[242] The perceptions of Iraq and Vietnam are germinating one another. There is a need to change the questions that are asked in this debate, to allow different answers to be generated, to be creative. Rather than having a formulaic approach to strategy, the Army and the nation needs to be creative, and less bound by myths of the past or fixed images of itself and what it can do.

CONCLUSION

The primary objective of this book has been to answer the questions of how and why the US changed its military intervention strategy after the Vietnam War. The main argument has been that US strategy traditionally relied upon national mobilisation to co-ordinate its political aims and military means. After the Vietnam War the approach changed to a formula of establishing militarily achievable political objectives prior to the use of military force. What was deemed militarily achievable was set by the Army. The change was embodied in the Weinberger doctrine. However, rather than seeing this as simply a negative response to the experience in Vietnam, this book argues that the lessons were also indicative of the changed nature of the Army, and this heavily influenced the strengths and weaknesses of policy. The reading of the development of US intervention strategy outlined in this book has important consequences for the debates on US foreign policy, and the literature examining strategic culture and military innovation.

US foreign policy

By placing the concept of identity at the centre of the analysis of the strategic learning, it is possible to bring together the two broad wings of the debate over the nature of the Army's learning after Vietnam. The Army sees itself as fundamentally different from its earlier nature, whilst many critics argue that it has hardly changed its thinking and concerns since the Vietnam War. By highlighting the social context of its thinking and the central importance of the new doctrine to it, one can see the parameters that limited the nature of the change in strategic thinking and the new avenues that were opened up. They were applied, crucially, to all levels of warfare.

By arguing that the Weinberger doctrine is not simply a summation of the negative 'never again' response to the experience in Vietnam, this book challenges the assumptions that the so-called 'Vietnam syndrome' is simply about the fear of casualties by the nation. The first Gulf War showed that the US was prepared for high casualties. The centrality of the issue of casualties needs to be recast in terms of civil–military relations, where the Army is deeply suspicious of the administration misusing it and not understanding what it means to use military force. The Army's efforts at force protection are reflective of this tension, a perception enhanced by the administration's reaction to Somalia, which made clear that national interests were not sufficiently large enough to justify a continued presence. In one sense, therefore, the Army is protecting itself from the administration rather than the enemy on the ground. In addition, the reliance on firepower to protect troops is actually part of a broader institutional requirement to compensate for the historically poorly trained conscripted troops; as the Vietnam War showed there were officers prepared to accept large numbers of casualties and to use heavy firepower. The saliency of casualties to the US intervention debate is not, therefore, simply a post-Vietnam phenomenum of the value of the individual but an expression of a broader tension in civil–military relations and congressional–executive relations. Casualties are a political problem for the executive as a product of broader issues, not simply a problem in themselves. This perception requires a recasting of the understanding of the Army's reaction to the intervention agenda of the Clinton administration.

The espousal of the new interventionism by President Clinton in the first year of his term of office and the difficulties he faced in bringing it to any sort of fruition is at the core of this book. Rather than seeing the Army as simply blocking the administration's aspirations, it has shown that the Army was promoting a particular set of criteria for its use which was in conflict with the administration's requirements. The administration's understanding of the utility of force was based on a top-down model of policy requirements, whilst the Army had a bottom-up view in which the nature of the Army established what it could achieve and the requirements for doing so. The self-referential nature of the Army's understanding was borne out by the Somalia intervention where it was unable to cope with the unravelling situation there, and in consequence limited the administration's ability to intervene in conflicts. The liberal interventionist aspirations of the administration were therefore curtailed by the Army's lack of ability, as were the responses to the war against terrorism by conventionally attacking the regimes and state leadership in Afghanistan and Iraq. In consequence, the intervention aspirations were recast into a debate held in terms of what the US, namely the Army, could actually do. The withdrawal from the originally assertive liberal interventionist position was actually more reflective of the realist tools available to the administration, rather than an inherent feature of US strategic culture; the culture was being defined in terms of a crucial sub-culture within it.

Strategic culture

The analysis of the development of the US norms of military intervention raises important issues for the development of strategic culture literature. Strategic culture highlights the norms and the predisposition of a culture in the use of force. This book has outlined how those norms can change due to a sub-culture within the nation. The understanding the Army had of its role and its strategic outlook was a product of the broader culture, but the synonymic nature of the strategic understanding was ruptured with the Vietnam War. With this split the reformed strategic culture shifted from a position where the broader culture determined the strategy, to one where the Army became an intervening variable and altered the broader culture. In terms of the literature it provides a detailed case study of change within a culture, and highlights the importance of including the organisational culture of the military within the analysis of a nation's strategic culture. A strategic culture is more than the product of inherent cultural features of a nation. This raises the question as to what the intervening variable, in this case the Army, draws upon for its own cultural tendencies.

The divorce from the broader society, which the Vietnam War occasioned for the Army, opened it to the increased importance of the concept of professionalism in the force of arms, a position it developed in relation to fellow military professionals in Israel and NATO countries. The cross-fertilisation, drawing upon its own historical traditions and studies of strategy, helped develop a unanimity in military thinking and the terms of debate for fellow professionals. In the initial stages American thinking had little conception of the importance of the operational level because it drew upon Israeli thinking, whilst later the US Army's thinking helped to develop manoeuvrist thinking in UK forces. The internationalisation of military professionalism has important consequences for the analysis of the sources and nature of strategic cultures.

The norms of military professionalism are not necessarily those of the domestic culture, and can, therefore, come into conflict with it. The Introduction to the book gave the outbreak of the First World War as an example of the military developing a role that was counter to the needs of the political requirements of the national policies. In Germany's case, the needs of the Kaiser were limited and then driven by the demands and ability of the Army. Therefore, at an extreme level, the very defence of the nation, for which the Army exists to protect, can be imperilled by a lack of dialogue between the civil and military natures inherent within a nation's military. To be an effective tool of policy in less vital situations, the Army still needs to reflect its home society or else policy, such as Somalia, will fail. Strategic coherence in the US was achieved by the executive agreeing to the Army's criteria in the years between Weinberger's announcement and the conclusion of the first Gulf War. However, this does not provide a long-term solution as an administration can challenge the criteria and unravel the strategic solution. For the post 9/11 period the coherence is only achieved at the operational level as victory in the campaign has become, in and of itself, national policy. In some countries the civil–military clash between the understanding of professionalism and the civil society has led to military coups, a situation unlikely in the US but indicative of the antagonism that can be the outcome of the tension. The outcome of the antagonism in the US has produced a shift in the centrality of the Army as a tool of US policy and altered its strategic culture as a result.

The failure in Somalia and the resurgence of the Weinberger doctrine has the Army withdrawing from a potentially pre-eminent position as regards peace support operations, to one of only being utilised once Weinberger can be invoked, as with Bosnia in 1995. This position by the Army, consistent with its understanding of its nature, role and utility as a professional force, means that the executive turns to the Air Force and Special Forces as the services of choice to carry out its policy when the situation does not allow the Weinberger doctrine be invoked. In consequence, the strategic coherence and synergistic strategic understanding developed after Vietnam unravels, as the Army is bypassed and the Weinberger doctrine can be ignored. This leaves US strategy similar to the Vietnam era, where force was used gradually, instrumentally but crucially without casualties. If not, then overwhelming victory becomes national policy, as Iraq shows. In sum, one can argue that the most prominent legacies, rather than lessons, of the Vietnam War some thirty years after its end is that of the question of casualties, and a formulaic model of strategy that can be bypassed.

The ability to bypass the Army and the Weinberger doctrine allows administrations to ignore the strategic lessons of Vietnam. The attractiveness of air power to provide a low/no-cost instrument of coercion, underpinned by Army reluctance, returns US strategy to its cultural emphasis on technology and logistical pre-eminence, rather than strategic adeptness. However, rather than returning the understanding of strategic culture to that of the first generation, who saw the broad culture determining the strategic one, the argument of this book requires an examination of the intervening variable, the Army, coming between the broad national culture and the strategic culture. Due regard has to be paid to how a nation's military innovates, and the potential this has for the future of US strategic culture.

Military innovation

The changes that the Army initiated after the Vietnam War, based upon its developing identity and professional resources, highlight the internal nature of some of the key motors of military innovation. How a military changes is an issue of great importance during such an unstable strategic period. Understanding that it is not necessarily the most commonly cited drivers of change, such as the strategic environment itself, or changes in the technology of warfare, which can be the dominant force for change has large consequences for future policies and adaptations to new strategic roles. As President Clinton found out with his policy on gays in the military, the influence of poor civil–military relations can permeate the whole administration's strategic policy, though on first sight it is a counter-intuitive analysis. Additionally, understanding the different aspects of innovation highlights that the learning process after strategic failure is a complex and highly layered process.

The perception of failure, and defining it, is a crucial aspect of how the US, in particular, will adapt and shape the emerging strategic environment. Defining the cause of failure and learning from it is not the only process involved, as the consequences for the organisations involved may have a higher priority in how they address the rebuilding. After the Vietnam War the Army's priority was the reconstitution of itself and the learning from the war was placed squarely within the process. Therefore, being clear as to how the key variable, in this case the Army, perceives the broader failure will be a crucial aspect of the learning that is undertaken to adapt to the new strategic environment. After Somalia the paucity of the civil–military relationship was of higher concern to the Army than the actual tactical and operational issues involved with peace support operations. This was most clearly shown with the force protection priorities of the mission to Haiti. As a consequence, the innovation undertaken by the military is not necessarily that of addressing the operational failure of a mission, or adapting to new strategic demands. Central to the perception of these important issues, and how they are addressed, is the question of the organisation's sense of identity.

This book has placed the Army's understanding of its identity at the centre of the innovation process that it undertook after the Vietnam War. The drivers behind the changes in the Army's doctrine, with the development and adoption of AirLand Battle, were significantly different from the most commonly accepted ones, as the doctrine changed during a period when the strategic environment did not alter. Additionally, it laid out the future technological requirements of the Army doctrine, rather than simply embodying current technical advancements. The internal development of a doctrine-based professional identity allowed the Army to change its traditional way of war independently of these two common factors. Doctrine was an explicit tool to change the culture within the Army and how it went about its business. However, the changes in doctrine could not be independent of the other developments and so it is necessary to recognise that the development and acceptance of the changes was due to the Army addressing a specific operational and strategic problem in Europe.

The consensus that existed about the importance of the role of Europe, and the problems it faced there, enabled reform. Crucially, consensus was not available to advocates of Low-Intensity Conflict (LIC), or the type of lessons that could be drawn from Vietnam, and once these issues began to be re-addressed it was only after the core identity had been rebuilt on the work from AirLand Battle doctrine. However, as the book shows, defining a specific problem, which can achieve consensual support, is not alone sufficient; central to the innovation process are the key individuals who design and manage the changes.

The complex interplay between the Army structure and the individual agents of change has been conceptualised as 'structuration', where the practices of the key individuals constitute the structure. There were key turning points in the development of the Army's approach to warfighting, its new culture and the nation's strategy after the Vietnam War. The decision by General Abrams to give the Reserves the logistical responsibility in the Total Force; the emphasis on training, leadership and doctrine manuals by DePuy; Starry's development of AirLand Battle doctrine and the systems approach he took to its development and adoption; Richardson's perpetuation of it and the operational art; and General Meyer's support as Army Chief of Staff, were vital. All these men had been members of the pre-Vietnam War Army, were steeped in its traditions, but were able to change the Army's outlook as a result of the disarray after the war. The Army, therefore, can change but it required men in key positions at a period of self-doubt to do so at this time.

The success of the first Gulf War and the confidence it brought has blocked the potential learning of the Army, leaving one to postulate that failure is necessary to the learning process, not to provide specific lessons but to open the organisation to change. However, changes have to be focused on the potential strategic environment and the Army's role, or else the sensitivity to the civil–military aspect of identity will be too distorting to the conclusions, as seen after Somalia. Distrust of the administration's support, after the failure in Somalia and the fear of the social reforms of gays and women in the Army, cut to the core of the Army's identity and limited its potential to respond to the new international environment and develop a role within it. This in turn restricted the broader culture's ability to adapt and act internationally. Namely, the Army's reluctance alters US strategy, and this in turn broadens the understanding of the nature and sources of strategy itself.

The nature of strategy

This book is a focused case study of how and why a nation changed its understanding of strategy after failure. The formula that the US developed was an example of strategic maturity, developing appropriate aspirations and capabilities to carry out foreign policy, but the sources of that learning indicate the need to account for internal rather than simply external pressures. Realism's stress on the irrelevancy of the internal characteristics of a state is shown to be inadequate to account for the changes in state strategy in the case examined. How the state responds to the international state system is not simply an unambiguous product of national interest in an anarchical system; the formulation of the national interest and capabilities to realise it are explicitly domestic. In the case of the US, the Clausewitzian model of strategy as the continuation of politics is shown to be reliant on how the identity of the Army perceives its utility, as political objectives have to be militarily achievable and what is achievable is a product of the Army's identity. The Weinberger doctrine reinforced this model and was shown to be self-justifying, so that as the 'broader' security issues arose the Army's ability to provide appropriate capabilities to address these issues limited the ability of the US to bring them to fruition. Not only that, the narrowness of the thinking weakened US policy in Iraq in its efforts to win the battles but not the peace.

The outcome of this trend is the reinforcement of the Clausewitzian tradition rather than an opening up to a broader understanding of security issues. The military role in broader security concerns is limited by the conceptualisation of professionalism in the Army. With the appropriate tools unavailable, the executive has to rely on alternatives, thereby changing the nature of the nation's strategy for essentially negative rather than operationally appropriate reasons. To change the nation's land power capability, and hence its strategy, includes a requirement to recast the Army's identity, as that understanding of identity is central to how the nation 'learns' its strategy.

However, the learning process outlined in this book did not simply rely on social constructivism to provide the framework. It showed that the sociology of knowledge and identity were central themes in the process, but that they accompanied more traditional realist issues of military power in the international system. Strategic demands for new roles and capabilities are formulated through the social aspects of the individuals and organisations involved, meaning that the process of adaptation is multifaceted. The pivotal dilemma of addressing the Soviet forces' second echelon attacks is a case in point where the two fields were involved. The response opened up new vistas in operational analysis, a new 'way of war' and provided the tools to bring to fruition ideas concerning jointery. Awareness of the factors involved in the making of strategy, and its response to strategic environmental changes, is vital, as the US's role in international affairs is so significant and influential that its response helps shape and establish the very nature of the relations.

The US response to the immediate novelty of the post-Cold War period was hampered by the time it took for its agents of policy to adapt to the new environment, and to develop a new and appropriate identity. The aspirations of the New World Order and the hope of 'assertive multilateralism' were surprisingly short-lived as US policy. The rapidity of change was too fast for the Army to adapt in time; the era began just as sufficient learning had taken place to address the strategic requirements of the previous strategic environment. The first Gulf War was the vindication for the Army, of the learning that had taken place over the nearly twenty-year period after the Vietnam War. The demands of the new interventionism appeared within four years of the major review process begun under President Bush at the end of the Cold War.

New policy, as Rumsfeld's experience shows, can be shaped by the anachronistic tools available to the executive power, requiring analysts of strategy to look beyond the demands of external policy aims and resources utilised to fulfil them, towards the domestic requirements that shape the resources themselves. The Weinberger doctrine is more than just a statement of the criteria for effective external use of force, but recognition of the domestic constituencies that need to be addressed for policy to be realised. In its original formulation it was an advance in US strategic understanding, but the speed of the new tasks shook the foundations of the Army's identity forcing the reassertion of the doctrine. It was a regressive step. rather than moving strategy on towards a more complex and nuanced understanding, it reinforced a formulaic approach to strategy.

In terms of the use of force debate within the US, this book has questioned the nature of the evolution and development of strategy and highlighted the key constituencies that are involved in its implementation. Rather than simply seeing the Weinberger doctrine as an expression of the adherence to classical principles of war, it outlines the broader issues that went into the learning of the principles and their domestic purpose. For the US debate on the use of force to move forward, the discussion needs to focus on the state of civil–military relations and clarify the limits and motives behind what is defining the limits of the 'militarily achievable'. As their contemporary roots have made clear, recourse to so-called 'timeless principles' is insufficient; appeal should instead be made to the demands of the greater society on the military it raises and pays for. The Army again needs to be the expression of the society from which it arises, as only then will the US be able to rebalance its political aims and military means as it did in the last years of the Cold War. This, of course, may only be possible serendipitously as in the Reagan years, but that does not absolve future administrations from asserting its requirements and demanding the capabilities to fulfil them. As the Introduction outlined, a more dialectical civil–military relationship is itself reflective of the paradoxical nature of strategy. The Army needs to develop an equally dialectical civil–professional identity to enable the dialogue to take place.

Strategic issues

Ultimately strategy is decided at the grand strategic level and very few states have a thought-out grand strategy.[1] The problems the US has had in bringing its political ends in line with its military means is a reiteration of the complex and paradoxical nature of strategy, and highlights how impressive the efforts after the Vietnam War had been. It also signals the dynamism of strategy, as it creates a continual need to keep on learning rather than settling for a formula that had previously proved successful. For the US, the domestic constituents (with civil–military relations at its core) rather than the international environment, have fundamentally shaped its learning of strategy; namely, US strategy is a 'self-referential' strategy.

A self-referential strategy is very vulnerable to self-deception. One of the fathers of Realism, the American Reinhold Niebuhr, warned the US long ago of the inherently self-deceptive nature of politics and the need to recognise it.[2] The American experience has also led to a particular foreign policy that sees itself as 'innocent'. This means for Niebuhr that the US

> Can understand the neat logic of either economic reciprocity or the show of pure power. But we are mystified by the endless complexities of human motives and the varied compounds of ethnic loyalties, cultural traditions, social hopes, envies and fears which enter into the policies of nations, and which lie at the foundation of their political cohesion.[3]

The self-referential route out of this dilemma is particularly difficult and dangerous in an era of the 'war against terrorism', when looking to address those outside of that particular way of seeing the world.

America's self-confidence in being the manifestation of the Enlightenment tradition, embodying reason and freedom, enshrined in the rule of law,[4] is not a universal or neutral way of looking at the world. In fact, the events on 9/11 2001 destroyed, for many, 'the West's ruling myth' of the secular, enlightened and inherently peaceful world.[5] After all, the century had been marked by America's belief in its gains from globalisation being mutually beneficial.[6] There needs to be an engagement with those who challenge the orthodoxy and raise large questions about America and what America is,[7] and the debate needs to draw on both sides of the argument as certainty and dogmaticism destroy constructive engagement.

The tensions that exist between ideals and violence are, of course, inherent within society as violence lies at the heart of the foundational myth of any state.[8] The US is no different, as it was born in the violence of the Revolutionary Wars and formed by the Civil War, and large-scale violence currently pervades it. The identity of the US has been put under great pressure by the violent events of 9/11 and its aftermath.

Terrorism is a very real danger but there is also the potential calamity due to an extreme response as America has always faced threats and always exaggerated them.[9] During the Cold War the US had a single enemy with the Soviet Union, a demonised monolith, which had the key features of ideology, intercontinental weaponry and geo-strategic interests. The current times are in danger of being recast in that mould, with Islam, terrorism and China taking the three roles in the traditional understanding of threat. As Tariq Ali so eloquently puts it, there is currently a danger of there being a clash of fundamentalisms: religious fundamentalism and imperial fundamentalism looking to discipline the world.[10] For example, the US enforcing one code of international conduct whilst following a permissive one itself has become a key issue for the US and international relations.[11] This is further complicated by the US being a technologically based culture – 'The more we become immersed in technology, the more difficult it is to be patient with the natural unevenness and unpredictability of living. We learn to close ourselves off.'[12] There is a need to ask open questions rather than simply rely on automatic and set answers.[13] Unreflective impositions of 'bounding' premises only polarise an issue – there is a clear need to be more reflexive to cope with the current age.[14] The US needs to accord dignity to those that are different – to feel enlarged, not threatened, by difference.[15] A closed attitude leads to demonisation.

The US faces the danger of defining what is outside itself, with the best of intentions, in the wrong terms. For example, 'Western man, becoming aware of the aggressive will to power of the East, sees himself forced to take extraordinary measures of defence, at the same time as he prides himself on his virtue and good intentions.'[16] With these words Carl Jung warned of the danger of the flaw in western thinking during the Cold War. For Jung the flaw was that the threat was the West's shadow being reflected back at it, thus the problem of the enemy was not simply a military or economic one, it was a moral one facing itself. Currently, the US has many resources at its disposal to address this problem of moral identity. David Campbell's advocacy that US security is defined by the 'other', the opposite, is flawed in not recognising how the inherent sense of self, and of America as an idea and ideal, is deeply embedded in American culture.[17] Walter Russell Mead's work, for example, outlines key trends of this sense of identity that run throughout US foreign policy.[18] But the sense of identity of the US is now deemed threatened by the events of 9/11. Regaining a clear sense of what America is, and not succumbing to the pressure to be defined by another, is one of the key political tasks for the US this century; recovering a sense of being a 'City on a hill' that is a home to refugees and a site of opportunity. This is not a perspective unique to neo-conservatism but it runs throughout the history of US foreign policy.

Finally, US culture has a problem coping with failure, and failures like Vietnam. To address the inability to deal with failure, there is a need, as the American writer Bill Holm says, for the focus to shift away from self-obsession and 'sympathetically imagine something outside itself'.[19] The need for empathy runs in the face of America's hegemonic power being understood simply as a unilateral opportunity. True, the US is burdened with enormous power and massive expectations. However, as Salman Rushdie's novel portrays, the expectations have generated *fury*, in and outside the US. As one of his characters says, America 'fears the fury of the world and renames it envy'.[20] The culture of fear pervades western society, which means that problems are inflated, potential solutions overlooked and new challenges are transformed into issues of survival.[21] There is still a need to come to terms with Vietnam, especially as 'We were humbled in Vietnam, purged, for a while, of a dangerous hubris.'[22] Exaggerated responses and avoiding risk is counter-productive, especially when linked to a lack of hubris. To re-establish solidarity within its borders and engage with those without, the US needs to turn back to its visionary resources and face the issue of failure and the risk of engagement.

The Army needs to express that as well, and not just focus on the technical aspects of the profession of war, or rely on its mythology of the Vietnam War and its lessons. It needs to be far more open in its innovation, to be a defender and embodiment of American values in an innovative fashion, and if that involves a lot of messy roles like peacekeeping and nation building, then so be it. That is why the nation pays for and raises an Army.

Ultimately, strategy, like virtue, is a product of the society from which it emerges; to be effective it cannot just be a product of only one aspect of the society, such as the administration or the military. Strategy reflects an understanding of past experiences, current dilemmas and future aspirations, and these tensions have different understandings that need to be kept in communication. For grand strategy this means that there is a need for political consensus building and an overall strategic direction, and the military to produce the means to fulfil this, with the politics permeating every level of military expertise. In these terms the Weinberger doctrine can be seen as the thesis, the virtuous aspirations as the anti-thesis, and the need for better civil–military relations and the resultant understanding of strategy as the synthesis. The inherent tension in this view creates a need for the US, in Alasdair MacIntyre's terms, to have a 'narrative unity' so that the necessary shared moral and political vision can bring together the practice, the understanding and the aim to create an understanding of virtuous behaviour that can gain authority.[23] The aims and the means cannot therefore be separated as in Weinberger's doctrine, neither does it mean that the past can be used to hobble developments. For the US this creates a dual task: internally, as with the Clinton administration's civil–military relations, and externally, as the George W. Bush administration found with its early posture of unilateralism and its current need to build international coalitions. There needs to be a more open approach to strategy rather than advocating a formula to ignore the inherent strains in addressing these issues. As Luttwak reminds us, strategy is not management because there is a reacting enemy; it is paradoxical.[24] Tensions are inevitable as perfection and predictable outcomes are not possible and what is thus necessary and inevitable should be embraced and not seen as wrong. American strategic thinking needs to be creative because creativity, by addressing the relation of internal and external issues, moderates those inherent tensions.[25] To paraphrase Grotowski, to be creative one must be dedicated, avoid the mechanical act and use the conjunction of spontaneity and discipline to mutually reinforce each other.[26]

This understanding of strategy is a long way from the current position of seeing strategy as a managerial task – where setting political objectives and having the clear means to achieve them is sufficient. Internal and external coalitions alone undo this formula. Strategy is inherently unstable, and coherence is generated by not treating the aims and means of policy as separate steps in a formula, but as part of a broader communal understanding of the past, present and future aspirations – and that lies in the realm of politics not military capability. As the American poet Wendell Berry says, 'the house is a shambles/ unless the vision of its perfection/ Upholds it like stone.'[27] What that vision is, and how the US addresses it, is crucial. Generating a vision is crucial for the simple reason that without one war will become a replacement elixir for the lack of fulfilment.

> As long as we think abstractly, as long as we find in patriotism and the exuberance of war our fulfillment [*sic*], we will never understand those who do battle against us, or how we are perceived by them, or finally those who battle for us and how we should respond to it all. . . . And we will court our own extermination.[28]

It is also crucial because there is no international institution that has proven capable of effective action without the power generated and exercised by the US.[29] America's need and ability to create a vision that generates a creative approach to strategy is thus an issue for the world.

NOTES

INTRODUCTION

1 Freeman, Chas. W. Jr. *Arts of Power: Statecraft and Diplomacy.* (Washington, DC: United States Institute of Peace Press, 1997) p. 3.
2 Hart, B.H. Liddell. *Strategy.* Second, revised edition (London: Faber and Faber, 1967) p. 321.
3 Luttwak, Edward N. *Strategy: The Logic of War and Peace.* (Cambridge, MA: Belknap Press, 1987) p. 8.
4 Luttwak, *Strategy*, p. 4.
5 Bridge, F.R. and Bullen, Roger. *The Great Powers and the European States System, 1815–1914.* (London: Longman, 1980) pp. 7–11.
6 Howard, Michael. *War in European History.* (Oxford: Oxford University Press, 1976) gives a marvellous overview in only 143 pages.
7 Tuchman, Barbara W. *The Guns of August.* (New York: Macmillan, 1962).
8 Clausewitz, Carl von. Ed. and trans. Howard, Michael and Paret, Peter. *On War.* (Princeton, NJ: Princeton Univerity Press, 1976) p. 87.
9 Keegan, John. *War and Our World: The Reith Lectures 1998.* (London: Hutchinson, 1998) p. 42.
10 Beaufre, Andre. *Introduction to Strategy.* (London: Faber and Faber, 1965) p. 13.
11 Kennan, George F. *Around the Cragged Hill.* (New York: W. W. Norton, 1993) p. 212.
12 'Text of Remarks by Secretary of Defense Caspar W. Weinberger to the National Press Club, November 28, 1984' in Weinberger, Caspar. *Fighting for Peace: Seven Critical Years in the Pentagon.* (New York: Warner Books, 1990) Appendix: pp. 433–45.
13 Stevenson, Charles A. 'The Evolving Clinton Doctrine on the Use of Force'. *Armed Forces and Society.* (Vol. 22, No. 4. 1996) p. 515.
14 Joint Chiefs of Staff. *National Military Strategy of the United States.* (Washington, DC: GPO, 1992) pp. 10, 26.
15 Les Aspin, 'Speech to the Jewish Institute for National Security Affairs, 21 September 1992' in Haass, Richard N. *Intervention: The Use of American Military Force in the Post-Cold War World.* (Washington, DC: Carnegie, 1994) Appendix D: pp. 183–190.
16 Mandelbaum, Michael. 'Foreign Policy as Social Work'. *Foreign Affairs.* Vol. 75, No. 1. 1996, p. 16. He refers to the intervention policy toward Bosnia, Somalia and Haiti.
17 White House. 'Clinton Administration Policy on Reforming Multilateral Peace Operations. (PDD 25.) May 5, 1994'. <http://www.fas.org/irp/offdocs/pdd25.htm>
18 Posen, Barry R. *The Sources of Military Doctrine: France, Britain, and Germany Between the World Wars.* (Ithaca, NY: Cornell University Press, 1984) p. 25. This issue was faced by the famous Weinberger–Schultz debate, where the respective Secretaries

of Defense and State argued over the use of US military force from different ends of the means/end axis. It is analysed in Chapter 5.

19 Betts, Richard K. 'Should Strategic Studies Survive?' *World Politics*. (Vol. 50, No. 1. 1997) pp. 7–8.

20 As Richard Betts explains: 'Foremost are political constraints that are essential (rooted in the U.S. Constitution), not peripheral [. . .] coherence may emerge if the process is well managed but it will always be suboptimal according to the logic of any particular philosopher king.' Betts, Richard K. 'Conventional Strategy: New Critics, Old Choices' in Miller, Steven E. (ed.) *Conventional Forces and American Defense Policy*. (Princeton, NJ: Princeton University Press, 1986) p. 196.

21 Posen, *The Sources of Military Doctrine*, p. 25.

22 Dessler, David. 'What's at Stake in the Agent–Structure Debate?' *International Organization*. (Vol. 43, No. 3. 1989) pp. 441–73.

23 'Structuration' is taken from Giddens, Antony. *The Constitution of Society: Outline Theory of the Theory of Structuration*. (Cambridge: Polity Press, 1984) pp. 1–40. Hay, Colin. 'Structure and Agency' in Marsh, David and Stoker, Gerry (eds) *Theory and Methods in Political Science*. (London: Macmillan, 1995) pp. 189–206 is an excellent analysis and Richardson, James L. *Crisis Diplomacy: The Great Powers since the Mid-Nineteenth Century*. (Cambridge: Cambridge University Press, 1994) is an example of how it can be fruitfully applied in international studies.

24 Preston, P.W. *Political/Cultural Identity: Citizens and Nations in a Global Era*. (London: SAGE 1997) p. 28.

25 Campbell, David. *Writing Security: United States Foreign Policy and the Politics of Identity*. (Manchester: Manchester University Press, 1992) p. 8.

26 Spiller, Roger J. 'In the Shadow of the Dragon: Doctrine and the US Army after Vietnam'. *RUSI Journal*. (Vol. 142, No. 6. 1997) pp. 41–54.

27 Galloway, Archie. 'FM 100-5: Who Influenced Whom?' *Military Review*. (Vol. 71, No. 3. 1986) p. 47.

28 Farrell, Theo. 'Making Sense of Doctrine' in Duffy, Michael, Farrell, Theo and Sloan, Geoffrey (eds) *Doctrine and Military Effectiveness: Strategic Policy Studies 1*. (Exeter: Strategic Policy Studies Group, 1997) p. 2.

29 Bacevich, A.J. *The Pentomic Era: The U.S. Army between Korea and Vietnam*. (Washington, DC: National Defense University Press, 1986) p. 5. See also Brodie, Bernard. *War and Politics*. (New York: Macmillan, 1973) pp. 479–96.

30 The key specialist journals were: *Military Review*, the journal of the Command and General Staff College and *Parameters*, the Army War College; the doctrinal debate was held in these journals and supplemented by the journals from separate arms of the Army: *Infantry, Armor, Field Artillery*. The *FM 100-5* editions of 1976, 1982, 1986, 1993 were of key relevance here. On the Vietnam War in particular, the lessons in Department of the Army. *A Study of Strategic Lessons Learned in Vietnam*. 8 vols. (McLean, VA: BDM Corporation, 1979) The Army's Vietnam Studies series and the Center for Military History studies were also valuable. The research was complemented by a series of confidential interviews with senior Army officers, civilian analysts and academics conducted in 1999, many of whom made relevant papers available.

31 Hay, Colin. *Political Analysis: A Critical Introduction*. (Basingstoke: Palgrave, 2002) p. 3.

32 Freedman, Lawrence. 'Mindless Eclecticism or Creative Synthesis?' in Clarke, Michael (ed.) *New Perspectives on Security*. (London: Brassey's, 1993) p. 131.

33 Freedman, Lawrence. 'The Professional and Political Context of Security Studies'. *Arms Control*. (Vol. 14, No. 2. 1993) pp. 204–5.

34 Hollis, Martin and Smith, Steve. *Explaining and Understanding International Relations*. (Oxford: Clarendon, 1990).

35 Betts, 'Should Strategic Studies Survive?' pp. 8–9.

36 Paret, Peter. 'The History of War and the New Military History' in his *Understanding War: Essays on Clausewitz and the History of Military Power*. (Princeton, NJ: Princeton University Press, 1992) pp. 209–26.
37 Catterall, Peter. 'What (if anything) is Distinctive about Contemporary History?' *Journal of Contemporary History*. (Vol. 32, No. 4. 1997) p. 445.
38 Travers, Tim. *The Killing Ground: The British Army, the Western Front and the Emergence of Modern Warfare, 1900–1918*. (London: Unwin Hyman, 1987) p xix. Marc Trachtenberg observes that the aim of the historian is to bring the interaction of the different strands together. See: Trachtenberg, Marc. *History and Strategy*. (Princeton, NJ: Princeton University Press, 1991) p. 278.
39 Important works outlining the changes include, Herbert, Paul H. *Deciding What Has To Be Done: General William E. DePuy and the 1976 Edition of FM 100-5, Operations*. Leavenworth Paper No. 16. (Fort Leavenworth, KS: Combat Studies Institute, 1988); Romjue, John L., et al. *Prepare the Army for War: A Historical Overview of the Army Training and Doctrine Command 1973–1993*. (Fort Monroe, VA: TRADOC. 1993); Romjue, John L. *From Active Defense to AirLand Battle: The Development of Army Doctrine, 1973–1982*. (Fort Monroe, VA: TRADOC, 1984); and his *The Army of Excellence: The Development of the 1980s Army*. (Fort Monroe, VA: TRADOC, 1993) outlines the doctrinal and later broader changes within the Army; Lovell, John P. 'Vietnam and the U.S. Army: Learning to Cope with Failure' in Osborn, George K., et al. (eds) *Democracy, Strategy, and Vietnam; Implications for American Policymaking*. (Lexington, MA: Lexington Books, 1987) pp. 121–54.
40 Scales, Robert H. *Certain Victory: The U.S. Army in the Gulf War*. (London: Brassey's, 1994) p. 36.
41 Sarkesian, Sam C., et al. *Soldiers, Society, and National Security*. (Boulder, CO: Lynne Rienner, 1995).
42 Gacek, Christopher M. *The Logic of Force: The Dilemma of Limited War in American Foreign Policy*. (New York: Columbia University Press, 1994); Hoffman, F.G. *Decisive Force: The New American Way of War*. (Westport, CT: Praeger, 1996).
43 Naveh, Shimon. *In Pursuit of Military Excellence: The Evolution of Operational Theory*. (London: Frank Cass 1997) pp. 250–331 covers the US developments.
44 Builder, Carl H. *The Masks of War: American Military Styles in Strategy and Analysis*. (Baltimore, MD: Johns Hopkins University Press, 1989).
45 Builder, *Masks of War*, pp. 3, 4, 8–9.
46 See: Allison, Graham and Zelikow, Philip. *Essence of Decision: Explaining the Cuban Missile Crisis*. Second edition. (New York: Longman, 1999) chapter 3 'Model II: Organizational Behaviour' pp. 143–253. Also for General Powell's very public rejection of a military role in Bosnia at time of great cutbacks: Powell, Colin L. 'U.S. Forces: Challenges Ahead'. *Foreign Affairs*. (Vol. 72, No. 5. 1992/3) pp. 32–45.
47 Carter, Ashton B. and Perry, William J. *Preventive Defense: A New Security Strategy for America*. (Washington, DC: Brookings Institution, 1999) pp. 191–2.
48 Avant, Deborah D. *Political Institutions and Military Change: Lessons From Peripheral Wars*. (Ithaca, NY: Cornell University Press, 1994).
49 Rosen, Stephen Peter. 'New Ways of War; Understanding Military Innovation'. *International Security* (Vol. 13, No. 1. 1988) p. 134.
50 Downie, Richard D. *Learning from Conflict: The U.S. Military in Vietnam, El Salvador, and the Drug War*. (Westport, CT: Praeger, 1998) and Bickel, Keith B. *Mars Learning: The Marine Corps' Development of Small Wars Doctrine, 1915–1940*. (Boulder, CO: Westview, 2001).
51 See: Posen, *The Sources of Military Doctrine*.
52 Kier, Elizabeth. *Imagining War; French and British Military Doctrine Between the Wars*. (Princeton, NJ: Princeton University Press, 1997) p. 12.

53 See: Farrell, Theo. 'Sliding into War: The Somalia Imbroglio and US Army Peace Operations Doctrine'. *International Peacekeeping*. (Vol. 2, No. 2. 1995) pp. 194–214.
54 Examples are: Fuller, J.F.C. *Armament and History: A Study of the Influence of Armaments on History from the Dawn of Warfare to the Second World War*. (London: Eyre and Spottiswoode, 1946); and Dupuy, Trevor N. *The Evolution of Weapons and Warfare*. (New York: Da Capo, 1984).
55 The Army Chief of Staff Creighton Abrams put the 'five' together and his successor outlined the Big Five as 'a coordinated set of major items'. They were: a modern tank; an infantry fighting vehicle; an attack helicopter; a utility helicopter; and a surface-to-air missile. See Weyand, Fred C. 'Shaping the Army for the Future'. *Strategic Review*. (Vol. 3, No. 2. 1975) p. 8. The 'five' became: the MI Abrams tank; the M2/3 Bradley; the AH-64 Apache; the UH-60 Blackhawk; and the Patriot missile. See Scales, *Certain Victory*, pp. 19–20.
56 Leonhard, Robert R. *The Art of Maneuver: Maneuver-Warfare Theory and AirLand Battle*. (Novato, CA: Presidio, 1991) pp. 138–55.
57 Scales, *Certain Victory*, p. 36.
58 Lind, William S., et al. 'The Changing Face of War: Into the Fourth Generation'. *Military Review*. (Vol. 69, No. 9. 1989) p. 4.
59 Kier, *Imagining War*, and 'Culture and French Military Doctrine before World War II' in Katzenstein, Peter J. (ed.) *The Culture of National Security; Norms and Identity in World Politics*. (New York: Columbia University Press, 1996) pp. 186–215; Farrell, Theo and Terriff, Terry (eds) *The Sources of Military Change: Culture, Politics, Technology*. (Boulder, CO: Lynne Rienner, 2002); Legro, Jeffrey W. *Cooperation Under Fire: Anglo-German Restraint During World War II*. (Ithaca, NJ: Cornell University Press, 1995); Rosen, Stephen Peter. *Societies and Military Power: India and Its Armies*. (Ithaca, NJ: Cornell University Press, 1996).
60 Posen, *The Sources of Military Doctrine* and Rosen, Stephen Peter. *Winning the Next War: Innovation and the Modern Military*. (Ithaca, NY: Cornell University Press, 1991).
61 Murray, Williamson and Millet, Allan R. (eds) *Military Innovation in the Interwar Period*. (Cambridge: Cambridge University Press, 1996); Kier, *Imagining War*; Trubowitz, Peter, et al. (eds) *The Politics of Strategic Adjustment: Ideas, Institutions, and Interests*. (New York: Columbia University Press, 1999). Work has not been confined to the US, there is important work looking at Soviet and post-Soviet issues: Zisk, Kimberly Martin. *Engaging the Enemy: Organizational Theory and Soviet Military Innovation, 1955–1991*. (Princeton, NJ: Princeton University Press, 1993).
62 Macmillan, Alan, et al. 'Strategic Culture.' in Booth, Ken and Trood, Russell (eds) *Strategic Cultures in the Asia-Pacific Region*. (London: Macmillan, 1999) p. 10.
63 Macmillan et al. 'Strategic Culture', p. 13.
64 Howard, Michael. *The Franco-Prussian War*. (London: Rupert Hart-Davis, 1961) p. 8. Howard later developed this idea by outlining four key aspects of strategy in his essay 'Forgotten Dimensions of Strategy' in his *The Causes of War*. (London: Unwin, 1984) pp. 101–15. He outlined the logistical, operational, social and technological elements.
65 Weigley, Russell F. *The American Way of War: A History of United States Military Strategy and Policy*. (New York: Macmillan, 1973). Also Shy, John. *A People Numerous and Armed: Reflections on the Military Struggle for American Independence*. Revised edition (Ann Arbor, MI: University of Michigan, 1990).
66 Linn, Brian M. 'The American Way of War Revisited'. *Journal of Military History*. (Vol. 66, No. 2, 2002) pp. 501–30.
67 Weigley has accepted the limitations of his 'attritional–annihilation' analysis and the under-emphasis on manoeuvre thinking. See: Weigley, Russell F. 'Response to Brian McAllister Linn'. *Journal of Military History*. (Vol. 66, No. 2. 2002) pp. 531–33.

The current study helps add to broadening the understanding of the American way of war by its emphasis on the development of manoeuvre thinking in the 1970s and 1980s.

68 Baritz, Loren. *Backfire: A History of How American Culture Led Us into Vietnam and Made Us Fight the Way We Did.* (Baltimore, MD: Johns Hopkins University Press. 1985). Baritz focuses upon the cultural myths, the political assumptions and nature of political and military bureacratic behaviour that produces an American way of war which is 'congruent' with American culture.

69 Jacobsen, Carl G. (ed.) *Strategic Power: USA/USSR.* (London: Macmillan, 1990). Gray, Colin S. *Nuclear Strategy and National Style.* (Lanham, MD: Hamilton Press, 1986) and his 'Strategic Culture as Context: The First Generation of Theory Strikes Back'. *Review of International Studies.* (Vol. 25, No. 1. 1999) pp. 49–69.

70 Johnston, Alaistair Iain. 'Thinking about Strategic Culture'. *International Security.* (Vol. 19, No. 4. 1995) pp. 36–8.

71 Howard, Michael. 'Review of *The Making of Strategy: Rulers, States and War.* (eds) Williamson Murray, Macgregor Knox, and Alvin Bernstein'. *War in History.* (Vol. 4, No. 1. 1997) pp. 105–10.

72 Johnston, 'Thinking about Strategic Culture', pp. 41–3 and Kier, *Imagining War,* pp. 3–9, 21.

73 Johnston, 'Thinking about Strategic Culture', p. 48.

74 The phrase 'way of war' referring to the military's operational style, rather than the national culture is also made in McInnes, Colin. *Hot War, Cold War: The British Army's Way in Warfare 1945–95.* (London: Brassey's, 1996) pp. 1–2; Hoffman, *Decisive Force,* pp. 1–3.

75 For example, the attritional failure of the First World War is often seen as the source of innovation for restoring manoeuvre and mobility to the battlefield, especially with the development of blitzkrieg by Germany. Rosen points out that failure can in fact lead not to innovation but to reinforcing more failure, especially as bureaucracies are designed not to change. Rosen, *Winning the Next War,* p. 4. Andrew Krepinevich's *The Army in Vietnam.* (Baltimore, MD: Johns Hopkins University Press, 1986) is really a study of this phenomena within the US Army during the Vietnam War.

76 Rosen, *Winning the Next War,* pp. 185–220, and Zisk, *Engaging the Enemy.*

77 Ellis, John. *Brute Force: Allied Strategy and Tactics in the Second World War.* (London: Andre Deutsch, 1990).

78 Weigley, *The American Way of War.*

1 THE US ARMY AND AMERICAN STRATEGIC CULTURE

1 Builder, *The Masks of War,* p. 86.

2 Booth, Ken. 'American Strategy: The Myths Revisited' in Booth, Ken and Wright, Moorhead (eds) *American Thinking about Peace and War.* (Hassocks, Sussex: Harvester, 1978) p. 14.

3 Mahan's classic work is: Mahan, Alfred Thayer. *The Influence of Sea Power Upon History 1660–1783.* Fifth edition. (Boston, MA: Little, Brown, 1890). On Mitchell, see MacIsaac, David. 'Voices from the Central Blue: The Airpower Theorists' in Paret, *Makers of Modern Strategy,* pp. 624–47.

4 Gray, Colin S. 'Strategy in the Nuclear Age: The United States, 1945–1991' in Murray, Williamson, et al. (eds) *The Making of Strategy: Rulers, States and War.* (Cambridge: Cambridge University Press, 1994) p. 583. Some have seen this tradition being compensated by 'overthink'. See: Coles, Harry L. 'Strategic Studies Since 1945, the Era of Overthink'. *Military Review.* (Vol. 53, No. 4. 1973) pp. 3–16.

5 Builder, *The Masks of War,* p. 87.

6 Synder, Jack. 'The Concept of Strategic Culture: Caveat Emptor' in Jacobsen, Carl G. (ed.) *Strategic Power: USA/USSR*. (London: Macmillan, 1990) p. 8.
7 Keegan, John. *The Mask of Command; A Study of Generalship*. (London: Jonathan Cape, 1987) pp. 1–2.
8 For the central importance of the nature of political institutions to military innovation see: Avant, *Political Institutions and Military Change*.
9 Anderson, Fred. *Crucible of War: The Seven Years' War and the Fate of Empire in British North America, 1754–1766*. (London: Faber and Faber. 2000) is very good in showing how independence would have been achieved without war was it not for the the Seven Years' War.
10 Palmer, Dave R. *1794: America, Its Army, and the Birth of the Nation*. (Novato, CA: Presidio, 1994) pp. 281–2.
11 'The Relationship between the American Revolutionary War and European Military Thought and Practice' in Paret, Peter. *Understanding War: Essays on Clausewitz and the History of Military Power*. (Princeton, NJ: Princeton University Press, 1992) p. 31.
12 Palmer, *1794*, p. 133.
13 'Oath of Commission' quoted in full in Department of the Army. *FM 100-1, The Army*. (Washington, DC: GPO, 1994) chapter 1.
14 FM 100-1 The Army. 1994. Foreword.
15 Moellering, John H. 'The Army Turns Inward?' *Military Review*. (Vol. 53, No. 7. 1973) p. 70.
16 The Civil War was the last great Napoleonic war as new technology was not as significant as often thought. See: Griffith, Paddy. *Battle Tactics of the American Civil War*. (Ramsbury: Crowood, 1987) pp. 189–92.
17 Howard, Michael. 'The Forgotten Dimensions of Strategy' in his *The Causes of War*. (London: Unwin, 1984) p. 103.
18 Starry, Donn A. 'A Perspective on American Military Thought'. *Military Review*. (Vol. 59, No. 7. 1989) p. 4.
19 McPherson, James M. *Battle Cry of Freedom: The Civil War Era*. (Oxford: Oxford University Press. 1988) gives a complete view of the war, placing it in the broader perspectives of the clashes between the different cultures of the North and South.
20 Ambrose, Stephen E. *Upton and the Army*. (Baton Rouge, LA: Louisiana State University Press, 1964) p. 112.
21 Hackett, John. *The Profession of Arms*. (London: Sidgwick and Jackson, 1983) p. 129.
22 Cunliffe, Marcus. *Soldiers and Civilians: The Martial Spirit in America, 1775–1865*. (London: Eyre and Spottiswoode, 1969) pp. 431–5.
23 Royster, Charles. 'Comment on John Shy "The Cultural Approach to the History of War" and on Russell Weigley, "The American Military and the Principle of Civilian Control from McClellan to Powell"'. *Journal of Military History*. (Vol. 57, No. 5. 1993) p. 61.
24 Upton, Emory. *The Military Policy of the United States from 1775*. (Washington, DC: GPO, 1904).
25 Royster, 'Comment on John Shy', p. 61.
26 Ambrose, *Upton and the Army*, pp. 112–35; Huntington, Samuel. *The Soldier and the State: The Theory and Politics of Civil–Military Relations*. (Cambridge, MA: Harvard University Press, 1957) pp. 230–7; Avant, *Political Institutions*, pp. 26–9.
27 Weigley, *History of the United States Army*, pp. 315–26.
28 The General Staff Act was passed on 12 February 1903. Congress had revised the 1792 Militia Act in the January (known as the Dick Act).
29 Hammond, Paul Y. *Organizing for Defense: The American Military Establishment in the Twentieth Century*. (Princeton, NJ: Princeton University Press, 1961) p. 10. For an analysis of the reforms see pp. 10–48.
30 Hackett, *The Profession of Arms*, p. 193.

31 Bergamini, Oliviero. 'Nation, Organization and the Individual: The Military Thought of Theodore Roosevelt' in Adams, David K. and Minnen, Cornelius A. van (eds) *Aspects of War in American History*. (Keele: Keele University Press, 1997) p. 114.
32 He was appointed in July 1910.
33 The Rough Riders was a citizen-volunteer regiment raised during the Spanish War of 1898. It was famously heroic, a perception magnified by its lieutenant colonel, one Theodore Roosevelt. See: Weigley, *History of the United States Army*, pp. 296, 305–6.
34 Wood, Leonard. *The Military Obligation of Citizenship*. (Princeton, NJ: Princeton University Press, 1915) p. 41.
35 Originally summer camps to provide paying college students with military training, Wood opened a camp in Plattsburg, New York, funded privately, to train business and professional men as part of the preparedness movement. The idea spread. See: Weigley, *History of the United States Army*, pp. 342–3.
36 Bergamini, 'Nation, Organization and the Individual', p. 119.
37 Wood, *The Military Obligation of Citizenship*.
38 Hodgson, Godfrey. *The Colonel: The Life and Wars of Henry Stimson, 1867–1950*. (New York: Alfred A. Knopf, 1990) pp. 82–4.
39 Stimson was Secretary of State under Hoover (1929–33), and Secretary of War (1940–45) in the Second World War and under President Truman. See Hodgson, *The Colonel*, pp. 77 and 388.
40 Isaacson, Walter and Thomas, Evan. *The Wise Men: Six Friends and the World They Made*. (New York: Simon and Schuster, 1986). A speech on public service by Stimson in 1942 inspired the young George Bush to enlist immediately in the Navy. See, 'Remarks at the United States Military Academy in West Point, New York. January 5, 1993'. <http://bushlibrary.tamu.edu/papers/1993/93010500.html>
41 Hunt, Michael H. *Ideology and U.S. Foreign Policy*. (New Haven, CT: Yale University Press, 1987) p. 137.
42 DePuy, William E. 'Letter to General Bruce C. Clarke from General DePuy, 18 August 1976' in Gilmore, Donald L. and Conway, Carolyn D. (eds). *Selected Papers of General William E. DePuy*. (Fort Leavenworth, KS: Combat Studies Institute, 1994) p. 197.
43 Weigley, Russell F. *Eisenhower's Lieutenants: The Campaign of France and Germany, 1944–1945*. (Bloomington, IN: Indiana University Press, 1981) p. 2. Weigley provides an excellent analysis of the Army of 1940 in pp. 1–31.
44 Cohen, Eliot A. 'The Strategy of Innocence? The United States, 1920–1945' in Murray et al. *The Making of Strategy*, p. 464.
45 Ellis, *Brute Force*, p. 535. A similar point is made in Weigley, *Eisenhower's Lieutenants*, pp. 837–40.
46 Ellis, *Brute Force*, p xviii.
47 DePuy, William E. 'Letter to General Bruce C. Clarke from General DePuy, 18 August 1976'. *Selected Papers*, p. 197.
48 For example: Phil Silver's television series 'Sergeant Bilko' and the 'Beetle Bailey' cartoon series.
49 Czege, Huba Wass de. 'Clausewitz: Historical Theories Remain Sound Compass References; The Catch Is Staying on Course'. *Army*. (September 1988) p. 42. The author was one of the writers of the 1986 manual.
50 Hoffman, *Decisive Force*, p. 1. The strategic culture's more apocalyptic aspects of the prosecution of the Second World War is outlined in Sherry, Michael S. *The Rise of American Air Power: The Creation of Armageddon*. (New Haven, CT: Yale University Press, 1987).
51 Wilmot, Chester. *The Struggle for Europe*. (London: Wm. Collins, 1954) p. 136.
52 Starry, 'A Perspective on American Military Thought', p. 6.
53 'Just as mass production was the core principle of industrial economies, mass

destruction became the core principle of industrial-age warfare. . . . Mass production was paralleled by . . . the conscription of mass armies . . . World War II showed the awesome potential for industrializing death.' Toffler, Alvin and Heidi. *War and Anti-War: Survival at the Dawn of the 21st Century.* (Boston, MA: Little, Brown, 1993) pp. 38 and 40; see chapter 6 'Second Wave War', pp. 38–43.

54 J.F.C. Fuller, the famous British writer on strategy, actually challenges this analysis of Grant's strategy but cites it in his book: Fuller, J.F.C. *The Generalship of Ulysses S. Grant.* (London. John Murray, 1929) p. 195.

55 Weigley, *Eisenhower's Lieutenants*, p. 6.

56 Clausewitz, *On War.*

57 Howard, Michael. 'The Influence of Clausewitz' in Clausewitz, Carl von. *On War* (Howard, Michael and Paret, Peter ed. and trans.) p. 42.

58 Sarkesian, Sam C. 'The American Response to Low-Intensity Conflict: The Formative Period' in Charters, David A. and Tugwell, Maurice (eds) *Armies in Low-Intensity Conflict: A Comparative Analysis* (London: Brassey's 1989) p. 27.

59 Howard, 'The Influence of Clausewitz', p. 42.

60 Summers, *On Strategy*, p. 93.

61 This tendency is critically examined by John Ellis in his magnificent study: *Brute Force.* He argues that it was the level of material resources that was critical in winning the war, and that the Allies made 'less than optimum use of the resources', p xviii.

62 Scales, Robert H. Jr. *Firepower in Limited War.* Revised Edition. (Novato, CA: Presidio, 1995) p. 4.

63 Gudmundsson, Bruce I. *On Artillery.* (Westport, CT: Praeger, 1993) pp. 146–53.

64 Scales, *Firepower*, p. 19.

65 Ibid., p. 4. See especially, pp. 3–22 on 'Firepower in American Way of War'. The same point is made in Krepinevich, *The Army and Vietnam*, p. 5.

66 Eisenhower, *Crusade in Europe*, pp. 510–11. This different approach to casualties did not mean Zhukov used less firepower. For his attack on Berlin in 1945 he used 2,500,000 men, 41,000 guns and mortars, 6,200 tanks and 7,500 aircraft. See: Seaton, Albert. *The Russo-German War 1941–45.* (Novato, CA: Presidio, 1971) p. 566.

67 Wilmot, *The Struggle For Europe*, p. 129.

68 Kinnard, Douglas. *The War Managers.* (Wayne, NJ: Avery, 1985) p. 112.

69 Weigley, *The American Way of War*, pp xvii–xviii.

70 Wilmot, *The Struggle for Europe*, p. 796.

71 For a brief account of this see: Eisenhower, *Crusade in Europe*, pp. 436–40; and Betts, Richard K. *Soldiers, Statesmen, and Cold War Crises.* (Cambridge, MA: Harvard University Press, 1977) pp. 77–8.

72 Lansdale, Edward. 'Contradictions in Military Culture' in Thompson, W. Scott and Frizzell, Donaldson D. (eds) *The Lessons of Vietnam.* (New York: Crane, Russack, 1977) p. 42.

73 Weigley, *History of the United States Army*, p. 340. General Wood is discussed in particular in pp. 327–41.

74 See: '*NSC 68.* April 14, 1950. United States Objectives and Programs for National Security' in Etzold, Thomas H. and Gaddis, John Lewis (eds) *Containment: Documents on American Policy and Strategy, 1945–1950.* (New York: Columbia University Press, 1978) pp. 385–442. See also: Acheson, Dean. *Present at the Creation: My Years in the State Department.* (New York: W. W. Norton, 1969) on the thinking behind it and how the Korean War moved it from being a theory to a budget issue where defence appropriations and powers grew massively. See: pp. 373–80, 420–2.

75 Bacevich, A.J. *The Pentomic Era: The U.S. Army Between Korea and Vietnam.* (Washington, DC: National University Press, 1986).

76 Cohen, 'The Strategy of Innocence?' pp. 435–6.

77 Leffler, Melvyn P. *A Preponderance of Power: National Security, the Truman*

Administration, and the Cold War. (Stanford, CA: Stanford University Press, 1992) p. 176.

78 For an analysis of the inter-service thinking and rivalry in the legislation, see: Hammond, *Organizing for Defense*, pp. 186–226.

79 Strachan, *European Armies*, p. 188.

80 Boyne, Walter J. *Beyond the Wild Blue: A History of the U.S. Air Force*. (New York: St Martin's Griffin, 1997) pp. 21–50.

81 See Chapter 5.

82 Leffler, *A Preponderance of Power*, p. 209.

83 Weigley, *A History of the United States Army*, pp. 496–504.

84 Stueck, William. *The Korean War: An International History*. (Princeton, NJ: Princeton University Press, 1995) p. 3.

85 Scales, *Firepower*, p. 16.

86 Moellering, John H. 'The Army Turns Inward?' *Military Review*. (Vol. 53, No. 7. 1973) p. 72, for example, points to the Army being criticised for lack of POW collaboration; lack of motivation; and lack of discipline.

87 Hastings, Max. *The Korean War*. (London: Michael Joseph, 1987) p. 414.

88 Christopher Gacek provides excellent analysis of limited war versus all-or-nothing thinking from the Korean War to the Vietnam War in *The Logic of Force*. pp. 53–219.

89 Department of the Army. *A Study of Strategic Lessons Learned in Vietnam*, Vol. 8. p Ex 7.

90 See: Spanier, John W. *The Truman–MacArthur Controversy and the Korean War*. (Cambridge, MA: Harvard University Press, 1959).

91 Department of the Army. *A Study of Strategic Lessons Learned in Vietnam*. Vol. 8. p Ex 7.

92 Hilsman, Roger. *To Move a Nation: The Politics of Foreign Policy in the Administration of John F. Kennedy*. (New York: Doubleday, 1967), especially pp. 128–9, and Craig, Gordon A. and George, Alexander L. *Force and Statecraft: Diplomatic Problems of Our Time*. Third edition. (Oxford: Oxford University Press, 1995) pp. 259–63.

93 Taylor, Maxwell D. *The Uncertain Trumpet*. (New York: Harper, 1959) pp. 15–22.

94 For example see: Davis, Vincent. 'Defense Reorganization and National Security' in Hays, Peter L., et al. (eds) *American Defense Policy*. Seventh edition. (Baltimore, MD: Johns Hopkins University Press, 1997) p. 122.

95 Smoke, Richard. 'Theories of Escalation' in Lauren, Paul Gordon (ed.) *Diplomacy: New Approaches in History, Theory, and Policy*. (London: Collier Macmillan, 1979) p. 169.

96 Freedman, Lawrence. *The Evolution of Nuclear Strategy*. Second edition. (London: Macmillan/IISS, 1989) covers Korea, limited war and massive retaliation thinking. See pp. 63–119.

97 Bacevich, *The Pentomic Era*.

98 Kissinger, Henry. *Diplomacy*. (London: Simon and Schuster, 1994) p. 778.

99 Smoke, 'Theories of Escalation', p. 169. As so often, Henry Kissinger was the exception to the rule and his PhD was published as *A World Restored; Metternich, Castlereagh and the Problems of Peace 1812–1822*. (Boston, MA: Houghton Mifflin, 1957).

100 Walter Millis. *Armies and Men: A Study of American Military History*. (London: Jonathan Cape, 1958) p. 364.

101 Kissinger, Henry. *Nuclear Weapons and Foreign Policy*. (New York: Council on Foreign Relations, 1957) pp. 225–6.

102 For example see: Gacek's *The Logic of Force* on the British difficulties during the Boer War, p. 341.

103 Smoke, 'Theories of Escalation', pp. 162–3.

104 Cable, Larry. 'Reinventing the Round Wheel: Insurgency, Counter-Insurgency, and

Peacekeeping Post Cold War'. *Small Wars and Insurgencies.* (Vol. 4, No. 2. 1993) p. 235.

105 Summers, Harry G. *The New World Strategy: A Military Policy for America's Future.* (New York: Simon and Schuster, 1995) pp. 95–6.

106 Russett and Stepan, *Military Force and American Society.*

107 Huntington, *The Soldier and the State.* This is taken from the title of part III, 'Crisis in American Civil–Military Relations, 1940–55', pp. 315–466.

108 Schwarzkopf, H. Norman. *It Doesn't Take A Hero*, p. 107. He discusses his experiences in pp. 107–14.

109 Millis, *Armies and Men*, pp. 359–60.

110 'The unwitting effect of this was the creation of a neo-18th century type Army answerable more to the Executive than to the American people.' Summers, *On Strategy*, p. 14.

111 'Many soldiers will spend their entire careers preparing for war without ever having the opportunity to learn from practice on the battlefield.' Handel, Michael I. *War, Strategy and Intelligence.* (London: Frank Cass, 1989) p. 6.

2 THE VIETNAM WAR AND THE US ARMY

1 Barnett, Correlli. *The Swordbearers: Studies in Supreme Command in the First World War.* (London: Eyre and Spottiswoode, 1963) p. 11.

2 See: Kattenburg, Paul M. *The American Trauma in American Foreign Policy, 1945–75.* (New Brunswick, NJ: Transaction Books, 1980).

3 There is an enormous literature on the Vietnam War. To clarify the Army viewpoints, particular attention is paid to the accounts given by the senior commanders of the war, studies produced by the Army after the war and interviews with officers who served. The Army Chief of Staff, General Westmoreland (1968–72), commissioned serving senior commanders to write 'Vietnam Studies', which were published during the later stages of the war. The BDM corporation wrote a study for the Army published as: Department of the Army. *A Study of Strategic Lessons Learned in Vietnam.* 8 vols. (McLean, VA. BDM Corporation, 1979) which was critical of its approach. The Center for Military History produced later historical studies of the Vietnam War, which have been used.

4 Department of the Army. *A Study of Strategic Lessons Learned in Vietnam.* Vol. 8 p Ex 3.

5 Kissinger, Henry. *Diplomacy.* (London: Simon and Schuster, 1994) p. 480. For Kissinger's analysis of Korea and Vietnam see: pp. 446–92, 643–73.

6 Presidents Kennedy, Nixon and Johnson's powers were in excess of predecessors and perhaps in excess of the Constitution. See: Gelb, Leslie H. with Betts, Richard K. *The Irony of Vietnam: The System Worked.* (Washington, DC: Brookings Institute, 1979) p. 362.

7 For example: Freedman, Lawrence. 'Escalation/Limited War: The US View' in Jacobsen, *Strategic Power*, p. 159.

8 Kennedy, Robert. *Thirteen Days: A Memoir of the Cuban Missile Crisis.* (New York: Norton, 1969) p. 36.

9 General Palmer saw this generating a dramatic change within the Army. See: Palmer, Bruce. Jr. *The 25 Year War: America's Military Role in Vietnam.* (New York: Da Capo, 1984) p. 11. Krepinevich, *The Army and Vietnam*, is far more sceptical. See, pp. 36–55.

10 Taylor, *The Uncertain Trumpet.*

11 Gaddis, John Lewis. *Strategies of Containment: A Critical Appraisal of Postwar American National Security Policy.* (Oxford: Oxford University Press, 1982) p. 237. President Roosevelt's generation had had a European first agenda, in contrast to John F. Kennedy and George Bush who placed greater emphasis on the Third World.

12 Hilsman, *To Move a Nation*, pp. 128–9. Freedman, Lawrence. *Kennedy's Wars: Berlin, Cuba, Laos, and Vietnam*. (New York: Oxford University Press, 2000) pp. 290–1.
13 For the papers of the Taylor mission see: Department of State. *Foreign Relations of the United States*. (Washington, DC: GPO, annual) 1961–63 vol 1. pp. 380–614. Hereafter abbreviated as *FRUS* with year, volume and pages.
14 Maclear, Michael. *Vietnam: The Ten Thousand Day War*. (London: Thames Methuen, 1981) p. 57.
15 Gelb and Betts, *The Irony of Vietnam*, p. 361.
16 Caputo, Philip. *A Rumor of War*. (London: Macmillan, 1977) p xiv. Colin Powell was later to write that he had gone off to Vietnam in 1962 'standing on a bedrock of principle and conviction. And I had watched that foundation eroded by euphemisms, lies, and self-deception. [. . .] We had lost touch with reality' and were deluded by technology. Powell, Colin L. *A Soldier's Way: An Autobiography*. (London: Hutchinson, 1995) pp. 145–6.
17 Gaddis, *Strategies of Containment*, p. 237.
18 Paddy Griffith sees the war as being so complex because it was actually five overlapping wars: 'the international political struggle, the strategic bombing campaign, the interdiction campaign, the mainforce battle, and the pacification or "Village war."' Griffith, Paddy. *Forward into Battle: Fighting Tactics from Waterloo to Vietnam*. (Chichester: Antony Bird, 1981) p. 105.
19 Komer, Robert W. 'Foreword.' to Thayer, Thomas C. *War Without Fronts: The American Experience in Vietnam*. (Boulder, CO: Westview, 1985) p xxi. Komer wrote an excellent book on the Vietnam War: Komer. Robert W. *Bureaucracy at War; U.S. Performance in the Vietnam Conflict*. (Boulder, CO: Westview Press, 1986).
20 Karnow, Stanley. *Vietnam: A History. Revised edition*. (London: Penguin, 1991) p. 33.
21 Ott, David Ewing. *Field Artillery 1954–1973*. Vietnam Studies. (Washington, DC: GPO, 1975) pp. 3–6.
22 DePuy, William E. 'Our Experience in Vietnam: Will We Be Beneficiaries or Victims?' p. 397 and Ott. *Field Artillery*, p. 7.
23 Collins, James Lawton, Jr. *The Development and Training of the South Vietnamese Army 1950–1972*. Vietnam Studies. (Washington, DC: GPO, 1975).
24 Logevall, Fredrik. *Choosing War: The Lost Chance for Peace and the Escalation of War in Vietnam*. (Berkerly, CA: University of California Press, 1999) p. 388.
25 Starry, Donn A. *Mounted Combat in Vietnam*. Vietnam Studies. (Washington, DC: GPO, 1978) pp. 14–16.
26 *FRUS* 1964–8, Vol. III, pp. 209–17.
27 Collins, *The Development and Training of the South Vietnamese Army*.
28 McMaster, H.R. *Dereliction of Duty: Lyndon Johnson, Robert McNamara, The Joint Chiefs of Staff, and The Lies That Led to Vietnam*. (New York: HarperCollins, 1997) pp. 323, 334.
29 Halberstam, David. *The Making of a Quagmire: America and Vietnam During the Kennedy Era*. Revised edition. (New York: Alfred A. Knopf, 1964/1988).
30 See Johnson's speeches such as 'Remarks to the American Alumni Council: United States Asian Policy' 12 July 1966. *Public Papers of the Presidents of the United States: Lyndon B. Johnson*. 1966 Vol. II. (Washington, DC: GPO, 1967) pp. 718–22.
31 Freedman, Lawrence. 'Vietnam and the Disillusioned Strategist'. *International Affairs*. (Vol. 72, No. 1. 1996) p. 136.
32 Clodfelter, Mark. *The Limits of Airpower: The American Bombing of North Vietnam*. (New York: Free Press, 1989) is a remarkable Clausewitzian analysis of why the early bombing campaigns did not work, and why it was later the appropriate instrument because of Nixon's specific goals and the political and military situation which then existed. For a sense of the decisions at the time see: *FRUS* 1964–8. Vol. II, pp. 521–2.
33 MacDonald, *Giap*, p. 316.

34 Sharp, U.S.G. *Strategy for Defeat: Vietnam in Retrospect*. (Novato, CA: Presidio, 1978) pp. 2, 4, 268.
35 Palmer, *The 25 Year War*, p. 30.
36 Eckhardt, George S. *Command and Control 1950–1969*. Vietnam Studies. (Washington, DC: GPO, 1974) p v.
37 Creveld, Martin van. *Command in War*. (Cambridge, MA: Harvard University Press, 1985) p. 260; 1963 figures given on p. 235. His chapter on the Vietnam War is an excellent analysis of how the technological tools provided to assist actually hindered the US by their growing complexity. See: 'The Helicopter and the Computer', pp. 232–60.
38 See: Eckhardt, *Command and Control*.
39 Westmoreland, William C. *A Soldier Reports*. (New York: Dell, 1976) pp. 198–9.
40 Westmoreland, William C. 'A Military War of Attrition' in Thompson, W. Scott and Frizzell, Donaldson D. (eds) *The Lessons of Vietnam*. (New York: Crane, Russak, 1977) p. 58 (and JCS p. 59).
41 General Palmer comments that the invasion came five years too late and blames Westmoreland whilst commending Abrams. Palmer makes a similar argument in *The 25 Year War*, p. 188. Sorley, Lewis. *A Better War: The Unexamined Victories and Final Tragedy of America's Last Years in Vietnam*. (New York: Harcourt Brace, 1999).
42 Westmoreland, *A Soldier Reports*, p. 296.
43 DePuy, 'FM 100-5 Revisited', p. 308.
44 Department of the Army. *A Study of Strategic Lessons* p Ex 5.
45 Millet, Allan R. 'The United States Armed Forces in the Second World War' in Millet, Allan R. and Murray, Williamson (eds) *Military Effectiveness, Volume III; The Second World War*. (Boston, MA; Unwin Hyman, 1988) p. 74.
46 Krepinevich, *The Army in Vietnam*, pp. 168–72.
47 For example: Rogers, Bernard William. *Cedar Falls–Junction City: A Turning Point*. Vietnam Studies. (Washington, DC: GPO, 1974) p. 156.
48 Macksey, Kenneth. *Tank Warfare: A History of Tanks in Battle*. (St Albans: Granada, 1976) pp. 141–7.
49 Ott, *Field Artillery*, pp. 55–72.
50 Gudmundsson, Bruce I. *On Artillery*. (Westport, CT: Praeger, 1993) p. 151.
51 Ott, *Field Artillery*, on the siege of Khe Sanh, pp. 148–57. One of the best pieces of war writing and example of 'new' journalism is the account of the siege of Khe Sanh in Herr, Michael. *Dispatches*. (London: Picador, 1978). See, 'Khe Sanh' pp. 86–166.
52 Ott, *Field Artillery*, p. 148.
53 Nalty, Bernard C. *Air Power and the Fight for Khe Sanh*. (Washington, DC: GPO, 1973) p. 103.
54 Schulzinger, Robert D. *A Time for War: The United States and Vietnam, 1941–1975*. (Oxford: Oxford University Press, 1997) p. 260.
55 Spark, Alasdair. 'Flight Controls: The Social History of the Helicopter as a Symbol of Vietnam' in Walsh, Jeffrey and Aulich, James (eds) *Vietnam Images: War and Representation*. (London: Macmillan, 1989) pp. 86–111.
56 Ott, *Field Artillery*, pp. 52–3.
57 Palmer, Bruce Jr. 'Introduction' to Matthews, Lloyd J. and Brown, Dale E. (eds) *Assessing the Vietnam War; A Collection from the Journal of the U.S. Army War College*. (London: Pergamon-Brassey's, 1987) pp. ix–xix.
58 Scales, Robert H. Jr. *Firepower in Limited War*. Revised edition. (Novato, CA: Presidio, 1995) pp. 21–2. See, pp. 3–22 on 'Firepower in American Way of War'. On airmobility developments see: Tolson, John J. *Airmobility, 1961–1971*, Vietnam Studies. (Washington, DC: GPO, 1973).
59 Rosen, *Winning the Next War*, pp. 85–95.

60 Matheny, Michael R. 'Armor in Low-Intensity Conflict: The U.S. Experience in Vietnam'. *Armor*. (July–August 1988) p. 9.
61 Macksey, *Tank Warfare*, p. 296.
62 Matheny, 'Armor in Low-Intensity Conflict', pp. 9–15.
63 Starry, *Mounted Combat in Vietnam*, p. 220.
64 Hastings, *The Korean War*, p. 416.
65 See: MacDonald, *Giap* for an account of Giap's strategy and tactics against French and American forces. The book is based on interviews by the author with Giap.
66 Ewell, Julian J. and Hunt, Ira A. Jr. *Sharpening the Combat Edge: The Use of Analysis to Reinforce Military Judgment*. Vietnam Studies. (Washington, DC: GPO, 1974) pp. 76–8.
67 Ewell and Hunt, *Sharpening the Combat Edge*, p. 83. Krepinevich is particularly scathing of Ewell personally, quoting his nickname of 'Delta Butcher' and showing his obsession with body counts. He feels that Ewell's methods were in effect given official sanction and perpetuated by his authoring of the Vietnam study. Krepinevich, *The Army in Vietnam*, pp. 203–5. However, the book Ewell wrote stressed the need for innovative light infantry operations, and the use of systemic analysis; surely a contribution to improving US counter-insurgency operations.
68 Sweeney, Jerry K. (ed.) *A Handbook of American Military History: From the Revolutionary War to the Present*. (Boulder, CO: Westview, 1996) p. 252.
69 Thompson, Leroy. *The U.S. Army in Vietnam*, (New York: David and Charles, 1990) p. 25.
70 Griffith, *Forward into Battle*, p. 135.
71 Gibson, James William. *The Perfect War: Technowar in Vietnam*. (Boston, MA: Atlantic Monthly, 1986).
72 Griffith, *Forward into Battle*, pp. 105–36.
73 Summers, *On Strategy*, p. 1.
74 Department of the Army. *A Study of Strategic Lessons*. Omnibus Executive Summary. p Ex 7–8.
75 For example, Congressional amendments to defence bills during the Nixon administration were part of a larger move by Congress to rein in executive power regarding the war in South-East Asia as advocated by critics such as Senator Fulbright. See: Woods, Randall Bennet. *J. William Fulbright, Vietnam, and the Search for a Cold War Foreign Policy*. (Cambridge: Cambridge University Press, 1998) pp. 223–9.
76 Figures provided in Thompson, *US Army in Vietnam*, p. 13.
77 Phrase taken from the opening chapter of Karnow, *Vietnam*, pp. 9–59.
78 Palmer, *The 25 Year War*, p. 169.
79 Ibid., pp. 169–70.
80 Summers, *On Strategy*, p. 13.
81 Kinnard, Douglas. *The War Managers*. (Wayne, NJ: Avery, 1985) p. 118.
82 Ibid., p. 112. Kinnard's book is based on his survey of senior American officers who served in Vietnam.
83 Lewy, Guenter. *America in Vietnam*. (New York: Oxford University Press, 1978) p. 330.
84 Powell, *A Soldier's Way*, p. 144.
85 General Nguyen Ngoc Loan's summary execution was to be very symbolic, captured as it was by an AP photographer on 3 February. See: Schulzinger, Robert D. *A Time for War: The United States and Vietnam, 1941–1975*. (New York: Oxford University Press, 1997) p. 261. See also: Hersh, Seymour. *My Lai 4: A Report on the Massacre and Its Aftermath*. (New York: Vintage Books, 1970).
86 After the Tet offensive one in five shifted from being a 'hawk' to being a 'dove'. Lewy, *America in Vietnam*. p. 434. The media's move away from supporting the war is

also linked to Johnson's change of heart and the loss of him as the war's principal spokesman. See: Hammond, William M. *Public Affairs: The Military and the Media, 1968–1973 The U.S. Army in Vietnam*. (Washington, DC: GPO, 1996) pp. 1–11, 620.

87 MacDonald, *Giap*, pp. 266 and 269.

88 There was a clear consensus among senior Army officers that the Army of South Vietnam and the media were weak links. Kinnard, *The War Managers*, p. 19.

89 Westmoreland, 'A Military War of Attrition', p. 61.

90 Garfinkle, Adam. *Telltale Hearts: The Origins and Impact of the Vietnam Antiwar Movement*. (London: Macmillan, 1995) p. 100.

91 Hammond, *Public Affairs*.

92 Lewy, *America in Vietnam*, p. 433.

93 Sweeney, *A Handbook of American Military History*, p. 272.

94 Garfinkle, *Telltale Hearts*, p. 100.

95 Spector, *After Tet*, p. xvii.

96 Wheeler, John. 'Coming to Grips with Vietnam'. *Foreign Affairs*. (Vol. 63, No. 4. 1984) p. 747. For example, see: Buzzanco, Robert. *Vietnam and the Transformation of American Life*. (Oxford: Blackwell, 1999).

97 Johnson, Lyndon B. 'The President's Address to the Nation Announcing Steps to Limit the War in Vietnam and Reporting His Decision Not To Seek Reelection. March 21, 1968' in *Public Papers of the Presidents. Lyndon B. Johnson 1968–69. Volume One*. (Washington, DC: GPO, 1970) pp. 469–76.

98 Johnson, 'The President's Address to the Nation', p. 476.

99 Nicholas, H.G. 'The 1968 Presidential Elections'. *Journal of American Studies*. (Vol. 3, No. 1. 1969) pp. 4–5.

100 Sorley, *A Better War*, p. xiv. For example Karnow, *Vietnam*, has 103 pages out of 670 on this period and Herring, George C. *America's Longest War: The United States and Vietnam 1950–1975*. Second edition. (New York: Alfred A. Knopf, 1986) has 60 out of a possible 281 pages.

101 Spector, *After Tet*, p. xv.

102 For an account based on new sources of Abram's changes, see: Sorley, *A Better War*. A Standard account is: Shawcross, William. *Sideshow: Nixon, Kissinger and the Destruction of Cambodia*. (New York: Simon and Schuster, 1979). For a current example of the controversy and its associated issues see: Hitchens, Christopher. *The Trial of Henry Kissinger*. (London: Verso, 2001) pp. 6–43.

103 Spector, *After Tet*, p. xvi.

104 It should be noted that the reserves were seen by this period to be a haven for draft dodgers. Kitfield, James. *Prodigal Soldiers*. (New York: Simon and Schuster, 1995) p. 150.

105 Palmer sees the performance as high quality till 1969–70. Palmer, *The 25 Year War*, p. 155. Stanton, Shelby L. *The Rise and Fall of an American Army: U.S. Ground Forces in Vietnam, 1965–1973*. (Novato, CA: Presidio, 1985) saw the decline as underway by the end of 1969. See, p. 280.

106 Karnow, *Vietnam*, p. 33.

107 Powell, *A Soldier's Way*, pp. 132–3.

108 *Congressional Quarterly Weekly Report*. (Vol. 30, No. 8. 19 Feb 1972) p. 391.

109 Ibid., p. 393.

110 Ambrose, Stephen E. *Nixon: The Triumph of a Politician, 1962–72*. (London: Simon and Schuster, 1989) pp. 190–1, 264–5.

111 Nixon, Richard M. 'Statement Announcing Appointment of the President's Commission on an All-Volunteer Armed Force. March 27 1969'. *Public Papers of the Presidents. Richard Nixon. 1969*. (Washington, DC: GPO, 1971) p. 258.

112 See: Gates, Thomas S. *The Report of the President's Commission on an All-Volunteer Armed Force*. (New York: Macmillan, 1970) and Latham, Willard. *The Modern*

Volunteer Army Program: The Benning Experiment, 1970–1972. (Washington, DC: GPO, 1974).

113 Nixon introduced changes to the draft deferment and made the lottery national rather than local. Nixon, Richard M. 'Special Message to the Congress on Draft Reform. April 23 1970'. *Public Papers of the Presidents. Richard Nixon. 1970*. (Washington, DC: GPO, 1971) p. 395.

114 See: Nixon, Richard M. 'Address to the Nation Announcing Conclusion of an Agreement on Ending the War and Restoring Peace in Vietnam. January 23, 1973'. *Public Papers of the Presidents. Richard Nixon. 1973*. (Washington, DC: GPO, 1975) pp. 18–20.

115 Jeffrey, Timothy B. 'Today's Army wants to Join You; Do We Really?' *Military Review*. (Vol. 53, No. 1. 1973) p. 63.

116 Jeffrey, 'Today's Army wants to Join You', p. 64.

117 This idea had been stressed earlier in Janowitz, Morris. *The Professional Soldier: A Social and Political Portrait*. (New York: Free Press. 1960).

118 Madigan, John J. and Hoy. Pat C. 'The Dialectical Imperative; Civil–Military Confrontation'. *Military Review*. (Vol. 53, No. 11. 1973) p. 44.

119 This observation opens Fred Ikle's classic post-Vietnam book on the issue. Ikle, Fred Charles. *Every War Must End*. Revised edition. (New York: Columbia University Press, 1991) Preface, p. vii.

120 Melanson, Richard A. *Reconstructing Consensus: American Foreign Policy since the Vietnam War*. (New York: St Martin's Press, 1991) p. 189.

121 Gelb and Betts, *The Irony of Vietnam*, p. 357.

122 Westmoreland, *A Soldier Reports*, p. 566.

123 Lewy, *America in Vietnam* was the first 'revisionist' history, using primary sources, to challenge the idea of the war being a 'moral failure' with the US burdened with a catalogue of evils. See the Preface. Chapter 7 is called: 'American Military Tactics and the Law of War'.

124 Garfinkle, *Telltale Hearts*, p. 214.

125 Smith, Gaddis. *Morality, Reason and Power: American Diplomacy in the Carter Years*. (New York: Hill and Wang, 1986) especially pp. 12–33; Gaddis, John Lewis. *The United States and the End of the Cold War: Implications, Reconsiderations, Provocations*. (Oxford: Oxford University Press, 1992) pp. 47–64.

126 Owens, Mackubin T. 'Strategy and Resources: Trends in the U.S. Defense Budget' in Murray, Williamson (ed.) *Brassey's Mershon American Defense Annual 1995–1996*. (London: Brassey's, 1995) p. 171.

127 Clark, Asa A. IV., et al. 'Did Vietnam Make a Difference? No! Conclusions and Implications' in Osborn, George K. et al. (eds) *Democracy, Strategy, and Vietnam: Implications for American Policymaking*. (Lexington, MA: Lexington Books, 1987) pp. 319–49.

128 Smith, *Morality, Reason and Power*, pp. 35–45 and Winik, *On the Brink*, p. 83.

129 Brzezinski, Zbigniew. *Power and Principle: Memoirs of the National Security Adviser 1977–1981*. Revised edition. (New York: Farrar, Strauss, Giroux, 1985) pp. 42–4.

130 For example: Dunn, David H. *The Politics of Threat: Minuteman Vulnerability in American National Security Policy*. (London: Macmillan, 1997) pp. 83–123. There is a marvellous biography of Jackson available: Kaufman, Robert G. *Henry M. Jackson: A Life in Politics*. (Seattle, WA: University of Washington Press, 2000).

131 Booth, 'American Strategy: The Myths Revisited', pp. 1–35.

132 Luttwak, Edward N. 'The Impact of Vietnam on Strategic Thinking in the United States' in Hearden, Patrick J. (ed.) *Vietnam: Four Perspectives*. (West Lafayette. IN: Purdue University Press, 1990) p. 71.

133 For example: Gaddis, John Lewis. *The United States and the Origins of the Cold War, 1941–1947*. (New York: Columbia University Press, 1972).

134 Nixon, Richard. *No More Vietnams*. (London: W. H. Allen, 1985) p. 13.

135 Bowen, Wyn Q. and Dunn, David H. *American Security Policy in the 1990s: Beyond Containment*. (Aldershot: Dartmouth, 1996.) p. 88.
136 The linkage between normative concerns and self-images is from: Smith, Steve. 'The Self-Images of a Discipline: A Genealogy of International Relations Theory' in Booth, Ken, and Smith, Steve (eds) *International Relations Theory Today*. (Oxford: Polity, 1995) p. 30. It is further analysed in the same collection: Vasquez, John A. 'The Post-Positivist Debate: Reconstructing Scientific Enquiry and International Relations Theory After Enlightenment's Fall', pp. 217–40.
137 The Navy and Air Force had different experiences of reform, especially as the Air Force emphasis shifted from its strategic role to a tactical one. See: Chapter 4, and Lovell, 'Vietnam and the U.S. Army: Learning to Cope with Failure', pp. 123–4.
138 An analysis of the need for systems analysis, and a defence of McNamara's use of it, is found in Brodie, *War and Politics*, pp. 453–79.
139 Buzzanco, *Masters of War*, pp. 14–19.
140 Palmer, Dave R. *Summons of the Trumpet: U.S.–Vietnam in Perspective*. (Novato, CA: Presidio, 1978) p. 204.
141 Shapley, Deborah. *Promise and Power: The Life and Times of Robert McNamara*. (Boston, MA: Little, Brown, 1993) p. 407.
142 Westmoreland, *A Soldier Reports*, p. 562.
143 Buzzanco categorised military leaders' views into: dissenters, doubters, critics, politicos and true believers. Buzzanco, *Masters of War*, pp. 9–11. He sees Westmoreland as a 'true believer' and 'politico'. General Abrams took a very different approach, see Sorley, *A Better War*, pp. 17–30. However, for all the diversity of views, Westmoreland's basic perception was in accord with the consensual perception as captured in Summers's *On Strategy*, a book which captures the mood of the time. Krepinevich's *The Army in Vietnam* expresses the alternative view from within the Army. Bruce Palmer, Army Vice Chief of Staff, sees that top-level military must share the onus of failure. See: Palmer, *The 25 Year War*, p. 201. It is important to remember that Westmoreland was the rising star of his generation in the Army. Betts, Richard K. *Soldiers, Statesmen, and Cold War Crises*. (Cambridge, MA: Harvard University Press, 1977) pp. 240–1. n. 10.
144 The growing alienation is tracked in Atkinson, Rick. *The Long Gray Line: The American Journey of West Point's Class of 1966*. (Boston, MA: Houghton Mifflin, 1989).
145 Westmoreland, *A Soldier Reports*, p. 565. See also, Thompson, W. Scott and Frizzell, Donaldson D. (eds) *The Lessons of Vietnam*. (New York: Crane, Russak, 1977) p. iv.
146 Summers, *On Strategy*.
147 Rose, Stephen Peter. 'Vietnam and the American Theory of Limited War'. *International Security*. (Vol. 7, No. 2. 1982) pp. 83–113.
148 Clark, Wesley K. 'Gradualism and American Military Strategy'. *Military Review*. (Vol. 60, No. 9. 1975) p. 7. See also, pp. 3–13.
149 DePuy, 'Infantry Combat', p. 453.
150 Sarkesian, 'The American Response to Low-Intensity Conflict: The Formative Period', p. 40.
151 Concept taken from the book and title; Gacek, Christopher M. *The Logic of Force: The Dilemma of Limited War in American Foreign Policy* (New York. Columbia University Press, 1994).
152 Clausewitz, *On War*, p. 75.
153 Deborah Avant sees the Army's separatist view as a product of its institutional position. Avant, *Political Institutions and Military Change*.
154 Cohen, Eliot. 'Dynamics of Military Intervention' in Levite, Ariel *et al*. (eds) *Foreign Military Intervention*. (New York: Columbia University Press, 1992) pp. 261–84. The same point is made in Freedman, Lawrence. 'Escalators and Quagmires: Expectations and the Use of Force'. *International Affairs*. (Vol. 67, No. 1. 1991) pp. 15–31.

155 Smoke, Richard. 'Theories of Escalation' in Lauren, Paul Gordon. (ed.) *Diplomacy: New Approaches in History, Theory and Policy*. (London: Collier Macmillan, 1979) pp. 43–68.
156 For an analysis of it being 'crisis management' rather than coercive diplomacy see: Simons, William E. 'U.S. Coercive Pressure on North Vietnam, Early 1965' in George, Alexander L. and Simons, William E. (eds) *The Limits of Coercive Diplomacy*. Second edition. (Boulder, CO: Westview, 1994) pp. 133–73, especially p. 163.
157 Clark, 'Gradualism and American Military Strategy', p. 3.
158 Summers, *On Strategy*, p. 173.
159 McNeill, Ian. *The Team: Australian Army Advisers in Vietnam 1962–1972*. (London: Leo Cooper, 1984) p. 481.
160 Krepinevich, *The Army in Vietnam*, p. 131.
161 Ibid., p. 5
162 Summers, *On Strategy*, p. 76.
163 Clutterbuck, Richard. *The Long, Long War: The Emergency in Malaya. 1948–1960*. (London: Cassell, 1966) p. 4.
164 Ewell and Hunt, *Sharpening the Combat Edge*. pp. 227–8. See also: McNeill, *The Team: Australian Army Advisers in Vietnam*. The Australian experience led to abandonment of forward defence and refocused on home defence and regional co-operation. See p. 484.
165 Shafer makes the point of US policy failings being due to formulaic response to insurgencies. Shafer, D. Michael. *Deadly Paradigms: The Failure of U.S. Counter-insurgency Policy*. (Leicester: Leicester University Press, 1988) pp. 280–3. See also: Blaufarb, Douglas S. *The Counterinsurgency Era: U.S. Doctrine and Performance, 1950 to the Present*. (New York: The Free Press, 1977) p. 310.
166 Avant, *Political Institutions and Military Change*, pp. 76–101. Krepinevich, *The Army in Vietnam*, pp. 172–7. For example see Stolfi, Russell H. *U.S. Marine Corps Civic Action Efforts in Vietnam March 1965–March 1966*. (Washington, DC: GPO, 1968).
167 Peterson, Michael E. *The Combined Action Platoons: The U.S. Marines' Other War in Vietnam*. (Westport, CT: Praeger, 1989) p. 123.
168 Peterson, *The Combined Action Platoons*, p. 123.
169 Stanton, *The Rise and Fall of an American Army*, p. xv.
170 Betts, *Soldiers, Statesmen, and Cold War Crises*, p. 138.
171 See: Kelly, Francis J. *U.S. Army Special Forces 1961–1971*. Vietnam Studies. (Washington, DC: GPO, 1985).
172 Howard, 'The Forgotten Dimensions of Strategy', p. 108.
173 Sarkesian, 'The American Response to Low-Intensity Conflict', p. 38.
174 Eckhardt, *Command and Control*, p. 69. In 1967 Robert Komer was appointed Westmoreland's deputy for CORDS and he wrote an important critique of the war. See: Komer, Robert W. *Bureaucracy at War; U.S. Performance in the Vietnam Conflict*. (Boulder, CO: Westview, 1986).
175 Department of the Army. *A Study of Strategic Lessons Learned*. Omnibus Executive Summary. p VI 11.
176 Palmer, *The 25 Year War*, pp. 180–1.
177 Pike, Douglas. *PAVN: People's Army of Vietnam*. (Novato, CA: Presidio, 1986) p. 217. This concept would be utilised by John Boyd in his work on the OODA loop which is examined in Chapter 4.
178 Gelb and Betts, *The Irony of Vietnam*, p. 2.
179 Gray, Colin S. *Weapons Don't Make War: Policy, Strategy, and Military Technology*. (Lawrence, KS: University of Kansas Press, 1993) p. 174.
180 Starry, Donn A. 'Changing Things: Keynote Remarks', Australian Chief of Army Annual exercise, Brisbane. 20 October 1998, p. 3.

181 The Army's perception of the particular nature of the 'logic of war' is covered in Gacek, *The Logic of Force*, whilst the model of professionalism contrasting with the broader society is examined in Avant, *Political Institutions and Military Change*.
182 A fundamental question after the war was the issue of the JCS not articulating its role. See: Palmer, *The 25 Year War*, p. 46 and p. 213 n. 26. on the failure of the JCS to articulate its concerns and General Johnson's inability to provide a logical rationale for this. The debate has been reignited by McMaster's *Dereliction of Duty*.
183 Weyand, Fred C. and Summers, Harry G. Jr. 'Vietnam Myths and Military Realities'. *Armor*. (September–October 1976) p. 35.
184 Cohen, Eliot A. *Supreme Command: Soldiers, Statesmen, and Leadership in Wartime*. (New York: The Free Press, 2002) especially pp. 175–88.
185 Weyand and Summers, 'Vietnam Myths and Military Realities', p. 36.
186 Starry, Donn A. 'TRADOC's Analysis of the Yom Kippur War', The Jaffee Center Military Doctrine Joint Conference, Casarea, Israel. 14–18 March 1999, p. 2.
187 Garfinkle shows that the protest movement actually extended the war by default. prolonging the Army's taking casualties, as most were taken after 1968 and the stated policy of withdrawal. Garfinkle, *Telltale Hearts*.
188 Stanton, *The Rise and Fall of an American Army*, p. 368.
189 Parrish, Robert D. and Andreacchio, N.A. *Schwarzkopf: An Insiders View of the Commander and His Victory*. (London: Bantam Books, 1991) p. 36.
190 Ten years after the war the figure was 58,022. See: Department of Defense. *U.S. Casualties in Southeast Asia, Statistics as of April 30, 1985*. (Washington. DC: GPO. 1985) p. 1.
191 For an analysis of the difficulty the US has with matching ends to means, that US counter-insurgency policy tends to be formulaic, and that the outcomes reflect the intentions of what the implementing agencies could and would do. See: Shafer, *Deadly Paradigms*, pp. 276–83.

3 THE ALL-VOLUNTEER ARMY

1 History generates generalisations rather than rigid laws. See: Evans, Richard J. *In Defence of History*. (London: Granta, 1997) pp. 58–62.
2 Abercrombie, Clarence L. III and Alcala, Raoul H. 'The New Military Professionalism' in Russett and Stepan, *Military Force and American Society*, pp. 34–57.
3 Nixon, Richard M. 'Address to the Nation Announcing Conclusion of An Agreement on Ending the War and Restoring Peace In Vietnam. January 23, 1973'. *Public Papers 1973*, pp. 18–20. See also: Berman, *No Peace, No Honor*.
4 Schulzinger, *A Time for War*, p. 308.
5 Thompson and Fizzell, *The Lessons of Vietnam*, p. iii.
6 This paragraph is drawn from interviews with Army officers of the period.
7 Richardson, William R. 'Officer Training and Education'. *Military Review*. (Vol. 64, No. 10. 1984) pp. 22–34, especially p. 28.
8 Moellering, John H. 'The Army Turns Inward?' *Military Review*. (Vol. 53, No. 7. 1973) pp. 68–83.
9 Atkinson, Rick. *The Long Gray Line: The American Journey of West Point's Class of 1966*. (Boston, MA: Houghton Mifflin, 1989) p. 369.
10 Richardson, 'Officer Training and Education', p. 30.
11 Downie, Richard Duncan. *Learning from Conflict: The U.S. Military in Vietnam, El Salvador, and the Drug War*. (Westport, CT: Praeger, 1998) shows that the Army innovates in learning cycles, building on previous Standard Operating Procedures.
12 Richardson, *Crisis Diplomacy*, p. 350. 'Structuration' is taken from the ideas in Giddens, Antony. *The Constitution of Society: Outline Theory of the Theory of Structuration*. (Cambridge: Polity Press, 1984) pp. 1–40. See Introduction n. 24 above.

This was true not only for the Army; foreign policy veterans cut teeth in the administrations of the war's era, e.g. George Bush, Brent Scowcroft, Lawrence Eagleburger, Cyrus Vance, Antony Lake, Richard Holbrooke.

13 Rosen, *Winning the Next War*, p. 58.
14 Betts, *Soldiers, Statesmen, and Cold War Crises*, p. 9.
15 *Congressional Quarterly Weekly Report.* (22 Sept. 1973) p. 2525.
16 Westmoreland, *A Soldier Reports*, p. 565.
17 *Congressional Quarterly Weekly Report.* (22 Sept. 1973) p. 2526.
18 Gray, George H. 'What Are US Reserve Forces Really For?' *Military Review.* (Vol. 55, No. 6. 1975) p. 87.
19 The Reserves and National Guard during this time included Dan Quayle and George W. Bush.
20 Ikeda, Moss M. 'Reserve Strength in Face of the Zero Draft'. *Military Review.* (Vol. 53, No. 5. 1973) pp. 58–66.
21 Gray, 'What Are US Reserve Forces Really For?' pp. 88–90.
22 Callaway, Howard H. 'The Army and the Future'. *Strategic Review.* (Vol. 3, No. 4. 1975) p. 16.
23 Department of Defense. *Statement of Secretary of Defense, Melvin R. Laird, on the Fiscal Year 1972–76 Defense Program and the 1972 Defense Budget. March 15 1971.* (Washington, DC: GPO, 1971) p. 21.
24 Summers, Harry G. Jr. *On Strategy II: A Critical Analysis of the Gulf War.* (New York: Dell, 1992) pp. 73–4.
25 Kitfield, *Prodigal Soldiers*, p. 150.
26 Gray, 'What Are US Reserve Forces Really For?' p. 90.
27 Kitfield, *Prodigal Soldiers*, p. 151.
28 Ibid., p. 351.
29 Scales, *Certain Victory*, p. 52.
30 Kitfield, *Prodigal Soldiers*, pp. 351–2.
31 Herring, George C. *America's Longest War: The United States and Vietnam 1950–1975.* Second edition. (New York: Alfred A. Knopf, 1986) p. 273.
32 Spiller, Roger J. 'In the Shadow of the Dragon: Doctrine and the US Army after Vietnam'. *RUSI Journal.* (Vol. 142, No. 6. 1997) p. 54 n. 41.
33 Ibid., p. 44.
34 Starry, Donn A. 'TRADOC's Analysis of the Yom Kippur War'. Unpublished address to The Jaffee Center, Military Doctrine Joint Conference, Casarea, Israel. 14–18 March 1999, pp. 1–2.
35 Palmer, *The 25 Year War*, pp. 169–70.
36 Starry, 'TRADOC's Analysis of the Yom Kippur War', pp. 1–2.
37 Scales, *Certain Victory*, pp. 6–7.
38 Summers, Harry G. *The Astarita Report: A Military Strategy for the Multipolar World.* (Carlisle Barracks, PA: Strategic Studies Institute, US Army War College, 1981) See: Spiller, 'In the Shadow of the Dragon', p. 53 n. 20.
39 Lovell, John P. 'Vietnam and the U.S. Army: Learning to Cope With Failure' in Osborn et al. *Democracy, Strategy, and Vietnam*, pp. 133 and 151 n. 44.
40 Friedman, Norman. *The US Maritime Strategy.* (London: Jane's, 1988) pp. 197–8.
41 Lovell, 'Vietnam and the U.S. Army', p. 133.
42 Starry, Donn A. 'A Tactical Evaluation – FM 100-5'. *Military Review.* (Vol. 58, No. 8. 1978) pp. 2–11.
43 DePuy, 'Talking Paper on Field Manual 100-5, Operations. 8 July 1976', p. 194.
44 For challenges to the consensus see: Williams, Phil. *The Senate and US Troops in Europe.* (London: Macmillan, 1985). There were frustrations with European allies, defence spending levels, centralisation of power in the Presidency, with attitudes, and the actions and policies of President Nixon. See: pp. 235, 256.

45 Department of Defense. *Statement of Secretary of Defense on the FY 1972–76 Defense Program. March 15 1971*, p. 25.
46 See: Downie, *Learning from Conflict* and Adams, Thomas K. *US Special Operations Forces in Action: The Challenge of Unconventional Warfare*. (London: Frank Cass, 1998). This was styled by one four-star general, in interview, as the 'ostrich' approach.
47 Freedman, *The Evolution of Nuclear Strategy*, pp. 359–95.
48 Terriff, Terry. *The Nixon Administration and the Making of U.S. Nuclear Strategy*. (Ithaca, NY: Cornell University Press, 1995) p. 191.
49 Kissinger also saw that NATO strategy was in urgent need of revision at this time. See: Kissinger, Henry. *Years of Upheaval*. (Boston, MA: Little, Brown, 1982) pp. 131, 134.
50 Cronin, James E. *The World the Cold War Made: Order, Chaos, and the Return of History*. (London: Routledge, 1996) p. 190.
51 The 'ostpolitik' developments in West Germany were rather independent of American policy orientations, see: Ash, Timothy Garton. *In Europe's Name: Germany and the Divided Continent*. (London: Jonathan Cape, 1993).
52 Johnson, Robert H. *Improbable Dangers: U.S. Conceptions of Threat in the Cold War and After*. (London: Macmillan, 1994) p. 70. Johnson sees a clear confusion over the military-means and political-ends relationship in Europe by the US, as the military programmes were politically driven, but the military rationales soon came to express the prevailing reality, p. 83.
53 Gray, 'Strategy in the Nuclear Age', p. 595.
54 Department of the Army. *FM 100-5, Operations*. (Washington, DC: GPO, 1976) p. 1–2.
55 The Carter doctrine was the name given to the declaration in the 1980 State of the Union Address that any attempt to control the Persian Gulf by an outside power would be deemed an assault on US vital interests. The speech was made in the wake of the Soviet invasion of Afghanistan and led to the creation of the Rapid Deployment Joint Task Force (RDF), which in January 1983 became the unified Central Command. Part of the reason for its peculiar composition was the fact that the US had difficulties finding host nations for the forces assigned to the RDF. The geographical region covered by Central Command stretched from Egypt to Pakistan and Iran to Kenya, leaving out Israel.
56 Coker, *US Military Power in the 1980s*, pp. 14–15.
57 Starry, 'The Kermit Roosevelt Lecture', pp. 6–7.
58 Schwarzkopf, *It Doesn't Take a Hero*, pp. 342–58.
59 *FM 100-5*. 1976, p. 1–2.
60 See: Bacevich, A.J. 'Old Myths, New Myths: Renewing American Military Thought'. *Parameters*. (Vol. 18, No. 1. 1988) pp. 15–25. Also see: Builder, *The Masks of War*, p. 185.
61 Bacevich, 'Old Myths, New Myths', p. 22.
62 Donald Vought made the important point that future markets and resources compelled the US not to avoid Vietnam-style conflicts. See: Vought, Donald B. 'Preparing for the Wrong War?' *Military Review*. (Vol. 57, No. 5. 1977) pp. 16–33.
63 See Chapter 5 below.
64 Murray, Williamson. 'Innovation Past and Present' in Murray, Williamson and Millet, Alan R. (eds) *Military Innovation in the Interwar Period*. (Cambridge: Cambridge University Press, 1996) pp. 311–12.
65 Romjue, *The Army of Excellence*, p. 3. The interview was held on 19 March 1993.
66 DePuy, 'Letter to General Frederick C. Weyand', p. 179.
67 Thompson and Frizzell, *The Lessons of Vietnam*, p. v.
68 Moellering, John H. 'The Army Turns Inward?' *Military Review*. (Vol. 53, No. 7. 1973) p. 73.
69 Douglas Kinnard's study in September 1974 mailed a 60-item questionnaire to the 173 Army generals who commanded in Vietnam. His book is very important and tells the

story from perspectives of the US Army General Officers who commanded there. Kinnard, Douglas. *The War Managers*. (Wayne, NJ: Avery, 1985).

70 Kinnard, *The War Managers*, p. 112.

71 US Army War College. *Leadership for the 1970s*. (Washington, DC: GPO, 1970).

72 Powell, *A Soldier's Way*, pp. 155–6.

73 *Congressional Quarterly Weekly Report*. (Vol. 30, No. 8. 19 Feb. 1972) p. 392.

74 Westmoreland, 'A Military War of Attrition', p. 60.

75 Spiller, 'In the Shadow of the Dragon', p. 43.

76 Summers, *On Strategy*, p. 194. Also see (on the findings and recommendations of Defense Manpower Commission): Bruce Palmer Jr. 'A Careful Look at Defense Manpower'. *Military Review*. (Sept 1976/ Vol. 77, No. 1. 1997) pp. 23–9.

77 Diehl, Richard P. 'Military Professionalism in the US Army Officer Corps'. *Military Review*. (Vol. 54, No. 3. 1974) p. 63.

78 For the discussion on the unique nature of the professional soldier see: Diehl, Richard P. 'Military Professionalism in the US Army Officer Corps', pp. 60–72; Toner, James A. 'The Military Ethic: On the Virtue of an Anachronism'. *Military Review*. (Vol. 54, No. 12. 1974) pp. 9–18; and Parham, Paul B. 'The American Military Profession; An Egalitarian View'. *Military Review*. (Vol. 54, No. 11. 1974) pp. 18–29.

79 Weyand, Fred C. and Summers, Harry G. 'Serving the People; The Need for Military Power'. *Military Review*. (Vol. 56, No. 12. 1976) pp. 8–18.

80 An explanation of the paradoxical and anti-rational nature of war, see: Luttwak, Edward N. *Strategy: The Logic of War and Peace*. (Cambridge, MA; Belknap Press, 1987). Gacek gives the clearest account of the US Army understanding that war had a logic of its own. Gacek, *The Logic of Force*.

81 Avant, *Political Institutions and Military Change*, pp. 26–7.

82 Wass de Czege, Huba. 'Clausewitz: Historical Theories Remain Sound Compass References; The Catch is Staying on Course'. *Army*. (September 1988) p. 37.

83 There was an enormous amount of literature published on the issue of military professionalism at this time, for example see: Bradford, Zeb B. Jr and Brown, Frederick J. *The United States Army in Transition*. (Beverley Hills, CA: Sage, 1973): Hauser. William L. *America's Army in Transition: A Study of Civil–Military Relations*. (Baltimore, MD: Johns Hopkins University Press, 1973); and Yarmolinsky, Adam. *The Military Establishment*. (New York: Harper Colophon, 1971).

84 Creighton Abrams was Army Chief of Staff, 1972–74, and Bruce Palmer was Army Vice Chief of Staff, 1968–73.

85 For the key literature see: Introduction n. 39 above, and Chapman, Anne W. *The Army's Training Revolution, 1973–1990: An Overview*. (Fort Monroe, VA: TRADOC, 1991) which summarises the innovations in training.

86 Palmer, *The 25 Year War*, pp. 138–9.

87 For DePuy's account of the establishment of TRADOC and his time as its commander see: Brownlee, Romie L. and Mulen, William J. III. *Changing an Army: An Oral History of General William E. DePuy, USA Retired*. (Washington, DC: GPO, nd) pp. 175–98.

88 Palmer, *The 25 Year War*, pp. 138–9. DePuy worked under Palmer, who was the Army Vice Chief of Staff at the time.

89 Schwarzkopf, *It Doesn't Take A Hero*, p. 240.

90 See: Brownlee and Mulen, *Changing an Army*; William E. DePuy. *Selected Papers of General William E. DePuy*. Gilmore, Donald L. and Conway, Carolyn D. (eds) (Fort Leavenworth, KS: Combat Studies Institute, 1994).

91 Hackett, John. *The Profession of Arms*. (London: Sidgwick and Jackson, 1983) p. 197.

92 General Starry was part of both the first and second generations of change, as was General Paul Gorman. General William Richardson was to lead the later revision of AirLand Battle. Shimon Naveh identifies two additional 'nuclei' of reform at lower levels: the tutorial staff at the Military Academy: A.A. Clark, T.W. Fagan and J.M.

Oseth; and the staff at the Command and Staff College: including Huba Wass de Czege and L.D. Holder. See: Naveh, Shimon. *In Pursuit of Military Excellence*, p. 280 n. 44. The last two on Naveh's list were the authors of *FM 100-5*, 1982 and 1986.

93 Confidential interview.
94 Rosen, *Winning the Next War*, p. 58.
95 Kitfield, *Prodigal Soldiers*, p. 157.
96 Ibid., p. 127.
97 Schwarzkopf, *It Doesn't Take A Hero*, p. 288.
98 Buzzanco, *Masters of War*, p. 11.
99 Kitfield, *Prodigal Soldiers*, pp. 70–1 gives a brief account.
100 Ibid., p. 156.
101 Brownlee and Mulen, *Changing an Army*. See pp. 156–61, 190.
102 Ibid., p. 138.
103 Ibid., p. 133.
104 *FM 100-5*, 1976, p. 2–2.
105 DePuy, William E. 'Letter to General Frederick C. Weyand', p. 179. DePuy wrote an important detailed paper on the 1973 war as TRADOC's presentation on the lessons of the war; see: 'Implications of the Middle East War on U.S. Army Tactics, Doctrine and Systems. A Presentation. N.d.' in *Selected Papers of General William E. DePuy*, pp. 75–112.
106 DePuy, 'Letter to General Frederick C. Weyand', pp. 179–84.
107 Ibid., p. 180.
108 Starry, 'TRADOC's Analysis of the Yom Kippur War', p. 3.
109 Starry outlined the key lessons of the Middle East War as:

1 'the staggering density of the battlefield at critical points'
2 'the presence on both sides of large numbers of modern weapons systems'
3 'the increased criticality of command and control'
4 'the increased likelihood of interrupted command and control due to large numbers of sophisticated electronic warfare means'
5 'the inability of any single weapon system to prevail – reaffirming the essentiality of all-arms combat'
6 'the outcome of the battle reflecting, more often than not, factors other than numbers'
7 additionally 'it was starkly obvious that large-scale destruction in a short time was a most likely outcome of first battles in war'.

See: Starry, Donn A. 'A Perspective on American Military Thought'. *Military Review*. (Vol. 69, No. 7. July 1989) p. 8. It is significant that the concerns with the command and control issues were not the major focus for DePuy, but were to be predominant for Starry and the development of AirLand Battle.

110 Starry, 'TRADOC's Analysis of the Yom Kippur War', p. 4.
111 Ibid., p. 4.
112 The US had to use NATO stocks to supply the high Israeli consumption. See: O'Balance, Edgar. *No Victor, No Vanquished* (Novato, CA: Presidio, 1978) pp. 331–3.
113 *FM 100-5*, 1976, pp. 2–17, 1–1, 1–2.
114 Ibid., p. 2–1.
115 Starry, 'A Perspective on American Military Thought', p. 8.
116 Ibid.
117 Heller, Charles E. and Stoft, William A. (eds) *America's First Battles 1776–1965*. (Lawrence, KS: University of Kansas Press, 1986). Starry supported the publication of *America's First Battles* from his TRADOC position, and the editors worked at Leavenworth.
118 Starry, 'TRADOC's Analysis of the Yom Kippur War', p. 6.

119 Toffler, *War and Anti-War*, pp. 33–56 for the three types of war. The Tofflers were in discussion with General Starry and his doctrine writing team when it came to the writing of the 1982 revision of *FM 100-5*. The Tofflers analyse war in a rather economically deterministic way, seeing that 'the way we make war reflects the way we make wealth' (p. 3). They also rather awkwardly refer to limited wars as 'anti-wars'.
120 Scales, *Certain Victory*, p. 9.
121 Department of the Army. *A Study of Strategic Lessons Learned in Vietnam*. Omnibus Executive Summary. p VI 9.
122 Brownlee and Mulen, *Changing an Army*, p. 90.
123 A detailed history of the command's training developments is given in Chapman, *The Army's Training Revolution, 1973–1990*, which summarises the innovations in training. Chapman, Anne W. *The Origins and Development of the National Training Center 1976–1984*. (Fort Monroe, VA: TRADOC, 1992) gives a detailed account of the training centre. Two articles by one of the leading advocates, General William, R. Richardson, give a good sense of the movement. See his articles: 'Training: Preparation for Combat'. *Military Review*. (June 1986/ Vol. 77. January 1997) pp. 84–6 and, 'The "Training Revolution" that Built Today's Army'. *Army*. (September 1996) pp. 8–12.
124 Brownlee and Mulen, *Changing an Army*, p. 202.
125 DePuy, William E. 'Presentation to the TRADOC Commanders' Vision '91 Conference. 5 October 1988', p. 430.
126 Ibid., p. 430.
127 Romjue et al., *Prepare the Army for War*, pp. 21–40.
128 The formal title of Army of Excellence came out of the TRADOC restructuring studies called Division 86. In 1983 General Wickham, Army Chief of Staff, looked to developing lighter infantry battalions; the study was called the 'Army of Excellence'. See: Romjue, *The Army of Excellence*, pp. 23–42.
129 Thomas, James A. 'On Moral Preparation'. *Military Review*. (Vol. 53, No. 8. 1973) p. 76.
130 Chapman, *The Origins and Development of the National Training Center*.
131 Brownlee and Mulen, *Changing an Army*, p. 186.
132 Ibid., p. 188.
133 William S. Lind is the author of *Maneuver Warfare Handbook* (London: Westview, 1985) and the key critical article on DePuy's 1976 FM 100-5, 'Some Doctrinal Questions for the United States Army'. *Military Review*. (Vol. 57, No. 3. 1977) pp. 54–65 which is discussed in detail in Chapter 4.
134 Spiller, 'In the Shadow of the Dragon', p. 48.
135 A sense of the debate can be found in Richardson, William R. 'The Leavenworth Influence on Today's Army'. *Military Review*. (Vol. 61, No. 5. 1981) pp. 16–23, Richardson, William R. 'Officer Training and Education'. *Military Review*. (Vol. 64, No. 10. 1984) pp. 22–34, and Wass de Czege, Huba. 'Challenge for the Future; Educating Field Grade Battle leaders and Staff Officers'. *Military Review*. (Vol. 64, No. 6. 1984) pp. 2–13.
136 Richardson, 'Training: Preparation for Combat', p. 84.
137 *FM 100-5*, 1976, p. 1–3.
138 Richardson, 'Officer Training and Education', p. 33.
139 Meyer, Edward C. 'Leadership: A Return to Basics'. *Military Review*. (Vol. 60, No. 7. 1980) pp. 4–9.
140 See: Coroalles, Antony M. 'Implementing a Maneuver Style of Warfare'. *Military Review*. (Vol. 62, No. 12. 1982) p. 23. Also Vandergriff, Don. 'The Culture Wars' in Bateman, Robert L. (ed.) *Digital War: A View from the Front Lines*. (Novato, CA: Presidio, 1999) pp. 222–3.
141 Vandergriff, 'The Culture Wars.' pp. 217–24.
142 See: Kitfield, *Prodigal Soldiers*, pp. 207–14.

143 Halliday, Fred. *The Making of the Second Cold War*. Second edition. (London: Verso, 1986) pp. 123–4.
144 *Congressional Quarterly Weekly Report*. (Vol. 39, No. 2. 10 Jan. 1981) p. 108.
145 Less than one-third identified themselves as Republican in a 1976 survey, two-thirds did in 1996. See: Holsti, Ole R. 'A Widening Gap between the U.S. Military and Civilian Society? Some Evidence, 1976–96'. *International Security*. (Vol. 23, No. 3. 1998) pp. 11–12.
146 Garthoff, Raymond L. *The Great Transition: American–Soviet Relations and the End of the Cold War*. (Washington, DC: Brookings Institution, 1994) p. 33.
147 Powell, *A Soldier's Way*, pp. 258–9.
148 This section is based on Kitfield's account of interviews with Thurman. See: Kitfield, *Prodigal Soldiers*, pp. 207–14, 339.
149 Thurman, Maxwell R. 'On Being All You Can Be: A Recruiting Perspective' in Fredland, J. Eric et al. (eds) *Professionals on the Front Line: Two Decades of the All-Volunteer Force*. (Washington, DC: Brassey's, 1996) pp. 56, 60.
150 Peters. Ralph. *Fighting for the Future; Will America Triumph?* (Mechanicsburg, PA: Stackpole. 1999) pp ix–xi.
151 DePuy, William E., 'Presentation to the TRADOC Commanders' Vision '91 Conference. 5 October 1988', p. 431.
152 Brownlee and Mulen, *Changing an Army*, p. 188.
153 Department of the Army, *FM 100-1, The Army*. (Washington, DC: GPO, 1994) Preface.
154 Janowitz, Morris. *The Professional Soldier: A Social and Political Portrait*. (New York: Free Press, 1960) p. 257.
155 Spiller, 'In the Shadow of the Dragon', p. 50.
156 *FM 100-5*, 1976, Preface. p i.
157 Ibid., p. i.
158 Scales, *Certain Victory*, p. 11.
159 *FM 100-5*, 1976, Appendix B.
160 Romjue, John L. *From Active Defense to AirLand Battle: The Development of Army Doctrine, 1973–1982*. (Fort Monroe, VA: TRADOC, 1984) p. 10.
161 *FM 100-5*, 1976, p. 1–5.
162 Ibid., p. 3–1.
163 DePuy, 'FM 100-5 Revisited', p. 303.
164 *FM 100-5*, 1976, p. 5–2.
165 Ibid., pp. 2–13 to 2–14.
166 Ibid., p. 2–32.
167 Ibid., p. 2–28.
168 Ibid., p. 1–2.
169 Starry, 'TRADOC's Analysis of the Yom Kippur War', p. 5.
170 DePuy, 'Implications of the Middle East War', pp. 75–111.
171 The attacker needed a 6:1 advantage to be successful. *FM 100-5*, 1976, p. 3–4.
172 *FM 100-5*, 1976, p. 5–2. Starry, 'A Perspective on American Military Thought', p. 8.
173 *FM 100-5*, 1976, p. 2–6.
174 Ibid., p. 2–3.
175 O'Ballance, *No Victor, No Vanquished*, p. 341. See also: Starry, 'TRADOC's Analysis of the Yom Kippur War', p. 3.
176 *FM 100-5*, 1976, p. 4–7
177 Ibid., p. 8–1. See: chapter 8 'Air-Land Battle', pp. 8–1 to 8–7.
178 Starry had raised combined arms as a key lesson from Vietnam in Starry, Donn A. *Mounted Combat in Vietnam*. Vietnam Studies. (Washington, DC: GPO, 1978).
179 *FM 100-5*. 1976, p. 1–1.
180 DePuy, 'Letter to General Frederick C. Weyand', p. 180.
181 Ibid., p. 180.

182 DePuy, 'Talking Paper on Field Manual 100-5, Operations', p. 195.
183 See, *FM 100-5*. 1976, chapter 2. 'Modern Weapons on the Modern Battlefield', pp. 2–1 to 2–32.
184 *FM 100-5*. 1976, p. 1–3.
185 Ibid., p. 1–4.
186 Ibid., p. 1–4.
187 Ibid., p. 3–11.
188 Ibid., p. 12–1.
189 Spiller, 'In the Shadow of the Dragon', p. 46.
190 *FM 100-5*, 1976, p. 2–2.
191 Ibid., p. 5–13.
192 Ibid., p. 5–7.
193 Ibid., p. 3–6.
194 This is a very frequently cited section of *FM 100-5*, 1976 (p. 3–6), and is quoted by 'managerial critics' such as James Fallows in his *National Defence* (New York: Random House, 1981) p. 32 as examples of attritional thinking and managerial logic; and 'maneouvrist critics' such as James Burton in his *Pentagon Wars*. (Annapolis, MD: Naval Institute Press, 1993) p. 2 who uses it as an example of 'dinosaur' thinking of the 1960s and 1970s.
195 Wass de Czege, 'Clausewitz: Historical Theories Remain Sound Compass References', p. 42.
196 Department of the Army. *A Study of Strategic Lessons Learned in Vietnam*. Executive summary. p VI–9.
197 Spiller, 'In the Shadow of the Dragon', p. 51.
198 Wass de Czege, Huba and Holder, L.D. 'The New FM 100-5', p. 54 and Tate. Clyde J. and Holder, L.D. 'New Doctrine for the Defense'. *Military Review*. (Vol. 61, No. 3. 1981) p. 4.
199 DePuy, 'Implications of the Middle East', p. 111.
200 Spiller, 'In the Shadow of the Dragon', p. 43.
201 Ibid., p. 52.
202 Naveh, *In Pursuit of Military Excellence*, p. 252.
203 Tate, 'New Doctrine for the Defense', pp. 2–3.
204 Lupfer shows that the resistance to change is less to do with conspiracies and more to do with inherent characteristics of the military. See: Lupfer, Timothy T. 'The Challenge of Military Reform' in Clark et al., *The Defense Reform Debate; Issues and Analysis*. (Baltimore, MD: Johns Hopkins University Press, 1984) pp. 23–32.
205 As noted in the Introduction, the official historiography does not recognise fully the role of the civilian thinkers in the developments and Chapter 4 covers this in detail.
206 Spiller, 'In the Shadow of the Dragon', p. 43.
207 Powell, *A Soldier's Way*, p. 325.
208 Spiller, 'In the Shadow of the Dragon', p. 43. Spiller sees that there is a post-Gulf consensus that this was the means of the transformation of the Army after Vietnam and that the Nixon doctrine provided insufficient strategic guidance for the rebuilding, p. 53 n. 17.

4 INNOVATION IN US ARMY DOCTRINE

1 Starry, Donn A. 'A Tactical Evolution – FM 100-5'. *Military Review*. (Vol. 68, No. 8. 1978) p. 3.
2 Wass de Czege, Huba and Holder, L.D. 'The New FM 100-5'. *Military Review*. (Vol. 62, No. 7. 1982) p. 53.
3 Thompson, John L. *Strategic Management: Awareness and Change*. Third edition. (London: International Thomson Business Press, 1997) p. 666.

4 Scales, *Certain Victory*, p. 14.
5 Starry, 'To Change an Army', p. 25. For a brief background on Starry and his library, see: Toffler, *War and Anti-War*, pp. 44–55.
6 Starry, 'To Change an Army', p. 25.
7 Wass de Czege, 'Army Doctrinal Reform' in Clark *et al.*, *The Defense Reform Debate*, p. 101.
8 Tate, Clyde J. and Holder, L.D. 'New Doctrine for the Defense'. *Military Review*. (Vol. 61, No. 3. 1981) p. 4.
9 Toffler, *War and Anti-War*, p. 52. For the Tofflers' analysis of AirLand Battle being an embodiment of 'third wave' social/technological thinking see, pp. 44–56. Starry's views are encapsulated in his 'Extending the Battlefield'. *Military Review*. (Vol. 61, No. 3. 1981) pp. 31–50. His record of the intellectual underpinings of the doctrinal changes is given in 'A Perspective on American Military Thought'. *Military Review*. (Vol. 69, No. 7. 1989) pp. 2–11. Other articles he wrote explaining separate emphases of the doctrine are: 'The Principles of War'. *Military Review*. (Vol. 61, No. 9. 1981) pp. 2–12, and 'Command and Control: An Overview'. *Military Review*. (Vol. 61, No. 11. 1981) pp. 2–3. General Starry gives accounts of how the doctrinal changes were brought about in 'To Change an Army', pp. 20–7; and 'Changing Things: Keynote Remarks' at the Australian Chief of Army Annual Exercise, Brisbane, 20 October 1998. The importance of the 1973 war to changes were outlined in, 'TRADOC's Analysis of the Yom Kippur War', the Jaffee Center Military Doctrine Joint Conference, Casarea, Israel, 14–18 March 1999.
10 Starry, 'A Perspective on American Military Thought', p. 3.
11 Wass de Czege and Holder, 'The New FM 100-5', p. 69.
12 Starry, 'Extending the Battlefield', p. 32.
13 Scales, *Certain Victory*, pp. 1–38, entitled 'Forging a New Army'. The book was first published by the Office of the Chief of Staff, United States Army, in 1993.
14 Downing, Wayne A. 'Firepower, Attrition, Maneuver – US Army Operations Doctrine: A Challenge for the 1980s and Beyond'. *Military Review*. (January 1981/ Vol. 77, No. 1. 1997) p. 144. As a result of this influential article Downing was consulted during the writing of the 1986 version of *FM 100-5*.
15 An example of what Starry refers to is: Starry, Donn A. 'The Kermit Roosevelt Lecture' at the Army Staff College, Camberley, UK. 10 May 1982.
16 Starry, Donn A. 'Preface to a reprinting of "Extending the Battlefield"'. *Military Review*. (Vol. 77, No. 1. 1997) p. 151.
17 Leonhard, Robert. *The Art of Maneuver: Maneuver-Warfare Theory and AirLand Battle*. (Novato, CA: Presidio, 1991) p. 138.
18 Morrelli was publicly acknowledge after his death; Toffler, *War and Anti-War*, pp. 9–12, 53–6 and Luttwak, Edward N. *The Pentagon and the Art of War*. (New York: Simon and Schuster, 1984) p. 7.
19 Burton, James G. *The Pentagon Wars: Reformers Challenge the Old Guard*. (Annapolis, MD: Naval Institute Press, 1993) p. 53.
20 Oseth, John M. 'An Overview of the Reform Debate' in Clark et al. *The Defense Reform Debate*, pp. 44–5.
21 Lind, William S. *Maneuver Warfare Handbook*. (Boulder, CO: Westview, 1985) pp. xi–xii.
22 Army officers often quoted Edward Luttwak, Steven Canby, John Boyd and William Lind whilst advocating a manoeuvrist approach. For example see: Coroalles, Antony M. 'Maneuver to Win: A Realistic Alternative'. *Military Review*. (Vol. 61, No. 9. 1981) pp. 35–46, Wass de Czege, Huba 'Army Doctrinal Reform' in, Clark et al., *The Defense Reform Debate*, pp. 101–20. Wayne Downing, who was involved in the 1986 *FM 100-5*, and was later the CINC Special Operations Command, drew on all of them in 'Firepower Attrition Maneuver', p. 150 n. 1, 13, 18, 25, 35, 37, 40.

23 See: chapter 1 'Operational Art and the General Theory of Systems' of Naveh, *In Pursuit of Military Excellence*, pp. 1–29.
24 For example, a seminal work was the criticism and proposals outlined in Luttwak, *The Pentagon and the Art of War*, especially pp. 23–92, 266–86.
25 Dating the start of the 'military reform' is impossible due to the disparate nature of the movement. The caucus was described by the *New York Times* as 'a bipartisan group of liberals and conservatives who seek a more highly maneuverable fighting force, with simpler weapons' *New York Times*. (1 March 1984 Sec B. p. 13). The caucus included: Newt Gingrich, Sam Nunn, William S. 'Bill' Cohen, Richard 'Dick' Cheney. See also: Hart, Gary and Lind, William S. *America Can Win: The Case for Military Reform*. (Bethesda, MD: Alder and Alder, 1986) pp. ix–xv, 1–25; Naveh, *In Pursuit of Military Excellence*, p. 279; and Burton, *The Pentagon Wars*, p. 237.
26 Clark et al., *The Defense Reform Debate*, p. xi. This book is the best on the military reform issues. Reformer Dina Rasor's edited volume, was a seminal work in the procurement aspects of the reform movement. See: *More Bucks, Less Bang: How the Pentagon Buys Ineffective Weapons*. (Washington, DC: Fund for Constitutional Government, 1983).
27 Mearsheimer, John J. 'Maneuver, Mobile Defense, and the NATO Central Front' in Miller, Steven (ed.) *Conventional Forces and American Defense Policy*. (Princeton, NJ: Princeton University Press, 1986) pp. 231–49, especially p. 231.
28 Fallows, James. *National Defense*. (New York: Random House, 1981) chapter 2, pp. 19–34.
29 Canby, Steven L. 'NATO Strategy: Political–Military Problems of Divergent Interests and Operational Concept'. *Military Review*. (Vol. 59, No. 4. 1979) pp. 50–8.
30 *Military Review* is the journal of the US Army's Command and General Staff College, and refers to itself as the Army's 'professional journal'.
31 Lind, *Maneuver Warfare Handbook*. Lind had written a white paper on defence in 1976 for Senator Taft and in 1977 Senator Gary Hart, who was the founder of the Military Reform Caucus, hired him.
32 William S. Lind. 'Some Doctrinal Questions for the United States Army'. *Military Review*. (Vol. 57, No. 3. 1977) pp. 54–65. Lind aimed to examine four aspects of the doctrine: 'fight outnumbered and win'; 'win the first battle'; attrition or manoeuvre doctrine; and tactics. See, p. 54. See also: Naveh, *In Pursuit of Military Excellence*. pp. 264 and 282 n. 82.
33 Clark et al., *The Defense Reform Debate*, p. 362.
34 Lind, 'Some Doctrinal Questions', p. 61.
35 Bond, Brian. *Liddell Hart* (London: Cassell, 1977) pp. 238–72. Naveh, *In Pursuit of Military Excellence*, argues that blitzrieg was a 'bastard' concept, driven by hyper-aggressive political ideology and manipulation of tactical patterns of combat, p xvii. See pp. 105–63.
36 Boyd's briefing was called 'A Discourse on Winning and Losing' and eventually grew to 13 hours in length. See: Burton, *The Pentagon Wars*, p. 273. Boyd was the 'father' of the F-16. See: Hammond, Grant T. *The Mind of War: John Boyd and American Security*. (Washington, DC: Smithsonian Institute, 2001); Coram, Robert. *Boyd: The Fighter Pilot Who Changed the Art of War*. (Boston, MA: Little, Brown, 2002). The presentation can be found at: <http://www.belisarius.com/modern_business_ strategy/boyd/boyd_papers.htm>
37 Lind, *Maneuver Warfare Handbook*, p. 5.
38 Ibid., p. 6.
39 Ibid., pp. 4–8.
40 Ibid., p. 6.
41 Lind, 'Some Doctrinal Questions for the United States Army', p. 58.
42 See: Gudmundsson, Bruce I. *On Artillery*. (London: Praeger, 1993), especially p. 137.

Scales, *Firepower in Limited War*, rather confusingly refers to an 'American style of blitzkrieg' in the Second World War, with the US tactical emphasis on artillery rather than armour providing the breakthroughs, p. 10.

43 Lind, 'Some Doctrinal Questions', pp. 54–65. In the seminal collection: Hooker, Richard D. Jr (ed.) *Maneuver Warfare; An Anthology*. (Novato, CA: Presidio, 1993), six of the eight essays on 'The Historical Basis of Maneuver Warfare' are of the German Army. See also: Doughty, Robert A. *Seeds of Disaster: The Development of French Army Doctrine, 1919–1939*. (Hamden, CT: Archon, 1985) and Gudmundsson, Bruce I. *Stormtroop Tactics: Innovation in the German Army, 1914–1918*. (New York: Praeger. 1989).

44 Lind, *Maneuver Warfare Handbook*, pp. 19–21.

45 Lind, 'Some Doctrinal Questions', p. 58.

46 Lind, *Maneuver Warfare Handbook*, pp. 12–19.

47 Ibid., p. 13.

48 Lind, 'Some Doctrinal Questions', p. 58.

49 Luttwak, Edward N. 'The Operational Level of War'. *International Security*. (Vol. 5, No. 3. 1980) sees blitzkrieg as 'an operational scheme', p. 67.

50 Luttwak, 'The Operational Level of War', pp. 61–79, and for a greater analysis of the relational-maneuver concept, see chapter 7 of his book *Strategy*, pp. 91–112. The development of the operational concept, and in particular roots in Soviet thinking, is outlined and analysed by Shimon Naveh in his book *In Pursuit of Military Excellence*.

51 Luttwak, 'The Operational Level of War', p. 62.

52 Leonhard, *The Art of Maneuver*, pp. 52–8 and Naveh, *Military Excellence*, pp. 164–249.

53 Weigley, Russell F. *The Age of Battles: The Quest for Decisive Warfare from Breitenfeld to Waterloo*. (London: Pimlico. 1993).

54 Naveh, *In Pursuit of Military Excellence*, p. xviii.

55 Naveh, *In Pursuit of Military Excellence*, pp. 11 and xviii. See also: Bellamy, Christopher. *The Evolution of Modern Land Warfare: Theory and Practice*. (London: Routledge. 1990) and Simpkin, Richard E. *Race to the Swift: Thoughts on Twenty-First Century Warfare*. (London: Brassey's, 1985).

56 Naveh. *In Pursuit of Military Excellence*, chapter 7 'From Tactical Destruction to Operational Manoeuvre: The Conceptual Revolution in American Military Thought', pp. 250–86.

57 Bolger questions the four key assumptions of manoeuvre warfare: understanding war through social science; war as war at any level; dislocating manoeuvre over killing firepower; use of military history to prove their case. He sees the prescriptions of avoiding strength and hitting weakness, and encouraging initiative as traditional military approaches. He also notes that the operational art can dangerously filter out political considerations. See: Bolger, Daniel P. 'Maneuver Warfare Reconsidered' in Hooker, *Maneuver Warfare*, pp. 19–41, especially p. 26.

58 DePuy, William E. '*The Future of Land Warfare*: A Book Review by General DePuy'. *Selected Papers of General William E. DePuy*, pp. 407–9.

59 DePuy, '*The Future of Land Warfare*: A Book Review', pp. 407–8.

60 Romjue, *From Active Defense to AirLand Battle*, pp. 57–8.

61 Mearsheimer, 'Maneuver, Mobile Defense, and the NATO Central Front', pp. 231–49.

62 Ibid., p. 234.

63 Ibid., p. 236.

64 Ibid., p. 247.

65 Wass de Czege, 'Army Doctrinal Reform', p. 103.

66 Betts, Richard K. 'Conventional Strategy: New Critics, Old Choices'. *International Security*. (Vol. 7, No. 4. 1983) p. 193.

67 Lind, 'Some Doctrinal Questions', p. 64.
68 This distinction is drawn from: Farrell, Theo. 'Figuring Out Fighting Organisations: The New Organisational Analysis in Strategic Studies'. *Journal of Strategic Studies*. (Vol. 19, No. 1. 1996) p. 124.
69 Lind, *Maneuver Warfare Handbook*, p. 50. He saw the Falklands war as an example of a clash between forces prepared for war, and those who were distracted by such issues as domestic politics.
70 Ibid., pp. 69–133.
71 Department of the Navy. *FMFM 1 Warfighting*. (Washington, DC: GPO, 1989) especially pp. 58–61 and Department of the Navy. *FMFM 1-1 Campaigning*. (Washington, DC: GPO, 1990).
72 *United States Code*: Title 10, Section 5063, ensures that there is 'not less than three combat divisions and three air wings'.
73 Keithly, David and Melshen, Paul. 'Past as Prologue: USMC Small Wars Doctrine'. *Small Wars and Insurgencies*. (Vol. 8, No. 2. 1997) pp. 87–108.
74 For a history of the USMC in the years from 1975 to the Gulf War see: Moskin, J. Robert. *The U.S. Marine Corps Story*. Third Revised Edition. (Boston, MA: Little, Brown, 1992) pp. 699–801.
75 Competition among different services and new technology can also threaten organisational essence. See: Mearsheimer, *Liddell Hart and the Weight of History*, p. 222.
76 Meese, Michael J. 'Institutionalizing Maneuver Warfare: The Process of Organizational Change' and Hooker, Richard D. Jr. 'Implementing Maneuver Warfare' both in Hooker, *Maneuver Warfare*, pp. 193–216, 217–35.
77 Westmoreland, *A Soldier Reports*, pp. 561–2.
78 DePuy, 'FM 100-5 Revisited', p. 304.
79 Betts, 'Conventional Strategy: New Critics, Old Choices', p. 193.
80 DePuy, 'FM 100-5 Revisited', p. 308.
81 *FM 100-5*, 1976, p. 4–5.
82 Starry, 'A Perspective on American Military Thought', pp. 8–9.
83 Confidential interview.
84 Tate, 'New Doctrine for the Defense', p. 3.
85 Bolger, 'Maneuver Warfare Reconsidered', p. 37.
86 Lind, William S. 'Defense Reform: A Reappraisal' in Clark et al., *The Defense Reform Debate*, pp. 327–33.
87 Betts, 'Conventional Strategy: New Critics, Old Choices', p. 199. A contemporary example was the deployment in 1983 to Grenada of a USMC detachment, which was at the time steaming to Lebanon to relieve Marines in Beirut.
88 Tate, 'New Doctrine for the Defense', pp. 2–9.
89 Luttwak, *Strategy*, p. 97. Luttwak first made this point with reference simply to the US, and it provoked much debate. See: Luttwak, Edward N. 'The American Style of Warfare and the Military Balance'. *Survival*. (Vol. 21, No. 2. 1979) pp. 57–60, and Karber, Phillip A., Wilcox, John G., Cabaniss, Edward H. and Canby, Steven L. 'Symposium on Military Strategy in Western Europe'. *Armed Forces and Society*. (Vol. 7, No. 1. 1980) pp. 69–86.
90 Palmer, *Summons of the Trumpet*, p. 117.
91 Naveh, *In Pursuit of Military Excellence*, p. 271.
92 Starry, 'To Change an Army', p. 25.
93 Starry, 'Extending the Battlefield', p. 34.
94 Tate, 'New Doctrine for the Defense', p. 8.
95 Frustration with the fact that the choke points, such as the Ho Chi Minh trail, were not hit, for example. See: Nicklas-Carter, M. 'Nato's Central Front' in Harris, J.P. and Toase, F.H. (eds) *Armoured Warfare*. (London: B. T. Batsford, 1990) pp. 205–29.

96 Holder, L.D. 'Maneuver in Deep Battle'. *Military Review*. (Vol. 62, No. 5. 1982) p. 60 n. 1.
97 Sutton, Boyd D., et al. 'Deep Attack Concepts and the Defense of Central Europe'. *Survival*. (Vol. 26, No. 2. 1984) pp. 50–70.
98 Rogers, Bernard W. 'Greater Flexibility for NATO's Flexible Response'. *Strategic Review*. (Vol. 11, No. 2. 1983) pp. 11–19. The FOFA concept was eventually overtaken by Soviet shifts in doctrine to address this difficulty, and they placed more emphasis on the decisive role of the first echelon: Bellamy, Chris. *The Future of Land Warfare*. (London: Croom Helm, 1987) p. 180.
99 Rogers, Bernard W. 'Follow-On Forces Attack (FOFA): Myths and Realities'. *NATO Review*. (Vol. 32, No. 6. 1984) p. 6.
100 Ibid., pp. 1–9.
101 Rogers, Bernard W. 'ACE Attack of Warsaw Pact Follow-on Forces'. *Military Technology*. (Vol. 83, No. 5. 1983) p. 40, and see pp. 38–50.
102 Rogers, 'Follow-On Forces Attack (FOFA)', p. 1.
103 Ibid., p. 2.
104 Especially: surveillance, target acquisition and intelligence means; survivable command, control and communications (C^3) systems; and conventional weapons. Rogers, 'ACE Attack of Warsaw Pact', pp. 42–5.
105 Department of the Army. *Field Manual 100-5, Operations*. (Washington, DC: Department of the Army, 1982).
106 Rogers, 'Greater Flexibility for NATO's Flexible Response', p. 17. For further analysis see: pp. 11–19.
107 Richardson, William R. 'FM 100-5: The AirLand Battle in 1986'. *Military Review*. (Vol. 66, No. 3. 1986) pp. 4–11.
108 NATO agreed this in May 1980. See: Coker, Christopher. *US Military Power in the 1980s*. (London: Macmillan/RUSI, 1983) pp. 14–16.
109 Department of the Army. *TRADOC Pamphlet 525–5. Military Operations: Operational Concepts for the AirLand Battle and Corps Operations, 1986*. (Fort Monroe, VA: TRADOC, 1981).
110 Sutton, 'Deep Attack Concepts and the Defense of Central Europe', pp. 60–2.
111 Rogers, 'Follow-On Forces Attack (FOFA)', p. 7.
112 *FM 100-5*, 1976, p. 4–6.
113 Ibid., p. 4–6.
114 *FM 100-5*, 1982, p. 2–2.
115 Doerfel, John S. 'The Operational Art of the AirLand Battle'. *Military Review*. (Vol. 62, No. 5. 1982) p. 6.
116 Starry, 'Extending the Battlefield', p. 46.
117 *FM 100-5*, 1982, p. 2–2.
118 Ibid., p. 2–2.
119 Starry, 'Extending the Battlefield', pp. 31–50.
120 Starry, 'A Perspective on American Military Thought', p. 9.
121 Starry, 'Extending the Battlefield', p. 32.
122 *FM 100-5*, 1986, p. 2.
123 Starry, 'TRADOC's Analysis of the Yom Kippur War', p. 4.
124 Starry, 'Extending the Battlefield', p. 32.
125 Ibid., p. 33.
126 Gorman, Paul F. 'Toward a Stronger Defense Establishment' in Clark et al., *The Defense Reform Debate*, p. 292.
127 Nicklas-Carter, 'Nato's Central Front', p. 205–29.
128 *FM 100-5*, 1982, p. 1–5.
129 Starry, 'TRADOC's Analysis of the Yom Kippur War', p. 5.
130 *FM 100-5*, 1982, p. 2–2.

131 Starry, 'A Perspective on American Military Thought', pp. 9–10.
132 *FM 100-5*, 1982, pp. 2–1, 2–3.
133 Naveh, *In Pursuit of Military Excellence*, p. 254.
134 Wass de Czege and Holder, 'The New FM 100-5', p. 55.
135 See above, n. 32. and, Doerfel, John S. 'The Operational Art of the AirLand Battle'. *Military Review*. (Vol. 62, No. 5. 1982) pp. 3–10. Newell, Clayton R. *The Framework of Operational Warfare*. (London: Routledge, 1991).
136 *FM 100-5*. 1982, p. 2–1.
137 Ibid., p. 2–1.
138 Gray, Colin S. 'Strategy in the Nuclear Age: The United States, 1945–1991' in, Murray *et al. The Making of Strategy*, pp. 592 and 579–613.
139 Erickson, John. 'The Development of Soviet Military Doctrine; The Significance of Operational Art and the Emergence of Deep Battle' in, Gooch, John (ed.) *The Origins of Contemporary Doctrine*. (Camberley: Strategic and Combat Studies Institute. 1997) p. 106.
140 *FM 100-5*, 1986, p. 10.
141 Ibid., p. 10.
142 Starry, 'The Principles of War', p. 10.
143 Naveh, *In Pursuit of Military Excellence*, p. 251.
144 *FM 100-5*, 1982, p. 2–4.
145 Ibid., p. 2–4.
146 Ibid., p. 9–1.
147 Downing, Wayne A. 'Firepower, Attrition, Maneuver – US Army Operations Doctrine: A Challenge for the 1980s and Beyond'. *Military Review*. (January 1981/ Vol. 77, No. 1. 1997) p. 146.
148 *FM 100-5*, 1982, p. 2–2.
149 Ibid., p. 2–2.
150 Simpkin, *Race to the Swift*.
151 Hackett, John. 'Foreword', to Perret, Bryan. *A History of Blitzkrieg*. (New York: Jove, 1983) pp. 11, 15.
152 Nicklas-Carter, 'Nato's Central Front', p. 216.
153 *FM 100-5*, 1982, p. 1–5.
154 *FM 100-5*, 1986, p. 6.
155 Behagg, A. 'Increasing Tempo on the Modern Battlefield' in Reid, Brian Holden (ed.) *The Science of War: Back to First Principles*. (London: Routledge, 1993) pp. 110–30.
156 Starry, 'Command and Control: An Overview', p. 2.
157 Ibid., p. 3.
158 For example: Gourley, Scott R. 'Tactical Intelligence is Key to the AirLand Battle Scenario'. *Defense Electronics*. (February 1988) pp. 43–53.
159 Starry, 'Command and Control: An Overview', p. 3.
160 Wass de Czege and Holder, 'The New FM 100-5', p. 56.
161 *FM 100-5*. 1982, p. 2–7.
162 Ibid., p. 2–1.
163 Ibid., p. 2–3.
164 Ibid., p. 2–3.
165 *FM 110-5*, 1986, p. 17.
166 *FM 100-5*, 1982, p. 2–1.
167 Naveh, *In Pursuit of Military Excellence*, p. 13.
168 *FM 100-5*, 1982, p. 2–6.
169 Ibid., p. 2–6.
170 Lind, William S., et al. 'The Changing Face of War: Into the Fourth Generation'. *Military Review*. (Vol. 69, No. 10. 1989) pp. 2–11, especially p. 4.

171 *FM 100-5*, 1982, p. 2–6.
172 Naveh, *In Pursuit of Military Excellence*, pp. 14–15.
173 Starry, 'To Change an Army', p. 26.
174 Confidential interview.
175 Starry, Donn A. 'Changing Things: Keynote Remarks'. Australian Chief of Army Annual exercise, Brisbane. 20 October 1998, p. 8.
176 *FM 100-5*, 1986, p. i.
177 Department of the Army. *TRADOC Pamphlet 525–5, Military Operations: Operational Concepts for the AirLand Battle and Corps Operations-1986*. (Fort Monroe, VA: TRADOC, 1981).
178 Romjue, *Prepare the Army for War*, p. 59.
179 Goose, Stephen D. 'Low-Intensity Warfare: The Warriors and Their Weapons' in Klare. Michael T. and Kornbluh, Peter (eds) *Low-Intensity Warfare: Counterinsurgency, Proinsurgency, and Antiterrorism in the Eighties*. (New York: Pantheon Books. 1988) pp. 98–104.
180 *FM 7-20*, 1992, p. 1–1.
181 McInnes, Colin. *Hot War, Cold War: The British Army's Way in Warfare 1945–95*. (London: Brassey's, 1996) pp. 60–75. See also: Kiszely, John. 'The British Army and Approaches to Warfare Since 1945' in Reid, Brian Holden (ed.) *Military Power: Land Warfare in Theory and Practice*. (London: Frank Cass, 1997) pp. 179–206. Also his 'The Meaning of Manoeuvre'. *RUSI Journal*. (Vol. 143, No. 6. 1998) pp. 36–40 for an analysis of the manoeuvrist debate in the UK Armed Forces.
182 On NATO unified doctrine, *Allied Tactical Publication (ATP)-35 (A)*, see: Bellamy, *The Future of Land Warfare*, pp. 124–9.
183 Starry, 'To Change an Army', p. 26.
184 Ibid., p. 26.
185 Wass de Czege, 'How to Change an Army', pp. 32–49.
186 Starry, 'Changing Things: Keynote Remarks', p. 8.
187 Beevor, Antony. *Inside the British Army*. Updated edition. (London: Corgi. 1991) p. 157. See also, Romjue, *Prepare the Army for War*, pp. 59–64.
188 Wass de Czege, 'How to Change an Army', pp. 32–49.
189 Wass de Czege and Holder, 'The New FM 100-5', p. 55 and *FM 100-5*, 1986, p. 6.
190 Wass de Czege, Huba 'Clausewitz: Historical Theories Remain Sound Compass References; The Catch Is Staying on Course'. *Army*. (September 1988) pp. 37–43. Gray, 'Strategy in the Nuclear Age: The United States. 1945–1991', p. 592 and Gacek. *The Logic of Force*.
191 *FM 100-5*, 1982, Appendix A lists: Ardant du Picq, Charles Jean Jacques Joseph. *Battle Studies: Ancient and Modern*. Trans. Greeley, John N. and Cotton, Robert C. (Harrisburg, PA: The Military Service Publishing, 1947); Clausewitz, Carl von. *On War*. Ed and trans. Howard, Michael and Paret, Peter (Princeton: Princeton University Press, 1976); Hart, B.H. Liddell. *Strategy: The Indirect Approach*. (New York: Praeger. 1954); Saxe, Marshall de. 'Reveries on the Art of War.' in Phillips, Thomas R. (ed.) *Roots of Strategy*. (Harrisburg, PA: The Military Service Publishing, 1955) pp. 177–300; Sun Tzu. 'The Art of War' in Phillips, Thomas R. (ed.) *Roots of Strategy*. (Harrisburg, PA: The Military Service Publishing, 1955) pp. 13–66. Interestingly Jomini is not listed, though he is often seen as the real father of US Army strategic thinking.
192 Scales, *Certain Victory*, p. 7.
193 Romjue, *Prepare the Army for War*, pp. 21–40.
194 See: Chapman, *The Origins and Development*, pp. 1–56.
195 Ibid., pp. 37–41.
196 Ibid., p. 141.
197 Ibid., p. 142.
198 Romjue, *Prepare the Army for War*. A further training centre was established in

Germany, at Hohenfels, called the Combat Maneuver Training Center (CMTC). Bolger, Daniel P. *The Battle for Hunger Hill: The 1st Battalion, 327th Infantry Regiment at the Joint Readiness Training Center*. (Novato, CA, Presidio: 1997.) p. 10.

199 See: Chapman, *The Origins and Development*, pp. 57–128.

200 Bolger, *The Battle for Hunger Hill*, p. 11. This book is an account of a battalion going through the JRTC training experience. Bolger, a Lieutenant Colonel, wrote of his experiences at the NTC in *Dragons at War: 2–34th Infantry in the Mojave*. (Novato, CA: Presidio, 1986).

201 Chapman, *The Origins and Development*, pp. 145–8.

202 *FM 100-5*, 1982, p. 2–4.

203 MacIsaac, David. 'Voices from the Central Blue: The Airpower Theorists' in Paret, *Makers of Modern Strategy*, pp. 624–47. The best analysis of Vietnam use of airpower is Clodfelter, Mark. *The Limits of Airpower: The American Bombing of North Vietnam*. (New York: Free Press, 1989).

204 Craig, Campbell. *Destroying the Village: Eisenhower and Thermonuclear War*. (New York: Columbia University Press, 1998) p. 111. On the broader issues see, Freedman, Lawrence. *The Evolution of Nuclear Strategy*. Second edition. (London: Macmillan, 1989).

205 Burton, *The Pentagon Wars*, p. 22.

206 Worden, Mike. *Rise of the Fighter Generals; The Problem of Air Force Leadership, 1945–1982*. (Maxwell, AL: Air University Press, 1998) p. x and pp. 211–34.

207 Ibid., p. 247.

208 Ibid., p. 220.

209 Hamilton, Robert J. *Green and Blue in the Wild Blue: An Examination of the Evolution of Army and Air Force Airpower Thinking and Doctrine since the Vietnam War*. (Maxwell, AL: Air University Press, 1993) p. 2.

210 Romjue, *From Active Defense to AirLand Battle*, p. 61.

211 See: Lambeth, Benjamin S. *The Transformation of American Air Power*. (Ithaca, NY: Cornell University Press, 2000) pp. 83–91.

212 Hamilton, *Green and Blue in the Wild Blue*, p. 22.

213 Worden, *Fighter Generals*, pp. 227, 238.

214 Lambeth, *The Transformation of American Air Power*.

215 Cardwell, Thomas A. III. 'Follow-On Forces Attack: Joint Interdiction by Another Name'. *Military Review*. (Vol. 66, No. 2. 1986) pp. 4–11.

216 Mason, R.A. *Airpower: A Centennial Appraisal*. (London: Brassey's, 1994) p. 99.

217 Wagner, Louis C. Jr. 'Modernization: Large Strides, Much to Do'. *Army*. (October 1986) pp. 212–25, especially pp. 214–15. Wagner was Deputy Chief of Staff for Research, Development and Acquisition.

218 Romjue, *Prepare the Army for War*, pp. 65–73.

219 Paschall, Rod. 'Low-Intensity Conflict Doctrine: Who Needs It?' in Matthews, *Assessing the Vietnam War*, p. 246.

220 Krepinevich, *The Army and Vietnam*, p. 260.

221 Waghelstein, John D. 'Post-Vietnam Counterinsurgency Doctrine'. *Military Review*. (Vol. 65, No. 5. 1985) pp. 42–9.

222 Downie, *Learning from Conflict*, p. 183.

223 *FM 100-5*, 1986, p. 6.

224 Meyer, Edward C. *White Paper 1980: A Framework for Molding the Army of the 1980s into a Disciplined, Well-Trained Fighting Force*. (Washington, DC: GPO, 1980).

225 Adams, *US Special Operations Forces*, p. 185.

226 Departments of the Army *Field Manual 7–85, Ranger Operations*. (Washington, DC: GPO, 1987) p iv.

227 Marquis, Susan L. *Unconventional Warfare: Rebuilding U.S. Special Operations Forces*. (Washington, DC: Brookings Institution, 1997).

228 Romjue, *Prepare the Army for War*, pp. 71–3.
229 Departments of the Army and Air Force. *FM 100-20/ AFP 3-20: Military Operations in Low Intensity Conflict*. (Washington, DC: GPO, 1990).
230 Morelli, Donald R. and Ferguson, Michael M. 'Low-Intensity Conflict: An Operational Perspective'. *Military Review*. (Vol. 64, No. 11. 1984) pp. 4, 5. Morelli was at the time the Deputy Chief of Staff for Doctrine, HQ TRADOC.
231 Ibid., pp. 4, 5, 7–8, 9, 15.
232 Metz, Steven. 'AirLand Battle and Counterinsurgency'. *Military Review*. (Vol. 70, No. 1. 1990) pp. 32–41.
233 Adams, Thomas K. 'LIC (Low-Intensity Clausewitz)'. *Small Wars and Insurgencies*. (Vol. 1, No. 3. 1990) pp. 266–75.
234 *FM 7-20*, 1992, p C-2.
235 Goose, 'Low-Intensity Warfare: The Warriors and Their Weapons', pp. 85–8.
236 See: Jablonsky, David. 'Strategy and the Operational Level of War: Part I'. *Parameters*. (Vol. 17, No. 1. 1987) pp. 65–76 and, 'Strategy and the Operational Level of War: Part II'. *Parameters*. (Vol. 17, No. 2. 1987) pp. 52–67.
237 *FM 100-5*, 1982, Appendix B, p B-2.
238 Ibid., p B-1.
239 Ibid., p B-5.
240 Lanir, 'The "Principles of War" and Military Thinking', p. 14.
241 Bolger, 'Maneuver Warfare Reconsidered', p. 36.
242 Builder, *The Masks of War*, p. 187.
243 Spiller, 'In the Shadow of the Dragon', p. 52.
244 Bacevich, A.J. 'Prospects for Military Reform'. *Parameters*. (Vol. 17, No. 1. 1987) pp. 29–42.
245 Rosen, Stephen Peter. 'New Ways of War: Understanding Military Innovation'. *International Security*. (Vol. 13, No. 1. 1988) p. 141.
246 Luttwak, *Strategy*, p. 98.
247 Snyder, Jack L. *The Ideology of the Offensive: Military Decision Making and the Disasters of 1914*. (Ithaca, NY: Cornell University Press, 1984) p. 210.

5 THE INFLUENCE OF ARMY THINKING

1 For example, Melanson, Richard A. *Reconstructing Consensus: American Foreign Policy since the Vietnam War*. (New York: St Martin's Press, 1991).
2 Schmitz, David F. and Walker, Vanessa. 'Jimmy Carter and the Foreign Policy of Human Rights: The Development of a Post-Cold War Foreign Policy'. *Diplomatic History*. (Vol. 28, No. 1. 2004) pp. 113–43.
3 See: Smith, Gaddis. *Morality, Reason and Power: American Diplomacy in the Carter Years*. (New York: Hill and Wang, 1986); Garfinkle, Adam. *Telltale Hearts: The Origins and Impact of the Vietnam Antiwar Movement*. (London: Macmillan, 1995) pp. 210–18; and Brzezinski, Zbigniew. *Power and Principle: Memoirs of the National Security Adviser 1977–1981*. Revised edition. (New York: Farrar Straus Giroux, 1985)
4 Garthoff, Raymond L. *Detente and Confrontation: American–Soviet Relations from Nixon to Reagan*. (Washington, DC: Brookings Institute, 1985) p. 945.
5 Smith, *Morality, Reason and Power*, pp. 218–47, and Garthoff, *Detente and Confrontation*, pp. 977–1121.
6 Tarr, David W. 'Political Restraints on US Intervention in Low-Intensity Conflicts'. *Parameters*. (Vol. 10, No. 3. 1980) p. 59.
7 Dallek, Robert. *Ronald Reagan: The Politics of Symbolism*. (Cambridge, MA: Harvard University Press, 1999) and Mervin, David. *Ronald Reagan and the American Presidency*. (London: Longman, 1990).

8 Halliday, Fred. *The Making of the Second Cold War*. Second edition. (London: Verso, 1986) pp. 105–33.
9 Melanson, *Reconstructing Consensus*, p. 149.
10 Ambrose, *Rise to Globalism*, p. 321.
11 Sherry, Michael S. *In the Shadow of War: The United States since the 1930s*. (New Haven, NJ: Yale University Press, 1995) p. 392. See, 'The Illusory Remilitarization, 1981–1988', pp. 391–430.
12 Lewy, Guenter. *America in Vietnam*. (New York: Oxford University Press, 1978). Summaries of the revisionist debate are found in Grinter, Lawrence, E. and Dunn, Peter M. (eds) *The American War in Vietnam: Lessons, Legacies, and Implications for Future Conflicts*. (New York: Greenwood Press, 1987) and Matthews, Lloyd J. and Brown, Dale E. (eds) *Assessing the Vietnam War: A Collection from the Journal of the U.S. Army War College*. (London: Pergamon-Brassey's, 1987).
13 *Congressional Quarterly Weekly Report*. (Vol. 39, No. 2. 24 January 1981) p. 188.
14 The presentation was on 24 February 1981. See: Weinberger, Caspar. *Fighting for Peace: Seven Critical Years in the Pentagon*. (New York: Warner, 1990) p. 56.
15 Shultz, George P. *Triumph and Turmoil: My Years as Secretary of State*. (New York: Charles Scribner, 1993) p. 553.
16 McKeever, Robert J. 'American Myths and the Impact of the Vietnam War: Revisionism in Foreign Policy and Popular Cinema in the 1980s' in Walsh, Jeffrey and Aulich, James (eds) *Vietnam Images: War and Representation*. (London: Macmillan, 1989) pp. 43–56, 44.
17 Melanson, *Reconstructing Consensus*, p. 188.
18 Schlesinger, Arthur M. *The Imperial Presidency*. (Boston, MA: Houghton Mifflin, 1973) p. 206.
19 'War Powers Resolution' Public Law 93–148, Joint Resolution, passed 7 November 1973. Congress did not always defer to the executive. See: Zoellick, Robert B. 'Congress and the Making of US Foreign Policy'. *Survival*. (Vol. 41, No. 4. 1999) pp. 20–41.
20 Public Law 93–148, Sec 3.
21 Mann. Thomas E. 'Making Foreign Policy: President and Congress' in Mann, Thomas E. (ed.) *A Question of Balance: The President, the Congress and Foreign Policy*. (Washington, DC: Brookings Institution, 1990) pp. 21–2. Political circumstances rather than the lack of constitutional or legal powers constrained Congress over Grenada. See: Rubner, Michael. 'The Reagan Administration, the 1973 War Powers Resolution, and the Invasion of Grenada'. *Political Science Quarterly*. (Vol. 100, No. 4. 1985) pp. 627–47. The US has only declared war on eight occasions: Germany, 6 April 1917; Austria–Hungary, 7 December 1917; Japan, 8 December 1941; Germany, 11 December 1941; Italy, 11 December 1941; Bulgaria, 5 June 1942; Hungary, 5 June 1942; Rumania, 5 June 1942.
22 Melanson, *Reconstructing Consensus*, p. 172.
23 Cronin, Thomas E. 'President, Congress, and American Foreign Policy' in Kegley, Charles W. and Wittkopf, Eugene R. (eds) *The Domestic Sources of American Foreign Policy: Insights and Evidence*. (New York: St Martin's Press, 1988) p. 157 and Katzmann. Robert A. 'War Powers: Toward a New Accomodation' in Mann, Thomas E. (ed.) *A Question of Balance*, p. 65.
24 Winik, Jay. *On The Brink*. (New York: Simon and Schuster, 1996) p. 261.
25 Sharpe, Kenneth E. 'The Post-Vietnam Formula under Siege: The Imperial Presidency and Central America'. *Political Science Quarterly*. (Vol. 102, No. 4. 1987) pp. 549–69.
26 Ambrose, *Rise to Globalism*, p. 326.
27 Melanson, *Reconstructing Consensus*, p. 195.
28 Reagan's policy in Nicaragua and how Congressional blocking helped initiate the Iran–Contra scandal is summarised by Kornbluh, Peter. 'Nicaragua' in, Schraeder,

Peter J. (ed.) *Intervention Into the 1990s: U.S. Foreign Policy in the Third World.* (Boulder, CO: Lynne Rienner, 1992) pp. 291–8.
29 Public Law 93–155, Sec 138 (a). Passed 16 November 1973.
30 Westmoreland, 'Vietnam in Perspective', p. 52.
31 Davis, 'Defense Reorganization and National Security', p. 128.
32 Sarkesian, *Soldiers, Society and National Security*, p. 114.
33 Korb, Lawrence J. 'Decision-Making in Defense: the US Case' in Jacobsen, Carl G. (ed.) *Strategic Power: USA/USSR*. (London: Macmillan, 1990) p. 235.
34 A clear account of the frustrations and procedures of Congress/White House defence budgetary issues is found in Weinberger, *Fighting for Peace*, pp. 42–52, 57–79.
35 Garfinkle, *Telltale Hearts*, p. 283.
36 Blechman, Barry M. *The Politics of National Security: Congress and U.S. Defense Policy*. (Oxford: Oxford University Press, 1990) pp. 20–1.
37 Fisher, Louis and Adler, David Gray. 'The War Powers Resolution: Time to Say Goodbye'. *Political Science Quarterly*. (Vol. 113, No. 1. 1998) p. 20.
38 Blechman, Barry M. 'The Congressional Role in U.S. Military Policy'. *Political Science Quarterly*. (Vol. 106, No. 1. 1991) pp. 17–32.
39 Adler, David Gray. 'The Constitution and Presidential Warmaking: The Enduring Debate'. *Political Science Quarterly*. (Vol. 103, No. 1. 1988) pp. 1–36. Congress cut the aid to South Vietnam and contributed to the idea that the Soviets had gained a huge advantage in inter-continental ballistic missiles (ICBMs). See: Dunn, David H. *The Politics of Threat: Minutemen Vulnerability in American National Security Policy*. (London: Macmillan, 1997).
40 Hart, Gary. 'Toward a New Consensus on Defense'. *Strategic Review*. (Vol. 8, No. 4. 1980) pp. 9–14. On the Military Reform Caucus see, Chapter 4, p. 80, above.
41 Fallows, James. 'Muscle-Bound Super Power: The State of America's Defense'. *Atlantic Monthly*. (October 1979) pp. 59–78. His *National Defense* was an expansion of the themes.
42 Reformers included John Boyd, Pierre Sprey and Chuck Spinney. See: Burton, *The Pentagon Wars*, p. 9.
43 Komer, Robert W. 'Strategy and Military Reform' in Clark et al. *The Defense Reform Debate*, pp. 5–15.
44 Kitfield, *Prodigal Soldiers*, pp. 246–53. *Congressional Quarterly Report*. (Vol. 40, No. 35. 28 August 1982) pp. 2132–3.
45 Jones, David C. 'What's Wrong With Our Defense Establishment' in Clark et al. *The Defense Reform Debate*, pp. 273, 283. See also: pp. 272–86.
46 Jones, 'What's Wrong With Our Defense Establishment', p. 276.
47 Kitfield, *Prodigal Soldiers*, p. 253.
48 Shultz, *Turmoil and Triumph*, p. 151.
49 O'Shaughnessy, Hugh. *Grenada: Revolution, Invasion and Aftermath*. (London: Sphere, 1984) p. 15.
50 Schwarzkopf, *It Doesn't Take a Hero*, p. 308.
51 Melanson, *Reconstructing Consensus*, p. 168.
52 Schultz, *Turmoil and Triumph*, p. 339.
53 Gray, 'Strategy in the Nuclear Age', p. 591.
54 Horowitz, David J. 'The Anti-War Movement: Vietnam Lessons' in Moore, John Norton (ed.) *The Vietnam Debate; A Fresh Look at the Arguments*. (Lanham, MD: University Press of America, 1990) p. 306.
55 Fromkin and Chace, 'What Are the Lessons of Vietnam?', p. 739.
56 Young, Peter, and Jesser, Peter. *The Media and the Military: From the Crimea to Desert Strike*. (London: Macmillan, 1997) p. 121. For an analysis of Grenada see: pp. 120–38.
57 Metcalfe, J. III. 'The Press and Grenada, 1983'. *Small Wars and Insurgencies*. (Vol. 2, No. 3. 1991) pp. 168–74.

58 Atkinson, *The Long Gray Line*, p. 491. See also: Handel, *Masters of War*, pp. 190, 192.
59 Ambrose, *Rise to Globalism*, pp. 311–12. The War Powers Act prevented the administration from publicly saying the mission was to support the Lebanese government. See: Lehman, John F. Jr. *Command of the Seas*. (New York: Charles Scribner's, 1988) pp. 318–19.
60 Weinberger, *Fighting for Peace*, pp. 133–74.
61 Department of Defense. *Report of the DOD Commission on Beirut International Airport Terrorist Act, October 23, 1983*. (Washington, DC: GPO, 1983) p. 40.
62 The success of the suicide bomber here was seen by terror groups as a model and led to the increasing use in Sri Lanka and then Israel.
63 See: Feldman, Shai. 'Israel's Involvement in Lebanon: 1975–1985' in Levite, Ariel E., et al. (eds) *Foreign Military Intervention: The Dynamics of Protracted Conflict*. (New York: Columbia University Press, 1992) pp. 129–61.
64 For example: *Newsweek*, 19 December 1983, had as its cover story 'The Marines in Lebanon: Right Men, Wrong Job'. See: pp. 8–13, 20–3.
65 Grant, Rebecca L. *Operation Just Cause and the U.S. Policy Process*. (Santa Monica, CA: RAND, 1991) p. 25.
66 Gacek, *The Logic of Force*, p. 3.
67 Weinberger's views on the Lebanon deployment and his conflicts with the rest of the administration are given in Weinberger, *Fighting for Peace*, pp. 135–74.
68 Weinberger, *Fighting for Peace*, pp. 144–5.
69 Ibid., pp. 155–8.
70 Ibid., p. 158.
71 Department of Defense, *Report on Beirut*.
72 Department of Defense, *Report on Beirut*, Executive Summary, pp. 2–15.
73 *U.S. News and World Report*, 1 October 1990, p. 32.
74 Weinberger, *Fighting for Peace*, pp. 163–5.
75 Hoffman, F.G. *Decisive Force: The New American Way of War*. (London: Praeger, 1996) pp. 39–56.
76 Powell, *A Soldier's Way*, pp. 302–3. Powell was his Military Assistant at the time.
77 The debate was somewhat aggravated by the fact that Weinberger had previously been Shultz's junior in government at the Office of Management and Budget and in the private sector at the Bechtel corporation. Winik, *On the Brink*, p. 328.
78 Luttwak, *The Pentagon and the Art of War*, pp. 50. 51–8.
79 Lehman, *Command of the Seas*, p. 329.
80 Ibid., p. 330.
81 Ibid., p. 337. For a full account see, pp. 306–38.
82 Kitfield, *Prodigal Soldiers*, pp. 263–8. For an analysis of the failings of special operations forces in Grenada and how this fed the Congressional debate see: Adams, *US Special Operations Forces*, pp. 189–94, and Marquis, *Unconventional Warfare*, pp. 91–106.
83 Lehman, *Command of the Seas*, pp. 291–305.
84 For the views of the protagonists and its context see: Weinberger, *Fighting for Peace*, pp. 159–61, 163–5, 401–2, and Shultz, *Turmoil and Triumph*, pp. 646–51.
85 Twining, David. 'The Weinberger Doctrine and the Use of Force in the Contemporary Era'. *Small Wars and Insurgencies*. (Vol. 1, No. 2. 1990) p. 115.
86 Gacek, *The Logic of Force*, pp. 262, 264. A good analysis of the whole debate is found in pp. 262–72.
87 Schultz, *Turmoil and Triumph*, p. 650.
88 See: Huntington, *The Soldier and the State*, p. 79; Betts, *Soldiers, Statesmen and Cold War Crises*; and Palmer, *The 25 Year War*, p. 209.
89 Unless otherwise stated, information in this and the following paragraph is drawn from confidential interviews.

90 Daggett, Stephen. 'Government and the Military Establishment' in Schraeder, *Intervention into the 1990s*, p. 428, n. 2. pp. 193–207.
91 Roth, David. *Sacred Honour: The Authorized Biography of General Sir Colin Powell.* (London: HarperCollins, 1994) p. 117.
92 Ibid., pp. 101–3. 208.
93 Summers, *On Strategy*. The information on the speech writers is drawn from interviews.
94 The War College was not part of TRADOC.
95 Weyand, Fred C. and Summers, Harry G. Jr. 'Vietnam Myths and Military Realities'. *Armor*. (September–October 1976) pp. 30–6.
96 Department of the Army, *Strategic Lessons Learned in Vietnam.*
97 See: Gates, John M. 'Vietnam: The Debate Goes On' in Matthews and Brown, *Assessing the Vietnam War*, pp. 43–56.
98 Summers, Harry G. Jr. *On Strategy II: A Critical Analysis of the Gulf War*. (New York: Dell, 1992) p. 132.
99 Confidential interview.
100 Schwarz, Benjamin C. *American Counterinsurgency Doctrine and El Salvador: The Frustrations of Reform and Illusions of Nation Building*. (Santa Monica, CA: RAND, 1991) pp. 2–3.
101 Downie, *Learning from Conflict*, pp. 129–62.
102 For the CGSC and War College reading lists see, Downie, R. *Learning from Conflict*, p. 74. See: the 'Chairman, Joint Chiefs of Staff Professional Military Reading List' in Joint Chiefs of Staff. *Joint Pub 1: Joint Warfare of the US Armed Forces*. (Washington, DC: GPO, 1991) pp. 71–2 and the 1995 edition, Appendix B.
103 See: <http://www.army.mil/cmh-pg/reference/csalist/list4.htm#summers> accessed 13 May 2004.
104 Villacres, Edward J. and Bassford, Christopher. 'Reclaiming the Clausewitzian Trinity'. *Parameters*. (Vol. 25, No. 3. 1995) p. 10.
105 Ibid., p. 15; Keegan and van Creveld do the same as Summers: see, p. 11. Also see, Keegan, John. *War and Our World; The Reith Lectures, 1998*. (London: Hutchinson, 1998) and Creveld, Martin van. 'What is Wrong with Clausewitz?' in, Nooy, Gert de (ed.) *The Clausewitzian Dictum and the Future of Western Military Strategy*. (The Hague: Kluwer Law International, 1997) pp. 7–23.
106 Handel, *Masters of War*, p. 246.
107 Eckhardt, William G. '"We the People" go to War: The Legal Significance of the Weinberger Doctrine'. *Small Wars and Insurgencies*. (Vol. 1, No. 2. 1990) pp. 131–45, especially p. 140.
108 Dauber, Cori E, 'Implications of the Weinberger Doctrine for American Military Intervention in a Post-Desert Storm Age'. *Contemporary Security Policy*, (Vol. 22, No. 2. 2001) pp. 66–90.
109 Martihinsen, Charles E. 'The Historical Significance of the Weinberger Doctrine'. *Small Wars and Insurgencies*. (Vol. 1, No. 2. 1990) pp. 118–30.
110 The speech is given in an appendix to his autobiography. See: Weinberger, *Fighting for Peace*, pp. 433–45.
111 Weinberger, *Fighting for Peace*, p. 434.
112 Ibid., p. 441.
113 Ibid., p. 441.
114 Ibid., p. 442.
115 Ibid., p. 442.
116 Ibid., p. 442.
117 Ibid., p. 442.
118 Weinberger, Caspar W. 'U.S. Defense Strategy'. *Foreign Affairs*. (Vol. 64, No. 4. 1986) pp. 675–97 and Department of Defense. *Report of Secretary of Defense Caspar W. Weinberger to the Congress on the FY 1987, FY 1988 Authorization Request and*

FY 1987–1991 Defense Programmes. (Washington, DC: Department of Defense, 1986) pp. 73–88.

119 Handel, *Masters of War*, pp. 189, 198.
120 Weinberger, *Fighting for Peace*, p. 444.
121 See: Cynkin, Thomas M. *Soviet and American Signalling in the Polish Crisis*. (London: Macmillan, 1988).
122 Zimmermann, Tim. 'Coercive Diplomacy and Libya' in George, Alexander L. and Simons, William E. (eds) *The Limits of Coercive Diplomacy*. Second edition. (Boulder, CO: Westview Press, 1994) pp. 201–28.
123 Buzzanco, *Masters of War*, p. 2.
124 Weinberger, *Fighting for Peace*, p. 433.
125 Handel, *Masters of War*, pp. 181–3, 185–203. See: pp. 99–117, 181–3 for his discussion of the contradictory nature of Clausewitz's thinking.
126 Clausewitz, *On War*, p. 570. Hall, George M. 'Culminating Points'. *Military Review*. (Vol. 69, No. 7. 1989) p. 80.
127 Handel, *Masters of War*, p. 182. As Handel says, Clausewitz 'seems to assume that the enlightened political leader will be overall command of the war, while refraining from direct interference in lower-level operational decisions', p. 57.
128 Franz, Wallace P. 'Two Letters on Strategy: Clausewitz' Contribution to the Operational Level of War' in Handel, Michael I. (ed.) *Clausewitz and Modern Strategy*. (London: Frank Cass, 1986) p. 171.
129 Showalter, Dennis E. 'Total War for Limited Objectives: An Interpretation of German Grand Strategy' in Kennedy, Paul (ed.) *Grand Strategies in War and Peace*. (New Haven, CT: Yale University Press, 1991) p. 107.
130 Danchev, Alex. 'Liddell Hart's Big Idea'. *Review of International Studies*. (Vol. 25, No. 1. 1999) p. 34.
131 Dauber, 'Implications of the Weinberger Doctrine', pp. 66–90.
132 For example: Klimow, Matthew S. *Moral versus Practical: The Future of US Armed Humanitarian Intervention*. (Kingston, Ontario: Centre of International Relations, Queen's University, 1996).
133 Krepinevich, *The Army and Vietnam*, p. 275.
134 Marquis, *Unconventional Warfare*, p. 136.
135 Spector, Ronald H. 'U.S. Army Strategy in the Vietnam War'. *International Security*. (Vol. 11, No. 4. 1987) p. 131.
136 Summers, Harry G. Jr. 'A War Is a War Is a War Is a War' in Thompson, Loren B. (ed.) *Low-Intensity Conflict: The Patterns of Warfare in the Modern World*. (Lexington, MA: Lexington Books, 1989) pp. 27, 31–3.
137 See: Shafer, *Deadly Paradigms*, p. 288 n. 28.
138 Ibid., especially pp. 276–90. This critique was not unique, for example, see: Shultz, Richard H. Jr, Pfaltzgraff, Robert L. Jr, Ra'anan, Uri, Olson, William J. and Lukes, Igor (eds) *Guerilla Warfare and Counterinsurgency: U.S.–Soviet Policy in the Third World*. (Lexington, MA: Lexington Books, 1989).
139 'National Security Decision Directive Number 277: National Policy and Strategy for Low Intensity Conflict. June 15, 1987' in Simpson, Christopher. *National Security Directives of the Reagan and Bush Administrations: The Declassified History of U.S. Political and Military Policy, 1981–1991*. (Boulder, CO: Westview Press, 1995) pp. 812–906.
140 Twinning, David T. 'Vietnam and the Six Criteria for the Use of Military Force' in Matthews and Brown, *Assessing the Vietnam War*, pp. 221–32.
141 Handel, *Masters of War*, p. 203.
142 Reagan, Ronald. *Ronald Reagan: An American Life*. (New York: Simon and Schuster, 1990) p. 466. Bush, George. 'Remarks at the United States Military Academy in West Point, New York' 5 January 1993. <http://bushlibrary.tamu.edu/papers/1993/93010500.html> especially pp. 3–4 of 4.

143 Craig and George, *Force and Statecraft*, pp. 268, 265–74.
144 Davis, 'Defense Reorganization', p. 128.
145 'Goldwater–Nichols Department of Defense Reorganization Act of 1986' Public Law, 99–433, passed 1 October 1986.
146 For example: General Bruce Palmer thought the DOD was in greater need than the JCS. See: Palmer, Bruce. Jr. 'The Case For Limited Reform of the JCS'. *Parameters*. (Vol. 15, No. 4. 1985) pp. 2–9. See also the article derived from the Center for Strategic and International Studies (CSIS) Defense Organization Project (which was aided by General David C. Jones and General Meyer): Lynn, William J. and Posen, Barry R. 'The Case for JCS Reform'. *International Security*. (Vol. 10, No. 3. 1985) pp. 69–97.
147 For analysis of the motives to pass the act see: *Congressional Quarterly Report*. (Vol. 44, No. 15. 12 April 1986) pp. 813–15 and Clark et al., *The Defense Reform Debate*, pp. 19–82, 211–359.
148 Burton, *The Pentagon Wars*, p. 9.
149 Gorman, Paul F. 'Toward a Stronger Defense Establishment' in Clark et al., *The Defense Reform Debate*, p. 294.
150 Oseth, John M. 'An Overview of the Reform Debate' in Clark et al., *The Defense Reform Debate*, p. 57.
151 The aims were to: reorganise the Department of Defense and strengthen the civil authority in the department; improve military advice to the president, the NSC, and the Secretary of Defense; place clear responsibility on commanders of combatant commands; unify commanders' authority; increase attention to formulation of strategy; provide more efficiency in the use of defence resources; improve joint officer management policies; and enhance effectiveness of military operations and improve management and administration of the department. See: Public Law 99–433, Sec 3 (1) to (8).
152 Public Law 99–143, Sec 151 (b).
153 Ibid., Sec 162 (4b) and Sec 163 (a 1)
154 Ibid., Sec 155 (e).
155 Ibid., Sec 153, (a 1).
156 Davis, 'Defense Reorganization', p. 122.
157 Palmer, *The 25 Year War*, p. 199.
158 Cohen, Eliot A. 'Civil–Military Relations'. *Orbis*. (Vol. 41, No. 2. 1997) p. 181.
159 Powell, *A Soldier's Way*, p. 444.
160 See Colin Powell's account of this in Powell, *A Soldier's Way*, pp. 440–4.
161 Hamilton, *Green and Blue in the Wild Blue*, p. 24.
162 See: Public Law 99–433, Secs 161–166. 'Combatant Commands'.
163 Ibid., Sec 404 (e)(1).
164 Davis, 'Defense Reorganization', p. 128. The process of developing joint doctrine began with a broad outline of what joint warfare meant, followed in 1993 by the first joint doctrine. See: Joint Chiefs of Staff, *Joint Pub 1: Joint Warfare of the US Armed Forces*. (Washington, DC: GPO, 1991) and Joint Chiefs of Staff, *Joint Pub 3–0: Doctrine for Joint Operations*. (Washington, DC: GPO, 1993).
165 Department of the Air Force. *AFM 1-1, Basic Aerospace Doctrine of the United States Air Force*. (Washington, DC: GPO, 1992).
166 Owens, MacKubin Thomas. 'The Hollow Promise of JCS Reform'. *International Security*. (Vol. 10, No. 3. 1985) p. 108.
167 Jones, 'What's Wrong With Our Defense Establishment', p. 203.
168 The problems the Navy faced in the 1990s, such as the Tailhook affair in 1991 and suicide of the Chief of Naval Operations (the Navy's most senior officer) Jeremy Boorda in June 1996, were linked to fact that the Navy 'never did the kind of soul searching' and institutional overhauls that other services did after Vietnam. See: Pine, Art. 'Moral Compass Key to Getting Navy on Course'. *Los Angeles Times*, 17 June 1996, p A–10.

169 The period of John Lehman's tenure as Secretary of the Navy (1981–87) saw a 'Rebirth of U.S. Naval Strategy' and the Naval War College as the site of much excellent strategic thinking, both of which fed the 'Maritime Strategy' released in 1986. See: Lehman, John F. Jr. 'Rebirth of U.S. Naval Strategy'. *Strategic Review*. (Vol. 9, No. 3. 1981) pp. 9–15, and Summers, 'Military Doctrine', p. 12. Watkins, James D. 'The Maritime Strategy'. *Proceedings*, Special Supplement (Vol. 112, No. 1. 1986) pp. 2–17.
170 For a naval point of view see: Friedman, Norman. *Desert Victory: The War For Kuwait*. Updated edition. (Annapolis, MD: Naval Institute Press, 1992) pp. 74–84, and Baer, *One Hundred Years of Seapower*, pp. 443–4.
171 Baer, *One Hundred Years of Seapower*, p. 444.
172 Friedman, *Desert Victory*, p. 78.
173 For example see: Yuknis, Christopher Allan. 'The Goldwater–Nichols Reorganization Act of 1986: An Interim Assessment' in Somerville, Mary A. (ed.) *Essays On Strategy: X*. (Washington, DC: National Defense University Press, 1993) pp. 75–103.
174 Roth, *Sacred Honour*, pp. 223–35.
175 Cohen, Eliot A. 'Review of *My American Journey* by Colin Powell'. *Foreign Affairs*. (Vol. 74, No. 6. 1995) p. 107.
176 Jaffe, Lorna S. *The Development of Base Force: 1989–1992*. (Washington, DC: Joint Chiefs of Staff, 1993) p. 49.
177 Ibid., pp. 49–50. The account of Powell's strategic vision and its implementation is found on pp. 11–50.
178 Cohen, 'Review of *My American Journey*', p. 104.
179 Confidential interview.
180 Roman, Peter J. and Tarr, David W. 'The Joint Chiefs of Staff: From Service Parochialism to Jointness'. *Political Science Quarterly*. (Vol. 113, No. 1. 1998) p. 109.
181 Buzzanco, *Masters of War*, p. 23.
182 Owens, MacKubin Thomas. 'The Hollow Promise of JCS Reform'. *International Security*. (Vol. 10, No. 3. 1985) p. 111. See also: pp. 98–111.
183 An excellent account of the bureaucratic battles involved and the subsequent effort to implement LIC has been provided by Marquis, *Unconventional Warfare*, especially pp. 107–226.
184 See: Chapter 4, p. 80, above.
185 Public Law 99–661.
186 Marquis, *Unconventional Warfare*, pp. 144–7.
187 US Code, Title 10, Sec 167 (4) (j) lists the nine specified tasks as: direct action; strategic reconnaissance; unconventional warfare; foreign internal defence; civil affairs; psychological operations; counter-terrorism; humanitarian assistance; theatre search and rescue.
188 Scott, James M. *Deciding to Intervene: The Reagan Doctrine and American Foreign Policy*. (London: Duke University Press, 1996) pp. 2, 1–39, 213–53.
189 Davis, 'Defense Reorganization', p. 128.
190 Adams, *US Special Operations Forces in Action*, pp. 233, 231–44. See also; Atkinson, *Crusade*, pp. 139–44, 180–1.
191 Cohen, 'Constraints on America's Conduct of Small Wars', p. 295.
192 Adams, *US Special Operations Forces in Action*, p. 226. See: Stiner, Carl W. 'US Special Operations Forces: A Strategic Perspective'. *Parameters*. (Vol. 22, No. 2. 1992) p. 4. See also: pp. 2–13.
193 Adams, *US Special Operations Forces in Action*, p. 259. Adams analyses Somalia and Haiti on pp. 258–86.
194 Koch, Noel. 'Objecting to Reality: The Struggle to Restore U.S. Special Operations Forces' in Thompson, Loren B. (ed.) *Low-Intensity Conflict: The Patterns of Warfare in the Modern World*. (Lexington, MA: Lexington Books, 1989) p. 52.

6 INTERVENTIONS

1 Buckley, Kevin. *Panama*. (New York: Touchstone, 1991) p. 225.
2 'Address to the Nation Announcing United States Military Action in Panama, December 20, 1989'. <http://bushlibrary.tamu.edu/papers/1989/89122000.html>
3 Confidential interview.
4 Noriega was seen as an asset by the Reagan administration for its fight against Marxism in Central America. To some departments he was a liability, to others an asset and overall there was no co-ordination of policy towards handling him. The US Senate and Department of Justice were concerned about the drug trade leading to indictments in a court in Florida. See: Grant, Rebecca L. *Operation Just Cause and the U.S. Policy Process*. (Santa Monica, CA: RAND, 1991) pp. 8–20.
5 Gilboa, Eytan. 'The Panama Invasion Revisited: Lessons for the Use of Force in the Post Cold War Era'. *Political Science Quarterly*. (Vol. 110, No. 4. 1995) p. 560.
6 Grant, *Operation Just Cause*, p. 39.
7 George, Alexander L. 'Coercive Diplomacy: Definition and Characteristics' in George and Simons, *The Limits of Coercive Diplomacy*, p. 10.
8 Freedman, Lawrence. 'Strategic Coercion' in Freedman, Lawrence (ed.) *Strategic Coercion: Concepts and Cases*. (Oxford: Oxford University Press, 1998) p. 36.
9 Downey, Frederick M. and Metz, Steven. 'The American Political Culture and Strategic Planning'. *Parameters*. (Vol. 18, No. 3. 1988) p. 39. Raymond Cohen highlights that the US is an individualistic, low-context culture, which causes it great problems when dealing with high-context collective cultures such as Japan. See, Cohen, Raymond. *Negotiating Across Cultures: International Communication in an Independent World*. Revised edition. (Washington, DC: United States Institute of Peace Press, 1997) pp. 9–43.
10 McNamara, Robert S. with VanDeMark, Brian. *In Retrospect: The Tragedy and Lessons of Vietnam*. (New York: Times Books, 1995) p. 322. US bureaucratic cultural ignorance has continued. See: Johnson, Wray R. 'War, Culture, and the Interpretation of History: The Vietnam War Reconsidered'. *Small Wars and Insurgencies*. (Vol. 9, No. 2. 1998) pp. 83–113.
11 For example see: Creveld, Martin van. *Command in War*. (Cambridge, MA: Harvard University Press, 1985) p. 253 and Leonhard, Robert R. *The Art of Maneuver: Maneuver-Warfare Theory and AirLand Battle*. (Novato, CA: Presidio, 1991) p. 141.
12 Donnelly, Thomas, et al. *Operation Just Cause: The Storming of Panama*. (New York: Lexington Books, 1991) p. 16. President Bush devotes approximately seven lines of text, out of 566 pages, to Panama in his memoirs. See: Bush, George and Scowcroft, Brent. *A World Transformed*. (New York: Alfred A. Knopf, 1998) pp. 23, 62, 166, 172, 324, 463, 489.
13 Woerner, Fred F. 'The Strategic Imperative for the United States in Latin America'. *Military Review*. (Vol. 69, No. 2. 1989) pp. 18–28. General Woerner was a light infantryman, fluent in Spanish, who had spent a large proportion of his career in Latin America and had worked for General Richardson at Fort Leavenworth.
14 Buckley, *Panama*, pp. 162–3.
15 Donnelly *et al.*, *Operation Just Cause*, pp. 33, 41.
16 Woodward, Bob. *The Commanders*. (London: Simon and Schuster, 1991) pp. 83–9.
17 Halloran, Richard. 'U.S. Military Chief is Replaced in the Central American Region'. *New York Times*. 21 July 1989, Sec A p. 5.
18 Buckley, *Panama*, p. 190.
19 Woodward, *The Commanders*, p. 97.
20 Ibid., p. 98.
21 Confidential interview. Thurman was trusted by the White House and Pentagon, having served as Army Vice Chief of Staff. See: Donnelly *et al.*, *Operation Just Cause*, p. 54.

22 Woodward, *The Commanders*, p. 93.
23 Buckley, *Panama*, p. 222.
24 The coup is outlined, and Thurman's role in it, in Buckley. *Panama*, pp. 197–208.
25 Confidential interview.
26 Grant, *Operation Just Cause*, pp. 31, 33.
27 The Joint Chiefs role in the Panama operation is covered in Cole, Ronald H. *Operation Just Cause: The Planning and Execution of Joint Operations in Panama, February 1988–January 1990.* (Washington, DC: GPO. 1995).
28 Grant, *Operation Just Cause*, p. 35.
29 Donnelly *et al.*, *Operation Just Cause*, p. 17.
30 Woerner, Fred F., Jr. 'Foreword' to Fishel, John T. *Civil Military Operations in the New World.* (Westport, CT: Praeger, 1997) p xi.
31 Confidential interview.
32 Buckley, *Panama*, pp. 222–3.
33 Woodward, *The Commanders*, p. 175.
34 See: Woodward, The Commanders. p. 178, and Young and Jesser, *The Media and the Military*, pp. 139–57.
35 Schulzinger, *American Diplomacy*, p. 369.
36 Thurman used psychological harassment against Noriega, including armoured vehicles gunning their engines, building a landing strip during the night and, most famously, blaring rock music at the nunciate at deafening levels for two days.
37 Woodward, *The Commanders*, p. 195.
38 Matloff, Maurice. (ed.) *American Military History, Volume 2: 1902–1996.* (Conshohocke, PA: Combined Books, 1996) p. 355.
39 Crowell, Lorenzo. 'The Anatomy of JUST CAUSE: The Forces Involved, the Adequacy of Intelligence, and Its Success as a Joint Operation' in Watson, Bruce and Tsouras, Peter G. (eds) *Operation Just Cause: The U.S. Intervention in Panama.* (Boulder, CO: Westview Press. 1991) p. 68.
40 Wallace, J.J.A. 'Manoeuvre Theory in Operations Other than War' in Reid, Brian Holden (ed.) *Military Power; Land Warfare in Theory and Practice.* (London: Frank Cass, 1997) p. 220.
41 Leonhard, *The Art of Maneuver*, pp. 208–20.
42 Powell, Colin L. 'U.S. Forces: Challenges Ahead'. *Foreign Affairs.* (Vol. 72. No. 5. 1992) p. 38, and especially pp. 36–41.
43 Crowell, 'The Anatomy of JUST CAUSE', p. 96.
44 Newell, Clayton R. *The Framework of Operational Warfare.* (London: Routledge, 1991) pp. 155–7.
45 Sweeney, *A Handbook of American Military History*, p. 255.
46 Briggs, Clarence E. III. *Operation Just Cause, Panama December 1989: A Soldier's Eyewitness Account.* (Harrisburg, PA: Stackpole Books, 1990) p. 17.
47 Briggs, *Operation Just Cause*, pp. 4, 142. This point is borne out in later analysis such as Metz, John M. 'Training the Way We Fight or for the Fight: Are Tactical Units Prepared for Post-Conflict Operations?' *Low Intensity Conflict and Law Enforcement.* (Vol. 5, No. 2. 1996) pp. 216–19.
48 Keefe, John M. 'The Operational Art of Peace Enforcement'. *Low Intensity Conflict and Law Enforcement.* (Vol. 5, No. 1. 1996) p. 64.
49 Hippel, Karin von. *Democracy by Force: US Military Intervention in the Post-Cold War World.* (Cambridge: Cambridge University Press, 2000.) pp. 43. 42–54. 117. See: Fishel, John T. *Civil Military Operations in the New World.* (Westport, CT: Praeger, 1997).
50 Calvert, Peter. 'The US Intervention in Panama'. *Small Wars and Insurgencies.* (Vol. 1, No. 3. 1990) p. 313.
51 Powell, *A Soldier's Way*, p. 434.
52 Hoffman, *Decisive Force*, p. 73.

53 Schwarzkopf. *It Doesn't Take A Hero*, p. 377.
54 Hippel, *Democracy by Force*, p. 122. For a fuller account from a reporter on the ground see: Shacochis, Bob. *The Immaculate Invasion*. (London: Bloomsbury, 1999).
55 See: Stiner, Carl W. 'US Special Operations Forces: A Strategic Perspective'. *Parameters*. (Vol. 22, No. 2. 1992) pp. 2–13, especially p. 4, and Adams, *US Special Operations Forces in Action*, p. 226.
56 Hoffman, *Decisive Force*, pp. 67, 73.
57 President Bush announced the commission on 5 November 1990, and it eventually recommended the closure of 130 bases. See, Department of Defense. *Defense Base Closure and Realignment Commission: 1993 Report to the President*. (Washington, DC: GPO, 1993) p viii.
58 Wallace, 'Manoeuvre Theory in Operations Other than War', p. 224.
59 Flanagan, Edward M. Jr. *Battle for Panama: Inside Operation Just Cause*. (Washington, DC: Brassey's, 1993) p. 232.
60 Ibid., p. 226. Flanagan was an Army Lieutenant General.
61 Important accounts of the Gulf War include: Freedman, Lawrence and Karsh, Efraim. *The Gulf Conflict* (London: Faber and Faber, 1993) for the political emphasis, the Army perspective is found in Scales, Robert H. Jr. *Certain Victory: The U.S. Army in the Gulf War*. (London: Brassey's, 1994), an air perspective in Hallion, Richard P. *Storm Over Iraq: Air Power and the Gulf War*. (Washington, DC: Smithsonian Institute Press, 1992); U.S. News and World Report. *Triumph Without Victory: The Unreported History of the Persian Gulf War*. (New York: Random House, 1992), Atkinson, Rick. *Crusade: The Untold Story of the Gulf War*. (London: HarperCollins, 1994) and Gordon, Michael R. and Trainor, Bernard E. *The General's War: The Inside Story of the Conflict in the Gulf*. (Boston, MA: Little, Brown, 1995) provide critical inside accounts.
62 For an analysis of the Gulf War as coercive diplomacy see: Jakobsen, Peter Viggo. *Western Use of Coercive Diplomacy After the Cold War: A Challenge for Theory and Practice*. (London: Macmillan, 1998) pp. 50–69.
63 Herrmann, Richard. 'Coercive Diplomacy and the Crisis over Kuwait, 1990–91' in George and Simons, *The Limits of Coercive Diplomacy*, p. 256.
64 'Remarks to the American Legislative Exchange Council, March 1, 1991'. <http://bushlibrary.tamu.edu/papers/1991/91030102.html>
65 Cohen, Eliot A. *Supreme Command: Soldiers, Statesmen, and Leadership in Wartime*. (New York: The Free Press, 2002) p. 199.
66 The cover of Kitfield, *Prodigal Soldiers*, says: 'How the Generation of Officers Born of Vietnam Revolutionized the American Style of War'. A similar tone is found in Powell, *A Soldier's Way* and Schwarzkopf, *It Doesn't Take a Hero*.
67 Freedman and Karsh, *The Gulf Conflict*, p. 283. In fact, the historical antecedent that concerned policy makers most was the Korean War, with its broadening of war aims during the fighting, and the inconclusive ending of the war. See: Atkinson, *Crusade*, pp. 297–300.
68 For example, Bowen and Dunn's list of political aspects includes: the clear-cut nature of the aggression; the commonality of interests of international coalition; a distracted Soviet Union; US leadership opportunity; costs borne by allies. See: Bowen, Wyn Q. and Dunn, David H. *American Security Policy in the 1990s: Beyond Containment*. (Aldershot: Dartmouth, 1996) pp. 9–14. Norman Friedman's military ones include: the terrain, the nature of the enemy forces, the theatre of operations, the availability of bases and the technology gap. See: Friedman, *Desert Victory*, pp. 236–50.
69 Betts, Richard K. *Military Readiness: Concepts, Choices, Consequences*. (Washington, DC: Brookings Institution, 1995) pp. 189–94.
70 Record, Jeffrey. *Hollow Victory: A Contrary View of the Gulf War*. (Washington, DC: Brassey's, 1993).

71 Record, *Hollow Victory*, p. 147. A full account is provided in Matthews, James K. and Holt, Cora J. *So Many, So Much, So Far, So Fast: The United States Transportation Command and Strategic Deployment for Operation Desert Shield/ Desert Storm.* (Washington, DC: GPO, n.d.).
72 Scales, *Certain Victory*, p. 5.
73 Spiller, *Shadow of the Dragon*, p. 53 n. 12.
74 Atkinson, *Crusade*, p. 2.
75 Meese, Michael J. 'Institutionalizing Maneuver Warfare: The Process of Organizational Change' in Hooker, *Maneuver Warfare: An Anthology*, p. 207.
76 Friedman, *Desert Victory*, p. 130.
77 Kitfield, *Prodigal Soldiers*, p. 24.
78 Romjue, *Prepare the Army for War*, p. 125.
79 Starry, 'TRADOC's Analysis of the Yom Kippur War', pp. 7 and 8.
80 Schubert, Frank N. and Kraus, Theresa L. (eds) *The Whirlwind War: The United States Army in Operations Desert Shield and Desert Storm.* (Washington, DC: GPO, 1995) pp. 25–45, 233.
81 For example, 'Top Guns: What America's Military Commanders Think about Waging War'. *U.S. News and World Report* (1 October 1990) pp. 28–36.
82 Dubois, Thomas R. 'The Weinberger Doctrine and the Liberation of Kuwait'. *Parameters*. (Vol. 24, No. 4. 1991) pp. 24–38. See the chart of interventions and the criteria used provided in Handel, *Masters of War*, p. 202.
83 Bush and Scowcroft, *A World Transformed*, p. 354.
84 Summers, Harry G. Jr. *On Strategy II: A Critical Analysis of the Gulf War.* (New York: Dell, 1992) pp. 153–247.
85 'Address to the Nation Announcing Allied Military Action in the Persian Gulf; January 16, 1991'. <http://bushlibrary.tamu.edu/papers/1991/91011602.html>
86 Freedman and Karsh, *The Gulf Conflict*, pp. 204–8.
87 Atkinson, *Crusade*, pp. 110–15.
88 Trainor, Bernard E. 'Jointness, Service Culture, and the Gulf War'. *Joint Force Quarterly*. (No. 3. 1993/4) p. 74. Disputes came to light in particular through the publication of Bob Woodward's *Commanders* and Gordon and Trainor's *The General's War*.
89 Senator Inouye of Hawaii told Bush. See: Bush and Scowcroft, *A World Transformed*, p. 435.
90 Bush and Scowcroft, *A World Transformed*, p. 371.
91 McMasters, *Dereliction of Duty*, pp. 323, 334.
92 Freedman and Karsh, *The Gulf Conflict*, pp. 211–74, 290–4.
93 Comment ascribed to Colin Powell by Bob Woodward in *Commanders*, p. 315.
94 For example, the media was used as part of the process of diplomatic signalling. See: Young and Jesser, *The Media and the Military*, pp. 158–91. See also the damning account of Hackworth, David H. 'The Gulf Crisis: The Media Point of View'. *Small Wars and Insurgencies*. (Vol. 2, No. 3. 1991) pp. 182–91.
95 Freedman, Lawrence and Karsh, Efraim. 'How Kuwait Was Won: Strategy in the Gulf War'. *International Security*. (Vol. 16, No. 2. 1991) p. 5. For the ambiguity of the casualty question see: pp. 17–19.
96 Watson, Bruce W. 'The Issue of Media Access to Information' in Watson, Bruce W. (ed.) *Military Lessons of the Gulf War.* (London: Greenhill Books, 1991) p. 208.
97 This was particularly the case with logistical and ethical problems. See: Fox, Terrance. 'The Media and the Military: An Historical Perspective on the Gulf War' in Walsh, Jeffrey (ed.) *The Gulf War Did Not Happen: Politics, Culture and Warfare Post-Vietnam.* (Aldershot: Arena, 1995) pp. 146–7.
98 For the close relationship between television and politicians in setting the news agenda see Mermin, Jonathan. 'Television News and American Intervention in Somalia:

The Myth of a Media-Driven Foreign Policy'. *Political Science Quarterly*. (Vol. 112, No. 3. 1997) pp. 385–403. Warren Strobel explains that the CNN effect is actually highly conditional, and that the media's influence depends on many factors, most of which are under government control; the nature of post-Gulf War peace operations reporting is due to the nature of the mission, rather than technological changes. See: Strobel, Warren P. *Late-Breaking Foreign Policy: The News Media's Influence on Peace Operations*. (Washington, DC: United States Institute of Peace Press, 1997) especially pp. 211–34.

99 Ignatieff, Michael. *Virtual War: Kosovo and Beyond*. (London: Chatto and Windus, 2000) pp. 137–9.

100 Borger, Julian. 'CNN Let Army Staff into Newsroom'. *The Guardian* 12 April 2000, p. 17.

101 See Chapter 2 above and Simons, Geoff. *Vietnam Syndrome: Impact on US Foreign Policy*. (New York: St Martin's Press, 1998) p xx.

102 'Address to the Nation on the Suspension of Allied Offensive Combat Operations in the Persian Gulf. February 27, 1991'. <http://bushlibrary.tamu.edu/papers/1991/91022702.html>

103 Bond, Brian. *The Pursuit of Victory: From Napoleon to Saddam Hussein*. (Oxford: Oxford University Press, 1996).

104 Cohen, Eliot A. 'A War That Was Not Left to the Generals'. *Joint Forces Quarterly*. (No. 8. 1995) p. 48.

105 A sustained reflection on this issue is provided in Cohen, *Supreme Command*.

106 Schwarzkopf, *It Doesn't Take a Hero*, pp. 575–80, 612–14. See: Powell, *A Soldier's Way*, pp. 520–2, 525.

107 Freedman and Karsh, *The Gulf Conflict*, pp. 402–9.

108 Dubois, 'The Weinberger Doctrine and the Liberation of Kuwait', p. 38.

109 Naveh, *In Pursuit of Military Excellence*, p xx.

110 Scales, *Certain Victory*, p. 358.

111 Ibid., p. 359.

112 Priest, *The Mission*, p. 95.

113 Cable, Larry E. 'Playing in the Sandbox: Doctrine, Combat, and Outcome on the Ground' in Head, William and Tilford, Earl H. Jr (eds) *The Eagle in the Desert: Looking Back on U.S. Involvement in the Persian Gulf War*. (Westport, CT: Praeger, 1996) pp. 175–200.

114 Scales, Robert H. Jr. *Firepower in Limited War*. Revised edition. (Novato, CA: Presidio, 1994) p. 249. See also: pp. 235–86.

115 Scales, *Certain Victory*, p. 366.

116 Clodfelter, Mark. 'Of Demons, Storms, and Thunder: A Preliminary Look at Vietnam's Impact on the the Persian Gulf Air Campaign'. *Airpower Journal*. (Vol. 5, No. 4. 1991) pp. 17–32.

117 See: Atkinson, *Crusade*, pp. 57–65, 216–228. Freedman and Karsh, *The Gulf Conflict*, pp. 301–30.

118 Freedman and Karsh, *The Gulf Conflict*, pp. 316–19. Atkinson, *Crusade*, pp. 56–65. Warden's ideas are outlined in Warden, John A. III. *The Air Campaign: Planning for Combat*. (Washington, DC: National Defense University Press, 1988).

119 Gordon and Trainor, *The General's War*, pp. 319–20.

120 Sarkesian, *Soldiers, Society and National Security*, p. 6. For example, see: Atkinson, *Crusade*, pp. 56–65, 216–28, 494.

121 Cohen, Eliot. 'The Mystique of U.S. Air Power'. *Foreign Affairs*. (Vol. 73, No. 1. 1994) pp. 109–24 and Keaney, Thomas A. and Cohen, Eliot. *Gulf War Air Power Survey*. 5 vols. (Washington, DC: GPO. 1993).

122 Warden, John A. III. 'Afterword: Challenges and Opportunities' in Hallion, Richard P. (ed.) *Air Power Confronts an Unstable World*. (London: Brassey's, 1997) pp. 227–40.

123 Mason, R.A. *Airpower; A Centennial Appraisal*. (London: Brassey's, 1994) p. 166.
124 Grant, Rebecca. 'Deep Strife'. *Air Force Magazine* (June 2001), pp. 54–8.
125 Bacevich, A.J. 'The Use of Force in Our Time'. *Wilson Quarterly*. (Winter. 1995) p. 58.
126 'Remarks at Maxwell Air Force Base War College in Montgomery, Alabama. April 13, 1991'. <http://csdl.tamu.edu/bushlib/papers/1991/91041300.html>
127 Krauthammer, Charles. 'The Unipolar Moment'. *Foreign Affairs*. (Vol. 70, No. 1. 1991) pp. 23–33.
128 McEvoy-Levy, Siobhan. *American Exceptionalism and US Foreign Policy: Public Diplomacy at the End of the Cold War*. (Basingstoke: Palgrave. 2001).
129 Joint Chiefs of Staff. *National Military Strategy of the United States*. (Washington, DC: GPO. 1992).
130 *National Military Strategy*. 1992, Foreword.
131 Ibid., p. 26. General Powell had wanted to call it 'overwhelming force' but on Paul Wolfowitz's advice it was modified to Decisive Force. Jaffe, Lorna S. *The Development of Base Force: 1989–1992*. (Washington, DC: GPO, 1993) p. 48.
132 See: *FM 100-7. Decisive Force: The Army in Theater Operations*. (Washington, DC: GPO. 1995)
133 *National Military Strategy*. 1992, p. 10.
134 The phrase is taken from Weigley, *The American Way of War*.
135 Huntington, Samuel P. *American Military Strategy*. (Berkeley, CA: Institute of International Studies, University of California, 1986) pp. 9–17.
136 Hoffman, *Decisive Force*, p. 94.
137 See Chapter 1 above.
138 Powell, Colin L. 'U.S. Forces: Challenges Ahead'. *Foreign Affairs*. (Vol. 72. No. 5. 1992/3) p. 38.
139 Powell, *A Soldier's Way*, p. 434.
140 Campbell, Kenneth J. 'Once Burned, Twice Cautious: Explaining the Weinberger–Powell Doctrine'. *Armed Forces and Society*, (Vol. 24, No. 3. 1998) p. 369.
141 Natsios, Andrew S. *U.S. Foreign Policy and the Four Horseman of the Apocalypse: Humanitarian Relief in Complex Emergencies*. (Westport, CT: Praeger/ CSIS, 1997) pp. 117 and 105–23.
142 Woodward, *Commanders*, pp. 230–1. See: Haass. Richard N. *Intervention: The Use of American Military Force in the Post-Cold War World*. (Washington, DC: Carnegie, 1994).
143 James McDonough. 'The Operational Art: Quo Vadis?' in Hooker, *Maneuver Warfare*, p. 116.
144 Creveld, Martin van. *The Transformation of War*. (New York: Free Press, 1991) pp. 57–8. See also: Creveld, Martin van. 'What is Wrong with Clausewitz' in, Nooy. Gert de (ed.) *The Clausewitzian Dictum and the Future of Western Military Strategy*. (The Hague: Kluwer Law International, 1997) p. 7.
145 Peters writes of the new warrior class, and the nature of future conflict as cultural. See: Peters, Ralph. *Fighting for the Future: Will America Triumph?* (Mechanicsburg, PA: Stackpole Books, 1999).
146 Kaldor, Mary. *New and Old Wars: Organized Violence in a Global Era*. (Cambridge: Polity, 1999) p. 11, esp. pp. 1–12. See also: Coker, Christopher. *Waging War Without Warriors? The Changing Culture of Military Conflict*. (London: Lynne Rienner, 2002).
147 Van Creveld, *Transformation of War*, p. 57.
148 See: <http://www.d-n-i.net/second_level/fourth_generation_warfare.htm>
149 Handel, *Masters of War*. p. 193. For a full examination of the Weinberger doctrine see: pp. 185–203.
150 Snow, Donald M. *Distant Thunder: Third World Conflict and the New International Order* (New York: St Martin's Press, 1993) p. 13. The Kosovo War was a response to

'victims' rather than national interest. See: Freedman, Lawrence. 'Victims and Victors: Reflections on the Kosovo War'. *Review of International Studies.* (Vol. 26, No. 3. 2000) pp. 335–58.

151 Ignatieff, Michael. *The Warriors Honor: Ethnic War and the Modern Conscience.* (London: Chatto and Windus, 1998.) p. 94. Freedman, 'Victims and Victors', refers to the 'bullying effect'.

152 Hippel, *Democracy by Force*, p. 204.

153 Stevenson, Jonathan. *Losing Mogadishu: Testing U.S. Policy in Somalia.* (Annapolis, MD: Naval Institute Press, 1995) pp xiv–xvi, 87–8, 100–3, 125–8.

154 Mackinlay, John. 'Military Response to Complex Emergencies' in Weiss, Thomas G. (ed.) *The United Nations and Civil War.* (London: Lynne Rienner, 1995) p. 52.

155 Thompson, Leroy. *Ragged War: The Story of Unconventional and Counter-Revolutionary Warfare.* (London: Arms and Armour Press, 1994).

156 Shacochis, Bob. *The Immaculate Invasion.* (London: Bloomsbury, 1999) pp. xi–xii.

157 Roberts, Adam and Kingsbury, Benedict (eds) *United Nations, Divided World: The UN's Roles in International Relations.* Second edition. (Oxford: Clarendon Press, 1993) provides good conceptual analysis, whilst Durch, William J. (ed.) *The Evolution of UN Peacekeeping: Cases Studies and Comparative Analysis.* (New York: St Martin's Press, 1993) provides a case specific approach.

158 Durch, William J. 'Keeping the Peace: Politics and Lessons of the 1990s' in Durch, *UN Peacekeeping*, p. 12 n. 14. For an analysis of Somalia see: pp. 193–216 and Durch, William J. 'Introduction to Anarchy: Humanitarian Intervention and "State-Building" in Somalia', pp. 311–66.

159 Clarke, Walter. 'Failed Visions and Uncertain Mandates in Somalia' in Clarke, Walter and Herbst, Jeffrey (eds) *Learning from Somalia: The Lessons of Armed Humanitarian Intervention.* (Boulder, CO: Westview, 1997) p. 18 n. 16.

160 Handel, *Masters of War*, p. 202.

161 Hoar, Joseph F. 'A CINC's Perspective'. *Joint Forces Quarterly.* (No. 2. 1993) p. 58.

162 Ganzglass, Martin R. 'The Restoration of the Somali Justice System' in Clarke and Herbst, *Learning from Somalia*, pp. 27–8. See also: pp. 99–117, 118–34. Hippel, *Democracy by Force*, pp. 55–91.

163 Taw and Peters, *Operations Other Than War*, p. 22.

164 Durch, 'Introduction to Anarchy: Humanitarian Intervention and "State-Building"', p. 323.

165 Woods, James L. 'U.S. Government Decisionmaking Processes During Humanitarian Operations in Somalia' in Clarke and Herbst, *Learning from Somalia*, p. 169. He highlights the aim of providing security without a political solution; no aim to 'defang' the warlords and the UN were aiming to put in institutions and resources to revitalise Somali society, even though they knew they would be unable to do so.

166 Williams, Michael C. *Civil–Military Relations and Peacekeeping*, Adelphi Paper 321. (Oxford: Oxford University Press/ IISS, 1998) p. 40.

167 For example, *Time* (4 October 1993).

168 Truehart, Charles. 'Canada Can't Shake Somali Scandal: New Military Chief Quizzed on Troop's 1993 Torture-Killing'. *Washington Post.* 30 December 1995, Sec A. p. 14.

169 Hillen, *Blue Helmets*, p. 4.

170 Mayall, James. 'Introduction' to Mayall, James (ed.) *The New Interventionism 1991–1994: United Nations Experience in Cambodia, former Yugoslavia and Somalia.* (Cambridge: Cambridge University Press, 1996) p. 17.

171 Howe, Jonathan T. 'Somalia: Frustration in a Failed Nation' in Benton, Barbara (ed.) *Soldiers for Peace.* (New York: Facts On File, 1996) p. 175. For his account of the operation see, pp. 159–85.

172 Allard, Kenneth. *Somali Operations: Lessons Learned.* (Washington, DC: National Defense University Press, 1995).

173 Boutros-Ghali, Boutros. *Unvanquished: A U.S.-U.N. Saga*. (London: I.B. Taurus, 1999) pp. 92–107.
174 Durch, 'Introduction to Anarchy: Humanitarian Intervention and "State-Building" in Somalia', p. 346.
175 Woods, 'U.S. Government Decisionmaking Processes During Humanitarian Operations in Somalia' in Clarke and Herbst, *Learning from Somalia*, p. 162.
176 Department of the Army. *FM 90-10, Military Operations on Urbanized Terrain (MOUT)* (Washington, DC: GPO, 1979) uses the central European setting to describe urbanisation. It concentrates on the physical rather than political aspects of urban warfare, fought against a centrally organised opposing force. The Army commissioned RAND to begin undertaking studies of this for it in the early 1990s. For example: Taw, Jennifer Morrison and Hoffman, Bruce. *The Urbanization of Insurgency: The Potential Challenge to U.S. Army Operations*. (Santa Monica, CA: RAND, 1994); Taw and Peters, *Operations Other Than War*.
177 *FM 100-20/AFP 3-20, Military Operations in Low Intensity Conflict*, 1990. and *FM 7-98, Operations in Low Intensity Conflict*, 1992.
178 *FM 100-20/ AFP 3-20*, 1992, Introduction.
179 Taw and Peters, *Operations Other Than War*, p. 43.
180 See *FM 7-20*, 1992, pp. 1–1, Appendix C.
181 Ibid., p C-1.
182 Confidential interview.
183 Farrell, Theo. 'Sliding into War: The Somalia Imbroglio and US Army Peace Operations Doctrine'. *International Peacekeeping*. (Vol. 2, No. 2. 1995) p. 211.
184 Ibid., p. 208.
185 Dobbie, Charles. 'A Concept for Post-Cold War Peacekeeping'. *Survival*. (Vol. 36, No. 3. 1994) p. 127. Dobbie was one of the authors of British peacekeeping doctrine.
186 Rose, Michael. *Fighting for Peace*. (London: Harvill Press, 1998) pp. 126, 201–3, 241–2.
187 Farrell, 'Sliding into War', p. 206.
188 The best account of the 3 October raid is given in Bowden, Mark. *Black Hawk Down: A Story of Modern War*. (New York: Atlantic Monthly Press, 1999).
189 Adams, *US Special Operations*, p. 259. Adams analyses Somalia and Haiti on pp. 258–86.
190 Bowden, *Black Hawk Down*, p. 16.
191 Boutros-Ghali, *Unvanquished*, p. 104.
192 President Clinton Report 'To The Congress of the United States. October 13, 1993.' <http://www.pub.whitehouse.gov/urires/I2R?urn:pdi://oma.eop.gov.us/1993/10/133.text.1>
193 Taw and Peters, *Operations Other Than War*, pp. 22–7.
194 Fishel, John T. *Civil Military Operations in the New World*. (Westport, CT: Praeger, 1997) p. xi.
195 Rosen, Stephen Peter. 'Vietnam and the American Theory of Limited War'. *International Security*. (Vol. 7, No. 2. 1982) p. 83. See: pp. 83–113.
196 Gray, Colin S. *Modern Strategy*. (Oxford: Oxford University Press, 1999) p. 279.
197 Sam Sarkesian captures this, albeit in reference to Special Forces, 'where personnel are trained as political soldiers skilled in military support of nonmilitary efforts. Underpinning this is an understanding of the causes and characteristics of unconventional conflicts. In a word, doctrine must support effective governance in accord with the indigenous culture.' Sarkesian, Sam C. *Unconventional Conflicts in a New Security Era: Lessons from Malaya and Vietnam*. (Westport, CT: Greenwood Press, 1993) p. 195.
198 *FM 100-5*, 1993. Chapter 13 covers OOTW, see: pp. 13–1 to 13–8.
199 *FM 100-5*, 1993, pp. 13–3 to 13–4. For a discussion of 'legitimacy' and the centrality

of civil–military relations to it, and the need for the US to develop military capabilities in line with this see: Barnes, Rudolph C. Jr. *Military Legitimacy: Might and Right in the New Millenium.* (London: Frank Cass, 1996).

200 *FM 100-20/AFP 3-20. Military Operations in Low Intensity Conflict*, 1990. The manual refers to the tenets of *FM 100-5* as characterising successful military operations, but in LIC other imperatives add other dimensions such as political dominance; legitimacy: unity of effort; adaptability; and perseverance. See: 'Introduction' and chapter 1. 'Fundamentals of Low Intensity Conflict'.

201 Russell Glenn argues that 'principles of operations other than war' should be dropped and 'principles of operations' adopted instead of 'principles of war'. See: Glenn, Russell W. 'No More Principles of War?' *Parameters.* (Vol. 28, No. 1. 1998) pp. 48–66.

202 Rinaldo, Richard J. 'Warfighting and Peace Ops: Do Real Soldiers Do MOOTW?' *Joint Forces Quarterly.* (No. 14. 1996) p. 111.

203 Fishel reiterates the Clausewitzian point that separating the 'military' from the 'political' is a key fault and that any catergorisation of conflict that does not see it as a continuum of political action is counterproductive. See: Fishel, John T. 'Little Wars, Small Wars, LIC, OOTW, The GAP, and Things That Go Bump in the Night'. *Low Intensity Conflict and Law Enforcement.* (Vol. 4, No. 3. 1995) pp. 372–98.

204 Mackinlay, John. 'Improving Multifunctional Forces.' *Survival.* (Vol. 36, No. 3. 1994) pp. 150–74.

205 Boutros-Ghali, *Unvanquished*, pp. 92–107.

206 Jakobsen, Peter Viggo. *Western Use of Coercive Diplomacy After The Cold War.* (London: Macmillan, 1998) p. 146.

207 Dandeker, Christopher and Gow, James. 'Military Culture and Strategic Peacekeeping' in Schmidl, Erwin A. (ed.) *Peace Operations between War and Peace.* (London: Frank Cass, 2000) pp. 58–79.

208 Title taken from Barnes, *Military Legitimacy.*

209 Adams, Thomas K. 'LIC (Low-Intensity Clausewitz)'. *Small Wars and Insurgencies.* (Vol. 1, No. 3. 1990) p. 273. See pp. 266–75.

210 Vasquez, John A. 'The Post-Positivist Debate: Reconstructing Scientific Enquiry and International Relations Theory After Enlightenment's Fall' in Booth, Ken, and Smith, Steve (eds) *International Relations Theory Today.* (Oxford: Polity, 1995) pp. 217–40, especially pp. 219–23.

211 Sarkesian, *Soldiers, Society and National Security*, p. 75.

212 Sullivan, Gordon R. 'Foreword' to, *FM 100-1, The Army*, 1994.

213 For example: Posen, Barry R. and Ross, Andrew L. 'Competing U.S. Grand Strategies' in Lieber, Robert J. (ed.) *Eagle Adrift: American Foreign Policy at the End of the Century.* (New York: Longman, 1997) pp. 100–34, and Mandelbaum, Michael. 'Foreign Policy as Social Work'. *Foreign Affairs.* (Vol. 75, No. 1. 1996) pp. 16–31.

214 Nooy, Gert de (ed.) *The Clausewitzian Dictum and the Future of Western Military Strategy.* (The Hague: Kluwer Law International, 1997).

215 Phrase from Bowen and Dunn, *American Security Policy in the 1990s*, p. 93.

7 RETURN TO THE GULF

1 Bacevich, Andrew J. *American Empire: The Realities and Consequences of U.S. Diplomacy.* (Cambridge, MA: Harvard University Press, 2002), p. 128. The other two premises were: a consensus on the desirability of military power, and a commitment to maintain US global military supremacy.

2 Cox, Michael. 'Wilsonian Resurgent? The Clinton Administration and the Promotion of Democracy' in Cox *et al.*, *American Democracy Promotion*, pp. 218–39.

3 Gordon, Philip H. and Shapiro, Jeremy. *Allies at War: America, Europe and the Crisis over Iraq.* (New York: Brookings Institute/ McGraw-Hill, 2004), p. 57.

4 Bellamy, Alex J. 'Lessons Unlearned: Why Coercive Diplomacy Failed at Rambouillet'. *International Peacekeeping*, (Vol. 7, No. 2. 2000) pp. 95–114. Art and Cronin's study of the ten cases of coercive diplomacy between 1992 and 2001, showed only two were successes. (The cases were Somalia, Haiti, North Korea, Bosnia, China, Iraq, Kosovo and terrorism (1993, 1998, 2001)). Art, Robert J. 'Coercive Diplomacy: What Do We Know?' in Art, Robert and Cronin, Patrick M. (eds) *The United States and Coercive Diplomacy* (Washington, DC: United States Institute of Peace, 2003) p. 378. See: pp. 359–420.

5 For example, see: Benbow, Tim. *The Magic Bullet? Understanding the Revolution in Military Affairs*. (London: Brassey's, 2004) pp. 55–103.

6 Owens, William A. 'The American Revolution in Military Affairs'. *Joint Forces Quarterly*. (No. 10. 1995/6) p. 37, pp. 37–8.

7 Owens, Bill, with Ed Offley. *Lifting the Fog of War*. (New York: Farrar. Straus and Giroux, 2000).

8 Owens, *Lifting the Fog of War*, p. 16.

9 Adams, James, *The Next World War: The Warriors and Weapons of the New Battlefields in Cyberspace*. (London: Hutchinson, 1998). For serving officers' views see: Bateman, Robert L. (ed.) *Digital War: A View From the Front Lines*. (Novato, CA: Presidio, 1999).

10 Gompert, David C., Kugler, Richard L. and Libicki, Martin C., *Mind the Gap; Promoting a Transatlantic Revolution in Military Affairs*. (Washington, DC: National Defense University, 1999) p. 3, 89.

11 O'Connell, Robert and Goldman, Alan. 'The Future of War: Implications for US Ground Forces'. *Low Intensity Conflict and Law Enforcement*. (Vol. 5, No. 2. 1996) p. 249, pp. 235–52.

12 *Joint Vision 2010*, and *NMS 1997*, p. 17.

13 Vickers, Michael G. and Kosiak, Steven M. *The Quadrennial Defense Review: An Assessment*. (Washington, DC: Center for Strategic and Budgetary Assessments, 1997) p. 15.

14 Downie, *Learning from Conflict*, p. 245.

15 Mearsheimer, John J. *Liddell Hart and the Weight of History*. (Ithaca, NY: Cornell University Press, 1988) p. 219. See also: work on organisational ideology: Snyder, Jack L. *The Ideology of the Offensive: Military Decision Making and the Disasters of 1914*. (Ithaca, NY: Cornell University Press, 1984).

16 See: Chapter 1.

17 Sorley, Lewis. 'Creighton Abrams and Active-Reserve Integration in Wartime'. *Parameters*. (Vol. 21, No. 2. 1991) p. 49.

18 Betts, Richard K. *Military Readiness: Concepts, Choices, Consequences*. (Washington, DC: Brookings Institution, 1995) p. 186.

19 Record, *Hollow Victory*, pp. 149, 151 and 153. Same point made four years later in Dunlap, Charles J. Jr. 'Joint Vision 2010: A Red Team Assessment'. *Joint Forces Quarterly*. (No. 17. 1997/8) pp. 47–9.

20 Krepinevich, 'The Clinton Defense Strategy', p. 115.

21 Helms, Robert F. II. *The Persian Gulf Crisis: Power in the Post-Cold War World*. (Westport, CT: Praeger, 1993). pp. 162, 168.

22 Gray, Chris Hables. *Postmodern War: The New Politics of Conflict*. (London: Routledge, 1997) pp. 248, 37 and especially pp. 36–50. Robert Leonhard argues that the classic 'principles of war' should be replaced with the principle of 'knowledge and ignorance', and six others. See: Leonhard, Robert R. *The Principles of War for the Information Age*. (Novato, CA: Presidio, 1998) pp. 3–34, 251–62.

23 Romjue, *American Army Doctrine for the Post-Cold War*, pp. 33–4, 37–8. John Romjue, chief historian at TRADOC, based his account on interviews with General Franks.

24 See: Sullivan, Gordon R. and Dubik, James M. 'Land Warfare in the 21st Century'. *Military Review*. (Vol. 73, No. 9. 1993) pp. 13–32.
25 Sullivan, Gordon R. and Dubik, James M. *Envisioning Future Warfare*. (Fort Leavenworth, KS: US Army Command and General Staff College Press, 1995).
26 See the Combined Arms Research Library bibliography on the Army after Next project. <http://www-cgsc.army.mil/carl/resources/biblio/AAN97.asp>
27 Sullivan, Gordon R. and Coroalles, Anthony M. *Seeing the Elephant: Leading America's Army Into the Twenty-First Century*. (Cambridge, MA: Institute for Foreign Policy Analysis, 1995) p. 40. Department of the Army. *TRADOC Pamphlet 525–5, Force XXI Operations* (Fort Monroe, VA: TRADOC, 1994).
28 Sullivan and Coroalles, *Seeing the Elephant*, especially pp. 39–46.
29 Reimer, Dennis J. 'The Army after Next: Knowledge, Speed and Power'. *Military Review*. (Vol. 79, No. 3, 1999) pp. 3–7.
30 *JV 2010*, p. 12.
31 Department of the Army. *FM 100-5, Operations*. (Washington, DC: GPO, 1993).
32 McCormick, Michael. 'FM 100-5: A Return to Operational Art'. *Military Review*. (Vol. 77, No. 5. 1997) pp. 5.
33 McDonough, James R. 'Building the New FM 100-5: Process and Product'. *Military Review*. (Vol. 71, No. 10. 1991) pp. 3–12.
34 *FM 100-5*, 1993, pp. 2–6 to 2–9.
35 McDonough, James R. 'Versatility: The Fifth Tenet'. *Military Review*. (Vol. 73, No. 12. 1993) p. 14.
36 *FM 100-5*, 1993, p. 3–1.
37 Ibid., p. 1–4 to 1–5.
38 Sullivan. Gordon R. 'Introduction' to: Bateman, Robert L. (ed.) *Digital War: A View from the Front Lines*. (Novato, CA: Presidio, 1999) p. xvii, pp. xvii–xx. The book is a discussion of Army views of the burgeoning technology, mainly by serving officers.
39 Franks. Frederick M. Jr. 'Full-Dimensional Operations: A Doctrine for an Era of Change'. *Military Review*. (Vol. 73, No. 12. 1993) pp. 7–8.
40 *FM 100-5*, 1993, p. 6–14 to 6–15.
41 See: *FM 100-5*, 1986, p. 16 and *FM 100-5*, 1993, p. 2–7.
42 *FM 100-5*, 1993, p. 2–8.
43 Downie, *Learning from Conflict*, p. 217.
44 Franks, 'Full-Dimensional Operations', pp. 7–8.
45 Department of the Army. *FM 3-0, Operations*. (Washington, DC: GPO, 2001).
46 McCormick, 'FM 100-5: A Return to Operational Art', pp. 3–14.
47 *FM 3-0, Operations*, 2001, p. 1–14 to 1–17.
48 Ibid., p. 9–5.
49 *FM 100-5*, 1993, p. 6–12.
50 *FM 3-0, Operations*, 2001, p. 4–20.
51 Ibid., p. 4–22 to 4–27.
52 Ibid., p. 4–19 to 4–20.
53 Macgregor, Douglas A. *Breaking the Phalanx: A New Design for Landpower in the 21st Century*. (Westport, CT: Praeger, 1997) pp. 59–93.
54 Burke, Michael D. 'FM 3-0: Doctrine for a Transforming Force'. *Military Review*, (Vol. 82, No. 2. 2002) pp. 91–7. See also: Nardulli, Bruce R. and McNaugher, Thomas L. 'The Army: Toward the Objective Force' in Binnendijk, Hans (ed.) *Transforming America's Military*. (Washington, DC: NDU Press, 2002) pp. 101–28.
55 Burke, 'FM 3-0: Doctrine for a Transforming Force', p. 93.
56 Latham, Andrew, 'Re-Imagining Warfare: The "Revolution in Military Affairs"' in Synder, Craig A. (ed.) *Contemporary Security and Strategy*. (London: Macmillan Press, 1999) p. 230, pp. 210–35.

57 Rosen, 'New Ways of War: Understanding Military Innovation', p. 141.
58 Lind *et al.* 'The Changing Face of War into the Fourth Generation', pp. 2–11 and Krepinevich, Andrew F. 'Cavalry to Computer: The Pattern of Military Revolutions'. *National Interest.* (No. 37. 1994) pp. 30–42.
59 For example on the divergence, see: Sarkesian, *Soldiers, Society and National Security*, p. 9.
60 Bacevich, A.J. 'The Use of Force in Our Time'. *Wilson Quarterly.* (Winter. 1995) p. 60 and pp. 50–63.
61 Bacevich, A.J. 'Preserving the Well-Bred Horse'. *National Interest.* (No. 37. 1994) pp. 48, 49.
62 Freedman, Lawrence. *The Revolution in Strategic Affairs.* Adelphi Paper 318. (London: Oxford University Press/ RIIA, 1998) p. 32.
63 Ibid., p. 78.
64 Gray, Colin S. *Weapons Don't Make War: Policy, Strategy, and Military Technology.* (Lawrence, KS: University of Kansas, 1993) p. 5.
65 For example: Steel, Chuck. 'Sullivan Sounds Off', *Rotor and Wing Magazine.* October 1999. <www.defensedaily.com/reports/sullivan.htm>
66 Bacevich, *American Empire*, p. 171.
67 For example see: Clinton's letter to Congress blaming the UN. 'To The Congress of the United States. October 13, 1993'. <http://www.pub.whitehouse.gov/uri-res/I2R?urn:pdi://oma.eop.gov.us/1993/10/13/3.text.1>
68 He was clearly following the unanimous Security Council resolution (837) of arresting and detaining the attackers of Pakistani peacekeepers. See: Lewis, Ioan and Mayall, James. 'Somalia' in Mayall, James (ed.) *The New Interventionism*, pp. 117–18.
69 For example see: Bolger, Daniel P. *Savage Peace: Americans at War in the 1990s.* (Novato, CA: Presidio, 1995) pp. 266–338. Bolger was a battalion commander in the 101st Airborne Division.
70 Confidential interview.
71 For an inside account of the blaming of Aspin, see: Drew, Elizabeth. *On the Edge: The Clinton Presidency.* (New York: Touchstone, 1994) pp. 315–37, 356–73.
72 Holbrooke, Richard. *To End a War.* (New York: Random House, 1998) p. 217.
73 Powell, *A Soldier's Way*, p. 576.
74 Confidential interview.
75 Powell, *A Soldier's Way*, p. 568.
76 For example his speeches: 'Remarks at the Aspen Institute Symposium in Aspen, Colorado'. 2 August 1990. <http://www.csdl.tamu.edu/bushlib/1990/90080206.html> 'Remarks at Maxwell Air Force Base War College in Montgomery, Alabama'. 13 April 1991. <http://csdl.tamu.edu/bushlib/papers/1991/91041300.html>
77 For example see: Bacevich, A.J. 'Tradition Abandoned: America's Military in a New Era'. *National Interest.* (No. 48. 1997) pp. 16–25; Johnson, Douglas and Metz, Steven. 'Civil–Military Relations in the United States: The State of the Debate'. *Washington Quarterly.* (Vol. 18, No. 1. 1995) pp. 197–213; Cohen, Eliot A. 'Civil–Military Relations'. *Orbis.* (Vol. 41, No. 2. 1997) pp. 177–86; Kohn, Richard H. 'Out of Control'. *National Interest.* (No. 35. 1994) pp. 3–17.
78 Holbrooke, *To End a War*, pp. 216–17.
79 Kitfield, *Prodigal Soldier*, pp. 429–33.
80 It was very common to defer, as Dick Cheney and Newt Gingrich did, and Clinton joined the ROTC (Reserve Officers Training Corps). Walker, Martin. *Clinton; The President They Deserve.* (London: Fourth Estate, 1996) pp. 31–4, 58–61.
81 Drew, *On the Edge*, pp. 42–8. Powell publicly opposed the administration policy in a speech on 12 January 1993; see *Time* 15 February 1993, p. 25. See also, Powell, *A Soldier's Way*, pp. 578–80.

82 Cohen, 'Civil–Military Relations', p. 177.
83 Dunlap, Charles J. Jr. 'The Origins of the American Military Coup of 2012'. *Parameters*. (Vol. 22, No. 4. 1992) pp. 2–20.
84 Summers, Harry G. Jr. *The New World Strategy: A Military Policy for America's Future*. (New York: Simon and Schuster, 1995) especially pp. 207–34.
85 Patterson, Robert B. Jr. *Dereliction of Duty: The Eyewitness Account of How Bill Clinton Compromised America's National Security*. (Washington, DC: Regnery, 2003) p. 147.
86 For example see: Snider, Don M. 'An Uniformed Debate on Military Cultures'. *Orbis*. (Vol. 43, No. 1. 1999) pp. 11–26; Feaver, Peter D. and Kohn, Richard H. (eds) *Soldiers and Civilians: The Civil–Military Gap and American National Security*. (Cambridge, MA: MIT Press, 2001).
87 See: Burk, James. 'Public Support for Peacekeeping in Lebanon and Somalia: Assessing the Casualties Hypothesis'. *Political Science Quarterly* (Vol. 114, No. 1. 1999) pp. 53–78.
88 Smith, Tony. *Foreign Attachments: The Power of Ethnic Groups in the Making of American Foreign Policy*. (Cambridge, MA: Harvard University Press, 2000) p. 71.
89 Shacochis, *The Immaculate Invasion*, pp. 30–4.
90 'Press Conference by the President, President Carter, Senator Sam Nunn and General Colin Powell. September 19, 1994'. <http://www.pub.whitehouse.gov/uri-res/I2R?urn:pdi://oma.oep.gov.us/1994/9/19/3.text.1>
91 Hackett, *The Profession of Arms*, p. 202.
92 'Press Conference by the President, President Carter, Senator Sam Nunn and General Colin Powell. September 19, 1994'. <http://www.pub.whitehouse.gov/uri-res/I2R?urn:pdi://oma.oep.gov.us/1994/9/19/3.text.1>
93 Peters, *Fighting for the Future*, p. 28.
94 Vertzberger, Yaacov Y.I. *Risk Taking and Decisionmaking: Foreign Military Intervention Decisions*. (Stanford, CA: Stanford University Press, 1998) p. 406.
95 Weinberger, *Fighting for Peace*, p. 437.
96 See: Luttwak, Edward N. 'Where Are the Great Powers? At Home with the Kids'. *Foreign Affairs*. (Vol. 73, No. 4. 1994) pp. 23–8, and his later 'A Post-Heroic Military Policy'. *Foreign Affairs*. (Vol. 75, No. 4. 1996) pp. 33–44.
97 Rosner, Jeremy D. *The New Tug of War: Congress, the Executive Branch, and National Security*. (Washington, DC: Carnegie Endowment for International Peace, 1995); MacKinnon, Michael G. *The Evolution of US Peacekeeping Policy Under Clinton: A Fairweather Friend?* (London: Frank Cass, 2000) pp. 62–104.
98 Avant, Deborah D. 'Are the Reluctant Warriors Out of Control? Why the U.S. Military is Adverse to Responding to Post-Cold War Low-Level Threats'. *Security Studies*. (Vol. 6, No. 2. 1996/7) pp. 51–90.
99 Priest, Dana. *The Mission: Waging War and Keeping the Peace with America's Military*. (New York: W.W. Norton, 2003), p. 91.
100 Ibid., pp. 71, 45.
101 Ibid., p. 67. On the CINCs see pp. 61–118. Andrew Bacevich also refers to the CINCs as Proconsuls, after Zinni's comments in 2000. See: Bacevich, *American Empire*, p. 280 n. 32, and pp. 167–97.
102 A copy of this memo can be found in Scarborough, Rowan. *Rumsfeld's War: The Untold Story of America's Anti-Terrorist Commander*. (Washington, DC: Regnery, 2004) p. 186.
103 Priest, *The Mission*, p. 14.
104 Holbrooke, *To End a War*. p. 219. Holbrooke lists eleven major differences between the State Department and the JCS a week before Dayton, including a rejection of any form of police functions. See: pp. 220–1.
105 White House. 'Clinton Administration Policy on Reforming Multilateral Peace

Operations (PDD 25). May 5, 1994' (released February 22, 1996). <http://www.fas.org/irp/offdocs/pdd25.htm>

106 Ibid., p. 5 of 11.

107 See: White House. 'Press Briefing by National Security Advisor Tony Lake and Director for Strategic Plans and Policy General Wesley Clark'. 5 May 1994. <http://www.fas.org/irp/offdocs/pdd25_brief.htm> Lake listed the four other areas as: (1) ensuring the US supports the right operations; (2) reduce the cost of peacekeeping operations; (3) ensure effective command and control of American forces; (4) improve the way American government manages the issue of peacekeeping.

108 See: Rosner, *The New Tug of War*.

109 See: White House. 'Press Briefing by National Security Advisor Tony Lake', p. 4 of 10.

110 Sewall, Sarah B. 'Peace Operations: A Department of Defense Perspective' in Hays et al., *American Defense Policy*, p. 413. See also, pp. 406–15.

111 Department of Defense. *The Annual Report of the Secretary of Defense to the President and Congress, 1995*. (Washington, DC: GPO, 1995) Part II, Challenges in the New Security Environment.

112 *National Military Strategy*, 1995, p. 305.

113 Ibid., p. 298.

114 Ibid., p. 305.

115 Department of Defense. *National Military Strategy of the United States of America*. (Washington, DC: GPO, 1997) p. 11.

116 MacKinnon, *The Evolution of US Peacekeeping Policy*, p. 119.

117 See: Sterling-Folker, Jennifer. 'Between a Rock and a Hard Place: Assertive Multilateralism and Post-Cold War U.S. Foreign Policy Making' in Scott, James M. (ed.) *After the End: Making U.S. Foreign Policy in the Post-Cold War World*. (Durham, NC: Duke University Press, 1998) pp. 277–304.

118 MacKinnon, *The Evolution of US Peacekeeping*, pp. 105–19.

119 Albright, Madeleine with Bill Woodward. *Madam Secretary: A Memoir*. (London: Macmillan, 2003) p. 152.

120 Kuperman, Alan J. *The Limits of Humanitarian Intervention: Genocide in Rwanda*. (Washington, DC: Brookings Institution, 2001).

121 Stevenson, Charles A. 'The Evolving Clinton Doctrine on the Use of Force'. *Armed Forces and Society*. (Vol. 22, No. 4. 1996) p. 529.

122 Power, Samantha. *A Problem from Hell: America and the Age of Genocide*. (London: Flamingo, 2003) p. 386.

123 Halberstam, David. *War in a Time of Peace: Bush, Clinton and the Generals*. (London: Bloomsbury, 2002) pp. 273–8.

124 Power, *A Problem from Hell*, p. 385.

125 Smith, Tony. 'National Security Liberalism and American Foreign Policy' in Cox, Michael, Ikenberry, G. John, and Inoguchi, Takashi (eds) *American Democracy Promotion: Impulses, Strategies, and Impacts*. (Oxford: Oxford University Press, 2000) pp. 85–102.

126 It could have deployed troops unilaterally or in support of Dallaire's beleaguered UN Assistance Mission to Rwanda (UNAMIR) forces, it could have used the Security Council to oppose the Rwandan government, determined it as genocide (rather than stay out or get involved everywhere argument), and avoided the Somalia fear and protected peacekeeping. See: Power, *A Problem from Hell*, p. 382–5.

127 Ignatieff, *The Warrior's Honor*, p. 89.

128 Project on Defense Alternatives website on the RMA and asymmetric warfare. <http://www.comw.org/rma/fulltext/asymmetric.html>

129 See Chapter 5 above. *United States Special Operations Command History: 15th Anniversary*. (MacDill AFB, FL: HQ USSOCOM, 2002) p. 17.

130 *United States Special Operations Forces Posture Statement 2003–04*. <http://www.socom.mil/Docs/2003_2004_SOF_Posture_Statement.pdf> p. 91.

131 Priest, *The Mission*, pp. 32, 28–34. Special Forces are examined on pp. 121–243.
132 *United States Special Operations Forces Posture Statement 2003–04*, p. 4.
133 See: Bert, Wayne. *The Reluctant Superpower: United States Policy in Bosnia, 1991–95*. (London: Macmillan, 1997); Stevenson, 'The Evolving Clinton Doctrine on the Use of Force', p. 522.
134 For example see: Glitman, Maynard. 'US Policy in Bosnia: Rethinking a Flawed Approach'. *Survival*. (Vol. 38, No. 4. 1996/7) pp. 66–83 and Clarke, Jonathan. 'Rhetoric Before Reality: Loose Lips Sink Ships'. *Foreign Affairs*. (Vol. 74, No. 5. 1995) p. 6, and Gacek, *The Logic of Force*, p. 335.
135 Woodward, Bob. *The Choice: How Clinton Won*. (New York: Simon and Schuster. 1996) p. 262.
136 'Statements by the President. November 27, 1995'. <http://www.pub.whitehouse.gov/urires/I2R?urn:pdi://oma.eop.gov.us/1995/11/28/1.text.1> See also: Stevenson, 'The Evolving Clinton Doctrine on the Use of Force', p. 530.
137 Gow, James. *Triumph of the Lack of Will: International Diplomacy and the Yugoslav War*. (London: Hurst, London. 1997) p. 307.
138 Luttwak, 'A Post-Heroic Military Policy', p. 36.
139 The frustrations with European prevarication helped feed the later unilateral turn of the Bush administration. Halper, Stephan and Clarke, Jonathan. *America Alone: The Neo-Conservatives and the Global Order*. (Cambridge: Cambridge University Press, 2004) pp. 93–4.
140 See: Clark, Wesley K. *Waging Modern War: Bosnia, Kosovo and the Future of Combat*. (New York: Public Affairs, 2001).
141 'Statement by the President to the Nation. March 24, 1999'. <http://www.pub.whitehouse.gov/uri-res/I2R?urn:pdi://oma.eop.gov.us/1999/3/25/1.text.1>
142 Zimm, Alan D. 'Desert Storm, Kosovo and "Doctrinal Schizophrenia"'. *Strategic Review*. (Vol. 28, No. 1. 2000) pp. 32–9.
143 Clark, Wesley K. *Waging Modern War: Bosnia, Kosovo and the Future of Combat*. (New York: Public Affairs, 2001) p. 243–4.
144 Grant, Rebecca. 'Deep Strife'. *Air Force Magazine* (June 2001) p. 58.
145 Glosson, Buster C. 'Impact of Precision Weapons on Air Combat Operations'. *Airpower Journal*. (Vol. 7, No. 2. 1993) p. 9.
146 Joint Forces Command Glossary <http://www.jfcom.mil/about/glossary.htm#EBO>
147 Cohen, Eliot A. 'Kosovo and the New American Way of War' in Bacevich, Andrew J. and Cohen, Eliot A. (eds) *War Over Kosovo: Politics and Strategy in a Global Age*. (New York: Columbia University Press, 2001) pp. 38–62.
148 Ignatieff, Michael. *Virtual War: Kosovo and Beyond*. (London: Chatto and Windus, 2000) pp. 164–76.
149 For example see: Clark, *Waging Modern War*, pp. 243–67.
150 Blair, Tony. 'Doctrine of the International Community' at the Economic Club, Chicago, 24 April 1999. <http://www.number-10.gov.uk/output/Page1297.asp> Kampfner, John. *Blair's Wars*. (London: Free Press, 2003) pp. 50–3.
151 Clark, Wesley K. 'Gradualism and American Military Strategy'. *Military Review*. (Vol. 60, No. 9. 1975) p. 10.
152 Bauman, Zygmunt. *Liquid Modernity*. (Cambridge: Polity, 2000) pp. 12–13.
153 Account taken from: Vickers, Michael G. 'Revolution Deferred: Kosovo and the Transformation of War' in Bacevich and Cohen, *War Over Kosovo*, pp. 189–209.
154 Ibid., p. 204.
155 Dunn, Richard J. 'Transformation: Let's Get it Right This Time'. *Parameters*. (Vol. 31, No. 1. 2001) pp. 22 and 22–8.
156 US Army. 'Army Completes Stryker Brigade Certification'. <http://www.army.mil/features/strykeroe/>
157 Cohen, Eliot A. 'Defending America in the Twenty-first Century'. *Foreign Affairs* (Vol. 79, No. 6. 2000).

158 Ibid., p. 41.
159 Rumsfeld, Donald H. 'Transforming the Military'. *Foreign Affairs* (Vol. 81, No. 3. 2002) p. 28.
160 Ibid., p. 27.
161 Nardulli, Bruce R. and McNaugher, Thomas L. 'The Army: Toward the Objective Force' in Binnendijk, Hans (ed.) *Transforming America's Military*. (Washington, DC: NDU Press, 2002) pp. 101–28.
162 Scarborough, *Rumsfeld's War*, pp. 119–20.
163 Loeb, Vernon and Ricks, Thomas E. 'Rumsfeld's Style, Goals Strain Ties In Pentagon "Transformation" Effort Spawns Issues of Control'. *Washington Post*, 16 October 2002. p. A01.
164 O'Hanlon, Michael. 'Rumsfeld's Defence Vision'. *Survival* (Vol. 44, No. 2. 2002) pp. 103–17; Cohen, Eliot A. 'A Tale of Two Secretaries'. *Foreign Affairs*. (Vol. 81, No. 3. 2002) pp. 33–46.
165 Borger, Julian and Teather, David. 'So Much for the Peace Dividend: Pentagon is Winning the Battle for a $400bn Budget'. *Guardian* (22 May 2003) p. 3.
166 A sense of the debate can be found in Kagan, Frederick W. 'A Dangerous Transformation'. Wall Street Journal On Line. (12 November 2003) <http://www.opinionjournal.com/extra/?id=110004289> and Hone, Tom. 'Understanding Transformation'. Office of Force Transformation, *Transformation Trends* (16 January 2004) <http://www.oft.osd.mil/library/library.cfm?libcol=9> The Army's process can be seen at: <http://www.army.mil/2003TransformationRoadmap/>
167 Office of Defense Transformation. *Network Centric Operations Conceptual Framework Version 1.0.* (November 2003) <http://www.oft.osd.mil/index.cfm> p. 2. The Office of Force Transformation, Department of Defense can be found at <http://www.oft.osd.mil/>
168 See: Daalder, Ivo H. and Lindsay, James M. *America Unbound: The Bush Revolution in Foreign Policy*. (Washington, DC: Brookings Institute, 2003) and Nye, Joseph S. Jr. *Soft Power: The Means to Success in World Politics*. (New York: Public Affairs, 2004).
169 Rice, Condoleezza. 'Promoting the National Interest'. *Foreign Affairs*, (Vol. 79, No. 1. 2000) p. 62.
170 Daalder and Lindsay, *America Unbound*. For a more critical reading of the shift from traditional interests to ideology in foreign policy, see: Halper and Clarke. *America Alone*.
171 Ibid., p. 138 and see chapter 4 'The Neo-Conservative Ascension' pp. 112–56.
172 Ibid., p. 2. See also pp. 31–5.
173 Woodward, Bob. *Plan of Attack*. (New York: Simon and Schuster, 2004) p. 63.
174 President Bush's 'Address to a Joint Session of Congress and the American People, 21st November 2001'. <http://www.whitehouse.gov/news/releases/2001/09/20010920-8.html>
175 Vaishnav, Milan. 'Afghanistan: The Chimera of the "Light Footprint"' in Orr, Robert C. (ed.) *Winning the Peace: An American Strategy for Post-Conflict Reconstruction*. (Washington, DC: Center for Strategic and International Studies, 2004) pp. 244–62.
176 Biddle, Stephen, *Afghanistan and the Future of Warfare: Implications for Army and Defense Policy*. (Carlisle, PA: Strategic Studies Institute, 2002).
177 Woodward, Bob. *Bush at War*. (New York: Simon and Schuster, 2002) pp. 43, 88.
178 Biddle, *Afghanistan and the Future of Warfare*, p vii.
179 Simons, Anna and Tucker, David. 'United States Special Operations Forces and the War on Terrorism' in Mockaitis, Thomas R. and Rich Paul B. (eds) *Grand Strategy in the War Against Terrorism*. (London: Frank Cass, 2003) pp. 84–5.
180 Chin, Warren. 'Operation "Enduring Freedom": A Victory for a Conventional Force

Fighting an Unconventional War'. *Small Wars and Insurgencies*. (Vol. 14, No. 1. 2003) pp. 57–76.

181 Biddle, *Afghanistan and the Future of Warfare*, p. 29. For example, most fire received by US forces in 'Operation Anaconda' came from unseen and unanticipated Al Qaeda fighting positions.

182 Friedman, Norman. *Terrorism, Afghanistan, and America's New Way of War*. (Annapolis, MD: Naval Institute Press, 2003) p. 223.

183 Chin, 'Operation "Enduring Freedom"', pp. 57–76.

184 House of Commons Foreign Affairs Committee. *Foreign Policy Aspects of the War against Terrorism. Seventh Report of Session 2003–04*. (London: Stationery Office, 29 July 2004) p. 72.

185 Vaishnav, 'Afghanistan: The Chimera of the "Light Footprint"' pp. 244–62.

186 Schmitt, Eric and Rohde, David. 'Taliban Fighters Increase Attacks', *New York Times*, 1 August 2004. <www.nytimes.com/2004/08/01/international/asia/01AFGH.html>

187 Vaishnav, 'Afghanistan: The Chimera of the "Light Footprint"', p. 258.

188 Ibid., p. 259.

189 Bailie, Gil. *Violence Unveiled: Humanity at the Crossroads*. (New York: Crossroads, 1995) p. 63, taken from the work of Girard. See: Girard, Rene. *Violence and the Sacred*. (London: Athlone Press, 1988).

190 Ignatieff, Michael. *Empire Lite: Nation-Building in Bosnia, Kosovo and Afghanistan*. (London: Vintage, 2003), p. 89.

191 For a view that sees the war as a hijack of policy by the Neo-conservatives see: Ramesh, Randeep (ed.). *The War We Could Not Stop: The Real Story of the Battle of Iraq*. (London: Faber and Faber 2003) pp. 3–22.

192 Dunn, David H. 'Myths, Motivations and "Misunderestimations": The Bush Administration and Iraq'. *International Affairs* (Vol. 79, No. 2. 2003) pp. 279–97.

193 White House. *The National Security Strategy of the United States of America*. (Washington, DC: GPO, September 2002) <www.whitehouse.gov/nsc/nss.html>

194 Record, Jeffrey. *Dark Victory: America's Second War Against Iraq*. (Annapolis, MD: Naval Institute Press, 2004) pp. 32–44.

195 *National Security Strategy 2002*, p. 1, iii.

196 Freedman, Lawrence. *Deterrence*. (Cambridge: Polity Press, 2004) p. 94.

197 Department of Defense. *Quadrennial Defense Review*. (Washington, DC: GPO, 2001). <http://www.defenselink.mil/pubs/qdr2001.pdf>

198 Freedman, *Deterrence*, pp. 84–108.

199 See: Gordon, Philip H. and Shapiro, Jeremy. *Allies at War: America, Europe and the Crisis over Iraq*. (New York: Brookings Institute/McGraw-Hill, 2004) and Lindley-French, Julian. *Terms of Engagement: The Paradox of American Power and the Transatlantic Dilemma post-11 September*. Challiot Papers 52, May 2002. <http://www.iss-eu.org/chaillot/chai52e.pdf>

200 Bush, George W. 'State of the Union Address'. 29 January 2002. <http://www.whitehouse.gov/news/releases/2002/01/20020129-11.html> See also: Frum, David. *The Right Man: An Inside Account of the Surprise Presidency of George W. Bush*. (London: Weidenfeld and Nicholson, 2003) pp. 224–45.

201 Frum, *The Right Man*, pp. 233–4.

202 Litwak, Robert S. *Rogue States and U.S. Foreign Policy: Containment after the Cold War*. (Washington, DC: Woodrow Wilson Center Press, 2000).

203 Clinton, *My Life*, p. 935. Clinton's list was: Osama Bin Laden and Al Qaeda, the lack of peace in the Middle East, nuclear stand-off between India and Pakistan, North Korea and, finally, Iraq.

204 Lopez, George A. and Cortright, David. 'Containing Iraq: Sanctions Worked'. *Foreign Affairs*. (Vol. 83, No. 4. 2004) p. 103.

205 Catan, Thomas and Huband, Mark. 'Report Confirms Iraq Had No Weapons of Mass Destruction'. *Financial Times* (7 October 2004) p. 1.

206 Murray, Williamson and Scales, Robert H. Jr. *The Iraq War: A Military History* (London: Belknap/Harvard University Press, 2003) pp. 89–90.

207 Confidential interview.

208 See: Murray and Scales, *The Iraq War*, pp. 184–233 for a narrative of the later phase of the campaign.

209 White House. 'President Discusses National, Economic Security in California, May 2nd 2003'. <http://www.whitehouse.gov/news/releases/2003/05/20030502-7.html>

210 Confidential sources.

211 <http://www.iraqbodycount.net/database/> at least 7,350 from coalition action prior to 1 May 2003. Total figures now (10 December 2004) are 14,620–16.805.

212 Filkins, Dexter and Berenson, Alex. 'Ayatollah Calls for Rally to End Fighting in Najaf' *New York Times*. 26 August 2004. <http://www.nytimes.com/2004/08/26/international middleeast/26iraq.html>

213 Kifner, John and Fisher, Ian. 'U.S. Weighs Falluja Pullback, Leaving Patrols to Iraq Troops'. *New York Times*. 30 April 2004. <http://www.nytimes.com/2004/04/30/international/middleeast/26iraq.html>

214 Sanger, David E. and Jehl, Douglas. 'Generals in Iraq Consider Options for More Troops'. *New York Times*. 6 April 2004. <http://www.nytimes.com/2004/04/06 politics/06PREX.html>

215 Crocker, Bethsheba N. 'Iraq: Going it Alone, Gone Wrong' in Orr, Robert C. (ed.) *Winning the Peace: An American Strategy for Post-Conflict Reconstruction*. (Washington, DC: Center for Strategic and International Studies, 2004) pp. 267–8.

216 Ibid., p. 266.

217 See for example: *BBC News*, 'Iraq is al-Qaeda battleground'. 29 July 2004. <http://news.bbc.co.uk/1/hi/uk_politics/3935755.stm>

218 See Chapter 6, 'A new national approach' above.

219 Callwell, C.E. *Small Wars: Their Principles and Practice*. Third edition. (Lincoln, NB: London: HMSO/University of Nebraska. 1906/96) p. 21.

220 Callwell, *Small Wars*, p. 42.

221 Thornton, Rod. 'The British Army and the Origins of its Minimum Force Philosophy' *Small Wars and Insurgencies*. (Vol. 15, No. 1. 2004) pp. 83–106.

222 Krulak, Charles C. 'The Strategic Corporal: Leadership in the Three Block War' *Marine Corps Gazette*. (Vol. 83, No. 1. 1999) pp. 18–22.

223 Bankus, Brent C. and Flavin, William R. 'Training US Army Peacekeepers'. *Small Wars and Insurgencies*. (Vol. 15, No. 1. 2004) pp. 129–39.

224 Hills, Alice. *Future War in Cities: Rethinking a Liberal Dilemma*. (London: Frank Cass, 2004) pp. 42–7.

225 Grossman, Elaine M. 'Army to Create "Asymmetric Warfare Group" to Prepare for New Threats'. *Inside the Pentagon*. (8 July 2004). <http://www.oft.osd.mil/index.cfm>

226 Marcus, Jonathan. 'US "emulates" Israeli tactics.' BBC News. 14 April 2004. <http://news.bbc.co.uk/1/hi/middle_east/3625315.stm>

227 Hills, *Future War in Cities*.

228 Jaffe, Greg. 'On Ground in Iraq, Capt. Ayers Writes His Own Playbook'. *Wall Street Journal*, 22 September 2004, p A1.

229 Macgregor, Douglas A. *Transformation Under Fire: Revolutionizing How America Fights*. (Westport, CT: Praeger, 2003) pp. 13, 15.

230 Department of Defense, *National Military Strategy of the United States of America*. (Washington, DC: GPO, 1997) p. 17.

231 Scales, Robert H. Jr. *Yellow Smoke: The Future of Land Warfare for America's Military*. (Lanham, MD: Rowman and Littlefield, 2003).

232 Gibson, James William. *The Perfect War: Technowar in Vietnam*. (Boston, MA: Atlantic Monthly, 1986).
233 McNamara, Robert S. with Van De Mark, Brian. *In Retrospect: The Tragedy and Lessons of Vietnam*. (Lexington, MA: D.C. Heath, 1995) p. 322.
234 Crocker, 'Iraq: Going it Alone, Gone Wrong', pp. 263–85.
235 Arendt, Hannah. *On Violence*. (New York: Harcourt Brace, 1970) p. 4.
236 Cable, Larry. 'Reinventing the Round Wheel: Insurgency, Counter-Insurgency, and Peacekeeping Post Cold War'. *Small Wars and Insurgencies*. (Vol. 4, No. 2. 1993) pp. 228–62.
237 Boot, Max. *The Savage Wars of Peace: Small Wars and the Rise of American Power*. (New York: Basic Books, 2002). See Brian Linn's critique of the Weigley thesis of the 'attritional' tradition in his 'The American Way of War Revisited', pp. 501–30.
238 Perceptual maps are 'how particular policy features are perceived by relevant interest groups or policy makers'. See, May, Peter J. 'Politics and Policy Analysis'. *Political Science Quarterly*. (Vol. 101, No. 1. 1986) p. 122. See also, pp. 109–25.
239 Moskos, Charles C. 'Towards a Postmodern Military: The United States as a Paradigm', in, Moskos, Charles C., Williams, John Allen and Segal, Donald R. *The Postmodern Military: Armed Forces after the Cold War*. (New York: Oxford University Press, 2000) pp.14–31.
240 Beaufre, Andre. *Introduction to Strategy*. (London: Faber and Faber, 1965).
241 Hart, B.H. Liddell. *Strategy*. Second revised edition. (London: Faber and Faber, 1967) p. 353.
242 Egan, Timothy. 'Wounds Open Anew as Vietnam Resurfaces'. *New York Times*. 26 August 2004. <www.nytimes.com/2004/08/26/politics/campaign/26voices.html>

CONCLUSION

1 Luttwak, Edward N. *Strategy: The Logic of War and Peace*. Revised and enlarged edition. (Cambridge, MA: Belknap Press, 2001) pp. 207–17.
2 Lovin, Robin W. *Reinhold Niebuhr and Christian Realism*. (Cambridge: Cambridge University Press, 1995) especially pp. 1–32.
3 Niebuhr, Reinhold. *The Irony of American History*. (London: Nisbet, 1952) p. 36.
4 See: Commager, Henry Steele. *The Empire of Reason: How Europe Imagined and America Realized the Enlightenment*. (London: Weidenfeld and Nicolson. 1978).
5 Gray, John. *Al Qaeda and What it Means to be Modern*. (London: Faber and Faber, 2003).
6 Eckes, Alfred E. Jr and Zeiler, Thomas W. *Globalization and the American Century*. (Cambridge: Cambridge University Press, 2003).
7 For example: Zinn, Howard. *A People's History of the United States 1492–Present*. Third edition. (London: Pearson Longman, 2003): 'There were themes of profound importance to me which I found missing in the orthodox histories that dominated American culture.' They included class, race, sexual inequality and national arrogance, pp. 684–86.
8 See: Girard, *Violence and the Sacred*, and a work based upon it: Bailie, *Violence Unveiled*. I would like to thank John Conway for bringing these to my attention.
9 Johnson, Robert H. *Improbable Dangers: U.S. Conceptions of Threat in the Cold War and After*. (London: Macmillan, 1994).
10 Ali, Tariq. *The Clash of Fundamentalisms: Crusades, Jihads and Modernity*. (London: Verso, 2002).
11 Freedman, *Deterrence*, pp. 84–108.
12 O'Donohue, John. *Eternal Echoes: Exploring Our Hunger to Belong*. (London: Bantam, 1998).
13 I would like to thank Jill Thornton for opening up this line of thinking to me.

14 Beck, Ulrich. *Risk Society: Towards a New Modernity*. (London: Sage, 1992).
15 Sacks, Jonathan. *The Dignity of Difference: How to Avoid the Clash of Civilisations*. Revised edition. (London: Continuum, 2003).
16 Jung, Carl G. *Man and his Symbols*. (London: Picador, 1964/78), p. 73.
17 Campbell, *Writing Security*.
18 Mead, Walter Russell. *Special Providence: American Foreign Policy and How It Changed the World*. (New York: Century Foundation/Alfred A. Knopf, 2001). He outlines the four schools of thought – Hamiltonian, Jeffersonian, Jacksonian and Wilsonian – as shaping the US's foreign policy debates, each with deep domestic roots and with a central concern, namely: protection of commerce, maintaining the democratic system, populist values and military might, and moral principle.
19 Holm, Bill. *The Music of Failure*. (Marshall, MN: Plains Press, 1985) p. 85.
20 Rushdie, Salman. *Fury*. (London: Jonathan Cape, 2001). It is an extended meditation on America.
21 Furedi, Frank. *Culture of Fear: Risk-taking and the Morality of Low Expectation*. Revised edition. (London: Continuum, 2002) especially pp. vii–xvii, 1–13, 169–93.
22 Hedges, Chris. *War Is Force That Gives Us Meaning*. (Oxford: PublicAffairs, 2002) p. 17.
23 Alasdair MacIntyre *After Virtue: A Study in Moral Theory*. Second edition. (London: Duckworth, 1985) p. 258.
24 Luttwak, *Strategy*.
25 Storr, Anthony. *The Dynamics of Creation*. (London: Secker and Warburg, 1972)
26 Grotowski, Jerzy. *Towards a Poor Theatre*. (London: Methuen, 1969). See especially pp. 85–93 and 211–18.
27 Berry, Wendell. 'The Design of a House', in *Collected Poems: 1957–1982*. (New York: North Point Press, 1985) p. 29.
28 Hedges, *War Is Force That Gives Us Meaning*, p. 180.
29 Cohen, Eliot A. 'History and the Hyperpower'. *Foreign Affairs*. (Vol. 83, No. 4, 2004) pp. 49–63, p. 63.

SELECT BIBLIOGRAPHY

(A full bibliography is available on application to the author.)

Government and officially commissioned sources

Blair, Tony. 'Doctrine of the International community' at the Economic Club, Chicago, 24 April 1999. http://www.number-10.gov.uk/output/Page1297.asp

Brownlee, Romie L. and Mulen, William J. III. *Changing an Army: An Oral History of General William E. DePuy, USA Retired.* (Washington, DC: GPO, n.d.).

Bush, George H.W. *National Security Strategy of the United States: 1990–1991.* (Washington, DC: GPO, 1990).

—— 'Address to the Nation Announcing Allied Military Action in the Persian Gulf. January 16, 1991'. http://bushlibrary.tamu.edu/papers/1991/91011602.html

—— 'Address to the Nation on the Suspension of Allied Combat Operations in the Persian Gulf. February 27, 1991'. http://bushlibrary.tamu.edu/papers/1991/91022702.html

—— 'Address Before a Joint Session of the Congress on the Cessation of the Persian Gulf Conflict. March 6, 1991'. http://bushlibrary.tamu.edu/papers/1991/91030600.html

—— 'Remarks at the United States Military Academy in West Point, New York. January 5, 1993'. http://bushlibrary.tamu.edu/papers/1993/93010500.html

Bush, George W. 'State of the Union Address'. 29 January 2002. http://www.whitehouse.gov/news/releases/2002/01/20020129-11.html

—— *The National Security Strategy of the United States of America.* (Washington, DC: GPO, September 2002) www.whitehouse.gov/nsc/nss.html

Clinton, William J. 'Message to the Congress Transmitting a Report on Somalia October 13, 1993'. http://frwebgate5.access.gpo.gov/cgi-bin/waisgate.cgi?WAISdocID=588521325342+4+0+0&WAISaction=retrieve

—— *National Security Strategy of the United States: 1994–1995. Engagement and Enlargement.* (Washington, DC: GPO, 1994).

—— 'Clinton Administration Policy on Reforming Multilateral Peace Operations. (PDD 25.) May 5, 1994'. http://www.fas.org/irp/offdocs/pdd25.htm

—— *National Security Strategy of Engagement and Enlargement. 1995–1996.* (Washington, DC: GPO, 1995).

—— *A National Security Strategy for a New Century.* (Washington, DC: GPO, 1998).

Department of Defense. *Report to the President and the Chairman of Armed Services Committees of the Senate and of the House of Representatives. Progress in Ending the Draft and Achieving The All-Volunteer Force.* (Washington, DC: GPO, 1971).

—— *Statement of Secretary of Defense Melvin R. Laird on the Fiscal Year 1972–76 Defense Program and the 1972 Defense Budget before the Senate Armed Services Committee, March 15 1971.* (Washington, DC: GPO, 1971).

—— *Report of the DOD Commission on Beirut International Airport Terrorist Act, October 23, 1983.* (Washington, DC: GPO. 1983).

—— *U.S. Casualties in Southeast Asia, Statistics as of April 30, 1985.* (Washington, DC: GPO, 1985).

—— *Report of Secretary of Defense Caspar W. Weinberger to the Congress on the FY 1987, FY 1988 Authorization Request and FY 1987–1991 Defense Programmes.* (Washington, DC: GPO, 1986).

—— *The National Military Strategy of the United States of America.* (Washington. DC: GPO, 1992).

—— *Defense Base Closure and Realignment Commission: 1993 Report to the President.* (Washington, DC: GPO, 1993).

—— *1995 Annual Defense Report.* http://www.dtic.mil/execsec/adr95/toc.html

—— *The National Military Strategy of the United States of America.* (Washington. DC: GPO, 1995).

—— *National Military Strategy of the United States of America.* (Washington, DC: GPO, 1997).

—— *Report of the Quadrennial Defense Review.* (Washington, DC: GPO, 1997).

—— *Quadrennial Defense Review.* (Washington, DC: GPO. 2001). http://www.defenselink.mil/pubs/qdr2001.pdf

Department of State. *Foreign Relations of the United States.* (Washington, DC: GPO, annual). (Abbreviated as *FRUS* with year, volume and pages.)

Department of the Air Force. *AFM 1-1, Basic Aerospace Doctrine of the United States Air Force.* (Washington, DC: GPO, 1992).

—— *Global Reach – Global Power: The Evolving Air Force Contribution to National Security.* (Washington. DC: GPO, 1992).

Department of the Army. *A Study of Strategic Lessons Learned in Vietnam.* 8 Vols. (McLean, VA: BDM Corporation, 1979).

—— *Bravo Company 1-325 Air TACSOP.* (Fort Bragg, NC: B Company, 1st Battalion, 325th Airborne Infantry Regiment, 1 August 1997).

—— *FM 100-5, Operations.* (Washington, DC: GPO, 1976).

—— *FM 100-1, The Army.* (Washington, DC: GPO, 1978).

—— *FM 90-10, Military Operations on Urbanized Terrain (MOUT)* (Washington, DC: GPO, 1979).

—— *FM 100-1, The Army.* (Washington, DC: GPO, 1981).

—— *FM 100-20, Low Intensity Conflict.* (Washington, DC: GPO, 1981).

—— *FM 100-5, Operations.* (Washington, DC: GPO, 1982).

—— *FM 21-75, Combat Skills of the Soldier.* (Washington, DC: GPO, 1984).

—— *FM 25-4, How to Conduct Training Exercises.* (Washington, DC: GPO, 1984).

—— *FM 100-5, Operations.* (Washington, DC: GPO, 1986).

—— *FM 7-85, Ranger Operations.* (Washington, DC: GPO, 1987).

—— *FM 7-20, The Infantry Battalion.* (Washington, DC: GPO, 1992).

—— *FM 7-98, Operations in Low Intensity Conflict.* (Washington, DC: GPO, 1992).

—— *FM 100-5, Operations.* (Washington, DC: GPO, 1993).

—— *FM 100-1, The Army.* (Washington, DC: GPO, 1994).

—— *FM 100-23, Peace Operations.* (Washington, DC: GPO, 1994).

——*FM 100-23-1, HA Multiservice Procedures for Humanitarian Assistance Operations.* (Washington, DC: GPO, 1994).

——*FM 100-7, Decisive Force: The Army in Theater Operations.* (Washington, DC: GPO. 1995).

——*FM 100-6, Information Warfare.* (Washington, DC: GPO, 1996).

—— *FM 100-6, Armor- and Mechanized-Based Opposing Force Operational Art.* (Washington, DC: GPO, 1998).

——*FM 22-100, Army Leadership: Be, Know, Do.* (Washington. DC: GPO, 1999).

——*FM 3-0, Operations.* (Washington, DC: GPO, 2001).

——*Force XXI Land Combat in the 21st Century.* (Fort Monroe, VA: TRADOC, 1997).

—— *Leaders Training Program JRTC.* (Fort Polk, LA: Joint Readiness Training Center. 1996).

—— *TOCSOP 2nd Battalion, 327th Infantry Regiment, 101st Airborne Division (Air Assault).* (Fort Campbell, KY: Headquarters, 2nd Battalion, 327th Infantry. 101st Airborne Division (Air Assault), 30 September 1996).

——*TRADOC Pamphlet 525-5, Military Operations: Operational Concepts for the AirLand Battle and Corps Operations, 1986.* (Fort Monroe, VA: TRADOC, 1981).

—— *TRADOC Pamphlet 525-5, Force XXI Operations* (Fort Monroe, VA: TRADOC, 1994).

—— and Air Force. *FM 100-20/ AFP 3-20, Military Operations in Low Intensity Conflict.* (Washington, DC: GPO, 1990).

Department of the Navy. *FMFM 1, Warfighting.* (Washington, DC: GPO, 1989).

——*FMFM 1-1, Campaigning.* (Washington, DC: GPO, 1990).

——*From the Sea: Preparing the Naval Service for the 21st Century.* (Washington. DC: GPO. 1992).

——*Forward . . . From the Sea.* (Washington, DC: GPO, 1995).

DePuy, William E. (eds Gilmore, Donald L. and Conway, Carolyn D.) *Selected Papers of General William E. DePuy.* (Fort Leavenworth, KS: Combat Studies Institute, 1994).

Eckhardt, George S. *Command and Control 1950–1969.* Vietnam Studies. (Washington, DC: GPO, 1974).

Grant, Rebecca L. *Operation Just Cause and the U.S. Policy Process.* (Santa Monica, CA: RAND, 1991).

Hoffman, Bruce and Taw, Jennifer Morrison. *A Strategic Framework for Countering Terrorism and Insurgency.* (Santa Monica, CA: RAND, 1992).

House of Commons Foreign Affairs Committee. *Foreign Policy Aspects of the War against Terrorism. Seventh Report of Session 2003–04.* (London: Stationery Office, 29 July 2004)

Jaffe, Lorna S. *The Development of Base Force: 1989–1992.* (Washington, DC: GPO, 1993).

Johnson, Lyndon B. *Public Papers of the Presidents of the United States.* 10 vols. (Washington, DC: GPO, 1965–70).

——'The President's Address to the Nation Announcing Steps to Limit the War in Vietnam and Reporting His Decision Not To Seek Reelection. March 21 1968'. *Public Papers of the Presidents: Lyndon B. Johnson 1968–69. Volume I.* (Washington, DC: GPO, 1970) pp. 469–76.

Joint Chiefs of Staff. *Joint Pub 1, Joint Warfare of the Armed Forces of the United States.* (Washington, DC: GPO, 1991).

——*Joint Pub 3-0, Doctrine for Joint Operations.* (Washington, DC: GPO, 1993).

——*Joint Pub 1, Joint Warfare of the Armed Forces of the United States.* (Washington, DC: GPO, 1995)

—— *Joint Pub 3-0, Doctrine for Joint Operations.* (Washington, DC: GPO, 1995).

—— *Joint Pub 3-07, Joint Doctrine for Military Operations Other Than War.* (Washington, DC: GPO, 1995).

—— *Joint Vision 2010.* (Washington, DC: GPO, 1995).

Kelly, Francis J. *U.S. Army Special Forces 1961–1971.* Vietnam Studies. (Washington, DC: GPO, 1985).

Kirkpatrick, Charles E. *The Army and the A-10: The Army's Role in Developing Close Air Support Aircraft, 1961–1971.* (Washington, DC: GPO, 1987).

Latham, Willard. *The Modern Volunteer Army Program: The Benning Experiment, 1970–1972.* (Washington, DC: GPO, 1974).

McChristian, Joseph A. *The Role of Military Intelligence 1965–1967.* Vietnam Studies. (Washington, DC: GPO, 1974).

Meyer, Edward C. *White Paper 1980: A Framework for Molding the Army of the 1980s into a Disciplined, Well Trained Fighting Force.* (Washington, DC: GPO, 1980).

Nixon, Richard M. *Public Papers of the Presidents, Vols 1970–73.* (Washington, DC: GPO, 1971–75).

Office of Defense Transformation. *Network Centric Operations Conceptual Framework Version 1.0.* (November 2003) http://www.oft.osd.mil/index.cfm

Ott, David Ewing. *Field Artillery 1954–1973.* Vietnam Studies. (Washington, DC: GPO, 1975).

Reagan, Ronald. *National Security Strategy of the United States.* (Washington, DC: GPO, 1988).

Rogers, Bernard William. *Cedar Falls–Junction City: A Turning Point.* Vietnam Studies. (Washington, DC: GPO, 1974).

Romjue, John L. *From Active Defense to AirLand Battle: The Development of Army Doctrine, 1973–1982.* (Fort Monroe, VA: TRADOC, 1984).

—— *The Army of Excellence: The Development of the 1980s Army.* (Fort Monroe, VA: TRADOC, 1993).

—— *American Army Doctrine for the Post-Cold War.* (Fort Monroe, VA: TRADOC, 1996).

——. Canedy, Susan and Chapman, Anne W. *Prepare the Army for War: A Historical Overview of the Army Training and Doctrine Command 1973–1993.* (Fort Monroe, VA: TRADOC, 1993).

Spector, Ronald H. *Advice and Support: The Early Years, 1941–1960. The U.S. Army in Vietnam.* (Washington, DC: GPO, 1983).

Starry, Donn A. *Mounted Combat in Vietnam.* Vietnam Studies. (Washington, DC: GPO, 1978).

Summers, Harry G. Jr. *The Astarita Report: A Military Strategy for the Multipolar World.* (Carlisle, PA: US Army War College, 1981).

Taw, Jennifer Morrison and Peters, John E. *Operations Other Than War: Implications for the U.S. Army.* (Santa Monica, CA: RAND, 1995).

US Army War College. *Leadership for the 1970's.* (Washington, DC: GPO, 1970).

US Special Operations Forces. *Posture Statement 2003–04,* http://www.socom.mil/Docs/2003_2004_SOF_Posture_Statement.pdf

Weinberger, Caspar W. *Annual Report to the Congress. Fiscal Year 1988.* (Washington, DC: GPO, 1987).

Articles in military journals

Allard, C. Kenneth. 'Lessons Unlearned: Somalia and Joint Doctrine'. *Joint Forces Quarterly*. (No. 9. 1995) pp. 105–9.

Bacevich, Andrew J. 'Prospects for Military Reform'. *Parameters*. (Vol. 17, No. 1. 1987) pp. 29–42.

—— 'Old Myths, New Myths: Renewing American Military Thought'. *Parameters*. (Vol. 18, No. 1. 1988) pp. 15–25.

—— 'The Army in the 1990s'. *Military Review*. (Vol. 69, No. 7. 1989) pp. 87–94.

—— 'Civilian Control: A Useful Fiction?' *Joint Forces Quarterly*. (No. 6. 1994/5) pp. 76–9.

Barber, James Alden. Jr. 'Military Force and Nonmilitary Threats'. *Military Review*. (Vol. 55, No. 2. 1975) pp. 3–13.

Barnett, Jeffrey R. 'Defeating Insurgents With Technology'. *Airpower Journal*. (Vol. 10, No. 2. 1996) pp. 69–75.

Barrett, Raymond J. 'Updating Civil Affairs Doctrine and Organization'. *Military Review*. (Vol. 54, No. 7. 1974) pp. 65–74.

Bingham, Price T. 'Ground Maneuver and Air Interdiction in the Operational Art'. *Parameters*. (Vol. 19, No. 1. 1989) pp. 16–31.

Bletz, Donald F. 'Military Professionalism: A Conceptual Approach'. *Military Review*. (Vol. 51, No. 5. 1971) pp. 9–17.

—— 'How Much Force to Defend Against What?' *Military Review*. (Vol. 54, No. 1. 1974) pp. 3–12.

Brown, Frederic J. 'The Army and Society'. *Military Review*. (Vol. 52, No. 3. 1972) pp. 3–17.

—— 'AirLand Battle Future; The Other Side of the Coin'. *Military Review*. (Vol. 71, No. 2. 1991) pp. 13–24.

Burgess, William H. III. 'Towards a More Complete Doctrine: SOF in AirLand Battle Future'. *Military Review*. (Vol. 71, No. 2. 1991) pp. 30–7.

Burke, Michael D. 'FM 3-0: Doctrine for a Transforming Force'. *Military Review*. (Vol. 82, No. 2. 2002) pp. 91–7.

Campbell, Kenneth J. 'Once Burned, Twice Cautious: Explaining the Weinberger–Powell Doctrine'. *Armed Forces and Society*. (Vol. 24, No. 3. 1998) pp. 357–74.

Canby, Steven L. 'NATO Strategy: Political-Military problems of Divergent Interests and Operational Concepts'. *Military Review*. (Vol. 59, No. 4. 1979) pp. 50–8.

Cardwell, Thomas A. III. 'AirLand Battle Revisited'. *Military Review*. (Vol. 65, No. 9. 1985) pp. 4–13.

—— 'Follow-On Forces Attack: Joint Interdiction by Another Name'. *Military Review*. (Vol. 66, No. 2. 1986) pp. 4–11.

Clark, Wesley K. 'Gradualism and American Military Strategy'. *Military Review*. (Vol. 60, No. 9. 1975) pp. 3–13.

Cohen, Eliot A. 'A War That Was Not Left to the Generals'. *Joint Forces Quarterly*. (No. 8, 1995) pp. 46–9.

Coles, Harry L. 'Strategic Studies Since 1945, the Era of Overthink'. *Military Review*. (Vol. 53, No. 4. 1973) pp. 3–16.

Coroalles, Anthony M. 'Maneuver to Win: A Realistic Alternative'. *Military Review*. (Vol. 61, No. 9. 1981) pp. 35–46.

—— 'Implementing a Maneuver Style of War'. *Military Review*. (Vol. 62, No. 12. 1982) pp. 20–5.

Corum, James S. 'Airpower and Peace Enforcement'. *Airpower Journal*. (Vol. 10, No. 4. 1996) pp. 10–26.

D'Amato, Martin J. 'Vigilant Warrior: General Donn A. Starry's AirLand Battle and How It Changed the Army'. *Armor*. (Vol. 109, No. 3. May–June 2000) pp. 18–22, 45–6.

Diehl, Richard P. 'Military Professionalism in the US Army Officer Corps'. *Military Review*. (Vol. 54, No. 3. 1974) pp. 60–72.

Doerfel, John S. 'The Operational Art of the AirLand Battle'. *Military Review*. (Vol. 62, No. 5. 1982) pp. 3–10.

Downey, Frederick M. and Metz, Steven. 'The American Political Culture and Strategic Planning'. *Parameters*. (Vol. 18, No. 3. 1988) pp. 34–42.

Downing, Wayne A. 'Firepower, Attrition, Maneuver – US Army Operations Doctrine: A Challenge for the 1980s and Beyond'. *Military Review*. (January 1981/ Vol. 77, No. 1. 1997) pp. 144–50.

Dubois, Thomas R. 'The Weinberger Doctrine and the Liberation of Kuwait'. *Parameters*. (Vol. 21, No. 4. 1991–2) pp. 24–38.

Dugan, Michael J. 'Air Power: Concentration, Responsiveness and the Operational Art'. *Military Review*. (Vol. 69, No. 7. 1989) pp. 12–21.

Dunlap, Charles J. Jr. 'The Origins of the American Military Coup of 2012'. *Parameters*. (Vol. 22, No. 4. 1992/3) pp. 2–20.

—— '21st-Century Land Warfare: Four Dangerous Myths'. *Parameters*. (Vol. 27, No. 3. 1997) pp. 27–37.

—— 'Joint Vision 2010: A Red Team Assessment'. *Joint Forces Quarterly*. (No. 17. 1997/8) pp. 47–9.

Dunn, Richard J. 'Transformation: Let's Get it Right This Time'. *Parameters*. (Vol. 31, No. 1. 2001) pp. 22–28.

Foss, John W. 'Advent of the Nonlinear Battlefield: AirLand Battle – Future'. *Army*. (February 1991) pp. 20–37.

Franks, Frederick M. Jr. 'Full-Dimensional Operations: A Doctrine for an Era of Change'. *Military Review*. (Vol. 73, No. 12. 1993) pp. 5–9.

Furlong, Raymond B. 'On War, Political Objectives, and Military Strategy'. *Parameters*. (Vol. 13, No. 4. 1983) pp. 2–10.

Galloway, Archie. 'FM 100-5: Who Influenced Whom?' *Military Review*. (Vol. 71, No. 3. 1986) pp. 46–51.

Glenn, Russell W. 'No More Principles of War?' *Parameters*. (Vol. 28, No. 1. 1998) pp. 48–66.

Glosson, Buster C. 'Impact of Precision Weapons on Air Combat Operations'. *Airpower Journal*. (Vol. 7, No. 2. 1993) pp. 4–10.

Gordon, John. IV. 'Operation Crusader; Preview of the Nonlinear Battlefield'. *Military Review*. (Vol. 71, No. 2. 1991) pp. 48–61.

Gourley, Scott R. 'Tactical Intelligence is Key to the AirLand Battle Scenario'. *Defense Electronics*. (February 1988) pp. 43–53.

Grant, Rebecca. 'Deep Strife'. *Air Force Magazine*. (June 2001) pp. 54–8.

Gray, Colin S. 'Comparative Strategic Culture'. *Parameters*. (Vol. 14, No. 4. 1984) pp. 26–33.

Gray, George H. 'What Are US Reserve Forces Really For?' *Military Review*. (Vol. 55, No. 6. 1975) pp. 82–91.

Hall, George M. 'Culminating Points'. *Military Review*. (Vol. 69, No. 7. 1989) pp. 79–83.

Helms, Robert F. II. 'A New Strategy for the US Army'. *Military Review*. (Vol. 55, No. 8. 1975) pp. 49–55.

Herring, George C. 'American Strategy in Vietnam: The Postwar Debate'. *Military Affairs*. (April 1982) pp. 57–63.

Hoar, Joseph F. 'A CINC's Perspective'. *Joint Forces Quarterly*. (No. 2. 1993) pp. 56–63.

Holder, L.D. 'Maneuver in Deep Battle'. *Military Review*. (Vol. 62, No. 5. 1982) pp. 54–61.

Ikeda, Moss M. 'Reserve Strength in Face of the Zero Draft'. *Military Review*. (Vol. 53, No. 5. 1973) pp. 58–66.

Jablonsky, David. 'Strategy and the Operational Level of War: Part I'. *Parameters*. (Vol. 17, No. 1. 1987) pp. 65–76.

—— 'Strategy and the Operational Level of War: Part II'. *Parameters*. (Vol. 17, No. 2. 1987) pp. 52–67.

—— 'US Military Doctrine and the Revolution in Military Affairs'. *Parameters*. (Vol. 24, No. 3. 1994) pp. 18–36.

Jeffrey, Timothy B. 'Today's Army Wants to Join You: Do We Really?' *Military Review*. (Vol. 53, No. 1. 1973) pp. 62–8.

Johnson, James R. 'People's War and Conventional Armies'. *Military Review*. (Vol. 54, No. 1. 1974) pp. 24–33.

Kiszely, John. 'The Meaning of Manoeuver'. *RUSI Journal*. (Vol. 143, No. 6. 1998) pp. 36–40.

Krulak, Charles C. 'The Strategic Corporal: Leadership in the Three Block War'. *Marine Corps Gazette*. (Vol. 83, No. 1. 1999) pp. 18–22.

Libbey, Miles A. III and Putignano, Patrick A. 'See Deep Shoot Deep; UAVs on the Future Battlefield'. *Military Review*. (Vol. 71, No. 2. 1991) pp. 38–47.

Lind, William S. 'Some Doctrinal Questions for the United States Army'. *Military Review*. (Vol. 57, No. 3. 1977) pp. 54–65.

—— 'An Operational Doctrine for Intervention'. *Parameters*. (Vol. 17, No. 4. 1987) pp. 30–6.

——, Nightengale, Keith M., Schmitt, John, Sutton, Joseph W. and Wilson, G.I. 'The Changing Face of War into the Fourth Generation'. *Military Review*. (Vol. 69, No. 9. 1989) pp. 2–11.

Lock-Pullan, Richard. '"And the Wall Came Tumbling Down": The Current Debate on the Changing Nature of the Military Professional'. *Journal of Defence Studies*. (Vol. 1, No. 3. 2001) pp. 122–32.

Loomis, Dan G. '[FM 100-5, Operations] A Review'. *Military Review*. (Vol. 57, No. 3. 1977) pp. 66–9.

Luttwak, Edward N. 'Notes on Low-Intensity Warfare'. *Parameters*. (Vol. 13, No. 4. 1983) pp. 11–18.

Machos, James A. 'Air–Land Battles or AirLand Battle?' *Military Review*. (Vol. 63, No. 7. 1983) pp. 33–40.

McDonough, James R. 'Building the New FM 100-5: Process and Product'. *Military Review*. (Vol. 71, No. 10. 1991) pp. 3–12.

—— 'Versatility: The Fifth Tenet'. *Military Review*. (Vol. 73, No. 12. 1993) pp. 11–14.

Maddox, David M. 'Projecting America's Power in Europe into the Future'. *Army*. (October 1994) pp. 77–83.

Madigan, John J. III and Hoy, Pat C. II. 'The Dialectical Imperative: Civil–Military Confrontation'. *Military Review*. (Vol. 53, No. 11. 1973) pp. 41–54.

Maechling, Charles Jr. 'Insurgency and Counterinsurgency: The Role of Strategic Theory'. *Parameters*. (Vol. 14, No. 3. 1984) pp. 32–41.

Maloney, Sean M. 'Afghanistan: From Here to Eternity?' *Parameters*. (Vol. 34, No. 1. 2004) pp. 4–15.

Matheny, Michael R. 'Armor in Low-Intensity Conflict: The U.S. Experience in Vietnam'. *Armor*. (July–August 1988) pp. 9–15.

Metz, Steven. 'AirLand Battle and Counterinsurgency'. *Military Review*. (Vol. 70, No. 1. 1990) pp. 32–41.

—— 'US Strategy and the Changing LIC Threat'. *Military Review*. (Vol. 71, No. 6. 1991) pp. 22–9.

—— 'Victory and Compromise in Counterinsurgency'. *Military Review*. (Vol. 72, No. 4. 1992) pp. 47–53.

—— 'A Wake for Clausewitz'. *Parameters*. (Vol. 24, No. 4. 1994/5) pp. 126–32.

—— 'A Flame Kept Burning: Counterinsurgency Support After the Cold War'. *Parameters*. (Vol. 25, No. 3. 1995) pp. 31–41.

Meyer, Edward C. 'Leadership: A Return to Basics'. *Military Review*. (Vol. 60, No. 7. 1980) pp. 4–9.

Moellering, John H. 'Future Civil–Military Relations; The Army Turns Inward?' *Military Review*. (Vol. 53, No. 7. 1973) pp. 68–83.

Morelli, Donald R. and Ferguson, Michael M. 'Low-Intensity Conflict: An Operational Perspective'. *Military Review*. (Vol. 64, No. 11. 1984) pp. 2–16.

Murry, William V. 'Clausewitz and Limited Nuclear War'. *Military Review*. (Vol. 55. No. 4. 1975) pp. 15–28.

Nadal, Ramon A. 'Status Quo: Enemy of Leadership'. *Military Review*. (Vol. 51, No. 6. 1971) pp. 24–30.

New, Larry D. 'Clausewitz's Theory: On War and Its Application Today'. *Airpower Journal*. (Vol. 10, No. 3. 1996) pp. 78–86.

New, Terry L. 'Where to Draw the Line between Air and Land Battle'. *Airpower Journal*. (Vol. 10, No. 3. 1996) pp. 34–49.

Newell, Clayton R. 'Modern Warfare: Balancing the Ends, Ways and Means'. *Army*. (August 1986) pp. 24–32.

O'Meara, Andrew P. 'Strategy and the Military Professional'. *Military Review*. (Vol. 60, No. 1. 1980) pp. 38–45.

Oakley, Robert B. 'An Envoy's Perspective'. *Joint Forces Quarterly*. (No. 2. 1993) pp. 44–55.

Ostovich, Rudolph III. 'Army Aviation in AirLand Battle Future'. *Military Review*. (Vol. 71, No. 2. 1991) pp. 25–33.

Owens, Mackubin Thomas. 'Civilian Control: A National Crisis?' *Joint Forces Quarterly*. (No. 6. 1994/5) pp. 80–3.

Owens, William A. 'The American Revolution in Military Affairs'. *Joint Forces Quarterly*. (No. 10. 1995/6) pp. 37–8.

Palmer, Bruce Jr. 'The Case for Limited Reform of the JCS'. *Parameters*. (Vol. 15, No. 4. 1985) pp. 2–9.

—— 'A Careful Look at Defense Manpower'. *Military Review*. (Sept 1976/ Vol. 77, No. 1. 1997) pp. 23–9.

Parham, Paul B. 'The American Military Profession: An Egalitarian View'. *Military Review*. (Vol. 54, No. 11. 1974) pp. 18–29.

Reimer, Dennis J. 'Leadership for the 21st Century: Empowerment, Environment and the Golden Rule'. *Military Review*. (Jan 1996/ Vol. 77, No. 1. 1997) pp. 47–51.

—— 'The Army after Next: Knowledge, Speed and Power'. *Military Review.* (Vol. 79, No. 3, 1999) pp. 3–7.
Reitz, John W. 'Managing Intellectual Change: Army's Revision of FM 100-5'. *Army.* (September 1992) pp. 45–7.
Richardson, William R. 'The Leavenworth Influence on Today's Army'. *Military Review.* (Vol. 61, No. 5. 1981) pp. 16–23.
—— 'Training for Maneuver Warfare'. *Armor.* (July–August 1981) pp. 31–4.
—— 'Officer Training and Education'. *Military Review.* (Vol. 64, No. 10. 1984) pp. 22–34.
—— 'FM 100-5: The AirLand Battle in 1986'. *Military Review.* (Vol. 66, No. 3. 1986) pp. 4–11.
—— 'The "Training Revolution" that Built Today's Army'. *Army.* (September 1996) pp. 8–12.
—— 'Training: Preparation for Combat'. *Military Review.* (June 1986/ Vol. 77, No. 1. 1997) pp. 84–6.
Rinaldo, Richard J. 'Warfighting and Peace Ops: Do Real Soldiers Do MOOTW?' *Joint Forces Quarterly.* (No. 14. 1996/7) pp. 111–16.
Rogers, Bernard W. 'ACE Attack of Warsaw Pact Follow-On Forces.' *Military Technology.* (Vol. 83, No. 5. 1983) pp. 38–50.
—— 'Follow-On Forces Attack (FOFA): Myths and Realities'. *NATO Review.* (Vol. 32, No. 6. 1984) pp. 1–9.
Silvasey, Stephen Jr. 'AirLand Battle; The Tactical Future'. *Military Review.* (Vol. 71, No. 2. 1991) pp. 2–12.
Sinnerich, Richard H. 'To Stand and Fight'. *Army.* (July 1997) pp. 15–19.
Sorley, Lewis. 'Creighton Abrams and Active-Reserve Integration in Wartime'. *Parameters.* (Vol. 21, No. 2. 1991) pp. 35–50.
Spiller, Roger J. 'In the Shadow of the Dragon: Doctrine and the US Army after Vietnam *RUSI Journal.* (Vol. 142, No. 6. 1997) pp. 41–54.
Starry, Donn A. 'A Tactical Evolution – FM 100-5'. *Military Review.* (Vol. 58, No. 8. 1978) pp. 2–11.
—— 'Extending the Battlefield'. *Military Review.* (Vol. 61, No. 3. 1981) pp. 33–50.
—— 'The Principles of War'. *Military Review.* (Vol. 61, No. 9. 1981) pp. 2–12.
—— 'Command and Control: An Overview'. *Military Review.* (Vol. 61, No. 11. 1981) pp. 2–3.
—— 'To Change an Army'. *Military Review.* (Vol. 63, No. 3. 1983) pp. 20–7.
—— 'Running Things'. *Military Review.* (Vol. 17, No. 3. 1987) pp. 13–20.
—— 'A Perspective on American Military Thought'. *Military Review.* (Vol. 69, No. 7. 1989) pp. 2–11.
Stevenson, Charles A. 'The Evolving Clinton Doctrine on the Use of Force'. *Armed Forces and Society.* (Vol. 22, No. 4. 1996) pp. 511–35.
Stiner, Carl W. 'US Special Operations Forces: A Strategic Perspective'. *Parameters.* (Vol. 22, No. 2. 1992) pp. 2–13.
Sullivan, Gordon R. and Dubik, James M. 'Land Warfare in the 21st Century'. *Military Review.* (Vol. 73, No. 9. 1993) pp. 13–32.
Summers, Harry G. Jr. 'Clausewitz: Eastern and Western Approaches to War'. *Air University Review.* (Vol. 37, No. 3. 1986) pp. 62–71.
Swain, Richard M. 'Clausewitz for the 20th Century: The Interpretation of Raymond Aron'. *Military Review.* (Vol. 71, No. 4. 1986) pp. 38–47.

Szafranski, Richard. 'Thinking about Small Wars'. *Parameters.* (Vol. 20, No. 3. 1990) pp. 39–49.

Tarr, David W. 'Political Constraints on US Intervention in Low-Intensity Conflicts'. *Parameters.* (Vol. 10, No. 3. 1980) pp. 51–60.

Tate, Clyde J. and Holder, L.D. 'New Doctrine for the Defense'. *Military Review.* (Vol. 61, No. 3. 1981) pp. 2–9.

Thomas, James A. 'Limited War; The Theory and Practice'. *Military Review.* (Vol. 53, No. 2. 1973) pp. 75–81.

—— 'Collapse of the Defensive War Argument'. *Military Review.* (Vol. 53, No. 5. 1973) pp. 35–8.

—— 'On Moral Preparation'. *Military Review.* (Vol. 53, No. 8. 1973) pp. 64–76.

Toner, James H. 'The Military Ethic: On the Virtue of an Anachronism'. *Military Review.* (Vol. 54, No. 12. 1974) pp. 9–18.

Trainor, Bernard E. 'Jointness, Service Culture, and the Gulf War'. *Joint Forces Quarterly.* (No. 3. 1993/4) pp. 71–4.

Tuttle, Henry S. 'Is AirLand Battle Compatible with NATO Doctrine?' *Military Review.* (Vol. 65, No. 12. 1985) pp. 5–11.

Ulmer, Walter F. 'Notes on Leadership for the 1980s'. *Military Review.* (July 1980/ Vol. 77, No. 1. 1997) pp. 76–7.

Villacres, Edward J. and Bassford, Christopher. 'Reclaiming the Clausewitzian Trinity'. *Parameters.* (Vol. 25, No. 3. 1995) pp. 9–19.

Vought, Donald B. 'Preparing for the Wrong War?' *Military Review.* (Vol. 57, No. 5. 1977) pp. 16–34.

Vuono, Carl E. 'The Strategic Value of Conventional Forces'. *Parameters.* (Vol. 21, No. 4. 1990) pp. 2–10.

—— 'National Strategy and the Army of the 1990s'. *Parameters.* (Vol. 21, No. 2. 1991) pp. 2–12.

Waghelstein, John D. 'Post-Vietnam Counterinsurgency Doctrine'. *Military Review.* (Vol. 65, No. 5. 1985) pp. 42–9.

Wagner, Louis C. 'Modernization: Large Strides, Much to Do'. *Army.* (October 1986) pp. 212–25.

Ward, James R. 'Vietnam: Insurgency or War?' *Military Review.* (Vol. 69, No. 1. 1989) pp. 15–23.

Wass de Czege, Huba. 'Challenge for the Future: Educating Field Grade Battle Leaders and Staff Officers'. *Military Review.* (Vol. 64, No. 6. 1984) pp. 2–13.

—— 'How to Change an Army'. *Military Review.* (Vol. 64, No. 11. 1984) pp. 32–49.

—— 'Clausewitz: Historical Theories Remain Sound Compass References; The Catch Is Staying on Course'. *Army.* (September 1988) pp. 37–43.

—— and Holder, L.D. 'The New FM 100-5'. *Military Review.* (Vol. 62, No. 7. 1982) pp. 53–70.

Watkins, James D. 'The Maritime Strategy'. *Proceedings.* Special Supplement. (Vol. 112, No. 1. 1986) pp. 2–17.

Weigley, Russell F. 'Shaping the American Army of World War II: Mobility versus Power'. *Parameters.* (Vol. 11, No. 3. 1981) pp. 13–21.

Weller, Jac. 'Sir Basil Liddell Hart's Disciples in Israel'. *Military Review.* (Vol. 54, No. 1. 1974) pp. 13–23.

Werrell, Kenneth P. 'Air War Victorious: The Gulf War vs. Vietnam'. *Parameters.* (Vol. 22, No. 2. 1992) pp. 41–54.

Weyand, Fred C. 'Serving the People: The Need for Military Power'. *Military Review.* (Vol. 56, No. 12. 1976) pp. 8–18.

—— and Summers, Harry G. Jr. 'Vietnam Myths and Military Realities'. *Armor.* (September–October 1976) pp. 30–6.

Woerner, Fred F. 'The Strategic Imperatives for the United States in Latin America'. *Military Review.* (Vol. 69, No. 2. 1989) pp. 18–28.

Zoll, Donald Atwell. 'A Crisis in Self-Image: The Role of the Military in American Culture'. *Parameters.* (Vol. 12, No. 4. 1982) pp. 24–31.

—— The Press and the Military: Some Thoughts After Grenada'. *Parameters.* (Vol. 14, No. 1. 1984) pp. 26–34.

Secondary material

Adams, Thomas K. 'LIC (Low-Intensity Clausewitz)'. *Small Wars and Insurgencies.* (Vol. 1, No. 3. 1990) pp. 266–75.

Ambrose, Stephen E. *Upton and the Army.* (Baton Rouge, LA: Louisiana State University Press, 1964)

Avant, Deborah D. *Political Institutions and Military Change: Lessons From Peripheral Wars.* (Ithaca, NY: Cornell University Press, 1994).

—— 'Are The Reluctant Warriors Out of Control? Why the U.S. Military is Adverse to Responding to Post-Cold War Low-Level Threats'. *Security Studies.* (Vol. 6, No. 2 1996/7) pp. 51–90.

Bacevich, Andrew J. *The Pentomic Era: The U.S. Army Between Korea and Vietnam.* (Washington, DC: National University Press, 1986).

—— 'Preserving the Well-Bred Horse'. *National Interest.* (No. 37. 1994) pp. 43–9.

—— *American Empire: The Realities and Consequences of U.S. Diplomacy.* (Cambridge, MA: Harvard University Press, 2002).

—— and Cohen, Eliot A. (eds) *War Over Kosovo: Politics and Strategy in a Global Age.* (New York: Columbia University Press, 2001).

Bankus, Brent C. and Flavin, William R. 'Training US Army Peacekeepers'. *Small Wars and Insurgencies,* (Vol. 15, No. 1. 2004) pp. 129–39.

Baritz, Loren. *Backfire.* (New York: William Morrow, 1985).

Bassford, Christopher. *Clausewitz in English: The Reception of Clausewitz in Britain and America 1815–1945.* (New York: Oxford University Press, 1994).

Bateman, Robert L. (ed.) *Digital War: A View from the Front Lines.* (Novato, CA: Presidio, 1999).

Bellamy, Alex J. 'Lessons Unlearned: Why Coercive Diplomacy Failed at Rambouillet'. *International Peacekeeping.* (Vol. 7, No. 2, 2000) pp. 95–114.

Bert, Wayne. *The Reluctant Superpower: United States Policy in Bosnia, 1991–95.* (London: Macmillan, 1997).

Betts, Richard K. *Soldiers, Statesmen, and Cold War Crises.* (Cambridge, MA: Harvard University Press, 1977).

—— 'Should Strategic Studies Survive?' *World Politics.* (Vol. 50, No. 1. 1997) pp. 7–33.

Bickel, Keith B. *Mars Learning: The Marine Corps' Development of Small Wars Doctrine, 1915–1940.* (Boulder, CO: Westview, 2001).

Blechman, Barry M. 'The Congressional Role in U.S. Military Policy'. *Political Science Quarterly.* (Vol. 106, No. 1. 1991) pp. 17–32.

Bolger, Daniel P. *Dragons at War: 2–34th Infantry in the Mojave.* (Novato, CA: Presidio, 1986).

—— *The Battle for Hunger Hill: The 1st Battalion, 327th Infantry Regiment at the Joint Readiness Training Center.* (Novato, CA: Presidio, 1997).

Booth, Ken. 'American Strategy: The Myths Revisited' in: Booth, Ken and Wright. Moorhead (eds) *American Thinking About Peace and War.* (Hassocks: The Harvester Press, 1978) pp. 1–35.

Boutros-Ghali, Boutros. *Unvanquished: A U.S.–U.N. Saga.* (London: I.B. Tauris, 1999).

Brodie, Bernard. *War and Politics.* (New York: Macmillan. 1973)

Builder, Carl H. *The Masks of War: American Military Styles in Strategy and Analysis.* (Baltimore, MD: Johns Hopkins University Press, 1989).

Burk, James. 'Public Support for Peacekeeping in Lebanon and Somalia: Assessing the Casualties Hypothesis'. *Political Science Quarterly.* (Vol. 114, No. 1. 1999) pp. 53–78.

Burton, James G. *The Pentagon Wars: Reformers Challenge the Old Guard.* (Annapolis, MD: Naval Institute Press, 1993).

Buzzanco, Robert. *Masters of War: Military Dissent and Politics in the Vietnam Era.* (Cambridge: Cambridge University Press, 1996).

Cable, Larry. 'Reinventing the Round Wheel: Insurgency, Counter-Insurgency, and Peacekeeping Post Cold War'. *Small Wars and Insurgencies.* (Vol. 4, No. 2. 1993) pp. 228–62.

Calvert, Peter. 'The US Intervention in Panama'. *Small Wars and Insurgencies.* (Vol. 1, No. 3. 1990) pp. 307–14.

Cameron, Craig M. *American Samurai: Myth, Imagination, and the Conduct of Battle in the First Marine Division, 1941–1951.* (New York: Cambridge University Press, 1994)

Chin, Warren. 'Operation "Enduring Freedom": A Victory for a Conventional Force Fighting an Unconventional War'. *Small Wars and Insurgencies.* (Vol. 14, No. 1. 2003) pp. 57–76.

Clark, Asa A. IV, Chiarelli, P.W., McKitrick, J.S. and Reed, J.W. (eds) *The Defense Reform Debate: Issues and Analysis.* (Baltimore, MD: Johns Hopkins University Press, 1984).

Clarke, Walter and Herbst, Jeffrey (eds) *Learning From Somalia: The Lessons of Armed Humanitarian Intervention.* (Boulder, CO: Westview Press, 1997).

Clausewitz, Carl von (Howard, Michael and Paret, Peter, ed. and trans.) *On War.* (Princeton. NJ: Princeton University Press, 1976).

Clodfelter, Mark. *The Limits of Airpower: The American Bombing of North Vietnam.* (New York: Free Press, 1989).

Cohen, Eliot A. 'Constraints on America's Conduct of Small Wars'. *International Security.* (Vol. 9, No. 2. 1984) pp. 277–307.

—— 'The Mystique of US Air Power'. *Foreign Affairs.* (Vol. 73, No. 1. 1994) pp. 109–24.

—— 'The Strategy of Innocence? The United States, 1920–1945' in: Murray *et al.* (eds) *The Making of Strategy: Rulers, States, and War.* (Cambridge: Cambridge University Press, 1994) pp. 428–65.

—— 'A Revolution in Warfare'. *Foreign Affairs.* (Vol. 75, No. 2. 1996) pp. 37–54.

—— 'Civil-Military Relations'. *Orbis.* (Vol. 41, No. 2. 1997) pp. 177–86.

—— 'Kosovo and the New American Way of War' in: Bacevich, Andrew J. and Cohen, Eliot A. (eds) *War Over Kosovo: Politics and Strategy in a Global Age.* (New York: Columbia University Press, 2001) pp. 38–62.

—— *Supreme Command: Soldiers, Statesmen, and Leadership in Wartime.* (New York: The Free Press, 2002).

—— 'A Tale of Two Secretaries'. *Foreign Affairs.* (Vol. 81, No. 3, 2002) pp. 33–46.

—— 'History and the Hyperpower'. *Foreign Affairs.* (Vol. 83, No. 4, 2004) pp. 49–63.

Collins, Joseph J. 'The Complex Context of American Military Culture: A Practitioners View'. *Washington Quarterly.* (Vol. 21, No. 4. 1998) pp. 213–28.

Cox, Michael. *US Foreign Policy after the Cold War: Superpower Without a Mission.* (London: Pinter/RIIA, 1995).

Craig, Gordon A. and George, Alexander L. *Force and Statecraft: Diplomatic Problems of Our Time.* Third edition. (Oxford: Oxford University Press, 1995)

Daalder, Ivo H. and Lindsay, James M. *America Unbound: The Bush Revolution in Foreign Policy.* (Washington, DC: Brookings Institute, 2003).

Dauber, Cori E. 'Implications of the Weinberger Doctrine for American Military Intervention in a Post-Desert Storm Age'. *Contemporary Security Policy,* (Vol. 22, No. 2. 2001) pp. 66–90.

Demchak, Chris C. *Military Organizations, Complex Machines: Modernization in the U.S. Armed Services.* (Ithaca, NY: Cornell University Press, 1991)

Downie, Richard Duncan. *Learning From Conflict: The U.S. Military in Vietnam, El Salvador, and the Drug War.* (Westport, CT: Praeger, 1998).

Drew, Elizabeth. *On the Edge: The Clinton Presidency.* (New York: Touchstone, 1994).

Dunn, David H. 'Anti-Internationalism and the New American Foreign Policy Debate'. *Contemporary Security Policy.* (Vol. 17, No. 2. 1996) pp. 238–63.

—— 'Myths, Motivations and "Misunderestimations": The Bush Administration and Iraq'. *International Affairs.* (Vol. 79, No. 2. 2003) pp. 279–97.

Durch, William J. (ed.) *The Evolution of UN Peacekeeping: Case Studies and Comparative Analysis.* (New York: St Martin's Press, 1993)

—— (ed.) *UN Peacekeeping, American Politics, and the Uncivil Wars of the 1990s.* (London: Macmillan, 1997)

Eckhardt, William G. '"We the People" Go to War: The Legal Significance of the Weinberger Doctrine'. *Small Wars and Insurgencies.* (Vol. 1, No. 2. 1990) pp. 131–45.

Erdmann, Andrew P.N. 'The U.S. Presumption of Quick, Costless Wars'. *Orbis.* (Vol. 43, No. 3. 1999) pp. 363–81.

Erickson, John. 'The Development of Soviet Military Doctrine; The Significance of Operational Art and the Emergence of Deep Battle' in: Gooch, John (ed.) *The Origins of Contemporary Doctrine.* SCSI, The Occasional, No. 30. (Camberley: Strategic and Combat Studies Institute, 1997).

Fallows, James. 'Muscle-Bound Super Power: The State of America's Defense'. *Atlantic Monthly.* (October 1979) pp. 59–78.

—— *National Defense.* (New York: Random House, 1981).

Farrell, Theo. 'Sliding into War: The Somalia Imbroglio and US Army Peace Operations Doctrine'. *International Peacekeeping.* (Vol. 2, No. 2. 1995) pp. 194–214.

—— 'Figuring Out Fighting Organisations: The New Organisational Analysis in Strategic Studies'. *Journal of Strategic Studies.* (Vol. 19, No. 1. 1996) pp. 122–35.

—— 'Making Sense of Doctrine' in: Duffy, Michael *et al.* (eds) *Doctrine and Military Effectiveness.* Strategic Policy Studies 1. (Exeter: Strategic Policy Studies Group, 1997) pp. 1–5.

—— 'Culture and Military Power'. *Review of International Studies.* (Vol. 24, No. 3. 1998) pp. 407–16.

—— and Terriff, Terry (eds) *The Sources of Military Change: Culture, Politics, Technology.* (Boulder, CO: Lynne Rienner, 2002).

Feaver, Peter D. and Kohn, Richard H. (eds) *Soldiers and Civilians: The Civil–Military Gap and American National Security*. (Cambridge, MA: MIT Press, 2001)

Fisher, Louis and Adler, David Gray. 'The War Powers Resolution: Time to Say Goodbye'. *Political Science Quarterly*. (Vol. 113, No. 1. 1998) pp. 1–20.

Freedman, Lawrence. 'Escalators and Quagmires: Expectations and the Use of Force'. *International Affairs*. (Vol. 67, No. 1. 1991) pp. 15–31.

—— 'The Professional and Political Context of Security Studies'. *Arms Control*. (Vol. 14, No. 2. 1993) pp. 198–205.

—— *The Revolution in Strategic Affairs*. Adelphi Paper 318. (Oxford: Oxford University Press/IISS, 1998).

—— (ed.) *Strategic Coercion: Concepts and Cases*. (Oxford: Oxford University Press, 1998).

—— 'Victims and Victors: Reflections on the Kosovo War'. *Review of International Studies*. (Vol. 26, No. 3. 2000) pp. 335–58.

—— *Kennedy's Wars: Berlin, Cuba, Laos, and Vietnam*. (New York: Oxford University Press. 2000).

—— and Karsh, Efraim. 'How Kuwait Was Won: Strategy in the Gulf War'. *International Security*. (Vol. 16, No. 2. 1991) pp. 5–41.

—— and Karsh, Efraim. *The Gulf Conflict* (London: Faber and Faber, 1993).

Fromkin, David and Chace, James. 'What Are the Lessons of Vietnam?' *Foreign Affairs*. (Vol. 63, No. 4. 1984) pp. 722–46.

Gacek, Christopher M. *The Logic of Force: The Dilemma of Limited War in American Foreign Policy*. (New York: Columbia University Press, 1994).

Garfinkle, Adam *Telltale Hearts: The Origins and Impact of the Vietnam Antiwar Movement*. (London: Macmillan 1995).

Gentry, John A. 'Military Force in an Age of National Cowardice'. *Washington Quarterly*. (Vol. 21, No. 4. 1998) pp. 179–91.

George, Alexander L. 'Case Studies and Theory Development: The Method of Structured, Focussed Comparison'. in: Lauren, Paul Gordon (ed.) *Diplomacy: New Approaches in History, Theory, and Policy*. (London: Collier Macmillan, 1979) pp. 43–68.

—— and Simons, William E. (eds) *The Limits of Coercive Diplomacy*. Second edition. (Oxford: Westview Press, 1994).

Gibson, James William. *The Perfect War: Technowar in Vietnam*. (Boston, MA: Atlantic Monthly, 1986).

Gilboa, Eytan. 'The Panama Invasion Revisited: Lessons for the Use of Force in the Post Cold War Era'. *Political Science Quarterly*. (Vol. 110, No. 4. 1995) pp. 539–62.

Goldman, Emily O. 'Mission Impossible: Organizational Learning in Peacetime' in: Trubowitz *et al.* (eds) *The Politics of Strategic Adjustment: Ideas, Institutions, and Interests*. (New York: Columbia University Press, 1999) pp. 233–66.

—— 'New Threats, New Identities, and New Ways of War: The Sources of Change in National Security Doctrine'. *Journal of Strategic Studies*. (Vol. 24, No. 2. 2001) pp. 43–76.

Gordon, Michael R. and Trainor, Bernard E., *The General's War: The Inside Story of the Conflict in the Gulf*. (Boston, MA: Little, Brown, 1995).

Gray, Colin S. 'National Style in Strategy. The American Example'. *International Security*. (Vol. 6, No. 2. 1981) pp. 21–47.

—— 'Villains, Victims, and Sheriffs: Strategic Studies and Security for an Interwar Period'. *Comparative Strategy*. (Vol. 13, No. 4. 1994) pp. 353–69.

—— 'Strategy in the Nuclear Age: The United States, 1945–1991' in: Murray *et al.* (eds) *The Making of Strategy: Rulers, States, and War.* (Cambridge: Cambridge University Press, 1994) pp. 579–613.

—— 'Strategic Culture as Context: The First Generation of Theory Strikes Back'. *Review of International Studies.* (Vol. 25, No. 1. 1999) pp. 49–69.

Grinter, Lawrence E. and Dunn, Peter M. (eds) *The American War in Vietnam: Lessons, Legacies, and Implications for Future Conflicts.* (New York: Greenwood Press, 1987).

Haass, Richard N. *Intervention: The Use of American Military Force in the Post-Cold War World.* (Washington, DC: Carnegie Endowment, 1994).

Halberstam, David. *The Making of a Quagmire: America and Vietnam During the Kennedy Era.* Revised edition. (New York: Alfred A. Knopf, 1964/1988).

—— *The Best and the Brightest.* (New York: Random House. 1969).

—— *War in a Time of Peace: Bush, Clinton and the Generals.* (London: Bloomsbury, 2002)

Handel, Michael I. (ed.) *Clausewitz and Modern Strategy.* (London: Frank Cass. 1986).

—— *Masters of War: Classical Strategic Thought.* Second revised edition. (London: Frank Cass, 1996).

Hart, Gary. 'Toward a New Consensus on Defense'. *Strategic Review.* (Vol. 8. No. 4. 1980) pp. 9–14.

—— and Lind, William S. *America Can Win: The Case for Military Reform.* (Bethesda, MD: Adler and Adler. 1986).

Hays, Peter L., Vallance, Brenda J. and Tassel, Alan R. Van. (eds) *American Defense Policy.* Seventh edition. (Baltimore. MD: Johns Hopkins University Press. 1997).

Hillen, John. 'Must U.S. Military Culture Reform?' *Orbis.* (Vol. 43, No. 1. 1999) pp. 43–57.

Hilsman, Roger. *To Move a Nation: The Politics of Foreign Policy in the Administration of John F. Kennedy.* (New York: Doubleday, 1967).

Hippel. Karin von. *Democracy by Force: US Military Intervention in the Post-Cold War World.* (Cambridge: Cambridge University Press, 2000).

Hoffman, F.G. *Decisive Force: The New American Way of War.* (London: Praeger, 1996).

Hoffman, Stanley, Huntington, Samuel P., May, Ernest R., Neustadt, Richard N., Schelling, Thomas C. 'Vietnam Reappraised'. *International Security.* (Vol. 6, No. 1. 1981) pp. 3–26.

Holsti, Ole R. 'A Widening Gap between the U.S. Military and Civilian Society? Some Evidence, 1976–96'. *International Security.* (Vol. 23, No. 3. 1998/9) pp. 5–42.

—— and Rosenau, James N. 'The Meaning of Vietnam: Belief Systems of American Leaders'. *International Journal.* (Vol. 32, No. 3. 1977) pp. 452–74.

Hooker, Richard D. Jr (ed.) *Maneuver Warfare: An Anthology.* (Novato, CA: Presidio, 1993).

Howard, Michael. 'The Influence of Clausewitz' in: Clausewitz, Carl von (Howard, Michael and Paret, Peter, ed. and trans.) *On War.* (Princeton, NJ: Princeton University Press, 1976).

—— *The Causes of War.* (London: Unwin, 1984).

—— 'The Forgotten Dimensions of Strategy' in his *The Causes of War.* (London: Unwin. 1984) pp. 101–15.

—— *The Lessons of History.* (Oxford: Oxford University Press, 1991).

Huntington, Samuel P. *The Soldier and the State: The Theory and Politics of Civil–Military Relations.* (Cambridge, MA: Harvard University Press, 1957).

—— 'Playing to Win'. *National Interest.* (No. 3. 1986) pp. 8–16.

—— *American Military Strategy.* Policy Papers in International Affairs, No. 28. (Berkeley, CA: Institute of International Studies, University of California, 1986).

—— *The Clash of Civilizations and the Remaking of World Order.* (London: Simon and Schuster, 1997).

Ignatieff, Michael. *The Warrior's Honor: Ethnic War and the Modern Conscience.* (London: Chatto and Windus, 1998).

—— *Virtual War: Kosovo and Beyond.* (London: Chatto and Windus, 2000).

—— *Empire Lite: Nation-Building in Bosnia, Kosovo and Afghanistan.* (London: Vintage, 2003)

Iriye, Akira. 'Culture and Power: International Relations as Intercultural Relations'. *Diplomatic History.* (Vol. 3, No. 2. 1979) pp. 115–28.

Jacobsen, Carl G. (ed.) *Strategic Power: USA/USSR.* (London: Macmillan, 1990).

Jakobsen, Peter Viggo. *Western Use of Coercive Diplomacy After the Cold War: A Challenge for Theory and Practice.* (London: Macmillan, 1998).

Janowitz, Morris. *The Professional Soldier: A Social and Political Portrait.* (New York: Free Press, 1960).

Jentleson, Bruce W. 'The Reagan Administration and Coercive Diplomacy: Restraining More Than Remaking Governments'. *Political Science Quarterly.* (Vol. 106, No. 1. 1991) pp. 57–82.

Johnson, David E. *Fast Tanks and Heavy Bombers: Innovation in the U.S. Army, 1917–1945.* (Ithaca, NY: Cornell University Press, 1998)

Johnson, Douglas and Metz, Steven. 'Civil–Military Relations in the United States: The State of the Debate'. *Washington Quarterly.* (Vol. 18, No. 1. 1995) pp. 197–213.

Johnson, James Turner. 'Just War Thinking and its Contemporary Application: The Moral Significance of the Weinberger Doctrine'. *Small Wars and Insurgencies.* (Vol. 1, No. 2. 1990) pp. 146–70.

Johnson, Wray R. 'War, Culture, and the Interpretation of History: The Vietnam War Reconsidered'. *Small Wars and Insurgencies.* (Vol. 9, No. 2. 1998) pp. 83–113.

Johnston, Alaistair Iain. 'Thinking about Strategic Culture'. *International Security.* (Vol. 19, No. 4. 1995) pp. 32–64.

—— *Cultural Realism: Strategic Culture and Grand Strategy in Chinese History.* (Princeton, NJ: Princeton University Press, 1995).

Kagan, Robert. *Paradise and Power: America and Europe in the New World Order.* (London: Atlantic Books, 2003).

Kaldor, Mary. *New and Old Wars: Organized Violence in a Global Era.* (Cambridge: Polity Press, 1999).

Katzenstein, Peter J. *Cultural Norms and National Security: Police and Military in Postwar Japan.* (Ithaca, NY: Cornell University Press, 1996).

—— (ed.) *The Culture of National Security: Norms and Identity in World Politics.* (New York: Columbia University Press, 1996).

Keefe, John M. 'The Operational Art of Peace Enforcement'. *Low Intensity Conflict & Law Enforcement.* (Vol. 5, No. 1. 1996) pp. 63–86.

Keegan, John. *The Face of Battle.* (London: Jonathan Cape, 1976)

Keithly, David. and Melshen, Paul. 'Past as Prologue: USMC Small Wars Doctrine'. *Small Wars and Insurgencies.* (Vol. 8, No. 2. 1997) pp. 87–108.

Kennedy, Paul. *Strategy and Diplomacy: 1870–1945.* (London: Allen and Unwin, 1983).

Kier, Elizabeth. 'Culture and Military Doctrine; France between the Wars'. *International Security.* (Vol. 19, No. 4. 1995) pp. 65–93.

—— *Imagining War: French and British Military Doctrine Between the Wars.* (Princeton, NJ: Princeton University Press 1997).

Kitfield, James. *Prodigal Soldiers*. (New York: Simon and Schuster, 1995).
Kohn, Richard H. 'Out of Control'. *National Interest.* (No. 35. 1994) pp. 3–17.
Komer, Robert W. *Bureaucracy at War: U.S. Performance in the Vietnam Conflict.* (Boulder, CO: Westview Press, 1986).
Krauthammer, Charles. 'The Unipolar Moment'. *Foreign Affairs.* (Vol. 70, No. 1. 1991) pp. 22–33.
Krepinevich, Andrew F. Jr. *The Army and Vietnam.* (Baltimore, MD: John Hopkins University Press, 1986).
—— 'Cavalry to Computer: The Pattern of Military Revolutions'. *National Interest.* (No. 37. 1994) pp. 30–42.
Krueger, Kimbra L. 'US Military Intervention in Third World Conflict: The Need for Integration of Total War and LIC Doctrine'. *Low Intensity Conflict and Law Enforcement.* (Vol. 4, No. 3. 1995) pp. 399–428.
Lanir, Zvi. 'The "Principles of War" and Military Thinking'. *Journal of Strategic Studies.* (Vol. 16, No. 1. 1993) pp. 1–17.
Legro, Jeffrey W. *Cooperation Under Fire: Anglo-German Restraint During World War II.* (Ithaca, NJ: Cornell University Press, 1995).
Lehman, John F. Jr. *Command of the Seas: Building the 600 Ship Navy.* (New York: Charles Scribner's, 1988)
Leonhard, Robert R. *The Art of Maneuver: Maneuver-Warfare Theory and AirLand Battle.* (Novato, CA: Presidio, 1991).
—— *The Principles of War for the Information Age.* (Novato, CA: Presidio, 1998).
Levite, Ariel E., Jentleson, Bruce W. and Berman, Larry (eds) *Foreign Military Intervention: The Dynamics of Protracted Conflict.* (New York: Columbia University Press, 1992).
Lewy, Guenter. *America in Vietnam.* (New York: Oxford University Press, 1978).
Licklider, Roy. 'The American Way of State Building: Germany, Japan, Somalia and Panama'. *Small Wars and Insurgencies.* (Vol. 10, No. 3. 1999) pp. 82–115.
Lind, William S. 'The Case for Maneuver Doctrine' and 'Defense Reform: A Reappraisal' in: Clark *et al.* (eds) *The Defense Reform Debate: Issues and Analysis.* (Baltimore, MD: Johns Hopkins University Press, 1984) pp. 88–100, 327–33.
—— *Maneuver Warfare Handbook.* (London: Westview Press, 1985).
—— 'The Theory and Practice of Maneuver Warfare' in: Hooker, Richard D. Jr. (ed.) *Maneuver Warfare: An Anthology.* (Novato, CA: Presidio, 1993) pp. 3–18.
Linn, Brian M. 'The American Way of War Revisited'. *Journal of Military History.* (Vol. 66, No. 2. 2002) pp. 501–30.
Lock-Pullan, Richard. 'Civilian Ideas and Military Innovation: Manoeuvre Warfare and Organisational Change in the US Army'. *War and Society.* (Vol. 20, No. 1. 2002) pp. 125–47.
—— '"An Inward Looking Time"; The US Army 1973–76'. *Journal of Military History.* (Vol. 67, No. 2. 2003) pp. 483–511.
—— 'Learning the Limits of Virtue: Clinton, the Army and the Criteria for the Use of Military Force'. *Contemporary Security Policy.* (Vol. 24, No. 2. 2003) pp. 133–56.
Lopez, George A. and Cortright, David. 'Containing Iraq: Sanctions Worked'. *Foreign Affairs.* (Vol. 83, No. 4, 2004) pp. 90–103.
Luttwak, Edward N. 'The American Style of Warfare and the Military Balance'. *Survival.* (Vol. 21, No. 2. 1979) pp. 57–60.
—— 'The Operational Level of War'. *International Security.* (Vol. 5, No. 3. 1980) pp. 61–79.

—— *The Pentagon and the Art of War.* (New York: Simon and Schuster, 1984).

—— *Strategy: The Logic of War and Peace.* (Cambridge, MA: Belknap Press, 1987).

—— 'The Impact of Vietnam on Strategic Thinking in the United States' in: Hearden, Patrick J. (ed.) *Vietnam; Four American Perspectives.* (West Lafayette, IN: Purdue University Press, 1990) pp. 59–80.

—— 'Where Are the Great Powers? At Home with the Kids'. *Foreign Affairs.* (Vol. 73, No. 4. 1994) pp. 23–8.

—— 'A Post-Heroic Military Policy'. *Foreign Affairs.* (Vol. 75, No. 4. 1996) pp. 33–44.

—— 'From Vietnam to Desert Fox: Civil–Military Relations in Modern Democracies'. *Survival.* (Vol. 41, No. 1. 1999) pp. 99–112.

Lynn, William J. and Posen, Barry R. 'The Case for JCS Reform'. *International Security.* (Vol. 10, No. 3. 1985) pp. 69–97.

MacDonald, Peter. *Giap: The Victor in Vietnam.* (London: Fourth Estate, 1993).

Macgregor, Douglas A. *Transformation Under Fire: Revolutionizing How America Fights.* (Westport, CT: Praeger, 2003)

McMaster, H.R. *Dereliction of Duty: Lyndon Johnson, Robert McNamara, The Joint Chiefs of Staff, and the Lies That Led to Vietnam.* (New York: HarperCollins, 1997).

Macmillan, Alan, Booth, Ken and Trood, Russell. 'Strategic Culture' in: Booth, Ken and Trood, Russell (eds) *Strategic Cultures in the Asia-Pacific Region.* (London: Macmillan, 1999) pp. 3–26.

Mandelbaum, Michael. 'Foreign Policy as Social Work'. *Foreign Affairs.* (Vol. 75, No. 1. 1996) pp. 16–31.

Marquis, Susan L. *Unconventional Warfare: Rebuilding U.S. Special Operations Forces.* (Washington, DC: Brookings Institution, 1997).

Marthinsen, Charles E. 'The Historical Significance of the Weinberger Doctrine'. *Small Wars and Insurgencies.* (Vol. 1, No. 2. 1990) pp. 118–30.

Matthews, Lloyd J. and Brown, Dale E. (eds) *Assessing the Vietnam War: A Collection from the Journal of the U.S. Army War College.* (London: Pergamon-Brassey's, 1987).

Mead, Walter Russell. *Special Providence: American Foreign Policy and How It Changed the World.* (New York: Century Foundation/Alfred A. Knopf, 2001).

Mermin, Jonathan. 'Television News and American Intervention in Somalia: The Myth of a Media-Driven Foreign Policy'. *Political Science Quarterly.* (Vol. 112, No. 3. 1997) pp. 385–403.

Metcalfe, J. III. 'The Press and Grenada, 1983'. *Small Wars and Insurgencies.* (Vol. 2, No. 3. 1991) pp. 168–74.

Metz, John M. 'Training the Way We Fight or For the Fight: Are Tactical Units Prepared for Post-Conflict Operations?' *Low Intensity Conflict and Law Enforcement.* (Vol. 5, No. 2. 1996) pp. 206–34.

Miller, Steven E. (ed.) *Conventional Forces and American Defense Policy.* (Princeton, NJ: Princeton University Press, 1986).

Millet, Allan R., Murray, Williamson and Watman, Kenneth H. 'The Effectiveness of Military Organizations'. *International Security.* (Vol. 11, No. 1. 1986) pp. 37–71.

Millis, Walter. *Armies and Men: A Study of American Military History.* (London: Jonathan Cape, 1958).

Mockaitis, Thomas R. and Rich, Paul B. (eds) *Grand Strategy in the War Against Terrorism.* (London: Frank Cass, 2003).

Morley, Morris and McGillion, Chris. '"Disobedient" Generals and the Politics of

Redemocratization: The Clinton Administration and Haiti'. *Political Science Quarterly.* (Vol. 112, No. 3. 1997) pp. 363–84.

Murray, Williamson, Knox, MacGregor and Bernstein, Alvin (eds) *The Making of Strategy: Rulers, States, and War.* (Cambridge: Cambridge University Press, 1994).

—— and Millet, Allan R. (eds) *Military Innovation in the Interwar Period.* (Cambridge: Cambridge University Press, 1996).

—— 'Does U.S. Military Culture Matter?' *Orbis.* (Vol. 43, No. 1. 1999) pp. 27–42.

Naveh. Shimon. *In Pursuit of Military Excellence: The Evolution of Operational Theory.* (London: Frank Cass, 1997).

Newland, Samuel J. and Johnson, Douglas V. II. 'The Military and Operational Significance of the Weinberger Doctrine'. *Small Wars and Insurgencies.* (Vol. 1, No. 2. 1990) pp. 171–90.

Nooy, Gert de (ed.) *The Clausewitzian Dictum and the Future of Western Military Strategy.* (The Hague: Kluwer Law International, 1997).

O'Connell, Robert and Goldman, Alan. 'The Future of War: Implications for US Ground Forces'. *Low Intensity Conflict and Law Enforcement.* (Vol. 5, No. 2. 1996) pp. 235–52.

O'Hanlon, Michael. 'Rumsfeld's Defence Vision'. *Survival* (Vol. 44, No. 2, 2002) pp. 103–17.

Orr, Robert C. (ed.) *Winning the Peace: An American Strategy for Post-Conflict Reconstruction.* (Washington, DC: Center for Strategic and International Studies, 2004).

Osborn, George K., Clark, Asa A. IV Kaufman, Daniel J. and Lute, Douglas E. (eds) *Democracy, Strategy, and Vietnam: Implications for American Policymaking.* (Lexington, MA: Lexington Books. 1987).

Owens, MacKubin Thomas. 'The Hollow Promise of JCS Reform'. *International Security.* (Vol. 10, No. 3. 1985) pp. 98–111.

Palmer, Bruce Jr. *The 25 Year War: America's Military Role in Vietnam.* (New York: Da Capo, 1984).

Paret, Peter (ed.) *Makers of Modern Strategy: From Machiavelli to the Nuclear Age.* (Princeton, NJ: Princeton University Press, 1986)

Peters, Ralph. *Fighting for the Future: Will America Triumph?* (Mechanicsburg, PA: Stackpole Books, 1999).

Peterson, Michael E. *The Combined Action Platoons: The U.S. Marines' Other War in Vietnam.* (Westport, CT: Praeger, 1989).

Posen, Barry R. *The Sources of Military Doctrine: France, Britain, and Germany Between the World Wars.* (Ithaca, NY: Cornell University Press, 1984).

Powell, Colin L. 'U.S. Forces: Challenges Ahead'. *Foreign Affairs.* (Vol. 72, No. 5. 1992/3) pp. 32–45.

—— *A Soldier's Way: An Autobiography.* (London: Hutchinson, 1995).

Priest. Dana. *The Mission: Waging War and Keeping the Peace with America's Military.* (New York: W.W. Norton, 2003)

Rasor, Dina (ed.) *More Bucks, Less Bang: How The Pentagon Buys Ineffective Weapons.* (Washington, DC: Fund for Constitutional Government, 1983).

Record, Jeffrey. 'Jousting with Unreality: Reagan's Military Strategy'. *International Security.* (Vol. 8, No. 3. 1983) pp. 63–78.

—— *Hollow Victory: A Contrary View of the Gulf War.* (London: Brassey's, 1993).

—— *Dark Victory: America's Second War Against Iraq.* (Annapolis, MD: Naval Institute Press, 2004).

Rice, Condoleezza. 'Promoting the National Interest'. *Foreign Affairs*. (Vol. 79, No. 1. 2000) pp. 45–62.

Rogers, Bernard W. 'Greater Flexibility for NATO's Flexible Response'. *Strategic Review*. (Vol. 11, No. 2. 1983) pp. 11–19.

Rogers, Clifford J. (ed.) *The Military Revolution Debate: Readings on the Military Transformation in Early Modern Europe*. (Boulder, CO: Westview Press, 1995).

Rogers, Paul. *Losing Control: Global Security in the Twenty-first Century*. (London: Pluto, 2000).

Roman, Peter J. and Tarr, David W. 'The Joint Chiefs of Staff: From Service Parochialism to Jointness'. *Political Science Quarterly*. (Vol. 113, No. 1. 1998) pp. 91–111.

Romjue, John L. 'The Evolution of American Army Doctrine' in: Gooch, John (ed.) *The Origins of Contemporary Doctrine*. SCSI, The Occasional, No. 30. (Camberley: Strategic and Combat Studies Institute, 1997).

Rosen, Stephen Peter. 'Vietnam and the American Theory of Limited War'. *International Security*. (Vol. 7, No. 2. 1982) pp. 83–113.

—— 'New Ways of War: Understanding Military Innovation'. *International Security*. (Vol. 13, No. 1. 1988) pp. 134–68.

—— *Winning the Next War: Innovation and the Modern Military*. (Ithaca, NY: Cornell University Press, 1991).

—— 'Military Effectiveness: Why Society Matters'. *International Security*. (Vol. 19, No. 4. 1995) pp. 5–31.

Royster, Charles. 'Comment on John Shy, "The Cultural Approach to the History of War" and on Russell Weigley, "The American Military and the Principle of Civilian Control from McClellan to Powell"'. *Journal of Military History*. (Vol. 57, No. 5. 1993) pp. 59–62.

Rubner, Michael. 'The Reagan Administration, the 1973 War Powers Resolution, and the Invasion of Grenada'. *Political Science Quarterly*. (Vol. 100, No. 4. 1985/6) pp. 627–47.

Ruggie, John Gerard. 'Interests, Identity, and American Foreign Policy' in his: *Constructing the World Polity: Essays on International Institutionalization*. (London: Routledge, 1998) pp. 203–28.

Rumsfeld, Donald H. 'Transforming the Military', *Foreign Affairs*. (Vol. 81, No. 3. 2002) pp. 20–32.

Rushdie, Salman. *Fury*. (London: Jonathan Cape, 2001)

Russett, Bruce M. and Stepan, Alfred (eds) *Military Force and American Society*. (New York: Harper and Row, 1973).

Ryan, Maria. 'Inventing the "Axis of Evil": The Myth and Reality of US Intelligence and Policy-Making After 9/11'. *Intelligence and National Security*. (Vol. 17, No. 4. 2002) pp. 55–76.

Sabrosky, Alan Ned. 'Panama 1989: Deposing a Dictator'. *Small Wars and Insurgencies*. (Vol. 1, No. 3. 1990) pp. 303–6.

Sacks, Jonathan. *The Dignity of Difference: How To Avoid the Clash of Civilisations*. Revised edition. (London: Continuum, 2003).

Sarkesian, Sam C., Williams, John Allen and Bryant, Fred B. *Soldiers, Society and National Security*. (London: Lynne Reinner, 1995).

Scales, Robert H. Jr. *Certain Victory: The U.S. Army in the Gulf War*. (London: Brassey's, 1994).

—— *Firepower in Limited War*. Revised edition. (Novato, CA: Presidio, 1995).

Schmitz, David F. and Walker, Vanessa. 'Jimmy Carter and the Foreign Policy of Human

Rights: The Development of a Post-Cold War Foreign Policy'. *Diplomatic History.* (Vol. 28, No. 1. 2004) pp. 113–43.

Schraeder, Peter J. (ed.) *Intervention into the 1990s: US Foreign Policy in the Third World.* Second edition. (Boulder, CO: Lynne Reinner, 1992).

Schwarzkopf, H. Norman. *The Autobiography: It Doesn't Take a Hero.* (London: Bantam Press, 1992).

Shacochis, Bob. *The Immaculate Invasion.* (London: Bloomsbury, 1999).

Shafer, D. Michael. 'The Unlearned Lessons of Counterinsurgency'. *Political Science Quarterly.* (Vol. 103, No. 1. 1988) pp. 57–80.

Sharp, U.S.G. *Strategy for Defeat: Vietnam in Retrospect.* (Novato, CA: Presidio, 1978/98).

Sharpe, Kenneth E. 'The Post-Vietnam Formula under Siege: The Imperial Presidency and Central America'. *Political Science Quarterly.* (Vol. 102, No. 4. 1987) pp. 549–69.

Shultz, George P. *Turmoil and Triumph: My Years as Secretary of State.* (New York: Macmillan, 1993).

Shy, John. *A People Numerous and Armed: Reflections on the Military Struggle for American Independence.* Revised edition. (Ann Arbor, MI: University of Michigan. 1990).

—— 'The Cultural Approach to the History of War'. *Journal of Military History.* (Vol. 57, No. 5. 1993) pp. 13–26.

Simpkin, Richard E. *Race to the Swift: Thoughts on Twenty-First Century Warfare.* (London: Brassey's, 1985).

Smith, Steve. 'The Self-Images of a Discipline: A Genealogy of International Relations Theory' in: Booth, Ken and Smith, Steve (eds) *International Relations Theory Today.* (Oxford: Polity Press, 1995) pp. 1–37.

Snider, Don M. 'An Uninformed Debate on Military Culture'. *Orbis.* (Vol. 43, No. 1. 1999) pp. 11–26.

Snyder, Jack. *The Ideology of the Offensive: Military Decision Making and the Disasters of 1914.* (Ithaca, NY: Cornell University Press, 1984).

Sorley, Lewis. *Thunderbolt: From the Battle of the Bulge to Vietnam and Beyond: General Creighton Abrams and the Army of his Times.* (New York: Simon and Schuster, 1992).

—— *A Better War: The Unexamined Victories and Final Tragedy of America's Last Years in Vietnam.* (New York: Harcourt Brace, 1999).

Spector, Ronald H. 'U.S. Army Strategy in the Vietnam War'. *International Security.* (Vol. 11, No. 4. 1987) pp. 130–4.

Starry, Donn A. 'Reflections' in: Hofman, George F. and Starry, Donn A. (eds) *Camp Colt to Desert Storm: The History of U.S. Armored Forces.* (Lexington, KY: University of Kentucky Press, 1999) pp. 531–61.

Summers, Harry G. Jr. *On Strategy: A Critical Analysis of the Vietnam War.* (Novato, CA: Presidio, 1982).

—— 'A War Is a War Is a War Is a War' in: Thompson, Loren B. (ed.) *Low-Intensity Conflict; Patterns of Warfare in the Modern World.* (Lexington, MA: Lexington Books, 1989) pp. 27–49.

—— 'On Strategy: Was Defeat Inevitable?' in: Moore, John Norton (ed.) *The Vietnam Debate: A Fresh Look at the Arguments.* (Lanham, MD: University Press of America, 1990) pp. 145–7.

—— 'Military Doctrine: Blueprint for Force Planning'. *Strategic Review.* (Vol. 22, No. 2. 1992) pp. 9–22.

Sutton, Boyd D., Landry, John R., Armstrong, Malcolm B., Estes, Howell M. III, and Clark,

Wesley K. 'Deep Attack Concepts and the Defense of Central Europe'. *Survival.* (Vol. 26, No. 2. 1984) pp. 50–70.

Taliaferro, Jeffrey W. 'Quagmires in the Periphery: Foreign Wars and Escalating Commitment in Interational Conflict'. *Security Studies.* (Vol. 7, No. 3. 1998) pp. 94–144.

Taw, Jennifer Morrison and Hoffman, Bruce. 'The Urbanisation of Insurgency: The Potential Challenge to US Army Operations'. *Small Wars and Insurgencies.* (Vol. 6, No. 1. 1995) pp. 68–97.

Taylor, Maxwell D. *The Uncertain Trumpet.* (New York: Harper, 1959).

Terriff, Terry and Keeley, James F. 'The United Nations, Conflict Management and Spheres of Interest'. *International Peacekeeping.* (Vol. 2, No. 4. 1995) pp. 510–35.

Thayer, Thomas C. *War Without Fronts: The American Experience in Vietnam.* (Boulder, CO: (Westview, 1985).

Thompson, W. Scott and Frizzell, Donaldson D. (eds) *The Lessons of Vietnam.* (New York: Crane, Russak, 1977).

Thornton, Rod. 'The British Army and the Origins of its Minimum Force Philosophy'. *Small Wars and Insurgencies.* (Vol. 15, No. 1. 2004) pp. 83–106.

Thurman, Maxwell R. 'On Being All You Can Be: A Recruiting Perspective' in: Fredland, J. Eric, Gilroy, C.L., Little, R.D. and Sellman, W.S. (eds) *Professionals on the Front Line: Two Decades of the All-Volunteer Force.* (Washington, DC: Brassey's, 1996).

Toffler, Alvin and Heidi. *War and Anti-War: Making Sense of Today's Global Chaos.* (London: Little, Brown, 1994).

Twining, David T. 'The Weinberger Doctrine and the Use of Force in the Contemporary Era'. *Small Wars and Insurgencies.* (Vol. 1, No. 2. 1990) pp. 97–117.

van Creveld, Martin. 'The Eternal Clausewitz' in: Handel, Michael I. (ed.) *Clausewitz and Modern Strategy.* (London: Frank Cass, 1986) pp. 35–50.

—— *The Transformation of War.* (London: Free Press, 1991).

—— 'What is Wrong with Clausewitz?' in: Nooy, Gert de (ed.) *The Clausewitzian Dictum and the Future of Western Military Strategy.* (The Hague: Kluwer Law International, 1997) pp. 7–23.

Vandergriff, Donald (ed.) *Spirit, Blood and Treasure: The American Cost of Battle in the 21st Century.* (Novato, CA: Presidio, 2001)

Walt, Stephen M. 'The Search for a Science of Strategy'. *International Security.* (Vol. 12, No. 1. 1987) pp. 140–65.

Warden, John A. III. *The Air Campaign: Planning for Combat.* (Washington, DC: National Defense University Press, 1988).

Wass de Czege, Huba. 'Army Doctrinal Reform' in: Clark *et al.* (eds) *The Defense Reform Debate: Issues and Analysis.* (Baltimore, MD: Johns Hopkins University Press, 1984) pp. 101–20.

Weigley, Russell F. *History of the United States Army.* (New York: Macmillan, 1967).

—— *The American Way of War: A History of United States Military Strategy and Policy.* (New York: Macmillan, 1973).

—— 'The American Military and the Principle of Civilian Control from McClellan to Powell'. *Journal of Military History.* (Vol. 57, No. 5. 1993) pp. 27–58.

—— 'Response to Brian McAllister Linn'. *Journal of Military History.* (Vol. 66, No. 2. 2002) pp. 531–3.

Weinberger, Caspar W. 'U.S. Defense Strategy'. *Foreign Affairs.* (Vol. 64, No. 4. 1986) pp. 675–97.

—— *Fighting for Peace: Seven Critical Years in the Pentagon.* (New York: Warner, 1990).

Westmoreland, William C. *A Soldier Reports.* (New York: Dell, 1976)

Weyand, Fred C. 'Shaping the Army For The Future'. *Strategic Review*. (Vol. 3, No. 2. 1975) pp. 7–11.
Wheeler, John. 'Coming to Grips with Vietnam'. *Foreign Affairs*. (Vol. 63, No. 4. 1984) pp. 747–58.
Williams, Michael C. 'Neo-Realism and the Future of Strategy'. *Review of International Studies*. (Vol. 19, No. 2. 1993) pp. 103–21.
Winik, Jay. *On the Brink*. (New York: Simon and Schuster, 1996).
Woerner, Fred F. Jr. 'Foreword' to, Fishel, John T. *Civil Military Operations in the New World*. (Westport, CT: Praeger, 1997).
Woods, Leonard. *The Military Obligations of Citizenship*. (Princeton, NJ: Princeton University Press, 1915).
Woodward, Bob. *The Commanders*. (London: Simon and Schuster, 1991).
—— *Bush at War*. (New York: Simon and Schuster, 2002).
—— *Plan of Attack*. (New York: Simon and Schuster, 2004).
Zimm, Alan D. 'Desert Storm, Kosovo and "Doctrinal Schizophrenia"'. *Strategic Review*. (Vol. 28, No. 1. 2000) pp. 32–9.
Zisk, Kimberly Marten. *Engaging the Enemy: Organizational Theory and Soviet Military Innovation, 1955–1991*. (Princeton, NJ: Princeton University Press, 1993).

Websites

Department of Defense – DefenseLINK
www.defenselink.mil
US Army – General Dennis J. Reimer Training and Doctrine Digital Library
www.adtdl.army.mil
Joint Doctrine
www.dtic.mil/doctrine/index.html
Office of Force Transformation, Department of Defense
www.oft.osd.mil/index.cfm

Defense Technical Information Center
www.dtic.mil
Project on Defense Alternatives
www.comw.org/rma/index.html
The Center for Defense Information
www.cdi.org
The Federation of American Scientists
www.fas.org
Institute for Security Studies, Paris
www.iss-eu.org

The White House
www.pub.whitehouse.gov
George H.W. Bush Presidential Library
http://bushlibrary.tamu.edu/index.php
Public Papers of the Presidents
www.gpo.gov/nara/pubpaps/srchpaps.html

John Boyd Papers
www.belisarius.com/modern_business_strategy/boyd/boyd_papers.htm

Unpublished material

Starry, Donn A. 'The Kermit Roosevelt Lecture', Army Staff College, Camberley. UK. 10 May 1982

—— 'Changing Things: Keynote Remarks', Australian Chief of Army Annual Exercise. Brisbane. 20 October 1998.

—— 'TRADOC's Analysis of the Yom Kippur War', The Jaffee Center Military Doctrine Joint Conference, Casarea, Israel. 14–18 March 1999.

INDEX

For Product Safety Concerns and Information please contact our EU representative GPSR@taylorandfrancis.com
Taylor & Francis Verlag GmbH, Kaufingerstraße 24, 80331 München, Germany

www.ingramcontent.com/pod-product-compliance
Ingram Content Group UK Ltd
Pitfield, Milton Keynes, MK11 3LW, UK
UKHW022014180926
475701UK00003B/355

* 9 7 8 0 4 1 5 4 0 7 8 7 8 *